T0316923

Competitiveness and Development

The Anthem Other Canon Series

Anthem Press and The Other Canon Foundation are pleased
to present **The Anthem Other Canon Series**. The Other Canon – also
described as 'reality economics' – studies the economy as a real object rather than as
the behaviour of a model economy based on core axioms, assumptions and techniques.
The series includes both classical and contemporary works in this tradition, spanning
evolutionary, institutional and Post-Keynesian economics, the history of economic
thought and economic policy, economic sociology and technology governance,
and works on the theory of uneven development and in the tradition of
the German historical school.

Other Titles in the Series

A 'Short Treatise' on the Wealth and Poverty of Nations (1613)
Antonio Serra, edited by Sophus A. Reinert

*Development and Semi-periphery: Post-neoliberal Trajectories
in South America and Central Eastern Europe*
Edited by Renato Boschi and Carlos Henrique Santana

*Economists and the Powerful:
Convenient Theories, Distorted Facts, Ample Rewards*
Norbert Häring and Niall Douglas

Knowledge Governance: Reasserting the Public Interest
Edited by Leonardo Burlamaqui, Ana Célia Castro
and Rainer Kattel, with a foreword by Richard Nelson

*The Politics of Enlightenment
Constitutionalism, Republicanism, and the Rights of Man in Gaetano Filangieri*
Vincenzo Ferrone, translated by Sophus A. Reinert

Thorstein Veblen: Economics for an Age of Crises
Edited by Erik S. Reinert and Francesca L. Viano

Competitiveness and Development

Myth and Realities

Mehdi Shafaeddin

Foreword by Erik S. Reinert

ANTHEM PRESS
LONDON · NEW YORK · DELHI

Anthem Press
An imprint of Wimbledon Publishing Company
www.anthempress.com
This edition first published in UK and USA 2012
by ANTHEM PRESS
75-76 Blackfriars Road, London SE1 8HA, UK
or PO Box 9779, London SW19 7ZG, UK
and
244 Madison Ave. #116, New York, NY 10016, USA

Copyright © Mehdi Shafaeddin 2012

The author asserts the moral right to be identified as the author of this work.

All rights reserved. Without limiting the rights under copyright reserved above,
no part of this publication may be reproduced, stored or introduced into
a retrieval system, or transmitted, in any form or by any means
(electronic, mechanical, photocopying, recording or otherwise),
without the prior written permission of both the copyright
owner and the above publisher of this book.

British Library Cataloguing-in-Publication Data
A catalogue record for this book is available from the British Library.

Library of Congress Cataloging-in-Publication Data
Shafaeddin, S. M. (S. Mehdi), 1945-
Competitiveness and development : myth and realities / Mehdi
Shafaeddin ; foreword by Erik S. Reinert.
p. cm.
Includes bibliographical references and index.
ISBN 978-0-85728-460-0 (hbk. : alk. paper)
1. Competition. 2. Economic development. I. Title.
HB238.S53 2012
338.9--dc23
2012024106

ISBN-13: 978 0 85728 460 0 (Hbk)
ISBN-10: 0 85728 460 6 (Hbk)

This title is also available as an eBook.

To Shahnaz, my wife, for her love and patience

CONTENTS

LIST OF TABLES, FIGURES AND BOXES

Tables

Figures

Boxes

FOREWORD

In the context of the financial crises and the crises of falling real wages in Europe and the United States, the zeitgeist of the West is in transition. In this context Mehdi Shafaeddin has written a very timely book, presenting for us the type of economic ideas that once made the West wealthy and which now need to be resurrected.

This book is part of a growing neodevelopmentalist tradition. Macro- and micro-level analyses are combined into a useful meso-level discourse, producing a level of abstraction where useful policy recommendations can be developed. Shafaeddin resurrects the eighteenth-century German and US concept of 'productive power', a power that – in the tradition of Friedrich List – is assumed to emanate from new knowledge, i.e., from mental rather than physical capital. In this book, economic development is created by dynamic imperfect competition of the Schumpeterian kind, not in a setting of perfect competition. Rather than a world of perfect information, this book sees the world far more realistically as one where barriers to entry abound. The static and unrealistic setting of mainstream economics is substituted by a dynamic one and, in the tradition of Edith Penrose, firms are seen as being unique. Economic development becomes a process of dynamic rent seeking by firms on behalf of nations, and the higher real wages at the core of economic development result from this dynamic process. Unceasing upgrading of technological skills and of economic activities – which are qualitatively different – is the name of the game in economic development.

Shafaeddin's approach is compatible with the German economics tradition in which capitalism was seen as consisting of three main elements: (1) the entrepreneur; (2) the modern state; and (3) the technological system, i.e., what we today would call the national innovation system. This perspective – defined by Werner Sombart – did not fit well in the Cold War perspective from left to right that has dominated Western discourse for so long. Stressing the entrepreneur would be seen as an analysis leaning to the political right, stressing the role of the state is definitely seen as a left-wing idea, while stressing technology has simply been unfashionable in mainstream economics.

Neoclassical economics failed to formalize any of these three elements of capitalism: entrepreneurship, state, and technology. In the West an ideological repudiation of the state is now often dominant, and there is a lack of political interest in technology policy. China's 'Market Leninism', however, appears to have recaptured what once was the Western formula for success: launching waves of industrial creation precisely based on entrepreneurship, on the state, and on technology. In this book, Shafaeddin urges other nations to follow the same example. In a very revealing case study he compares the respective fates of China and Mexico as these nations opened up to global competition.

We can witness how Western society itself slowly seems to be absorbing the assumptions of neoclassical economics as being reflections of reality. Mrs Thatcher's famous comment on the nonexistence of society is essentially just an assumption in neoclassical economics, and US Tea Party candidates, who are applauded when they indicate that the unemployed are just lazy, are implicitly basing their views on an assumption of labour markets that automatically clear. What were once unrealistic assumptions, purportedly made in order 'to sharpen the analyses', take on an independent life of their own as 'truths'.

Today's economic theory has lost key features of what built Western civilization, both of the Renaissance and of the Enlightenment. The core of what I call The Other Canon of Economics lies in qualitative features of Renaissance societies that are not compatible – not possible to include – in the excessively formal structures of today's mainstream economics. These qualities are brought back in Mehdi Shafaeddin's book.

The core of the Renaissance was über-Schumpeterian: the *magna facere* that created great innovations in art and in the production of everything from weaponry to irrigation canals was a way of thinking big that went far beyond profit making. What came to characterize the Western economy was that creating firms and organizations did not stop when the owner had enough money to feed his family. Creation continued beyond the satisfaction of personal needs. Renaissance *magna facere* thus went far beyond greed, and already in the 1200s the wealth of Florence was seen as emerging from a *ben commune*, a synergic common weal that was in itself a unit of analysis. These are perspectives contained in Friedrich List's work and in this book.

Two key features of the Enlightenment are also lost in today's economics: the ability to build classification systems, as Linnaeus did, and to understand the limits that need to be set for private greed. A key feature of mainstream economics is its inability to distinguish qualitatively among economic activities. The apparent accuracy of neoclassical economics is a direct result of its failure to make qualitative distinctions. We all understand that if all medical doctors in London are put in one country and all the people who wash the floors of London hospitals in another, we get one rich country of medical doctors and one poor country of cleaning ladies. This common-sense proposition is unfathomable in Ricardian trade theory, where world trade is modelled as the bartering of labour hours, all assumed to be of the same quality. This was the English way of trying to persuade the colonies to stay with their comparative advantage in being poor and ignorant. Now, when this same theory is boomeranging and making the West poorer, it is time for the developing world to rediscover it, as Shafaeddin invites us to do in this book.

Today's problems in the financial sector are often attributed to 'greed', and in order to set the agenda for development straight I think it is important to get the record on greed straight. With neoliberalism, the key Enlightenment debate on the limits of self-interest – a debate which lasted virtually through the whole of the eighteenth century – was lost. Having unlearned the wisdom that came out of this debate, the present discussion more often than not totally misses the point by discussing greed per se as an evil. The conclusion of the Enlightenment debate was boiled down to one sentence by Milanese economist Pietro Verri in 1771: '...the private interest of each individual, when it coincides with the public interests, is always the safest guarantor of public happiness'. In other words, greed – or *magna facere* for any other reason – is good as long as the end effect contributes to making the economic pie larger. As noted, with neoclassical economics the public interest – society – ceased to exist as a unit of analysis. This opened up for today's view that all greed is good, even the present greed of the financial sector which creates huge private wealth while shrinking the real economy to the detriment of the public interest. We must better understand the distinction between entrepreneurship that makes the economic pie bigger – which also has an element of greed because companies need to make money to survive – and the type of financial greed that feeds on shrinking the economic pie.

At its nucleus, mainstream economics describes Adam Smith's savage who has learned to barter, not Schumpeter's savage who has learned to innovate. Like new medicines which fail to get government approval, sophisticated economic models that may approach reality generally fail to reach policy level. The world is mostly ruled by the crudest of economic models. It is in this perspective that Mehdi Shafaeddin's book offers policy perspectives that are compatible both with the Renaissance and the Enlightenment.

Erik S. Reinert, President,
The Other Canon Foundation, Hvasser, Norway,
and the author of *How Rich Countries got Rich...and Why Poor Countries Stay Poor* (London: Constable, 2007)
December 2011

PREFACE

Almost all industrial countries have been concerned with their competitiveness in the international market, particularly during the last quarter century; they have established competitiveness commissions, or councils, in the offices of the presidents, or prime ministers. In all cases they have argued in favour of competitiveness at the high level of development. Government intervention for technological development and upgrading of the industrial structure and services has been their focus of attention. In all cases, they have argued, competitiveness should, in particular, serve the purpose of raising the standard of living of their citizens. The contents of the text of the US Presidential Commission on Industrial Competitiveness (1985, 7) is one example; refuting the narrow approaches to competitiveness based on exchange rate and trade balance, it advocates that competitiveness is the basis for raising a nation's standard of living and the expansion of employment. It should contribute, it is added, to labour productivity, real wage growth, and real return on capital employed in the industry in addition to improving the position of the country in world trade. The Organisation for Economic Co-operation and Development (OECD) Secretariat confirms this approach to competitiveness (OECD 1992, ch. 11). In 2006, the Bush administration approved an extensive policy framework for technological development under the 'American Competitiveness Initiative' with a Federal budget of $137 billion covering a wide range of activities. In a speech to the United Nations Economic and Social Council (ECOSOC) in 2007, the US representative clearly defended the need for protection of technology; he stated: '...technological change is driven by protection of IPRs [intellectual property rights]'.

According to the UK government's third white paper on competitiveness:

> Improving competitiveness is central to raising the underlying rate of growth of the economy and enhancing living standards... Improving competitiveness is not about driving down living standards. It is about creating a high skills, high productivity and therefore high wage economy where enterprise can flourish...
> (UK Government 1998, 10)

This approach is further confirmed in the UK government's white paper on competitiveness issued in 1998, in which it emphasizes the need for producing high-value goods by constant creativity, innovation and enhanced performance. According to the then UK prime minister: 'Old fashioned state intervention did not and cannot work. But neither does naïve reliance on markets' (UK Government 1998, 1–2). The related framework contains a new approach to industrial policy based on four main pillars: actively seeking new ideas and knowledge, innovating new products and services, investing in the workforce, utilizing knowledge and skills to the full (UK Government 1998).

The EU also adopted, through the Lisbon European Councils, a decision in March 2000 containing a strategy for strengthening a knowledge-based economy, which includes stepping-up the process of reform for competitiveness and innovation by R&D, training, etc.

While we have provided a couple of examples here, other developed countries also have had some sort of policy on competitiveness. Yet developed countries have been imposing competitiveness at the low level of development on developing countries through the advocacy of neoliberal ideology, e.g., the Washington Consensus, and the practices of international organizations such as the IMF, World Bank and WTO, or through bilateral, or regional, trade agreements. In other words, they have been imposing their market-oriented approach to competitiveness based on the theory of static comparative advantage, lack of government intervention, budget cuts, premature trade liberalization, absence of performance requirements from TNCs, etc. John Williamson, the advocate of the Washington Consensus, admits that 'none of the ideas spawned by the development literature…plays an essential role in motivating the Washington Consensus' (1990, 19–20).

Such an approach to competitiveness tends to lock the structure of production and exports of those developing countries, which are at early stages of industrialization, in primary commodities, resource-based industries and at best in assembly operation. In other words, it locks them at a low level of development. It also creates constraints on those developing countries which already have some industrial base to make their industries efficient and upgrade their industrial structure in order to enhance the value added and the standard of living of their citizens.

Having observed such contradictions and asymmetries, I was motivated to open up the 'black box' of competitiveness as advocated by developed countries and look into its impact on developing countries.

Mehdi Shafaeddin

ACKNOWLEDGEMENTS

The confusion surrounding the concept of competitiveness in the context of developing countries motivated me to write this book. The views of neoliberals on the issue have dominated the economic literature, as well as the provision of policy advice to developing countries by the international financial institutions since the early 1980s with the introduction of Structural Adjustment and Stabilization Programs. It was further intensified in the mid-1990s with the coming into effect of the Uruguay Round agreements. The philosophy behind both was the static version of the comparative cost hypothesis. The result: deindustrialization in many low-income countries. Thus, I was motivated to go 'against the stream' to explore the issue and come up with alternative views on competitiveness. My value judgement and premise was that competitiveness should be achieved in a way that would also contribute to development and a high standard of living for the mass population in developing countries, and that it should not be envisaged in a way that would lock them at low levels of industrialization and development. In doing so, I have benefited, *inter alia*, from writings of Joseph Schumpeter, F. List, Michael Kalecki, William Lazonick, Michael Best, Albert O. Hirschman, Michael Porter and last, but not least, Erik Reinert.

I am indebted to my wife Shahnaz for her continuous encouragement and support. My retirement from UNCTAD provided me time to concentrate on research for the preparation of the draft, and my long years of experience in the organization made me closely familiar with the critical situation and frustration of developing countries – particularly low-income ones – in their processes of industrialization and development.

Some chapters of the book were initially prepared for presentation in training courses for policy makers of developing countries, which provided me the opportunity to benefit from the views of such an audience. It also provided me with the opportunity to get to know more closely their educational background – some had been influenced strongly by the dominant views of neoliberals. Such educational deficiencies made me more determined to go 'against the stream' in the preparation of this book.

I have also benefited from views and comments of many friends and colleagues. Chapter 9 is based mainly on earlier works undertaken together with Kevin Gallagher and Juan Pizarro. I am particularly indebted to Ms Myriam Velia, of the TIPS (Trade and Industrial Policy Strategies) of South Africa, who read most chapters of the draft carefully and provided me with her valuable comments. I have also benefited from comments by Thomas Ganiatsos (an ex-colleague of mine) and Kamal Malhotra (of the UNDP) and his colleagues, and I am also indebted to the anonymous referees who read the draft carefully and provided very constructive comments. The production editors at Anthem Press also checked the draft carefully and brought to my attention the need for some correction. I am grateful to them.

My gratitude goes also to Mr Keith Povey for editing the draft.

Finally, I remain, however, solely responsible for any shortcomings and errors.

Mehdi Shafaeddin

LIST OF ABBREVIATIONS

ACP	African, Caribbean and Pacific
ASCM	Agreement on Subsidies and Countervailing Measures
BCG	Boston Consulting Group
CA	comparative cost advantage
CIS	Commonwealth of Independent States
DCs	developed countries
DMECs	developed market-economy countries
DSB	Dispute Settlement Body of the WTO
DVA	domestic value added
ECLAC	Economic Commission for Latin America and the Caribbean
EPA	Economic Partnership Agreement
EU	European Union
FDI	foreign direct investment
FMS	flexible manufacturing system
FTA	free trade agreement
GATS	General Agreement on Trade in Services
GATT	General Agreement on Tariffs and Trade
GDP	gross domestic product
GE	General Electric
GFCF	gross fixed capital formation
GSP	Generalized System of Preferences
GVC	global value chain
H&S	Hofer and Schendel
HFC	high fixed cost
IBM	International Business Machines
IBRD	International Bank for Reconstruction and Development
IFIs	international financial institutions
ILO	International Labour Organization
IMF	International Monetary Fund
INEGI	Instituto Nacionale de Estadistica y Geografia (Mexican National Institute of Statistics and Geography)
IPPC	International Plant Protection Convention
IPR	intellectual property right
IT	information technology
ITC	indigenous technological capability
ITO	International Trade Organization

JIT	just-in-time delivery system
LDCs	least developed countries
LFC	low fixed cost
METI	Ministry of Economy, Trade and Industry (Japan)
MEXT	Ministry of Education, Culture, Sports, Science and Technology (Japan)
MFN	most-favoured-nation
MITI	Ministry of International Trade and Industry (Japan)
MOST	Ministry of Science and Technology (People's Republic of China)
MVA	manufacture value added
NAFTA	North American Free Trade Agreement
NAMA	nonagricultural market access
NBER	National Bureau of Economic Research
NDP	national development plan
NICs	newly industrialized countries
NIEs	newly industrialized economies
NSI	national system of innovation
OBM	original brand manufacturer
ODM	original design manufacturer
OECD	Organisation for Economic Co-operation and Development
OEM	original equipment manufacturer
OIE	Office International des Epizooties
P&C	parts and components
PPP	public–private partnership
R&D	research and development
RCA	revealed comparative advantage
RULC	relative unit labour cost
S&T	science and technology
SAP	Structural Adjustment Program (World Bank)
SMEs	small and medium-sized enterprises
SOEs	state-owned enterprises
SP	Stabilization Program (IMF)
SPS	Sanitary and Phytosanitary Agreement (WTO agreement)
TBT	Technical Barriers to Trade Agreement (WTO agreement)
TC	technological capability
TCA	theory of competitive advantage
TCB	theory of capability building
TH	Triple Helix (model of innovation)
TNCs	transnational corporations or companies
TQC	total quality control
TQM	total quality management
TRIMs	Trade-Related Investment Measures (WTO agreement)

TRIPs	Trade-Related Aspects of Intellectual Property Rights (WTO agreement)
UK	United Kingdom
UN	United Nations
UNCTAD	United Nations Conference on Trade and Development
UNDP	United Nations Development Programme
UNESCO	United Nations Educational, Science and Cultural Organization
UNIDO	United Nations Industrial Development Organization
UR	Uruguay Round
URAs	Uruguay Round agreements
USA	United States of America
WIP	work-in-progress
WTO	World Trade Organization

1

INTRODUCTION: FRAMEWORK OF ANALYSIS

> The problem that is usually being visualized is how capitalism administers existing structure, whereas the relevant problem is how it creates and destroys them. As long as this is not recognized, the investigator does a meaningless job. (Schumpeter 1934, 84)

The issue of competitiveness has attracted a lot of attention, both at the academic and practical levels, during the last quarter-century, i.e. since the emergence of the new economic philosophy in favour of market orientation and trade liberalization. Such development has, in turn, resulted in changes in the rules of the game in business and in international trade. Some have regarded competitiveness as an important element of success in economic performance (e.g. OECD 1992); others have considered it as a misplaced concept and an obsession (e.g. Krugman 1994). The problem is that when the concept of competitiveness is applied to developing countries, it is often delinked to economic development as though competitiveness is an end per se. If this were the case one could go to the extreme in arguing that one could sell everything at zero prices on the international market!

Some proponents of the neoclassical theory of international trade do refer to the prevalence of some market failure, particularly in the case of developing countries. Nevertheless, the orthodox theoretical background to competitiveness is the pure neoclassical theory of static comparative cost advantage (CA), which is the philosophical and ideological basis of the 'Washington Consensus', activities of international financial institutions and their recommendations for economic reform and universal, across-the-board trade liberalization in developing countries. It is also the philosophy behind the GATT/WTO as a multilateral trade organization which sets rules on international trade.

According to the neoclassical theory, inherited and evolved from Adam Smith's theory of international trade, comparative advantage is rooted in resource endowment: capital, including natural resources, and labour. Material capital is the main source of specialization, division of labour and growth. The doctrine of CA, as it is applied, however, is a static theory, based on a number of unrealistic assumptions, and does not contribute to long-term development. For example it is assumed *inter alia* that technological knowledge is freely available in the market, and that the firm, which is a nucleus of economic activities in modern world, is atomistic and passive. This theory disregards the fact that economic development requires the upgrading of the production structure, which is a policy-induced activity requiring government intervention for specialization based on dynamic comparative advantage.

While a number of alternative theories have been developed to explain competitiveness, there is no satisfactory theoretical framework relevant to the case of developing countries. We will develop a framework of analysis based on Reinert's view on competitiveness. To him competitiveness is an element of development; it refers to activities, which, while 'being competitive' in the micro sense, also contribute to development, raising income, and contribute to the improvement in the standard of living of the population of a nation (Reinert 1995, 26). To do so, we have benefited from the views and theories of a number of economists such as F. List (1856), Kalecki (1955), Schumpeter (1934), Penrose (1959), Hirschman (1958) and Lazonick (1991), proponents of the theory of capability building, and Shafaeddin (2005c).

According to List (1856) productive power is the main source of comparative advantage, and development and mental capital (knowledge), rather than material capital, is the main source of productive power. Division of labour and accumulation of capital are the results of development. Knowledge is not given; it is to be acquired through education, science, training, discoveries, inventions, experience and division of labour. Further, according to List, knowledge is determined by social order, i.e. sociopolitical and institutional factors (Shafaeddin 2005a). List's theory is a dynamic one and, though it is an important step forward, the role of the firm in his theory is not well developed.

Kalecki (1955), like List, gives importance to sociopolitical and institutional factors in economic development. According to him, the contribution of capital accumulation to capacity building and development is limited by sociopolitical, institutional, infrastructural and other structural factors. In particular he maintains that the interest of the government might not necessarily coincide with the interest of the public at large. In other words, the government 'indifference decision curves' may diverge from the community's indifference curves (Kalecki 1971). However, he ignores the important role of the firm in his theory of capacity building and development even though in his theory of capitalist economy, designed for the case of developed countries, firms play an important role.

Schumpeter (1934) pioneered in placing the role of the firm and entrepreneurship in the centre of his theory of competitiveness and development. In his theory, a firm is active, has a strategy, and may have the knowledge and capabilities to change technology. Further, it influences not only the market but also the performance of other firms through its 'creative destruction'.

The Schumpeterian concept of firm is the centrepiece in our analysis of firm activities. Nevertheless, using elements of, and developing on, the theories of dynamic comparative advantage, productive power of F. List, competitive advantage of M. Porter, business organization of Lazonick, and the theory of capability building, we will argue that the firm is not an abstract concept. It is the main coordinator of economic activities; it has links with other firms, market, government and consumers (Shafaeddin 2005c). Furthermore, entrepreneurs not only play the coordinating role, but also perform 'creative' and 'cooperative' functions as suggested by Hirschman (1958). Moreover, like

Penrose (1959), we regard a firm as a collective learning unit. According to her, firms are 'living organs', with their own specific culture, collective capabilities and specific knowledge. Therefore, knowledge is firm specific.

Finally we regard competitiveness as a means to development, not an end per se. To increase income, and the rent accrued to a firm and a country, a firm can be operated in such a way as to make it difficult for others to compete with it – that is, by creating a unique situation that cannot be replicated easily. Creating barriers to entry is often considered as a means of achieving this objective. Moreover, it is important to create value for buyers in a unique way. This can be done through a number of measures of which creating favourable reputation and unique culture is the most important one.

Let us define the concept of competitive advantage (as distinct from comparative advantage) before going further. The theory of comparative advantage, whether in its static or dynamic version, is basically concerned with the role of cost and prices in completion under restrictive assumptions – particularly the assumption of the prevalence of a competitive market. In contrast, the concept of 'competitive advantage' also takes into account the role of non-cost/price factors. Further, it deals with the issue of competitiveness of a firm or country under imperfect competition and oligopolistic market structure.

To continue, competitive advantage is a dynamic concept requiring development of knowledge, technology and organization, which can be acquired, enhanced and utilized through learning. As a dynamic concept, competitive advantage can change over time requiring upgrading, which in turn necessitates the upgrading of products, process, knowledge and organization. Achieving competitiveness is a moving target. Competitiveness is a relative concept as others also try to improve their advantage. Such changes, however, cannot take place automatically through the operation of an allocative function of market forces, which is the sphere of static comparative advantage. Competitiveness, as a dynamic concept and as a means to development, is in the sphere of the theory of dynamic comparative advantage and 'creative function' of the market. Developing the necessary capabilities in turn requires taking policy measures and actions based on strategies at the level of firm, sectors and the national economy.

Competitiveness is not an abstract concept: it occurs through the actions of a firm, located in a specific country with specific characteristics and environment, against other national as well as international firms, with a particular product or products, in a marketplace with a specific structure, under certain world economic conditions; its aim is to obtain certain development objectives at the level of firm and nation. To obtain their objectives, firms and their governments take some specific actions and pursue a strategy over time.

Therefore, to put competitiveness in its proper context, one may refer to related issues by a triple 'C': 'concepts' (theories of competitiveness); 'context' or conditions under which countries compete in international market; and the way firms and countries 'cope with', or should cope with, the issue of competitiveness in their development strategy. In each case a number of questions arise. What does competitiveness mean? Why has it attracted increasing attention during recent decades? What is the relevance of different approaches to competitiveness to the economic development of developing countries? Is the objective of competitiveness to gain market share or to raise the standard of living of the citizens of the exporting country? What does competitiveness strategy mean? How do changes in economic philosophy, liberalization of trade and foreign direct investment (FDI), rapid technological changes, and new organization of production and changes in market structure affect the competitive position of developing countries? What sort of competitive strategy is envisaged for developing countries, both at the firm and national levels, to cope with the new situation without sacrificing their sustainable growth and development?

The answer to these questions occupies the minds of policy makers in developing countries and a thorough treatment of the issues involved is beyond the scope of one volume. Nevertheless, our main purpose in this book is to provide a framework for the analysis by taking up the main question: how can competitiveness contribute to the aspiration of the people of developing countries to raising their standard of living?

In the remainder of this chapter we will clarify the main concept and develop the analytical framework applied in this study. To do so, we will start by explaining the different approaches, static and dynamic, to competitiveness as applied in the literature. Such distinction is extremely important in our analysis. This is so particularly because, while developed countries have been concerned with competitiveness at the high level of development through technological development and concomitant upgrading of their industrial structure and services, they have been imposing competitiveness at the low level of development on developing countries. This is done through advocacy of neoliberal ideology, e.g. the Washington Consensus, and is imposed on developing countries through international organizations such as the IMF (International Monetary Fund), World Bank and WTO, or through bilateral and regional trade agreements. As firms are the coordinator of economic activities at the micro-level and play the central role in competitiveness of a country, we will then take up the conceptual issues related to firms before clarifying the meaning of strategy and productivity at the level of firms and national economy as employed in the study. Finally we will introduce the theme and the plan of the study.

Approaches to Competitiveness

The literature contains two different approaches to competitiveness related, *inter alia*, to the assumptions made on the structure and the behaviour of firms:

1. Static in which firms are small and passive, and competition is cost and price-led.
2. Dynamic in which firms are large with an active strategy, competition is a dynamic process, in its Schumpeterian sense.

The theoretical foundations behind these approaches are different.

Static approach

The static approach to competitiveness is based on the neoclassical theory of static comparative cost advantage (CA). Accordingly, in its Heckscher-Ohlian version, the comparative advantage is determined by its factor endowment – material capital and labour. Hence, countries specialize in the production and exports of those goods in production of which their most abundant factor of production is intensively used. On the basis of such specialization therefore they compete with each other. This approach to competitiveness is a theoretical abstraction with little practical value; it is based on a number of unrealistic assumptions as follows: product market is perfectly competitive; in each industry a large number of small firms operate without having any power over market prices; constant return to scale prevails at the firm level, which implies that as inputs to the firm increase by a certain proportion its output increases by the same proportion; firms are identical at the country and international levels; firms are passive, thus they take no strategic action; there are no firm- or industry-specific learning and other specific characteristics; there are no externalities; there are no barriers to entry to the market and exit from the market is costless; the products produced by various firms in the same industry are homogeneous; firms face a fixed set of technologies which are freely available to them; present cost and prices are independent of past (future) cost and prices; experience plays no role in cost determination; perfect competition also prevails in the factor market and factors of production are fully mobile both geographically and from one industry to another; perfect market information is available on supply, demand and future prices for all products and all factors of production; thus there is no uncertainty and no risks; buyers are numerous and have no power over the market; taste is given for a set of known products; economic institutions and organizations are given and are conducive to the operation of market forces.

The theory of static CA has several important implications for competitiveness. First, since firms are passive: that is they have no strategy and they cannot influence the market, they react to the market and compete with each other through cost. There is no rivalry on prices. Secondly there is no role for innovation and entrepreneurship. Thirdly economies of scale have no role to play in cost reduction and competitiveness – except Marshallian external economies of scale, i.e. scale of the manufacturing sector as a whole, which is compatible with perfect competition. Fourthly nonprice factors play no role in competitiveness whether at the level of firm or national economy. Sixthly as products in an industry are identical, nonprice attributes of a product have no role in competitiveness. Seventhly comparative advantage, thus, competitiveness, is explained by national and macroeconomic factors such as current market-determined factor costs, i.e. wages, interest rate, price of raw materials and exchange rates. Exchange rate is crucial in attaining international competitiveness since it translates internal prices into international ones. There is also no market failure in either the product market or factor market. Therefore, this implies that economic policy should be confined to the macro-level issues related to wage cost, or at best relative unit labour cost (RULC),[1] and exchange rate.

Critiques of the static approach

The static approach to competitiveness is, however, flawed with certain deficiencies for both theoretical and empirical reasons. In reality, outside agriculture, perfect competition is the

---

[1] In the Heckscher-Ohlian version of international trade theory, productivity plays no role either.

exception, not the rule (Schumpeter 1934, 78–9). Most industrial firms are large and dominate the market; economies of scales and scope prevail at the level of firms and plants in most industries; barriers to entry do exist; technology is not freely available; products produced by different firms are not necessarily homogeneous; accumulation of production over time does affect both cost and prices through gaining experience; market information is not perfect and uncertainties and risks are rampant. Firms are different, each having its own culture, specialized skills and other specific characteristics. There are also ample sources of market failures in the product and factor markets, particularly in developing countries at early stages of their industrialization and development. Moreover, the available theoretical empirical evidence indicates that other factors than costs, prices and exchange rate are also important in competitiveness. For example technology has been regarded a powerful main source of growth and the technology gap explains 'a major part of the difference in growth performance of countries (Krugman 1986; Fagerberg 1997). Similarly Fagerberg (1988), studying 15 industrial countries for the period 1960–83, concluded that '…the main factors influencing differences in international competitiveness [gaining market share] and growth across countries are technological competitiveness and the ability to compete on delivery' (1988, 371), which to a large extent depends on creating new production capacity requiring investment.[2] In contrast, the contribution of cost competitiveness was far less than other factors. In fact, in the particular case of Japan, while the country gained considerable market share *vis-à-vis* the UK and the USA during the 1960s and 1970s, at the same time its RULC increased significantly while those of the UK and USA declined.

The simultaneous increase in RULC and market share is referred to as 'Kaldor's paradox' in the literature. In a study for the period 1963–75, Kaldor (1982) concluded that countries with the fastest rate of growth of exports were those which at the same time experienced faster rates of increase in their RULC than others. On the basis of these results, he also concluded that in the long run relative changes in exchange rate can be the result of competitiveness, rather than its cause. Furthermore, relying on changes in RULC alone as a policy tool for improving competitiveness was, he argued, a simplistic view.[3]

In another study, Amendola et al. (1993), applying a dynamic approach to competitiveness, studied 16 developed countries for the period 1967–87 and reached similar results. The authors concluded that changes in unit labour costs and exchange (rate) 'display only short-run effects on changes in competitiveness' (1993, 463). These short-run effects are, however, reabsorbed in the longer run by more significant effects of technological learning, innovations[4] and country-specific factors, such as institutions, industrial organizations and policies (Amendola et al. 1993, 465–8). Amable and Verspagen (1995), studying 5 OECD countries and 18 industries, concluded that while price variables are important, nonprice variables, particularly technology – presented by patent – are also very important in export

---

2 Over two-thirds of growth in market share was accounted for by technological factors and the ability to deliver, respectively while the contribution of the RULC was slightly negative (ibid., table 4).

3 See also Fetherston et al. (1977) and Kellman (1983) for similar views expressed in the late 1970s and early 1980s.

4 Technological adaptation is embodied in new equipment and facilitated by investment but constrained by patents.

competitiveness. According to another empirical study, product quality and reputation are two other important factors in competitiveness (Esfahani 1991).

According to the OECD (Organisation for Economic Co-operation and Development), also in the long run, trends in relative exchange rates are explained by the competitive position of the country (OECD 1992, 241). The OECD adds that '[C]ountries which have a large number of industries in which they have a relatively high rate of innovation by international standards tend to experience a systematic appreciation of currencies over long periods, while less innovating countries witness persistent trade deficits and long-term currency depreciation' (Cantwell 1989, 181, cited in OECD 1992, 241).

Finally the environment within which firms operate, including structural characteristics of the country and government policies, has an important bearing on the competitiveness of firms (Best 1990; Porter 1990).

In a nutshell, competitiveness is a dynamic concept which is influenced by many factors at the level of firm and national economy – as it is also influenced by international factors. In a world where production and international trade are characterized by economies of scale, imperfect competition, barriers to entry and imperfect information, being competitive in the static neoclassical terms (relying solely on price and cost factors) would imply low value added and losses in terms of trade, income and employment. Competitive edge in exports of simple products based on low wage (static comparative advantage) is short lived and fails to produce sustainable growth. There is a need for:

> ...an industrial sector that develops a broad competitive base which is capable of remaining competitive as income rises. Building industrial competitiveness consists of moving away from static sources of cost advantage, and competitiveness strategy does not consist of simply cutting wages or retaining a market position in labour-intensive exports. (Lall 1990, 13)

The dynamic approach

The world of perfect competition is static. In reality, as already mentioned, competition is a process and firms are not passive; entrepreneurs take initiative to innovate and take strategic actions to change products, prices and technology and to influence tastes and market structure, etc. Hence, competitiveness is a dynamic concept. The dynamic approach to competitiveness has implications for the definitions of and factors contributing to competitiveness at both firm and country levels. At the firm level, gaining market share alone is not an objective; profit and growth are other main objectives. At the national level, the expansion of export per se is not to be regarded as a country's policy aim; rather competitiveness should contribute to the improvement in the standard of living of the population and growth of employment. Further, the definition of productivity takes a different dimension, as will be shortly explained. Another implication is that the role of both price/cost and nonprice factors in competitiveness should be envisaged in a dynamic context. It is within this framework and context that we can define competitiveness at the firm and national levels, linking it to the process of industrialization and development as is done in developed countries.

The Schumpeterian Approach

Firm level

At the level of firm, 'competitiveness' is referred to as the capacity of firms to compete and on the basis of their success in 'competitiveness', to gain market shares, increase their profits and grow (OECD 1992, 239). Hence, gaining market share alone is not regarded by the think-tank organization of developed countries as the objective of competitiveness. The OECD definition is close to the Schumpeterian approach to competitiveness. In its dynamic (Schumpeterian) sense, competition is a process of moving from one disequilibrium situation to another rather than a tendency towards equilibrium as is envisaged in the neoclassical theory. To Schumpeter, competition is a process of 'creative destruction' and discontinuous change. As production is a process of combing materials with other inputs, creative destruction means creating new combinations implying the 'competitive elimination of the old [combination]' (Schumpeter 1934, 67). According to him the new combination, whether by combining existing resources in a new way or with new resources, could include:

- The introduction of a new good – that is, one with which the consumers are not yet familiar – or of a new quality of existing goods;
- The introduction of a new method of production, that is, one not yet tested by experience in the branch of manufacture concerned, which by no means need be founded upon a discovery of scientifically new method; it can also take the form of a new way of handling a commodity commercially;
- The opening of a new market, that is, a market into which the particular branch of manufacture of the country in question has not previously entered, whether or not this market has existed before;
- The conquest of a new source of supply of raw materials or half-manufactured goods again irrespective of whether this source already exists or whether it has first to be created;
- The carrying out of the new organization of any industry, such as the creation of a monopoly position (for example through trustification) or the breaking up of a monopoly position (Schumpeter 1934, 66).

According to Schumpeter, such a process of competition:

…commands decisive cost or quality advantage and which strikes not at the margins of the profits and the output of existing firms but at their foundations and their very lives. This kind of competition is as much more effective than the other [competition on price] as a bombardment is in comparison with forcing a door, and so much more important that it becomes a matter of comparative indifference whether competition in the ordinary sense functions more or less promptly; the powerful lever that in the long run expands output and brings down prices is in any case made of other stuff. (Schumpeter 1934, 85)

By the 'other stuff', Schumpeter implies the process of 'creative destruction': '…the same process of industrial mutation…that incessantly revolutionizes the economic structure from within, incessantly destroying the old one, incessantly creating a new one. This process of Creative Destruction is the essential fact about capitalism' (Schumpeter 1934, 83).

In such a dynamic world, firms have different capabilities: different access to factor market, inputs and technology; different innovating, entrepreneurial and organizational abilities; different rate of in-job skill creation; different information about the market and marketing channels and distribution network. Such firm-specific capabilities provide them with a capacity to take strategic actions, through various Schumpeterian means outlined above, in order to create profit opportunities in the form of rents by developing a temporary monopoly position. The monopoly position would be temporary as other firms in the same industry are also engaged in a process of creative destruction to break that monopoly position or develop a 'new combination' superior to that of their rival in order to create profit opportunities and rents. This type of rent is a sort of 'entrepreneurial' rent different from monopoly rent arising from ownership of natural resources or windfall rent created by chance.

Therefore, the most important implications of the Schumpeterian approach to competitiveness are that: the firm is a driving force in economic activities; competition is a process through which a firm has to deal with disequilibrium; and firms shape the market through their activities by changing the cost curve and creating value for the consumers. According to Best such a firm has three main characteristics:

1 It 'does not seek to maximize profit simply by minimizing costs but seeks strategic advantage on the basis of Schumpeterian innovation in product, process, or organization';
2. Its goal 'is to gain strategic competitive advantage by continuous improvement in process and products';
3. It maintains organizational flexibility in order to adjust its competitive strategy 'depending upon the strength and weakness of its competitors at any point in time' (Best 1990, 11–12).

National level

At the national level also, developed countries consider competitiveness as a dynamic concept and as a means to raising the standard of living of their population. For example the OECD accepts fully the definition proposed in the 1985 Report of the US Presidential Commission on Industrial Competitiveness (vol. 2, 7). Accordingly:

Competitiveness for a nation is the degree to which it can, under *free* [my italics] and fair market conditions, produce goods and services that meets the test of international markets while simultaneously maintaining and expanding the real income of its citizens. Competitiveness is the basis for a nation's standard of living.

It is also fundamental to the expansion of employment opportunities and a nation's ability to meet its international obligations. (OECD 1992, 237)

This definition is largely similar to the one provided by Bruce Scott, a scholar of Harvard Business School with one exceptional difference. According to him:

> National competitiveness refers to a nation state's ability to produce, distribute and service goods in international economy in competition with goods and services produced in other countries, and to do so in a way that earns a rising standard of living. The ultimate measure of success is not a 'favourable' balance of trade, a positive current account, or an increase in foreign exchange reserves: it is an increase in standard of living. To be competitive as a country means to be able to employ national resources, notably the nation's labour force, in such a way as to earn rising level of real income through specialization and trade in the world economy. (Scott 1985, 14–15)

In Scott's definition producing and selling goods in competition with others – gaining or maintaining market share – is a necessary condition, but it is not sufficient. The sufficient condition is that it also improves the standard of living, i.e. it contributes to income growth of the population – in the form of return to both labour and capital and to the creation of employment (Scott 1985, 15). He also refers to the question of income distribution. Therefore, if increase in sales and market share is accompanied by decreased real wages and/or profit…it either reduces total income of the population or leads to deterioration in income inequality. He emphasizes that 'ordinarily the competitive challenge for a nation is to maintain or increase market share while enhancing wages and salaries as well as the returns on capital' (Scott 1985, 16).

The exceptional difference between the definition of competitiveness by Scott and the OECD/US presidential commission is that in the latter case reference is made to the free market, which seems unrealistic under a current market structure dominated by large firms and influenced by government policies.

According to a more realistic definition by Scott, the key indicators of competitiveness include: 'market share, profitability, real incomes for employees, employment, productivity, relative unit cost levels both for capital and labour and investment for the future in new technologies (R&D), new equipment, and enhanced skills for employees' (1985, 16). In this sense of the term, national competitiveness is an element of development; it refers to activities that, while 'being competitive' in the micro sense, also contribute to development, raising income and improvement in the standard of living (Reinert 1995, 26). Otherwise, one could think of a situation where the improvement in efficiency and productivity is transferred entirely to other countries, as argued by Prebisch in the case of primary commodities. In the case of manufactured goods also, many light (generic) manufactured goods exported by developing countries have similar features to primary commodities. In such cases one may talk of commoditization of manufactured goods. Reinert argues,

> the very idea of a nation lifting itself to higher levels of living standards through competitiveness – being engaged in activities that raise the national living

standards more than other activities – goes directly against the assumptions and beliefs which form the foundation of the neoclassical economic edifice. (Reinert 1995, 26)

Growth in productivity due to technological change, innovation and other factors is obviously beneficial. What is important, however, according to Reinert is that '…an important portion of the benefits is being distributed inside the producing nations through higher profits, higher wages, and higher taxable income overall' (1995, 27). Choosing activities that carry high rents, appropriating such rent and continuously upgrading, can contribute to achieving this goal. Incidentally, the question of appropriation of rent, explains the registration of patents and protection of technology governed by Intellectual Property Right (IPR) Agreement (see Appendix 1), through the WTO and other forums, by developed countries.

According to Oxley and Yeung (1998a, xxvi), upgrading is essential for maintaining or improving value added. 'In policy discussion, the term [competitiveness] usually refers to the ability to capture high value added industries which possibly generate rents and positive externalities that spill over to the rest of the economy.' Hence, activities that support the competitiveness of a national economy include those that '…retain the high value-added production activities which can lead to higher factor earnings and improving living standards' (Oxley and Yeung 1998a, xiv). Competitiveness, is not about 'one of overall competitiveness but of competition over those sectors that are of special value to the economy', referred to as strategic sectors by Krugman (1987, 208). Sectors which have special value to the economy include 'high-value-added sectors, linkages sectors, sunrise industries, and catalyst industries' (Krugman 1987, 208). In a more general term, one may speak of supply dynamic and demand dynamic industries. Supply dynamic industries are those which provide linkages and spill-overs, and thus externalities, to other activities. Demand dynamic industries include those for which demand rises fast in the international and domestic economy because of their high income elasticity (UNCTAD 2002, ch. 3). Thus upgrading is required to sustain competitiveness.

The upgrading of the production structure is a feature of the Schumpeterian approach to competition which implies mobility, that is, 'movement of factors of production from low occupation to high reward ones' (Reekie 1979, 11), or upgrading from low-value uses towards high-value uses (Reekie 1979, 82). The process of upgrading from low occupation to high rewards activities is depicted in the following figure. As is shown, low-quality activities are the characteristics of a situation where static comparative advantage and perfect competition prevail. Slow growth, and low wages and income are two main results of low-quality activities, which require little technological progress, R&D, learning and thus knowledge, and scale economies. In contrast, the high-quality activities take place under dynamic imperfect competition involving steep learning, rapid technological change, R&D, important economies of scale and high growth of output and income. Nevertheless, such characteristics and outcome are irrelevant in the world of static comparative advantage and perfect competition (see Figure 1.1).

Figure 1.1. The process of upgrading and moving from low-paid to high-paid occupation

BLACK:

Dynamic imperfect competition (high-quality activity)

Characteristics of high-quality activities:
– Steep learning curves
– High growth in output
– Rapid technological progress
– High R&D contents
– Necessitates and generates "learning-by-doing"
– Imperfect information

DARK GREY: – Investments come in large "chunks"/are indivisible (drugs)
Shoes (1850–1900) – Imperfect, but dynamic, competition
                   – High wage level
Golf balls   – Possibilities of important economies of scale and scope
Automotive paint   – High industry concentration
                   – High stakes: high barriers to entry and exit
                   – Branded product
                   – Standard neoclassical assumptions completely irrelevant

Characteristics of low-quality activities:
– Flat learning curves
– Low growth in output
– Little technological progress
– Low R&D contents
– Little personal or institutional learning required
– Perfect information
– Divisible investments (tools for a baseball factory)
– Perfect competition

LIGHT GREY: – Low wage level
                   – Little or no economies of scale/risk of diminishing returns
House paint   – Fragmented industry
                   – Low stakes: low barriers to entry and exit
Shoes (1993)   – Neoclassical assumptions a reasonable approximation of reality
Baseballs

WHITE:

Perfect competition (low-quality activity)

Source: Reinert (1995, 39).

Moving up from competitiveness at low-quality activities to high-quality activities does not take place through the operation of invisible hands of market forces and passive firms and passive government of the type envisaged by neoliberals. To achieve competitiveness by pursuing policies for attaining dynamic comparative advantage requires firms with specific characteristics and strategies; it also requires strategies at the national level.

The Schumpeterian/Penrosian Firm

Following Penrose (1959), we will consider a firm as an important agent for coordinating economic activities and as a growing social organ with collective learning capabilities and specific skills.

Beyond the world of neoclassical theory there are two different ways, in the literature, of looking at a firm as a basic unit for organization of business:

1. Firm as an administrative and management unit;
2. Firm as a 'living social organism' or unit with its own culture.

In the first sense of the term, a firm is a planning unit; economic activities within a firm are performed without going through the market. The larger the size of the firm, the greater will be the importance of activities undertaken within the firm rather than through the market. The question of size takes importance, as large firms, particularly transnational companies (TNCs), are different from small firms in their organization, administration and management, strategic behaviour and performance, as well as their impact on the market and other firms.

In the second sense a firm is more than an administrative-organizational unit. It is also a growing organ 'not as a price and-output decision maker for given products' (Penrose 1959, 14). It is 'a collection of productive resources the disposal of which between different uses and over time is determined by administrative decisions' (Penrose 1959, 24). Accordingly, a firm has the following main characteristics:

- A collective nature: A firm is a collection of productive resources, i.e. human resources and physical resources. Physical resources consist of tangible materials such as capital and inputs and human resources comprise managerial, technical, administrative staff, etc. The productive resources of the firm are inputs to the operation of the firm for providing productive services.
- A social organism with its unique culture: The managers and employees of the firm have constant contact with each other and with others outside the firm; they work as a team and also have cooperative functions with others outside the firm.
- A distinctive culture of learning: The learning culture of the firm together with its teamwork contributes to continuous improvement in capabilities and organizational aspects of the firm. That distinctive culture of learning implies that knowledge and experience is firm specific.

Implications for Competitiveness

The above approach to the definition of the firm has important implications for the accumulation of knowledge and experience, and entrepreneurship, which are two crucial factors in competitiveness and in achieving dynamic comparative advantage. Knowledge and experience have become increasingly significant in the present system of global production and distribution (see Chapter 7). Therefore, the role of human resources and the culture of the firm in learning, development of specialized skills, knowledge creation and competitiveness are crucial. Specialized skill and knowledge have a few main characteristics:

- They are embodied in individual workers as well as managers.
- They are firm specific and often personalized.

- They are a sort of 'capital stock that can be accumulated only through investment in education and training and through gaining experience' (Odigari 1992, 1). The knowledge and experience do not transmit through the market entirely.
- They are the combination of services provided by various individuals, rather than the collection of individuals' knowledge, that gives firms their unique characteristics. In other words, any firm has the knowledge of being in a unique situation, i.e. different from other firms (Reekie 1979, 7). The new knowledge developed within a firm through specialization, learning and experience is essential for the process of innovation and productivity growth needed for competition in the marketplace.
- The implication of our approach to the definition of the firm for the function of entrepreneurs and managers is also important; as a social organism, a firm does not operate in isolation; it is connected to other firms, government, market, institutions.

According to Hirschman (1958, 16–17), entrepreneurs have two functions: 'creative and cooperative'. The creative function of entrepreneurship is an individualistic characteristic: an entrepreneur is prepared to take risks by breaking through old practices and to introduce new approaches to production, distribution and marketing, and organization (Schumpeter 1934). The cooperative function of an entrepreneur involves attracting the cooperation of various parties involved in activities of the firm both inside and outside the firm. Those outside the firm include suppliers of inputs, intermediate products and services, transportation and distribution; government agencies; officials of various institutions and consumers, etc. The ability of an entrepreneur to mobilize a sense of cooperation inside the firm, however, is somewhat more important than the relation with the outside as far as competitiveness of the firm is concerned, for two main reasons. First whatever agreement is reached with the outside parties has to be implemented inside the firm. Secondly issues of innovation and knowledge development are internal ones requiring coordination and close cooperation of the employees at large. The cooperative function of a firm is closely related to its function as a coordinator of economic activities.

The Firm as a Coordinating Agency[5]

The traditional theoretical literature to coordination of economic activities, regards, explicitly or implicitly, market and/or government as the only coordination mechanism. In practice, the coordination of economic activities in an economy takes place through a combination of markets, state and firms, complemented by 'nonprice factors'. The nonprice factors include institutions, organizations and infrastructure. Such a coordination system is also influenced by the outside world. None of these mechanisms is, however, perfect on its own and cannot succeed without interaction with others and without the complementary role played by nonprice factors. Figure 1.2 shows the interrelation among various mechanisms. The nature of that combination, the relative role of each mechanism and the degree of the interaction among various mechanisms vary from one country to another and over time in each country, depending on the level

---

5 The following pages are based mainly on Shafaeddin (2005c).

Figure 1.2. Interlinkages of market, firm, government and nonprice factors

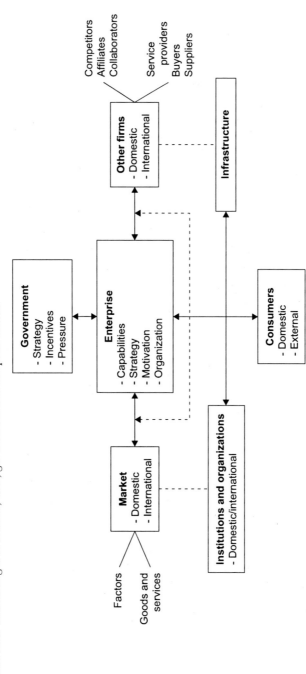

Source: Shafaeddin (2005c, 113).

of development, structural, historical and sociopolitical conditions of the country. It is also influenced by the interrelation among various sectors of the economy.

No generalization can be made. Nevertheless, contrary to the assumption made in the neoclassical theory, Figure 1.2 indicates that the firm is an active and driving force in such a coordination system, around which the other coordination agents operate (see Shafaeddin 2005c, ch. 4 for details).

To explain further, in a world where large firms increasingly dominate production and international trade, coordination of certain transactions or economic activities increasingly takes place through a nonmarket coordinating mechanism (firm) rather than through the market. This mechanism includes strategic planning – the planning system – and vertical and horizontal coordination among firms through networking, long-term supply and purchase contracts, technological alliance, etc. (Galbraith 1975; O. Williamson 1975; Lazonick 1991; Best 1990; Porter 1990).

At the turn of the twenty-first century 70 per cent of world trade was undertaken by 500 companies, and 200 and 1,000 firms dominated 28 per cent of total world output and 80 per cent of industrial output respectively (Mooney 2000, 74). Since the early twenty-first century, the degree of concentration of firms has further increased significantly because of merger and acquisition as shown in Table 1.1. As a result, a few of the largest TNCs dominated each industry, as is shown in Table 1.2, which depicts the largest 100 nonfinancial TNCs. Furthermore, these TNCs are owned predominantly by developed countries (20 of them are owned by the USA alone); only 7 of them are owned by developing countries, out of which only 3 (2 in the Republic of Korea and 1 in Hong Kong) are involved in manufacturing, with the rest in primary commodities. No developing country owns a company in the list of 50 largest financial TNCs (based on www.UNCTAD.org/ WIR, 2011, table 29).

To continue, the relative role and success of firms depends on three main factors: motivation (incentives), pressure and the internal organization of the firm – which in turn would depend, *inter alia*, on the degree of entrepreneurship. The market, through forces of competition and the government, through other incentives and/or disciplines, provides motivation of and pressure on the entrepreneurs. The success of entrepreneurs

Table 1.1. Annual average cross-border mergers and acquisitions with value of more than $1 billion (1987–2010)

Period	No. of deals	Value ($billion)
1987–96	29.3	60.7
1997–99	107	377.8
2000–2004	127.6	438.2
2005–2008	228	814.9
2010	152	324
Of which:		
Mergers with values of $5–18.8 billion	14	110

Source: Based on UNCTAD (2008a; 2009a; http://www.UNCTAD.org/WIR).

Table 1.2. Top 100 nonfinancial TNCs in terms of their foreign assets in 2010

Industry	No. of firms	Industry	No. of firms
Chemicals	3	Pharmaceuticals	8
Electrical/electronic equipment	10	Automotive	12
Petroleum[a]	9	Utilities	12
Telecommunications/utilities	6	Retail and wholesale trade	5
Construction and real estate	2	Metal and metal products	4
Mining and quarrying	6	Nonmetal minerals	3
Food, beverage and tobacco	8	Aircraft	2
Transport and storage	2	Machinery and equipment	2
Diversified	4	Business and engineering services	2

Note: [a] Refining/distribution and mining.
Source: Based on http://www.UNCTAD.org/WIR (accessed 10 July 2012).

depends on three main factors: their capabilities to develop and update the firm's strategic behaviour, thus their ability to compete on price and 'nonprice attributes'; their capabilities within the internal organization of the firm to attain efficiency, productivity and upgrading; the environment within which they operate, which to a large extent is influenced by government policies and strategies at the macro, sectorial and micro-levels. In other words, the strategic actions of a firm and its active behaviour towards other firms, market, government and the outside world affect its performance.

Interaction with other firms

The interaction of a firm with other firms might take place, either directly or indirectly, through the market; it also comprises relations with competitors or with firms involved in both upstream and downstream activities of the firm. Long-term supply contracts, outsourcing, clustering, etc. are examples of the latter. Clustering, which contributes to collective efficiency, is a vehicle providing framework for cooperation between the firm and its supply providers, its marketing channels as well as its competitors. The direct interaction of a firm with other firms replaces the coordination function of the market in the activities concerned. In their interaction with the market, or with other firms, however, the nonprice factors play the role of catalyst. For example the implementation of an input purchase contract is not easily possible without the availability of sufficient infrastructural and institutional facilities for transport, credit financing, insurance, etc.

In performing its function, a firm is connected with other firms in a chain of activities for design and product development, production, marketing and distribution, consumption and recycling. 'The value chain describes the full range of activities which are required to bring a product or service from conception, through the different phases of production (involving a combination of physical transformation and input of various producer services), delivery to final consumers, and final disposal after use' (Kaplinsky and Morris 2000, 4). In this sense, we may refer to it as the supply chain, which is different from M. Porter's concept of value chain (see Chapter 4). Hereafter, we use 'value chain' to mean 'the supply chain' unless otherwise explicitly mentioned.

The concept of value chain is important for two main reasons. First, it is believed that the competitiveness of a firm depends not only on the efficiency of the firm itself but also on the externalities created by the other firms involved, including those involved in the supply chain. Secondly, as knowledge and skill are firm specific, each firm has a core competence which cannot easily be copied by others. Therefore, it is recommended that each firm concentrates on activities in which it has core competence and should outsource the remaining competences to other firms in the value chain (Kaplinsky and Morris 2000, 10), e.g. through production sharing.

A firm may also be connected to other firms through 'clustering' or an industrial district. Clustering means rival firms are geographically concentrated in a region constituting a cluster of industries linked with each other. The industrial district is a wider concept where rival firms and/or firms involved in downstream or upstream activities of an industry are located in a region. In both cases the firms involved enjoy a sort of external economies – or what is called 'collective efficiency'. Firms in an industry may also collaborate with each other through industrial or trade associations.

Interaction with government

The activities and capabilities of a firm in a country are influenced by the activities and policies of the government directly or indirectly through the market and 'nonprice factors' with their influence on cost, prices and profits of firms. The government takes action through allocating resources, creating and developing markets or remedying market failure. It also takes measures for providing an appropriate institutional, infrastructural and organizational framework as well as other 'nonprice factors' for the smooth operation of the market. Through provision of incentives and pressures as well, the government may influence both cost and profits of a firm. Hence, government actions and policies influence market structure, firms' behaviour and their performance. The interaction between firms and the government machinery improves where there is a formal, or informal, mechanism for private–public relations.

The external environment

The external (international) environment influences the behaviour and capacities of a firm. The power and policies of TNCs, the government of main trading partners and international institutions influence the behaviour of firms not only directly but also indirectly through their impact on other elements of the coordinating system, i.e. government and market. For example the degree of international market concentration in an industry affects the ability of a developing country firm to enter the international market. The strategy and behaviour of large TNCs affects the ability of the existing firms to compete in that market. Further, the involvement of TNCs, through FDI, in a developing country affects the structure of the domestic market, the autonomy of decision making of the government and puts the independent national firms in an unfavourable competitive position. Similarly trade policies of the trading partners and the rules and regulations drawn by international trade and financial institutions, namely WTO, World Bank and IMF, limit the policy autonomy of the government in a developing country. Further, they influence the access of national firms to the international market, positively or negatively, depending on the rules they set or measures they take.

Dynamics of change

The relative role of firms in relation to market and government may vary from one country to another and over time in each country. Nevertheless, at the early stages of their development, developing countries face a dilemma because all coordination mechanisms run the high risk of failure. In these countries, market failure is pervasive because of the lack, or underdevelopment, of markets. The risk of entrepreneurship failure is high because of the lack of experienced entrepreneurs and underdevelopment of the formal sector. Similarly the risk of government failure is significant because of the low capacity of the government. The lower the level of development, the higher is the risk of coordination failure. Moreover, there is a vicious circle. The country is underdeveloped because of the failure of the coordination mechanisms; the coordination mechanisms fail because of the low level of development. Such vicious circle, however, does not justify the elimination of government intervention or the role of firms or market. In fact, to break this circle, action should be taken on all fronts: to create or improve markets; to increase the organizational capacity of entrepreneurs; to develop the necessary infrastructure and institutional framework of the country; and last not least, to increase the capacity of the state in policy formulation and decision making.

Nevertheless, to break the vicious circle, initially a key role is to be played by the government as indicated by the experience of all developed countries, newly industrialized economies (NIEs) and next-tier NIEs (see Shafaeddin 1998). Neither the market nor the nonprice factors, such as institutions, organizations and infrastructure, will be developed rapidly by market forces per se. The development of the state capacity and its efficiency requires education, training, motivation, sense of responsibility in the civil service, discipline and, most of all, the enhancement of the learning capacity, i.e. 'learning to learn', representation and accountability.

Since the design of industrial policy for achieving competitiveness with development differs from one country to another, nobody knows what the 'right policy' should be in each specific case. It is a question of trial and error – learning by doing. As markets, firms and nonprice factors are developed, government intervention may be gradually reduced, not only in international trade but also in all spheres of economic activities, in favour of market and firms.

Relation with consumers

As goods and services are produced for customers in internal and international markets, it is important that a firm, as well as a country, takes measures which creates and maintains 'value' to the consumers. While taking those measures, a firm also contributes to its own profit and income of the factors of production used. In addition to reputation for quality and after-sale services at the firm level, once again there is a need for long-term strategy at the level of both firm and country.

Strategy

Although strategy is defined differently by different scholars, we prefer the definition provided by Fahey (1994) and Davies et al. (2003). According to Fahey: 'Strategy [of a firm] is the means by which the organization creates and leverages changes in and around the market place' (1994, 7). Davies et al. define it in a similar fashion: 'strategy is about matching the competence of the organization to [the opportunities and challenges of] its environment. A strategy describes how an organization aims to meet its objectives' (Davies et al. 2003, 4). More precisely, strategy is about the direction of the firm to guide business over a long time period. Thus, the term 'strategy' implies initiating changes not only in response to internal and external events and environment, but also, more importantly, in anticipation of related changes. However, while their definition is a micro-concept, we can generalize it as a strategy that is not confined to firm-level issues. It is necessary to have strategy at various levels: business unit, corporation, industry and particularly country, i.e. national industrial strategy. As upgrading is essential in competitiveness in its dynamic sense, a strategy should also encompass issues related to upgrading at all levels.

A lot of emphasis has been placed, in recent decades, on the need for a strategy at the firm level. In contrast, the need for a national strategy has been downplayed. In fact, according to neoliberals there is no need for industrial strategy.

Further, one may also refer to strategies according to different functions of a firm: production (manufacturing) strategy comprising mass production; vertical integration; production sharing; diversification and flexible production; marketing strategy; advertisement strategy; human resource strategy; information strategy; financial strategy; R&D and technological strategy. The target of a strategy may be either the domestic or external market. The external environment may create both risks and opportunities for a firm as well as the country. Development in the global economy, changes in the market structure of an industry, technological changes as well as policies of other governments, and international rules and regulations are relevant at all levels: country, industry, firm and business unit. Therefore, for the sake of analysis, one should distinguish production strategy in general from export strategy – although production strategy and export strategy have many elements in common. Many of the elements of the firm-level strategy are also relevant at the national level.

For a firm or business unit, changes in competitive strategies of rival firms, possibility of new entrants, policies of buyers and suppliers and of product and factor markets, and changes in national environment, both economic and sociopolitical, are also to be considered. The strategy of a firm is also linked to both the creative and cooperative functions of an entrepreneur. The strategies related to creative functions are the domain of economics and business as outlined under different functional strategies above. The cooperative function of entrepreneurs requires sociopolitical and external relation strategy. The sociopolitical situation changes, and so do the relations with suppliers, buyers and others.

A national competitive strategy is as important as, if not more important than, a firm-level strategy in the process of industrialization and development of competitive industrial capacity. In such as strategy, trade and industrial policies, technological learning, R&D and training for technological development take the central role.

Following a strategic approach at any level – country, industry, firm or business unit – requires vision; mission; organization and structure. Further, it also involves a process which includes various stages, i.e. formulation, implementation and control/revision.

In the traditional economic theory, a firm has cost strategy and the government is supposed to have no industrial strategy. In perfect competition, cost minimization is the strategy of a firm as it does not have control on prices and products are homogeneous; in oligopolistic competition, price competition is the strategy of the firm and cost minimization is its organizational means. In the Schumpeterian approach, a manager chooses from among its various strategies – price and nonprice competition – and adjusts its organization accordingly (Best 1990, 139).

Productivity

In its normal sense, productivity depends only on the physical volume of goods produced. In the Schumpeterian forms of competition, productivity is influenced by two additional factors: value created for consumers and the allocation of income generated along the value chain to the producing firms. Thus the questions are how one is to create value for the consumers and how one is to allocate more a resulting rent to the firm and the factors of production.

Implications for Developing Countries

The very existence of Schumpeterian competition in the international market has implications not only for established firms, but more importantly for newcomer firms, particularly the firms of developing countries. It has implication for established firms because, as Schumpeter states: 'It disciplines before it attacks' (Schumpeter 1934, 85). In other words, each firm is constantly under competitive pressure. But the newcomer firms, particularly those from developing countries, are in an extremely inferior position. They face the barriers to entry in international markets and have no economy of scale, economy of scope, experience, technological capabilities, market information and managerial skills. Yet they have to compete with large, established firms in the international as well as national market. In particular, to be able eventually to compete at a high level of development, they will face a proportionately greater task ahead for which they will have to prepare themselves.

The Theme and Plan of the Book

We will argue in the rest of this book that: competitiveness at a high level of development cannot be achieved through specialization based on static cost comparative advantage advocated by neoliberals; such a specialization will lock low-income countries into production of primary commodities and, at best, assembly operation, making them compete at a low level of development. We will also explain that achieving competitiveness at a high level of development requires creating supply capacity in high-value-added activities, making the established capacity efficient and continuously upgrading the industrial structure. Developing countries are a diverse group: some have to develop supply capacity, some already have developed some capacity but have to make it efficient, while yet others have to upgrade their industrial structure. Prospects for achieving competitiveness at a high level of development for each group are limited if they rely on the operation of market forces alone. Also, proactive and conducive government policies and strategies are required, *inter alia*, for the development of indigenous capabilities of national enterprise. To achieve it, the policy space of developing countries should not become further limited and, in fact, should be enhanced by changes in international trade rules and the practices of international financial institutions (IFIs) and developed country donors in their bilateral and regional trade agreement with developing countries.

Within this framework, Chapter 2 will be devoted to the context and conditions under which competition takes place. We will explain that since the early 1980s a number of developments have taken place in the international economy which have made entry into and competition within international markets more difficult for new enterprises, particularly the firms of developing countries. Such developments include: changes in the economic philosophy in favour of market orientation and trade liberalization; the organization of international production in favour of globalization facilitated by liberalization of trade and FDI flows; rapid technological changes and a decrease in transport and transaction costs; increased risks in new investments due to enhanced complexity and rapidity of technological changes resulting in increases in the length and cost of learning; increases in the scale of production and market concentration enhancing barriers to entry; the emergence of new methods of organization and production, e.g. flexible manufacturing; emergence of China as a massive producer of labour-intensive products and assembly operation of technology-intensive goods. Such changes in the international economy have increased the need for government support to newcomer firms of developing countries. Yet, their policy space has been limited by international trade rules, the practices of IFIs and pressure from developed countries through bilateral and regional trade agreements.

In Chapter 3, after describing the deficiencies in the neoclassical theory, alternative theories of competitiveness will be reviewed. It will be argued that there is a lacuna for a comprehensive dynamic policy framework to achieve competitive advantage at a high level of development in developing countries. A critical view of M. Porter's theory of competitive advantage and Lazonick's theory of interaction between organization and innovation will be presented. Subsequently, the theory of productive power of F. List and the theory of capability building will be discussed. We will explain that Porter's theory does not go far enough to explain the implication of increasing return to scale; that Lazonick's theory remedies this problem but lacks macro-foundation and development perspective and does not consider the firm as a sociocultural unit. F. List's theory is one step forward as it has development perspectives but it lacks a micro-foundation. This problem is dealt with by the proponents of the theory of capability building (TCB). The micro-foundation of TCB, however, is based on the theory of perfect completion, which is in contrast to the practical reality of the international market for manufactured products dominated by large TNCs.

In Chapters 4–6, we will develop our own framework of analysis presented earlier in this chapter. In Chapter 4 we will explain other factors than factor cost and prices in competitiveness, including internal and external economies of scale and economies of scope. The importance of X-efficiencies and 'nonprice attributes' of products and the strategic behaviour of large firms in the competitiveness of firms is explained. Through 'three pronged investment' (à la Chandler) in manufacturing, marketing and management, and R&D, large global firms create barriers to entry for newcomer firms of developing countries. Further, new methods of organization of firms, such as the 'flexible manufacturing system', and their implications for the competitiveness of established firms as well as firms of developing countries will be explained. In Chapter 5, we will explain the external economies arising from vertical and horizontal interfirm relations and their implications for competitiveness. In particular, external economies related to clustering and production sharing will be discussed. Chapter 6 is devoted to the discussion of the external economies of reputation and the question of trust between a firm and its stakeholders, including consumers, government, its suppliers of inputs and distributors of its products.

The role of technology and innovation in competitiveness and upgrading will be discussed in Chapter 7. Explanation of the concept and features of innovation will be followed by the impact of innovation on export competitiveness. Subsequently, factors important in the national system of innovation (NSI), including entrepreneurship, R&D, intangible assets such as human capital and element of core competences, and their role in competitiveness and upgrading, will be illustrated. In the last part of the chapter, the difference between innovation by the followers (incumbents) and by leaders in an industry will be explained in order to develop some ideas on the strategies of newcomer firms of developing countries in their approach to innovation.

Chapter 8 explains in detail the macro-aspects of competitiveness, particularly the role of government policies. In doing so, three groups of developing countries will be distinguished: low-income countries with limited industrial capacity; those with some industrial base developed through import-substitutions; and others with substantial industrial capacity. While the eventual objective of all groups is to develop a competitive industrial base at a high level of development, at each point the burning issue for the first group of countries is to accelerate the development of their supply capacity. The dominant preoccupation of the second group is to make their production capacity efficient. The third group's burning issue is to upgrade their industrial structure, requiring special attention to technological development and innovation. Accordingly, after reviewing various theories of supply capacity building, including neoclassical theory, catch-up theories and the Kaleckian approach to acceleration of supply capacity, the needs and modalities of trade and industrial policies for capacity building and competitiveness will be reviewed. Subsequently, technological policies for upgrading will be discussed. Finally the possibilities of and constraints, both internal and external, on achieving competitiveness at a high level of development will be identified. In this connection, the need for changes in WTO rules, practices of IFIs and bilateral donors will be explained. Reference will also be made to avoiding further loss of policy space of developing countries through Doha and the Economic Partnership Agreement (EPA) negotiation.

Chapter 9 is devoted to the analysis of the comparative experience of China and Mexico since the early 1980s. We have chosen these countries for our case studies for two main reasons. First both started the process of economic liberalization and integration into the world economy through globalization more or less at the same period, i.e. around the early 1980s. Further, Mexico has had the added advantage of privileged market access to the USA through the North American Free Trade Agreement (NAFTA) since 1995. Both aimed at similar objectives, but show significant differences in their economic performance in enhancing value added in exports and growth of gross domestic product (GDP). Secondly while countries such as Singapore, South Korea and the territories of Taiwan and Hong Kong provinces of China (so-called Gang of Four) have succeeded in rapid industrialization and development, during the period concerned they had considerable policy space. China, unlike Mexico, has succeeded despite limitations imposed on its policy space due to its accession to the WTO. Thirdly there have been a number of studies on the 'Gang of Four' (e.g. Amsden 1989; Wade 1990; Shafaeddin 2006b, 2009c) for the aforementioned period. In earlier time series studies of a sample of 45 developing countries for the period 1980–2005, I have concluded that, for the development of competitive industrial capacity, developing countries should follow a dynamic and flexible trade and industrial strategy rather than universal and across-the-board liberalization (Shafaeddin 2005b). In such a context, I have grouped them into three categories. The first group consists of those at early stages of industrialization and development. For them the crucial issue is development of supply capabilities for which some infant industry support is needed. The second group are those with some industrial capacity developed through government support. Their industrial capacity needs to become competitive in the internal and international market by gradual liberalization. The third group includes those with some industrial production and export capabilities but whose industrial bases need upgrading. Mexico and China were at such a stage. Both countries had some industrial capacity in the early 1980s when they started liberalization. They provide a good comparative case study of their performance during the liberalization and globalization era, particularly following the conclusion of the Uruguay Round agreements (URA) in 1995. Of course, an important difference between the two countries is the role of government policies, i.e. the change in the role of the government in relation to market and enterprises over time during the course of industrialization, and this is precisely the important issue for consideration.

Reviewing the performance of the two countries, i.e. China and Mexico, in the development of competitive advantage in industrial production and exports, it will be shown that both countries, particularly Mexico, initially attracted a significant amount of

FDI in relation to GDP. Yet Mexico, unlike China, has achieved little in increasing value added in exports, growth of GDP and the upgrading of its industrial structure, despite its privileged access to the USA through NAFTA, beyond certain industries which had been developed through import-substitution, growth of GDP, exports and competitiveness at a high level of development are bleak.

The difference in the performance of the two countries is explained, we will argue, in their different approach to development. Mexico's government has relied on market operation alone, believing that trade liberalization and FDI will automatically lead to the attainment of its objective for industrialization and competitiveness at a high level of development. In contrast, while the government of China reacted to market signals, it has followed a 'developmentalist' approach by: targeting demand and supply dynamic industries; managing FDI; developing indigenous technological and other capabilities of national enterprises, establishing an institutional set-up for interrelation between public–private and academic institutions; paying close attention to the development of human capital through education and training, etc.

The concluding chapter will shed some light on the implications of the contrasting experience of China and Mexico in industrial and development strategy, and in achieving competitiveness at a high level of development for other developing countries. The caveats of this study will be highlighted and the need for further research outlined.

2

CONTEXT AND CONDITIONS OF INTERNATIONAL COMPETITION

> In the long-run, specialization based on static comparative advantage, i.e. low wages, will not lead to the development of competitive industries which can be highly rewarding to the factors of production. (List 1856)

Introduction

Changes in the global economy during the last quarter-century or so have intensified competition in the international and internal markets of developing countries. Such changes have increased the need for government support for infant industries in developing countries which are at the early stages of development and industrialization. Yet, the means for it has decreased because of the limits imposed on policy space of developing countries by international trade rules and conditions imposed on developing countries by IFIs and bilateral donors. To explain, since the early 1980s a number of factors have changed which have led to intensification of competition in international and internal markets, particularly for developing countries. The first and most important of all is the changes in the economic philosophy in favour of market orientation at the cost of the withdrawal of government from economic decision making and resource allocation. Such a change in philosophy has been accompanied by liberalization of international trade and FDI.

Secondly there have been changes in the organization of international production in favour of globalization, networking and production sharing. Globalization has been facilitated by the liberalization of FDI flows and trade liberalization; change in international trade rules, rapid technological changes, and decreases in transport and communication costs. The rapid technological changes have increased the length of learning, cost of acquisition and development of technology, and the risks of investment in new activities by the firms of developing countries. The expansion of skill- and knowledge-intensive production, the increased importance of economies of scale in production, marketing and distribution together with increased market concentration in favour of established firms have increased the power and competitive advantage of TNCs *vis-à-vis* the newcomer firms of developing countries. These newcomer firms may benefit from factor cost advantage, the importance of which to competitive advantage has declined in relation to the strategic advantage of the established transnational corporations (TNCs), which also compete on the nonprice attributes of products. The increase in the market power of TNCs has in turn intensified the barriers to entry into new lines of production and exports for independent firms from developing countries.

Thirdly the emergence of 'new methods of organization and production' such as flexible manufacturing, etc. has also contributed to the changes in the rules of the game on competition in the marketplace.

Fourthly there has been a growing shift in labour-intensive production and assembly operation, with the help of TNCs, to a limited number of countries, particularly China. The growing importance of China in international trade has been pronounced not only in labour-intensive products, but also particularly in exports of high-tech products in final forms through assembly operation. The likelihood of the fallacy of composition, increased instability in exchange rates and the increased volatility in the world economy, resulting in volatility in external demand, have all increased the risks of investment.

The aforementioned factors have more and more increased the need of the newcomer firms from developing countries, which are at early stages of industrialization and development, for support of their government. Yet the international trade rules and the practices of IFIs and bilateral donors have limited the policy space of the governments of developing countries to provide their newcomer firms with the necessary support.

Changes in Economic Philosophy

The change in the dominant economic philosophy was ignited by the publication of *Industry and Trade in Some Developing Countries* (Little et al. 1970) by the OECD, followed by a series of publications by distinguished neoliberals (e.g. Bhagwati 1978; Krueger 1978; Balassa 1980). The new philosophy and strategy proposed by these neoliberals and their followers had two main features: market orientation and outward orientation. This strategy was in sharp contrast with the industrial strategy that had prevailed during the previous decades, which had been based on government intervention and import-substitution. This interventionist strategy was in turn influenced by the dominant ideological positions, in the economic literature, during the post–World War II period till the early 1970s. The need for a change in economic philosophy, the neoliberals argued, was due to the failure of import-substitution strategies and inefficiencies of government intervention in allocation of resources. At the same time, misinterpreting the success of East Asian countries, the neoliberals attributed the success of these countries to the operation of market forces, activities of the private sector and pursuit of export promotion strategies (e.g. World Bank 1993a; Krueger 1978). The neoliberals' interpretation of the success of East Asian countries was, indeed, the falsification of historical facts. These countries followed strategies for support of their infant industries and exports prior to their entry into the international market and gradual trade liberalization (Shafaeddin 2005b).

The unsatisfactory performance of 'traditional' import-substitution strategies by many Latin American and some other developing countries increased the need for foreign exchange of many (non-oil) developing countries. The increases in the price of petroleum and industrial imports in the 1970s exacerbated the balance-of-payments problems of non-oil exporting developing countries, other than East Asian countries, and led to the debt crisis of the late 1970s and early 1980s.

Since then the new economic philosophy has become the official position of IFIs, i.e. the World Bank and IMF, in their relations with developing countries. These institutions subjected provision of loans to developing countries to the imposition of various conditions in favour of market-oriented approaches to allocation of resources, trade liberalization and export-oriented industrial development. It was argued that market-based allocation of resources and trade liberalization would change the incentive structure in favour of exports; the change in the incentive structure in turn would lead to allocative efficiencies with their positive influence on international competitiveness. The competitiveness in the international market in particular would improve, it was argued, due to the provision of neutral incentive for exports and imports, access to imported inputs at world prices and allocative efficiencies in favour of products in which the country had (static) comparative advantage.

The change in philosophy was further intensified by the publication of the *World Development Report* (1987) by the World Bank and the emergence of the so-called 'Washington Consensus' in the late 1980s (J. Williamson 1990). Williamson explicitly ignores the 'creative function' of the market totally as he admits that: 'none of the ideas spawned by...development literature...plays an essential role in motivating the Washington Consensus' (J. Williamson 1990, 19–20).

Allocative efficiency has also been the dominant philosophy behind GATT/WTO rules. This organization has been dominated by developed countries which have been concerned with allocative efficiency, particularly since the inception of the Uruguay Round; developed countries have been trying to impose conditions on developing countries based on such a philosophy, which in turn is based on the theory of static comparative advantage advocated by neoliberals. In particular, the proposals made by developed countries during the negotiation on nonagricultural market access (NAMA) in the Doha Round are a clear indication of the neoliberal economic philosophy – despite the rhetoric label of 'Development' given to the round. Developed countries proposed a drastic reduction in the level and dispersion of tariff rates for individual products imported by developing countries. Further, they proposed binding their tariffs at low levels. The result is to limit the policy space of developing countries further, particularly those which are at early stages of industrialization (see Wade 2005; Shafaeddin 2010c).

Therefore, while the emphasis was placed on the 'creative function' of the market in the 1950s and 1960s, according to the new philosophy the focus is on the allocative function of the market. In other words, since the early 1980s the emphasis has changed in favour of 'competitiveness' in its static sense, as against achieving competitiveness at the higher level of development through policies based on attaining dynamic comparative advantage.

Globalization

There have been numerous definitions of globalization (see Carras 2001 for a review survey). Further, globalization has various dimensions: economic, political, cultural, environmental, etc. We are concerned here mainly with the economic dimension of globalization, albeit we do not consider its other dimensions unimportant. The definition of globalization depends on whether one looks at it from the viewpoint of global firms or from the perspective of the economic development of developing countries. From the viewpoint of global firms involved, globalization implies the expansion of their activities across frontiers.[1] In other words, globalization 'pertains to a set of conditions in which an increasing fraction of value and wealth is produced and distributed world-wide through a system of interlinking private networks' (OECD 1992, 210, based on Bressand 1990) and production sharing. To explain, one may distinguish three types of established firms: domestic, TNCs and global. A domestic firm produces in the home country for the home or foreign markets. As an established firm it may enjoy home-based advantages resulting from factor endowment and other local conditions, economies of scale, technology and experience. A TNC also usually undertakes production and sales abroad in specific foreign market(s). So, in addition to home-based advantages, it enjoys host country advantages, such as access to cheap labour and raw materials, and benefits from closeness to local markets.

A global firm, like a TNC, produces and sells in different markets. It also organizes its activities through production sharing and networking with its own affiliates and/or other firms in different countries; it collaborates with other firms to share its activities such as R&D, production or procurement of inputs, intermediate products and assembly operation, marketing, distribution, product development, and design at the global level without necessarily investing abroad directly for these activities (Best 1990, 259–62 and Porter 1990, 54). Hence, global firms in addition enjoy advantages from networking, intrafirm trade, interfirm cooperation and other new forms of business organization some of which do not involve going through the market (Porter 1990, 60–62; Best 1990).

Production sharing is defined as 'the internationalization of a manufacturing process in which several countries participate in different stages of a specific good's fabrication' (Ng and Yeats 1999, 1). This definition is incomplete as it may give the impression that it is necessarily independent local firms of countries which are involved in product sharing. Components of a finished product may cross different countries before they are assembled, and some local firms may be involved in the process. Nevertheless, in practice, various components of a particular product originate mostly from a network of subsidiaries of a TNC or TNCs located in different countries, as well as the parent company. In this sense production sharing is a facet of the globalization of production,[2] which takes place among the TNCs through vertical integration, industrial collaboration and interindustry trade.

Networking may also involve firms other than subsidiaries of the same TNC, and more often than production sharing. It allows the obtaining of cheaper sources of inputs,

---

1 Some French scholars define 'globalization' as expanding market space and 'internationalization' as enlargement of functional space where the firm's input providers and human resources are located (Fuguet et al., cited in Justo 2003, 12). These definitions are incomplete as they give the impression that the global firm produces at home and sells abroad and the international firm produces at home and abroad but sells at home.
2 For a more comprehensive definition see Chapter 5.

technology, intermediate products, distribution channels etc., through international consortia, cross-licensing agreements, joint ventures, strategic alliance and other forms of interfirm cooperation (Best 1990, 260). It also allows expanding the scope of the market to enjoy economies of scale. Further, networking could allow economies of scope and agglomeration (see Chapter 5). Growth in world exports of parts and components in relation to growth of world exports of manufactured goods as a whole is an indicator of the evolution in networking and production sharing. Accordingly, their differential in the related growth rates increased from 1.5 per cent during 1981 to 2.4 per cent during 1990–2000 (World Bank, 2003, 55). Since then it has increased even further (see Gallagher and Shafaeddin 2010).

The fragmentation of industrial activities and increased specialization in the production of parts and components have been important factors in the expansion of networking and trade in parts and components, particularly in high-tech and other fragmented industries, processing and assembly operations. The following industries are ranked according to their importance of processing trade in total exports of the related industry: telecoms (SITC 76), electrics (SITC 77), office equipment (SITC 75), machinery (SITC 74), road vehicles (SITC 78), power generation (SITC 71), specialized industries (SITC 72), transport (SITC 79), metalworking (SITC 73) (Yu and Nijkamp 2009, 21).

A network of firms cooperate through sourcing, i.e. purchase of intermediate inputs from other firms or through interfirm transaction, subcontracting, technology alliance and supply contracts for the provisions of inputs and intermediate goods. Nevertheless, they may also compete in the market for their final products. Such methods of collaborative competition provide global firms with additional advantages *vis-à-vis* TNCs and domestic firms.

From the point of view of developing countries or developing country firms, globalization is the process of integration into the global production network. There are two main channels through which such integration is facilitated: the inflow of foreign direct investment (FDI) and international trade. Therefore, trade liberalization together with the removal of, reduction in or restriction on the flow of FDI facilitates globalization. Nevertheless, the liberalization of the FDI regime and international trade does not necessarily lead to the globalization of a firm from a developing country. Many African countries have liberalized their trade and FDI regimes, yet they have not succeeded in globalizing. FDI was not attracted to their countries much because the industrial supply capabilities of the local firms were, *inter alia*, insufficient. In fact, their competitive position in the international market has deteriorated and they have become marginalized in international trade (Shafaeddin 2009b).

Liberalization of trade and FDI

Globalization has been facilitated by the liberalization of international trade and FDI, which has allowed movements of goods and finance across the borders and facilitated activities of TNCs in host countries. The unweighted tariff rates on average declined from about 10 per cent in 1980 to around 5 per cent in 1998 following the

Table 2.1. FDI by region, 1980–2010 ($ billion)

	Inward						Outward					
	1980	2000	2006	2007	2009	2010	1980	2000	2006	2007	2009	2010
Value ($ billion)												
Developing countries	7.7	256	434	573	511	574	3	133	229	294	271	328
Developed market economies	48	1148	625	1307	603	601	51	1103	1158	1829	851	935
Economies in transition	0.02	7	31	91	72	68	0	3	24	52	49	61
World	55	1411	1459	1971	1185	1243	54	1239	1410	22175	1171	1323
Share of developing countries (%)	14	18.1	29.7	29.1	43.1	5.6	10.7	16.2	12.8	13.5	23.1	26.6
Ratios: 2007/1980												
World				35.8						42.3		
Developing countries				74.7						98		

Source: UNCTAD, *Handbook of Statistics*, 2010, table 7.3.1, and http://unctadstat.unctad.org/TableViewer/tableView.aspx

Uruguay Round in the case of industrial countries; that of developing countries declined from about 27 per cent to around 12 per cent over the same period (World Bank 2003, fig. 2.12).

Between 1980 and 2007, i.e. before the emergence of recent global economic crisis, the FDI inflow to the world and developing countries increased by about 36 times and over 75 times respectively (Table 2.1). As a percentage of global GDP, exports and gross fixed capital formation (GFCF), FDI inflows increased from 0.48, 2.42 and 2.1 in 1982 to 3.4, 10.7 and 14.8 in 2007 respectively (UNCTAD 2008a, table 1.4). The bulk of the investment took place in the manufacturing sector and service activities which were directly or indirectly related to trade. Thus during 2005–7, manufacturing, trade, business activities and finance accounted for over 68 per cent of FDI inflows (based on UNCTAD 2008a, table A.1.6). Although FDI inflows to developing countries have increased a lot faster than the total, the bulk of them have been attracted by a handful of countries, particularly China (see below), where exports of labour-intensive activities, including assembly operation, expanded very fast putting further competitive pressure on other developing countries. For example China together with Hong Kong alone accounted for over 23 per cent and 30 per cent of FDI inflow to developing countries in 2007 and 2010 respectively (Table 2.1).

Transport and communication costs

The globalization of the business structure has been facilitated in recent decades, in particular by reduction in transaction costs, including transport costs. Between 1950 and 1990 the freight costs and cargo transport costs have declined by 15 per cent and 58 per cent respectively. During the 1990s the transport cost declined further. For example freight cost as a percentage of world import value declined by about 6 per cent during this period; as a percentage of import value of developing countries, it fell by over 23 per cent. Only in recent years has there been a slight increase due to the rise in petroleum prices. Similarly a sharp decline in communication cost and the evolution of information technology has contributed to the decline in the cost of, and time necessary for, transaction. For example the average cost of a three-minute telephone call between New York and London declined from $300 in 1930 to $53.20 in 1950, $3.22 in 1990 and less than 20 cents in recent years (World Bank 1992b). With advance in information technology (IT) and the liberalization of telecommunications services, such declines in costs have become feasible.

Information technology has also brought about other gains in the form of better product quality, greater flexibility, customer service and the speed and reduced life cycle of production, the reduction in inventories, etc. (Cane 1992).

Other New Methods of Production

Flexible specialization is another form of new business organization. While mass production is emphasized in the case of globalization, in flexible specialization the emphasis is on innovation and rapid adaptation to changes in the market. It requires multi-use equipment and skilled manpower. Hence, small and medium-sized firms exploit their advantages in strategic thinking rather than strategic planning, which is common in global firms. Nevertheless, to internalize various externalities, a group of firms consult and cooperate with each other through industrial districts, regional conglomerations, federated enterprises and technological alliance. Such firms basically compete on differentiated products (Best 1990, chs 1 and 8).

Globalization basically emphasizes cost reduction through networking and economies of scale and mass production in intermediate goods, particularly parts and components. Flexible specialization stresses product-led competition, speedy production and delivery, and cost reduction through capacity utilization (see Chapter 4). Integration into the world economy through globalization requires, *inter alia*, mainly sophisticated technology and a large amount of capital. Flexible specialization requires sophisticated technology and highly skilled manpower. None is easily available to new developing country firms particularly at the early stages of their development. They are faced with barriers to entry and restrictive clauses under WTO rules.

Barriers to Entry[3]

In a perfectly competitive market there is no barrier to entry. In practice the sheer existence and strategic behaviour of TNCs and other established firms limit prospect for entry into the international market for the newcomers. Generally speaking there are two types of entry barriers: firm-related and government-based. We are concerned in this section mainly with the former, although government-related barriers in the form of tariff and nontariff measures and other regulatory barriers are also important (see below).

Firm-related barriers include the use of price and nonprice instruments. J. S. Bain distinguished three main sources of barriers: absolute cost advantages, internal economies of scale and product differentials (or barriers to product differentiation, Reekie 1979, 90). Absolute cost advantages may arise due to access to low-cost resources, both natural and financial,[4] patented technology, a favourable location in terms of closeness to market or to the sources of inputs requiring heavy transport cost and, most important of all, access to 'learning effect', i.e. experience. Experience-related cost advantage is mostly due to product-specific economies associated with learning by doing.

Globalization and new methods of organization are also sources of cost advantage to the established firms because of economies related to 'networking' and interfirm collaboration, which are often denied to a developing country firm. For example during the 1980s about 95 per cent of all strategic alliance was between firms from developed countries (UN 1992, 102–3). The established firms of developed countries have advantages in technological knowledge and experience as well as marketing channels, and benefit from their strategic advantages *vis-à-vis* firms of developing countries which are sources of low labour cost and, in some cases, natural resources.

---

3 The following passages are based on Clarke (1985, ch. 4), Davies et al. (2003, 99 and 223–8) and
   Scherer (1990, ch. 10).
4 Larger firms have access to cheaper loans than smaller firms and entrants (see Chapter 8).

While strategic alliance with TNCs provides technology, means of finance and marketing channels for newcomer firms from developing countries, the division of benefits is unequally in favour of TNCs. The available empirical studies indicate that:

> [G]reater rents accrue to those 'lead firms' in the value chain that control branding and product conception, on the one hand, and to the 'platform leaders' that provide core technologies and advance components, on the other... Firms that provide routine assembly tasks and other simple services within GVCs [global value chain] earn less, pay their workers less, and are more vulnerable to business cycles because they tend to hold large-scale employment and fixed capital. (Stugeon and Memedovic 2011, 4; see also the sources cited therein)

The problem is that independent local firms of developing countries have little option if they stay isolated as the GVC itself can create barriers to learning and entry. When these firms get involved in the GVC, e.g. through production sharing, it is mainly for the production of some intermediate goods or assembly operation. The producers of intermediate goods are more vulnerable to the international business cycle. Their greater vulnerability, as compared with producers of finished products, is due to the fact that they have derived demand, i.e. the demand for intermediate goods depends on the demand for final products. For example there is some evidence that the East Asian exporters of parts and components to China have become more vulnerable to the international business cycle. The correlation between growth in East Asia's interregional exports and the USA's imports increased from −0.01 during the 1990s to 0.83 during the 2000–August 2009 period (Kim et al. 2009, 8).[5]

Note here that dynamic economies of learning can also be internal to the firm. Firm-level economies of scale and scope could also act as barriers to entry even where external economies (to the firm) are absent.

Both absolute cost advantages and scale economies provide means of strategic behaviour in the form of 'limit pricing'. Accordingly, enjoying the scale economies, established firms can set a price at a level which prevents new firms from making profits as their average cost of production is higher than that of larger firms because of their smaller scale of production, lack of experience and other relative disadvantages. Established firms may also practise their price-related strategic deterrent behaviour through transfer pricing, marginal cost pricing or price discrimination. Alternatively, or more importantly, the established firms may charge high prices (which allows the entrants to make a profit) but threaten cut-throat pricing if there is an entrant. In this case, the incumbent firm needs to develop and maintain some excess capacity to expand production as required. In an oligopolistic market structure, where there is already some rivalry among incumbents and mark-up pricing prevails, the sheer existence of absolute cost advantage and/or economies of scale act as 'entry-deterring barriers'.

Product differentiation is the main nonprice instrument for entry deterring. Established firms may enjoy consumer preferences for products of an established firm. Such preferences

---

5 See also Shafaeddin (2010b, section V).

may arise not only from exclusive control of superior design and quality through patent protection, but also from consumer loyalty towards a brand name. A company may develop a reputation over time for providing high-quality products at competitive prices, after-sale services and timely delivery. Flexible specialization facilitates attaining such an objective. Moreover, massive advertisement over time may contribute to the development of consumer preference. In this case advertisement itself may involve economies of scale or scope denied to new entrants. Additionally, established firms may use product or brand proliferation as an instrument of deterrent entry. The established firms may supply varieties of products, or brands, to satisfy various tastes and prevent a newcomer firm from establishing a niche market in one or a number of geographical locations.

In the various cases of barriers to entry described above, a new firm wishing to enter the market may need to acquire a large amount of capital, which may not easily be available through the capital market to a new firm from developing countries. As a result, capital requirement may be regarded as an entry barrier in large-scale industries, which require a large amount of fixed assets.

It has been shown that in practice a firm may enjoy several sources of barriers to entry depending on the characteristics of the industry and the structure of the market concerned. Patented technology and product differentials (and scale economies in advertising) are the most important single source of entry barriers. However, in some industries such as automobiles, tractors, etc. scale economies in production and capital requirements are also crucial (Clarke 1985, 76–81). Moreover there is strong evidence that experience-related cost advantage is also important (Scherer and Ross 1990, 373).

In fact, a deterring entry strategy of a firm may consist of a number of elements. According to a survey of 293 product managers provided by R. Smiley and cited by Scherer and Ross (1990, 392) these elements include attempts by incumbent firms, through their restrictive business practice (behaviour), to:

- set prices at a low level by exploiting learning and scale economy effects aggressively;
- expand capacity;
- advertise to cement customer loyalty;
- seek patents on likely substitute products and technologies;
- talk tough about responding to entry;
- set limit prices to block entry;
- set limit prices to slow the rate of entry;
- introduce new product varieties to fill all product niches; or
- avoid disclosing profit data on individual lines.

According to the same survey, 58 per cent of respondents used one or more of these elements frequently, and 98 per cent used it at least occasionally. Advertising, patent protection, disguising profitability and other information were among most the commonly used elements (Scherer and Ross 1990, 392–3).

It would not be incorrect to say that 'the most plausible entrants into some markets are those companies already well established in another market or less closely related field' (Scherer and Ross 1990, 391). This is so because they have a better access to sources of funds and often enjoy economies of scope and reputation as well as learning effects to the extent that is relevant in production, distribution, marketing, or after-sale services for a new product. Hence any experience in industrialization would also be beneficial for entry into new activities.

A developing country may try, through competition law and policy, to regulate the behaviour of both national and foreign enterprises in order to prevent restrictive business practices by dominant firms, including foreign firms, in its domestic market. Nevertheless, competition policy is ineffective to deal with the practices of TNCs in the international market as there is no international agreement on the 'code of conduct' of TNCs. Moreover competition policy is totally irrelevant as far as the absolute cost and strategic advantages of established foreign firms, resulting from the economies of scale, speed and experience is concerned (see Chapter 4). The issue of competition policy and its relation to trade and industrial policies is a complicated one requiring in-depth analysis. We have mentioned a few related comments in Appendix 2. It should also be noted that the WTO rules restrict the policy space of the government *vis-à-vis* TNCs and create some barriers to entry, e.g. through Trade-Related Aspects of Intellectual Property Rights (TRIPs) etc., as will be explained below.

Implications of WTO Rules for Competitiveness

WTO rules are comprehensive and include several agreements the most relevant one of which is discussed in Appendix 1. Here we will discuss the way main agreements restrict the policy space of developing countries in entering new activities and upgrading for achieving competitiveness at a high level of development. Further, the rules increase the exposure of domestic firms from developing countries to competition with established TNCs, which influence the market through their strategies in the process of globalization and/or flexible specialization and dynamic competition as already explained.[6] Generally speaking WTO rules facilitate international trade as well as the operation of TNCs in different countries. At the same time these rules restrict the operation of local firms of developing countries in manufacturing *vis-à-vis* TNCs and in relation to imports. In other words, while the rules favour trade, they are biased against local production and development of supply capabilities and upgrading by national firms in many respects. Therefore, while they reduce the policy space of firms and governments of developing countries with little or insufficient industrial base, they favour the established firms of developed countries. More specifically, the WTO rules have three general implications for competitiveness:

- They expose national companies to more competition in the domestic and international markets;
- They impose certain restrictive measures on producers and exporters, and render attaining competitiveness on the basis of dynamic comparative advantages difficult;
- At the same time they provide certain privileges to producers and traders, and some opportunities to exporters to compete in foreign markets more easily.

---

6 The following pages are based on Shafaeddin (1998).

Exposure to competition

There is a basic difference between production under the regime of import-substitution and production under a liberalized trade regime. When a country follows an import-substituting strategy, a producing firm enjoys a lot of incentives with little risk because the domestic market is protected. Nevertheless, if protection prolongs, the import-substitution strategy will lack competitive pressure on the producers to become competitive in the international market.

Under the liberalized trade regime, while the incentive for production is reduced, its risk is increased. The competitive pressure will result in reduced profit margin, thus incentives, and at the same time it will increase the risks of investment. It will increase such risks because of the uncertainty regarding the sale prospects and unknown behaviour of the competitors. Of course the WTO rules will provide new opportunities in the international market but also involve risks in trade in the international market.

Opportunities and privileges

Trade liberalization and WTO rules provide a batter market access to contracting parties (member states). Nevertheless, not only do they involve certain risks, but they also limit the policy space of domestic firms. Trade liberalization improves the relative incentive for exports as against sale in the domestic market. Further, the WTO rules provide a number of privileges to exporters. First the reduction in trade barriers in the importing countries not only enhances the access to international markets, but also contributes to the expansion of international trades in general due to the income effects of reduction in international prices.

Secondly it improves the security in market access for the exporting firms for three reasons. One reason is that international trade will be subject to agreed rules by all contracting parties and the existing trade barriers will be known to the investors and exporters. For example in the case of trade in goods the use of quantitative restrictions is prohibited except under very special circumstances; tariffs are allowed but are to be restricted; any advantage provided by any country to another country will be automatically provided to others through most-favoured-nation (MFN) treatment. Another reason is that when any dispute arises between two trading partners they can settle it through the 'procedures for Dispute Settlement Mechanism' envisaged under GATT/WTO rules. These procedures include, in the first place, bilateral consultation but, in case the consultations fail, it can be resolved through the Dispute Settlement Panel and Appellate Body of the WTO. Moreover the WTO rules subject all governments to regulation of custom valuation in the case of imports. These regulations benefit the importers because they dictate that the value of goods for custom purposes should be determined by the price paid, or to be paid, by the importer. The Custom Valuation Agreement outlines ways of settling those differences that may arise between the importer and the custom authorities. Finally, if producing firms in an industry feel that imports compete with their products in an unfair manner they can request their government to take necessary measures through safeguard actions and the imposition of antidumping and countervailing duties. Safeguard actions can be taken if it is proven that sudden increase in the flow of imports of a product causes, or threatens to cause, injury to a domestic industry. The action would involve temporary restrictions (by tariffs or quantitative measures) for a maximum period of eight years. Antidumping or countervailing duties can be imposed, under certain conditions, on imports of a product from a specific country if its exporter resorts to unfair trading and imports cause, or threaten to cause, injury to producers of a domestic industry. Antidumping duties can be imposed on imports of a product when the exporter charges prices less than the prices charged in the domestic or third market. Similarly countervailing duties can be applied when the exporter subsidizes its export to reduce the export price.

Thirdly reduction in tariff rates on imported inputs contributes to the reduction in the cost of production of producing firms.

Nevertheless, the newcomer firms may not have the necessary production capabilities, except for products in which they have static comparative advantage, market information and marketing channels in foreign countries. Thus they may not be able to take advantage of opportunities provided by global trade liberalization. Even when they do, they may incur higher marketing cost due to their lack of experience, smaller scale and the lack of marketing and distribution channels.

More importantly, the WTO rules limit the policy space of developing countries for the expansion of supply capabilities and upgrading. Further, even when developing countries achieve competitive export capabilities, developed countries often abuse sanitary and phytosanitary (SPS), technical barriers to trade (TBT) and antidumping measures against their imports. We will turn to these issues below.

Restrictive measures on exports, supply capabilities and upgrading

The trade liberalization of recent years has limited the policy space of developing countries, necessary for diversifying and upgrading their production structure, in a number of ways. For example there are restrictions on the use of local inputs, infant industry protection and targeted export subsidies. Moreover, while the imposition of performance requirements clauses on foreign firms are relaxed, domestic companies have become subject to restrictive measures and regulations imposed through the Agreement on Trade-Related Investment Measures (TRIMs), the Agreement on Subsidy, Countervailing Measures (ASCM) and the TRIPs agreement.

WTO rules contain a number of restrictive measures that limit the exporting of goods for which a developing country already has production capabilities. More importantly, they reduce the policy space of a developing country to develop supply capabilities in new products for exports and to upgrade its production structure. Exporters have to observe mandatory product standards and sanitary and phytosanitary regulations imposed not only by WTO rules but also through additional requirements imposed by either importing firms or the governments of importing countries. Both exporting and importing countries should follow related agreed international rules to avoid unnecessary barriers to trade. Nevertheless, the observation of these standards is often costly and difficult for developing countries (Shafaeddin 2009c). Product standards are imposed on imports of industrial goods to protect the health and safety of consumers and are subject to the TBT Agreement. The regulations governed by the SPS Agreement are applied to imported goods to protect, plant, animal and human life from the spread of diseases. Importers sometimes use the SPS and TBT measures as pretexts for protectionist measures (Shafaeddin 2009c).

TRIPs agreement as a barrier to entry

The Trade-Related Intellectual Property Rights Agreement (TRIPs) provides an important competitive advantage for companies which invent and innovate. In contrast, it restricts the transfer of technology to developing countries; the related rules protect the holders of intellectual property, including patents, copyright, trademarks, industrial design, trade secrets and other undisclosed information, etc. In particular the use of any new invention is patented and cannot be used freely by others for 20 years. As a result those in the possession of new technology, mainly TNCs, will have a sort of monopolistic/oligopolistic power in technology (see Appendix 1). Firms from developing countries either will be deprived of the transfer of technology or they will have to incur the high costs of licensing and technology purchases. According to a World Bank estimate the full implementation of TRIPs would lead to a net transfer (in the form of patent rent) of about $41 billion a year, in constant 2000 prices, to seven major developed countries. The increase in the price of patented products could be significant. For example in the case of drugs it could range from 12 per cent to 68 per cent of the product price; in fact, in the case of antiretroviral (ARV) drugs the patented product could cost over 30 times more than the generic ones. The sum of costs of patent rents and deadweight loss for TRIPs is 1.6, 2.7 and 7.7 billion dollars, at 2000 prices, for Brazil, India and Mexico respectively. One should also add the cost of implementation of the TRIPs Agreement to these items. Therefore, while TRIPs does not encourage development of endogenous technology and innovation in developing countries, it is a vehicle for the transfer of resources from these countries to developed countries and it inhibits development of supply capabilities for upgrading the production structure in developing countries.[7] In particular R&D is concentrated in developed countries and the regulations related to the patent regime are all binding. Such provision in essence acts as a sort of infant industry protection for technology producers of developed countries, who also can benefit from the resulting monopoly right. In contrast, the provisions which are beneficial to developing countries, such as transfer of technology and technical cooperation, are not binding. Such asymmetries obviously increase the technological gap between the established firms of developed countries and those of developing countries, affecting the competitive position of the last. It also has a detrimental impact on their ability to diversify and upgrade their productive structure.

---

7 For details and references see Shafaeddin (2010c).

ASCM agreement

The Agreement on Subsidy and Countervailing Measures (ASCM), favours the development of new technology, which is in the interest of developed countries, but it is against infant industry protection and 'infant export protection' in developing countries. To explain, under URAs subsidies provided for R&D on specific activities are allowed, implying infant industry protection of new technology (articles 3 and 8). Para. 8.2a of the Agreement provides exceptions to the specificity clause. It covers research activities undertaken by firms and/or research and educational establishments, up to 75 per cent of costs of industrial research, or 50 per cent of the costs of precompetitive development activity. In contrast, infant industry protection for producing a new product in developing countries is practically impossible and subsidies provided for the expansion of exports and export supply capabilities are not permitted.

Regarding infant industry protection, developing countries are still subject to article XVIII of GATT. To explain, this article allows, under certain conditions, the use of protective measures for the '*particular* industries' in the case of countries which are at early stages of development. In other words, not only was infant industry protection allowed, but the principle of 'selectivity' was also accepted. Thus, developing countries could eventually apply, in principle, a dynamic trade policy for the diversification and development of their industrial base by selecting specific industries for protection and others for liberalization at each point in time. Nevertheless, in practice, infant industry protection is not so easy for them to achieve. To do so, a developing country should first obtain agreement from other affected WTO members and pay them compensation if requested. Apart from the fact that obtaining such agreement is uncertain and cumbersome, it is not clear how the compensation would be calculated, creating further uncertainty even when an agreement is obtained. If an agreement on compensation is not reached, any other contracting party 'shall be free to notify or withdraw equivalent consensus'.

Regarding the expansion of exports by newcomers to the international market, the use of subsidies contingent on exports is not allowed at all; the contents of article 3 of ASCM prohibit subsidies to be paid to firms (except for agricultural products) 'upon export performance' and 'upon the use of domestic over imported goods' (e.g. inputs). Subsidies contingent on export performance are defined such that they include any sort, whether direct or indirect (ASCM, appendix I).[8] Further, while production subsidies paid only to specific firms are prohibited, in the case of exports even if all industries were provided with subsidies tied to export performance or which favour domestically produced goods the subsidy would be regarded as specific (para. 2.3 of ASCM). In other words, a country cannot support its infant industries, whether or not for exports, either across the board or on a selective basis when the subsidy is tied to export performance.

---

8 If, however, subsidy is provided to an enterprise without being made legally contingent upon export performance, it would not be prohibited: 'The mere fact that a subsidy is granted to enterprises which export shall not for that reason alone be considered to be an export subsidy...' (ASCM, para. 3.1a, footnote 4).

R&D activities are concentrated in developed countries for the development of new technologies, new products and new processes – a development which is, in a sense, an 'infant' activity involving risks and requiring provision of extra incentive to the firms concerned. In developing countries, in contrast, 'application' rather than 'development' of a new technology or a new process is important in the enhancing of supply capabilities and export expansion. The transfer and efficient application of technology for the expansion of export capacity takes time and involves costs and risks, as does the development of marketing, brand names, etc., before an industry can mature and export products become internationally competitive. During this period infant industry protection is often required.

Furthermore, in applying import licences, export subsidies and subsidies which encourage the use of domestic products *vis-à-vis* imports are prohibited (except for agricultural goods, and on a temporary basis for countries with per capita income of less than $1,000 listed in the agreement).

TRIMs

According to the Agreement on Trade-Related Investment Measures (TRIMs), FDI and domestic investment should be treated equally. Therefore, the agreement prohibits local content requirement (i.e. it prohibits making foreign companies obliged to use local inputs); trade balancing requirement, i.e. limiting the use of imported products to an equivalent amount of exports; restricting imports to an amount equivalent to the exports of the product; restricting access to foreign exchange which would result in restriction on imports; restricting exports as a proportion of domestic production implying imposition of domestic sale requirement. Under certain conditions, however, countries can take 'safeguard' actions and impose antidumping and countervailing duties as mentioned before.

Other restrictions

While we have referred to main WTO agreements which restrict the policy space of developing countries, there are further restrictive clauses in the other agreements such as the General Agreement on Trade in Services (GATS), the rule of origin, antidumping and particularly in the area of tariffs. In this case tariff peak and tariff escalation seriously restricts the upgrading of the industrial structure of developing countries (UNCTAD 2003).

The UR has hardly corrected the traditional bias against finished products of exports interest to developing countries. Imports of these products to developed market-economy countries (DMECs) had faced protective measures that were three times higher than those related to intraindustry trade, which takes place basically among developed countries (de Castro 1989, 9–15). This situation was not corrected in the URAs. For example processed agricultural products face a tariff rate of 20.9 per cent as against 12.1 per cent for primary agricultural products. Even for a simple product like coffee, tariff escalation is significant. The percentage tariff rates on processed and raw coffee are 5.35 and 0.37 in the USA; 8 and

0.11 in the European Union (EU), and 20.02 and 1.63 in Japan. Developing countries also suffer from tariff escalation on textiles and clothing in somewhat similar ways. Similarly manufactured goods of developing countries faced a tariff peak of 110 per cent in North America. Further, tariff peaks are more common for medium- and low-technology products, which constitute the major export products of developing countries (UNCTAD 2003, tables 4, 7, 8 and 9).

Summarizing the impact of three UR agreements (TRIPs, TRIMs and GATS) on the domestic capabilities of developing countries, Professor Wade concludes that 'with a touch of hyperbole the agreements could be called a slow-motion Great Train Robbery' (Wade 2005, 89) against developing countries. Linda Weiss sees '...the WTO as an upgrading device for developed economies', but it '...acts as a development-constraining device for the countries still trying to climb the development ladder' (Weiss 2005, 745). Further, while developed countries advocate the lack of government intervention in the economy, '...the effects of the international economic system – an intensification of international competition in the context of increased multinational disciplines – are renewing the [need for] state's role in economic governance' (Weiss 2005, 745). In fact, as we have explained earlier on, the changes in the global economy during recent decades has increased the need for government supports for building up competitive industrial structure, but the WTO rules as well as other international rules and practices of IFIs and bilateral donors has reduced the policy space of developing countries. Further, even the existing rules are not always respected by developed countries, as explained below.

Abuse of WTO rules and the lack of implementation

Another problem is arbitrary application and abuse of some of the UR agreements, such as the SPS or antidumping agreements, as a means of protection by developed countries (Shafaeddin 2005c, 2009c; UNCTAD 2001). In the case of the antidumping agreement the USA's repeated use of zeroing practices against imports from developing countries, despite verdicts of the Dispute Settlement Mechanism of WTO, is an example (Shafaeddin 2010c). To explain, the dumping margin is the difference between the export price (FoB) and normal value of a product.[9] If the export price of a product to a destination is less than its normal value, dumping exists. Zeroing overestimates the dumping margins or even fabricates them. The US Department of Commerce is supposed to calculate the weighted average of net prices (after allowing for transport and other business margins) of various transactions for each imported product and compare it with the normal value of a product. In calculating the weighted average, however, the negative dumping margins are set to zero, i.e. in cases where the selling price of an imported product is higher than its normal value it is not taken into

---

9 The normal value is 'the comparable price, in the ordinary course of trade, for the like product when destined for consumption in the exporting country', or the highest comparable price for the like product for export to a third country, or the cost of production in the exporting country plus a reasonable selling cost and profit (para. 1 of article VI of GATT 1947).

account. Thus the negative dumping margins are excluded from the calculation of the dumping margin.

It is estimated that in 17 determinations, out of a sample of 18, '...the dumping margin was inflated by zeroing. In 5 cases, the overall dumping margin would have been negative. On average the dumping margins in the 17 cases would have been 86.4 per cent lower, if zeroing had not been employed' (Ikenson 2004, 2). Hence zeroing is a sort of selective protection tool which shields domestic producers from competitive imports (for details see Shafaeddin 2009a). The United States has continued zeroing despite numerous verdicts against its practice by the WTO (for details see Shafaeddin 2010c).

The arbitrary implementation of the trade rules by developed countries affects the predictability and the security of the world trading system and thus increases the risks of investment for newcomer firms and threatens their potential competitiveness in the international market. Hence it could be regarded as a type of barrier to entry. The increased instability in exchange rates, resulting from speculative activities in the financial markets, the increased volatility in the world economy, the increased exposure of developing countries to world demand and the 'fallacy of composition' when a large number of countries expand exports of the same products all add to the risks in investment for newcomer firms. In the particular case of volatility in the world economy it should be noted that since the early 1980s there have been four severe downturns in the world economy, the worst of which is the current economic recession caused by a financial crisis that is unprecedented since the Great Depression.

While the increased risks require compensation by higher return, or by support from the government, the profitability of domestic firms has in fact declined due to their increased exposure to competition (see, e.g., Shafaeddin 2005c, ch. 3 and Gallagher and Shafaeddin 2010 for the case of Latin America). Unfortunately there is also a double standard in tackling the crisis. While developed countries have embarked on extensive Keynesian-type stimulant programmes, many developing countries which are severely affected by the crisis are left at the mercy of the IMF and the World Bank, which impose budget cuts and conditions containing deflationary measures on developing countries, leading to the closure of some manufacturing enterprises. The case of Malawi is only one example (Shafaeddin 2009d).

All-in-all, the philosophy behind GATT/WTO rule is the theory of static cost comparative advantage, which is based on unrealistic assumptions and is not conducive to industrialization and development in developing countries. But the related rules also suffer from a number of contradictions with detrimental effects on the industrialization of developing countries. For example, while the objective of the GATT/WTO rule is liberalization of international trade, yet the power of governments in trade intervention and restriction of monopoly/oligopoly power of TNCs is not considered. Similarly while trade in manufactured goods is to be liberalized, agricultural products are exempted; further, in the category of manufactured goods labour-intensive products are to be liberalized, but technology development is subject to protection through IPR. Yet further, even the agreed rules are not implemented properly by developed countries (see also Shafaeddin 2010c for more details).

While we have discussed the restrictive nature of some WTO agreements, it should be mentioned that developed countries also impose 'WTO plus' conditions/'Singapore issues' on developing countries through regional and bilateral free trade agreements. The implications of such agreements for the industrialization and development of developing countries, particularly low-income ones, needs to be analysed in detail that is beyond the space available in this volume. Let us mention here, however, that WTO plus conditions are those which are either more demanding in terms of trade, financial liberalization or obligations contained in other agreements such as TRIPs, SPS, TBT etc., or contain issues which are not covered in the WTO agreements such as Singapore issues, namely government procurement, competition policy, investment, labour and environmental standards. NAFTA and EPA are two examples of regional agreements, and many bilateral FTAs also contain similar clauses (see Shafaeddin 2010c; Kelsey 2010; South Centre 2009, 2010a, 2010b and 2011). As a result, the related developing countries lose the remaining policy space available under WTO rules.

The Emergence of China

The emergence of China has intensified competition in the international market for products of interest to developing countries for a number of reasons. First the relative magnitude and the rate of growth of export of China are significant. As is shown in Table 2.2, in 2010 exports of goods from China were equivalent to over 42 per cent of exports from other developing countries excluding oil-exporting countries. When Hong Kong is included, the ratio reaches 47.6 per cent. More importantly, exports of manufactured goods from China and Hong Kong are nearly equivalent to about 82 per cent of exports of manufactured goods from other developing countries (Table 2.3). In 2009 manufactured goods accounted for over 93.5 per cent of exports from China.

Secondly light manufactured goods and assembled products, both of which are mainly labour-intensive, account for the bulk of exports of manufactured goods from China as shown in Table 2.4. These products are mainly those which are also exported by most other developing countries. While exports of machinery and equipment account for 49.5 per cent of total exports from the country, the bulk of these are assembled items based on imports of parts and components.

Thirdly while assembly operations still constitute the bulk of industrial plants in China, the country has also developed the capabilities of domestic firms in production of a number of technology-intensive products (see Chapter 9). In other words, the country is pioneering in upgrading its industrial structure by rapid expansion of value added in production and exports of technology-intensive goods. Such development makes attempts at upgrading the export structure of other developing countries for competition in the international market more risky.

Table 2.2. Total exports of goods from China (1980–2010)

	1980	1990	2000	2010 China	2010 China and HK
Value ($ billion):	18.1	62.1	249.2	1578	1970
As % of word exports	0.89	1.8	3.9	10.4	12.9
As a % of exports of developing countries	3	7.3	12.1	24.6	30.8
As a % of exports of developing (excluding oil exporting countries)	6	9.6	14.6	29.9	37.3
As a % of exports of developing countries (excluding oil exporting countries, China and Hong Kong)	6.3	10.6	17.1	42.6	47.6

	1980–90	1990–2000	2000–2007	2007–2010
Average annual growth rate (China):				
All exports	13.1	14.9	25.4	9.1
Manufactured goods	17.4	16.7	28.1	12.3

Source: Based on UNCTAD, Handbook of Statistics, 2008 and UNCTAD, STAT database online, http://unctadstat.unctad.org/TableViewer/tableView.aspx (accessed 24 September 2010).

Table 2.3. Export of manufactured goods of China and Hong Kong as a percentage of exports of manufactured goods of various groups (2010)

	China	China plus Hong Kong
World	14.5	18.1
Developing countries	36.1	45
Developing countries excluding China	56.4	70.4
Developing countries ex. China and HK	66.5	81.9

Source: Based on UNCTAD, STAT database, http://unctadstat.unctad.org/TableViewer/tableView.aspx (accessed 24 September 2010).

Table 2.4. Percentage share of manufactured goods in total exports of China (2010)

Goods	2010
SITC 7	49.5
Other (light)	38.3
Chemicals	5.6
Total	93.4

Source: Based on UNCTAD, STAT database, http://unctadstat.unctad.org/TableViewer/tableView.aspx (accessed 24 September 2010).

Conclusions

The changes in the global economic situation during the last quarter-century have increased the need for government support for newcomer firms from developing countries to develop supply capabilities and eventually enter the international market. Yet changes in the economic philosophy and international trade rules and practices of IFIs and bilateral donors have restricted the means of doing so by limiting the policy space of developing countries. Globalization and other new methods of production and organization have changed the nature of competition in the international market in three main ways. First they have enhanced the relative importance of the 'strategic competitive advantage' of large established firms *vis-à-vis* the comparative cost advantage of the firms of developing countries. Secondly thus it has intensified the process of Schumpeterian 'dynamic competition' and 'creative destruction'. In such a process firms are continuously active in innovation, product development, quality improvement, shortening of delivery time, etc. as stated in the previous chapter. As a result the role of 'nonprice attributes' of products in competitive advantages has increased, reducing the relative importance of labour cost. Finally the growing size, market concentration, rapid technological development and the oligopolistic power and strategic behaviour of established firms have increased barriers to entry into the international market for new independent firms of developing countries. It is true that the process of globalization and trade liberalization has also improved possibilities and opportunities for developing countries to enter the international market for the products which they already produce, based on their static comparative advantage, particularly in cases where global firms have relocated plants in these countries. Nevertheless, the limited supply capabilities of domestic firms in many developing countries constrains their ability to attract FDI. Moreover when they do attract FDI, the process of globalization increases the vulnerability of these countries to decisions of global firms in relocation of these plants from one country to another and to changes in external demand. The recent global financial and economic crisis has also revealed their extreme vulnerability to external sources of demand due to changes in the world economic situation.

All in all, during the last thirty years or so, the policy space of developing countries for expanding supply capabilities and upgrading their industrial structure based on 'dynamic comparative advantage' has become limited. With this background in mind, let us examine the alternative theories of competitiveness and their relevance to the case of developing countries in the following chapter.

3

ALTERNATIVE THEORIES
OF COMPETITIVENESS

> ...the objective [of a given nation] is not to
> increase directly, by means of commercial
> restrictions, the sum of exchangeable
> values in a country, but its productive
> power. (List 1856, 253)

Introduction

Some attempts have been made during recent decades to develop alternative theories of
competitiveness for the theory of static comparative advantage. The common features
of these theories consist of two main issues: the distinction between static and dynamic
considerations, and envisaging an important role for 'nonprice/cost' *vis-à-vis* cost factors.
Most of these theories are developed in the context of developed countries where
established firms operate. Capability-building theory is the only exception. Nevertheless,
as developing country firms ought to compete with established firms and would like to
join them eventually, it is necessary to review those theories as well.

Before proceeding further, let us emphasize that our extensive discussion of the
nonprice/cost factors is by no means the denial of the importance of price and cost for a
given product quality in competitiveness. In fact it has been shown, for example, that each
10 per cent cost reduction by a US manufacturing firm would increase its market share
by 2 per cent (Eckward 1992). In a similar study of 14 developed countries Carlin et al.
(2001) have shown that while the sensitivity of export market shares to RULC varies from
one country to another, on average every 10 per cent reduction in relative costs leads to
a 2.7 per cent increase in export market shares. Nevertheless, a number of other factors
also play important roles in competitiveness. These include technology, investment,
quality, human capital accumulation, institutions and ownership concentration.

In the particular case of developing countries, labour cost plays a more significant role
in determining the cost of production of their exports of manufactured goods (Riveros
1992) than in the case of developed countries. Globalization provides firms of developed
countries with the opportunity to locate plants in developing countries enjoying host country
advantages in wage costs in addition to their 'home advantage' as stated in the introductory
chapter. Meanwhile it has provided the host country with the opportunity to increase its
export of products in which the country has static comparative advantage through the
channel of TNCs. Nevertheless, to continue exporting on the basis of static comparative
advantage does not provide the opportunity for competitiveness at the high level of

development in the long run. Competitiveness at the high level of development requires upgrading the industrial structure on the basis of dynamic comparative advantage and competition with the established firms in the international market. The strategic behaviour of the established firms affects the price they can charge; the nonprice attributes of products and innovation play an important role in international competitiveness. Moreover it has also been shown that new methods of production organization, such as 'flexible specialization' and 'collaborative competition', affect the ability of firms in time delivery and in product and process innovation. These issues are mainly in the domain of industrial economics and have not been sufficiently integrated into international trade theory.

More recently some industrial economists have developed analysis of Schumpeterian methods of competition, which are based not only on cost but also on product quality and attributes, availability and delivery time. The common features of their analysis are an active role of firm, prevalence of economies of scale and production of differentiated products. Moreover they regard competition as a dynamic and evolving concept, and innovation, in its broad sense, plays an important role in sustainability of competitiveness (see e.g. Porter, 1990; Best 1990; Lazonick 1991; Odigari 1992). Such theoretical analysis has been backed by some evidence. For example it has been shown that the technological factors and the ability to compete on delivery are more important in international competitiveness than cost factors (Fagerberg 1988); that product quality and reputation are two other important factors (Esfahani 1991).

In the following pages we will first outline the theory of competitive advantage of M. Porter and the Lazonick theory of interaction between scale and innovation before reviewing the theory of productive power of F. List and its development by capability-building theorists.

The Theory of Competitive Advantage (TCA) of M. Porter

Dissatisfied with a partial explanation of international trade, the founder of the theory of competitive advantage (Porter 1990) takes a more comprehensive and practical approach in explaining international comparative, or rather competitive, advantage. Porter's theory is a dynamic one. He also presents a micro-foundation for competitiveness; allows a role for the government; emphasizes the importance of the environment within which firms operate; gives importance to skill formation, experience and training; and denotes the important role of upgrading the competitive structure. Drawing on various fields in social science, particularly industrial economics, he argues that the competitive advantage should be explained at the level of the particular industry where the firms involved engage in export operations. Thus, beginning from individual industries, he builds up to the economy as a whole. In other words, he provides a micro-foundation to competitive advantage at the national level without denying the role of the government and the environment within which firms operate. Accordingly competitive advantage within an industry results from an effective combination of two main sets of factors: the firm's 'competitive strategy' and the national (macro-) environment within which it operates. Such environment, would include, *inter alia*, government policies and national institutions. The way 'national environment' influences competitive advantage is, however, different from that of traditional theories. According to Porter, the firms are active and the behaviour of each firm varies from those of the others. Moreover firms do not necessarily produce homogeneous goods. Consequently competitive advantage results not only from cost but also from product attributes. Moreover competition is dynamic and evolving, and improvement, innovation in methods, technology and upgrading of competitive strategy play an important role in sustaining competitive advantage. Both firms and the government can contribute to the creation, and improvement, of factors of production and other elements which influence competitive advantage.

Competitive strategy of firms

An industry is the basic unit in the analysis of competition. The choice of a competitive strategy by a firm depends on the structure of the industry in which the firm competes, and on the way in which it positions itself within that structure. The industry structure influences five competitive forces, as shown in Figure 3.1. These forces determine industry profitability through their impact on price, cost and the required investment. Firms also influence the industry structure through their behaviour strategies – affecting the competitive forces.

To position itself within an industry, a firm should have a generic strategy. A generic strategy involves two elements: competitive advantage and competitive scope. Competitive advantage is of two types: lower cost and differentiation (see Figure 3.2). Lower cost is determined by the physical efficiency with which a firm produces goods. Differentiation is related to the product attributes, i.e. 'the ability to provide unique and superior *value* [my italics] to the buyers in terms of product quality, special features, or after sale services' (Porter 1990, 37). For given cost, 'differentiation allows a firm to command a premium price' (Porter 1990, 37). In technical terms it reduces the elasticity of demand facing a firm.

Competitive scope determines the segment(s) of the industry in which a firm chooses to operate. Such requirement relates to the choice of products, types of buyers, the distribution channels and the geographical area in which the firm operates. A firm could aim equally at a broad or narrow target.

A cost leadership strategy aims at producing various types of a particular product, not of particularly high quality, at a low cost. A differentiation strategy concentrates on producing high-quality varieties of a good at a premium price. Focused differentiation concentrates on very specialized types of a product, for a particular purpose, and a very high premium price. Finally a cost focus strategy offers a relatively simple standard good at a *very* low cost – through mass production.

The choice of a strategy by a firm depends on the structure of the industry and capabilities of the firm in organizing and performing its various activities. Such capabilities are the sources of competitive advantage of a firm which determine the value it creates for its buyers. Such 'value' is 'measured by the amount buyers are willing to pay for its product or service' (Porter 1990, 40). The activities of a firm involved in competing in an industry include two categories: primary and support. Primary activities include: inbound logistic; provision of inputs; operations; manufacturing; outbound logistic, e.g. transport and

Figure 3.1. Porter's five competitive forces of industry competition

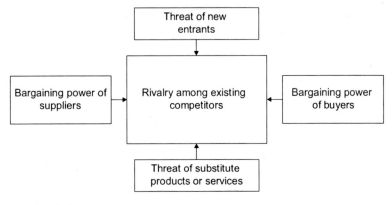

Source: Porter (1990, 35).

Figure 3.2. Generic firm strategies

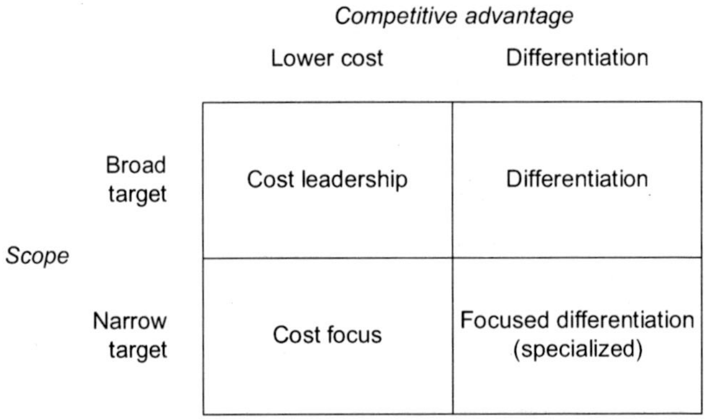

		Competitive advantage	
		Lower cost	Differentiation
Scope	Broad target	Cost leadership	Differentiation
	Narrow target	Cost focus	Focused differentiation (specialized)

Source: Porter (1990, 35).

delivery; marketing; and after-sale service. Support activities include: infrastructure; finance; planning; human resource management; technology development; and procurement. These activities, their coordination and interactions, contribute to buyers' value, so they are called 'value chains' by Porter.[1]

The value created for the buyers depends not only on the value chain of a firm, competing in an industry, but also on the value chains of the supplier of inputs to the firm and the distributors of goods produced by the firm.[2] Hence the existence of clusters of industries and the management of the linkages of the firm with its supplier and distribution channel is also a contributing factor to its competitive advantage.

---

1 In this sense 'value chain' is different from that which we have already defined.
2 Porter refers to 'value system' as the combination of the value chains of the firm and its suppliers, distributors and buyers (ibid., 42–3).

Sources of competitive advantage

The value chain exposes the sources of cost advantage, differentiation and competitive scope. Firms create, or improve, their competitive advantage through innovation, in its broad Schumpeterian sense (see Chapter 1), in any activity in the value chain. However, the ability to sustain competitive advantage depends on the source of advantage, the number of distinct sources of advantage a firm possesses and the extent of upgrading of the competitive strategy. There are two types of sources of competitive advantage in terms of their sustainability. First is the lower-order advantage originating from factor cost advantage, which is the low labour cost domain of static comparative advantage. This type is very vulnerable to competition from other locations or the emergence of new sources of supply of raw materials. Hence it is usually not sustainable. Second is higher-order advantage related to proprietary process technology, product differentiation and product attributes which are more durable. These are related to 'unique products or services, brand reputations based on cumulative marketing efforts, and customer relationships protected by higher customers costs of switching vendors' (Porter 1990, 50). These sources of product attributes could also create barriers to entry. High-order advantages require advanced skills, cumulative investment in physical equipment, human resources, R&D and marketing. If a firm is in possession of both 'low-cost' and 'high-order' advantages it will be in a more privileged position than one which is in the possession of one source of advantage alone. TNCs enjoy such advantages as they benefit from both their home advantage resulting from proprietary technology and experience, and from the low-cost advantage of the host country such as China. But China is trying to build up the capabilities of its domestic firms in order not only to enjoy its low factor cost advantage, but also to obtain high-order advantage by developing proprietary technology. Hence the success of China can be attributed to pursuing such a policy (see Chapter 9). Moreover continuous innovation is necessary to improve and upgrade competitive advantage.

However, continuous innovation requires 'change', which may be impeded by resistance to change and innovation. To overcome such an obstacle, upgrading an advantage should be stimulated by a threat of one kind or another from outside, such as competitive pressure, technological progress or innovation or by buyers' demand.

To compete internationally a firm should also have an 'international strategy' reinforcing its home-based competitive advantage. For global firms the competitive advantage of firms is decoupled from the comparative advantage of nations. Global firms can locate their activities in different places, drawing on the competitive advantage of different nations, and coordinate such dispersed activities. The aim of a global firm is to optimize its cost and/or differentiate advantages. A global firm thus makes two strategic choices: where to locate its various activities; and how to coordinate its dispersed activities (see Porter 1990, 55–61 for details). Hence such choices would include decisions both on trade and foreign direct investment, which involve innovation in organization of production, and on interfirm linkages such as strategic alliance, networking, supply contacts, etc.

Hence global firms, which can combine their home-based 'higher-order' advantage with that of 'low-cost' advantage in developing countries, are in a more competitive position than the local firms of developing countries.

National environment

The environment in which firms compete influences their competitive advantage. Four factors determine national advantage: factor conditions, home demand, related and supporting industries, and firm strategy, structure and rivalry. These determinants, together with their interaction, constitute a 'system' of national advantage referred to as 'diamond' by Porter. Generally speaking, factors of production also include knowledge and infrastructure not considered in the neoclassical theory. Factors of production are of two types: basic and advanced. Basic factors include 'natural resources, climate, locations, unskilled labour and semi-skilled labour and capital. Advance factors include modern digital data communications infrastructure, highly educated personnel…and university research institutes in sophisticated disciplines' (Porter 1990, 77). The returns on basic factors are low; these factors are usually deployed in the case of 'low-cost' advantages. In contrast, advanced factors are necessary for 'higher-order' competitive advantage. Moreover factors of production may be either generalized or specialized. Generalized factors are those which can be used in a wide range of activities; specialized factors are those relevant to a particular field or industry. Advanced/specialized factors contribute more to sustainability of competitive advantage than to basic/generalized factors. While most basic factors are inherited, advanced factors could be created and improved. Accordingly, in contrast to the neoclassical theory, Porter argues that abundance in factor endowment could in fact undermine competitive advantage.[3] On the contrary, selective disadvantage in factors, which create bottlenecks in the firm's operation, could contribute to competitive advantage positively because it puts pressure on the firms to innovate and stimulates them to develop a strategy for remedying the situation. The successful Japan, Taiwan and Republic of Korea are good examples of countries which are poor in natural resources.

Although the literature on economies of scale refers to the importance of the size (and the rate of growth) of the home demand in reaping efficient scales of production and low cost, Porter regards the composition of demand as more important. The more demanding the home buyers are on the variety, quality and features of products, the more a firm is stimulated to gain competitive advantage of a higher order that, as stated earlier, is more durable.

The contribution of related[4] and supporting industries is basically through externalities provided via their 'linkages' and 'learning' effects – although Porter does not use such terminologies. For example the contribution of supplier industries could take the form of the provision of efficient, rapid, low-cost and sometimes preferential access to inputs including machinery (Porter 1990, 102–3). More importantly, they could contribute through coordination of their activities with the purchasing firm and their cooperation in the process of innovation and upgrading through concerted and mutual efforts. An industry may also benefit from the opportunities for information flows, distribution channels and technological know-how available in related industries.

---

3 This issue is also considered in the literature on mineral economies and Dutch disease.

4 'Related industries are those in which firms can coordinate or share activities in the value chain when competing, or those which involve products that are complimentary' (ibid., 105).

The way firms are created, organized and managed, together with their goals, strategies and the pattern of their rivalry, may vary from one nation to another because it depends on specific national circumstances. For example American management practices have been different from Japanese ones. Such differences are noticed in training, orientation of leaders, group versus hierarchical style, the individual initiatives, tools for decision making, the nature of the relationship between firms and customers, and that between labour and management. Cultural and social factors affect the nature of goal, behaviour, strategy and the structure of firms. Likewise it affects the behaviour and goals of individuals working for the firm.

The nature of domestic rivalry among firms is one of the important factors in competitive advantage. Domestic competition at home puts pressure on firms to improve, innovate and upgrade. Competition should not be restricted to price; competition in other nonprice attributes and technological development contributes to attaining 'high-order' competitive advantage abroad, particularly if rivals are geographically concentrated in a region constituting a *cluster* of industries linked with each other. Moreover the competitors may also cooperate with each other in the form of trade associations, etc. The number of firms in each industry, however, is influenced by the related scale economies in the concerned industry.

Various determinants of competitive advantage explained above interact with and reinforce each other in such a way that the impact of one depends on the situation of others constituting a system (see Porter 1990, ch. 4). For example factor conditions are affected by domestic rivalry through stimulating development of skilled human resources, specialized knowledge and technology. Similarly, sophisticated domestic demand conditions could stimulate development of the specialized skilled labour necessary for product development. The presence of related and supporting industries contributes to the creation and upgrading of factors of production through training, learning by doing, etc.

In particular, domestic rivalry, geographical concentration and the availability of skilled labour are important for the realization of other conditions. Rivalry and the threat of entry upgrade the entire national 'diamond' contributing to sustainability of competitive advantage, and geographical concentration magnifies the interaction within the 'diamond'.

In addition to the determinant factors explained above, 'chance' and 'government policies' also play important roles in competitive advantage. The role of government policies are explained below. Chance is related to changes in factors beyond a firm's control: inventions, availability and price of inputs, shifts in international financial markets and exchange rates, shift in world demand, wars, and intervention in the market by foreign governments, etc.

The system of 'diamond' explained above is basically influenced by investment, in physical, human resources and infrastructure, and by innovation over time emerging from pressure and challenge.

Implications for developing countries

The theory of competitive advantage (TCA) has a number of implications for building up competitive industrial capacity thus for industrial policies of developing countries.

These include definition of productivity, terms of trade, government policies and the role of endogenous firms.

Productivity and terms of trade

In the neoclassical theory productivity depends only on the physical volume of production per unit of input because goods produced by firms in an industry are homogeneous. The productivity by which the resources of a firm are employed affects the cost of production, and not the price – at least in the short run.[5] According to the TCA productivity is defined differently; it also depends on the type of goods produced, i.e. the degree of product differentiation. Product attributes, in terms of quality and features,[6] affect the value chain and thus the premium price which the firm can charge. As a result the factors of production are rewarded more than the case where productivity depends only on the volume of production of homogeneous goods.[7]

Developing countries, at least at early stages of industrialization, produce standardized manufactured goods and trade them for sophisticated and differentiated goods exported by the industrialized countries. So their terms of trade, or rather relative rewards of factors of production, may turn against them unless they upgrade their competitive advantage to a 'higher order'.

To explain, Porter distinguished four stages in the competitiveness of nations over time: factor driven, investment driven, innovation driven and wealth driven. In the initial stage of industrialization nations draw almost entirely from basic factors of production in the 'diamond'. They produce goods requiring simple technology. Hence they compete basically on cost and price, and are vulnerable to changes in external demand, exchange rate, etc.

In the investment-driven stage competitive advantage is still drawn mainly from basic factors of production but factor conditions are important, i.e. more advanced factors are created and used, home demand will increase, but is still unsophisticated, and home rivalry increases. Foreign technology is applied after it has been improved upon. The range of industries is broadened by heavy investment, and the type of industries developed are 'those with significant scale economies and capital requirements, but still [with] a large labour cost component, standardized product, [and] technology which is readily transferable' (Porter 1990, 551). Hence, despite some improvement, such an economy still remains fragile because it competes basically through 'low cost'.

In the innovation-driven stage competitive advantage is drawn from all elements of the 'diamond'. The composition of consumer demand becomes sophisticated, domestic rivalry intensifies, products become more service-intensive and the role of factor cost in competitive advantage diminishes considerably. The economy competes on a 'higher

---

5 If, however, productivity is increased by all firms, the market price will decrease given the level of demand.

6 One also may add delivery time and reputation.

7 Profit depends positively on the value produced for the consumer and negatively on the cost of production. Labour is also rewarded more due to a sort of quasi-rent the labourers get because of working in that particular industry.

order'. The distinctive feature of this stage is that firms develop technology and rely on innovation intensively for upgrading and sustaining their competitive advantage. Firms develop the ability not only to compete abroad, but also to invest abroad intensifying their competitive position.

Finally, in the wealth-driven stage, 'the wealth that has *already* been achieved' is the driving force behind competitive advantage. The 'wealth' here implies the stock of various determinants of competitive advantage in the 'diamond'. Since in this stage firms attempt to maintain, rather than improve, their competitive advantage, they tend to lose their high-order competitive advantage. The erosion of 'higher-order' competitive advantage leads to resort to competing on cost and price. Porter gives the example of the situation of Great Britain as a wealth-driven nation.

Most developing countries are presently at the factor-driven stage, except newly industrialized countries (NICs) and the next-tier NICs which are at investment-driven stage, with a few of them, e.g. South Korea, at innovation-driven stage. Hence their rapid transition to higher stages is essential if their competitive advantage is to be enhanced.[8] 'Resting on factor-driven advantage…does not provide a solid foundation for sustained productivity growth or for expanding the range of successful industries' (Porter 1990, 564).

If they do resort to factor-driven activities, they will be trapped in the first phase of industrialization where they produce standardized goods, compete on price with each other, and lose, as a group and individually, on their terms of trade with the North. Moreover even their sustainability of 'low-cost' advantage is at risk because there are always possibilities that cheaper sources of factors, e.g. new reserves of natural resources, are found elsewhere or new cost-reducing technology is discovered. They may also risk protectionism by importers and dumping and subsidies by competitors.

Government policies

The upgrading of competitive advantage does not take place automatically. Both firms and the government have a role to play by concerted effort to escape from 'factor-driven' national advantages. Competitive advantage cannot be created, or controlled, by the government; it is attained at the firm level. The government can, however, influence it.[9] The impact of government policies should be measured through their influence on productivity growth. Such policies ought to affect various determinants of 'diamond' and cannot be confined to those which affect the prices of factors of production alone. Which determinants of the 'diamond' the government should concentrate on depends on the stage of competitive advantage through which the country is going. For example if the country is at the factor-driven stage, creating and upgrading factors of production through training and education, upgrading technology and R&D within and without firms, and upgrading infrastructure, capital investment and provision of information takes priority. In the investment-driven stage the expansion of the industrial base is to be

---

8 Normally a country moves from one stage to the next, but it is also possible that a country skips a stage, e.g. from stage 1 to 3 (ibid., 562–4).

9 See ibid., ch. 12 for details on the role of the government.

given priority. Nevertheless, in both stages policies to upgrade home demand conditions and firm strategy, structure and rivalry should not be ignored.

Porter emphasizes two points. First, if factor endowment alone cannot explain national success in most industries, policies aiming at changing factor cost and price incentives alone will be inefficient in the long run unless they are accompanied by those which aim at quality improvement, rapid product development, advanced features, etc. Those policies will include measures affecting interest rates and wages, subsidies, depreciation allowances, trade policies, devaluation and fiscal and monetary policies, etc. In fact, these policies could be counterproductive to the extent that they remove pressure on the firms to improve their competitive advantage through upgrading and innovation. Advocating these policies is based on a static view of competition. For example devaluation may work to increase exports and reduce imports. Nevertheless, it also lowers standard of living of the devaluing nation. More importantly, overreliance on devaluation will have a negative impact on the upgrading of competitive advantage. 'The expectations of a lower exchange rate lead firms towards dependence on price competition and towards competing in price-sensitive segments and industries' (Porter 1990, 642). It will have a negative impact on productivity and attainment of 'higher-order advantage'. 'Devaluation, then, may well lead to pressure for further devaluation' (Porter 1990, 642). Hence 'currency pressure needs to be strong enough to promote upgrading but not so great to run ahead of factor quality and other preconditions for upgrading to succeed' (Porter 1990, 642).

The currency incentive could work better if other determinants of 'diamond' are favourable. One such condition is the domestic rivalry which, in turn, can be affected by government policies through regulation of competition and trade policy. The infant industry protection can be effective 'in nations lacking [a strong industrial base and] well-established competitors in an industry in which foreign rivals are present' (Porter 1990, 665). However, domestic rivalry should prevail to reinforce the upgrading of the national 'diamond'.

In addition to the presence of domestic rivalry, two other conditions are essential for the success of infant industry protection. One is 'the presence in the nation of the potential for a favourable national diamond'. Another is that protection be of limited duration (Porter 1990, 665–6). The liberalization process should start with 'less sophisticated segments' if the aim is to reinforce industry upgrading. Such process requires stability and continuity in government.

The first conditions just described lead to the second point emphasized by Porter: there is a need for a comprehensive industrial strategy, where policies aiming at factor cost and incentive would be an integral part of it, aiming at improving all determinants of the 'diamond' where weaknesses and bottlenecks exist. The complementary influence of various determinants reinforces each; and any weakness in the system constrains the effectiveness of other determinants. Porter believes in change in the relative role of the government and firms over the course of development.

The nature of government policies and the degree of targeting, *vis-à-vis* functional intervention, depends on the stage of competitive advantage. At the first and second stages government intervention is more direct, e.g. through channelling resources to *related industries*, promoting risk taking, protection, upgrading and devaluations. At this stage 'targeting' is more likely to succeed than at a higher stage of competitive advantage. In the innovation-driven stage, however, firms would be the prime movers and the government role would be indirect by creating 'an environment in which firms are and continue to be innovative and dynamic' (Porter 1990, 672). At this stage creating advanced factors, upgrading demand conditions and increasing rivalry are among policies to concentrate on. To do so the government should move ahead of firms.

Endogenous firms

Throughout the process of industrialization, while foreign firms may participate in development of the country, creation and upgrading of capabilities of endogenous firms should be encouraged. FDI may provide sources of finance and technology, and facilitate access to marketing and distribution channels. Nevertheless:

> [I]t is rarely in a multinational's interest to make a developing country a major centre for producing sophisticated components or for conducting R&D. These are activities, first and foremost, for either the multinational's home base, nations with markets large enough to justify significant concession to local governments, or nations with attributes (such as demand conditions) that make locating in them important innovation... In addition, foreign subsidiaries do not necessarily breed managers with an orientation toward exports and international competition. (Porter 1990, 679)

Critique of the TCA

The TCA has sometimes been criticized on the ground that international 'competitiveness' is not a major issue since in most countries exports constitute only a small part of GDP. Moreover exports are not an objective in themselves. What is required is the rate of productivity growth in domestic economic activities (see, e.g., Krugman 1994). It should be stated, however, that TCA, at least Porter's version, does in fact emphasize the crucial role of productivity growth at the national level in general for raising the standard of living. However, for attaining international competitiveness, he refers to the relative productivity growth – in relation to other nations in specific industries since a country cannot be competitive in all industries. More importantly TCA aims at providing an alternative to the doctrine of CA. Hence the doctrine of CA could be, in that regard, subject to the same criticism as TCA.

Others have mentioned that differentiation is difficult to achieve and market focus is not as easy as product focus (Davies et al. 2003, 13). Such criticisms, however, are not fully justified. It is true that differentiation is not easy to achieve but some firms have done so by differentiating either their products or after-sale services or through reputation and branding. Sony is a good example in this respect as it has developed a reputation in the electronic industries.

Dell has developed its reputation for, *inter alia*, its direct sale and after-sale services. Similarly many firms restrict their market to a specific segment. Further, achieving quality advantage is a form of differentiation. As a result, differentiation contributes to competitive advantage through higher value created for buyers.

Another critique of Porter's theory cited in the literature is that 'differences of performance [of firms] are more important within individual industries, than between industries, considering that such differences are to be attributed to the type of combination of resources, mainly intangibles, developed by firms, rather than to industry structures', which is emphasized by Porter.

Note also that being the most efficient producer of a product (i.e. through a high level of productivity) does not necessarily means that it enables the country to raise the standard of living of its population (Reinert 1994, 3), for example if the fruits of productivity are reaped by the importing countries as argued by Raul Prebisch (1949). Prebisch's argument was in the context of primary products. Nevertheless, standard (generic) manufactured goods could also suffer from the same problem; one could talk of the 'commoditization' of manufactured goods. The benefits of productivity in production of these goods could accrue to the importing developed countries when a large number of developing countries specialize in production of the same goods and compete with each other in the international market. In such a situation they will suffer from the 'fallacy of composition' (UNCTAD, *TDR*, 2000). Thus, unless such countries try to upgrade their industrial structure, they will suffer from the terms of trade losses.

A more serious economic criticism of Porter's theory is that he does not take into account the operation of TNCs; he is silent about market failure in development of technological capabilities and 'the limited and indirect role for the Government [through their impacts on the element of 'diamond'] to promote competitiveness lacks economic rationale' (Wignaraja 2003).

The theory of competitive advantage of Porter is a business theory not presented in technical terms for economists. Nevertheless, it removes many of the weaknesses of the doctrine of competitive advantage. Unfortunately it does not go far enough to investigate the implications of increasing return at the firm level over time. Further, it does not expound sufficiently on the relative role of market, governments, firms and their changes over the course of development. Neither does it fully explain the complementary role played by institutions. Some of the implications of increasing returns and the interaction between organization and innovation is taken up by Lazonick (1991).

Interaction between Organization and Innovation (Lazonick's Theory)

Lazonick's theory of competitiveness is concerned with dynamic interaction among innovation, organization, economies of scale and experience. His theory is in sharp contrast with that of the neoclassical theory of competitiveness in many ways. As stated before, in the neoclassical theory technology is given and freely available (it is manna from heaven), goods produced are homogeneous and prices are given by market (a firm has no control over the price of the product it produces). In contrast, the main point emphasized by Lazonick (1991) is that an enterprise can change the technology it uses and it affects cost, price as well as the nonprice attributes of the product(s) it produces. A firm may follow an investment strategy that involves either a high fixed cost (HFC) or low fixed cost (LFC). Assume that an HFC and an LFC enterprise compete in an industry. Normally an established large firm is in a better position to follow an HFC strategy than a small and particularly new firm. The large established firm enjoys not only the economies of scale, but also benefits from experience.

According to W. Lazonick (1991, 95–101) it is the HFC investment in innovation and organization and their interaction that allow the firm to develop and utilize productive resources which can bring about new products with higher quality and/or new processes with lower costs. In other words, the combination of technological innovation and organizational capabilities of large firms provides them with the possibility of pursuing what he calls an 'innovative strategy' rather than an 'adaptive strategy'. In the former case the entrepreneur invests large amounts in R&D to develop a new product. Such investment would take a long time and involves a high fixed cost of innovation, which requires a large volume of sales to enable the enterprise to convert its high fixed cost into low average cost of production. In fact the enterprise must produce and sell high volumes of (high-quality) output per unit of time (high throughput); that is, it should achieve economies of scale together with economies of speed. To utilize the productive resources and human capabilities it has developed, to sell a large volume and to achieve high throughput, requires further fixed expenditure on planning and coordination of organizational activities including expenditures on advertisement and marketing. Such an enterprise may also sell its products at a loss temporarily in order to drive its competitors out. So price becomes a strategic variable which can contribute to achieving low unit cost. In this case the product price is independent of product cost.

If it succeeds in transferring 'high fixed cost' into low unit cost of production, the firm will be at a more favourable competitive advantage than an 'adaptive' firm which relies on low cost of production emancipating from factor cost advantage. Ex post the cost curve of the HFC enterprise would look like curve HH and that of the LFC firm would be curve LL in Figure 3.3a. The comparison of the two curves would imply that when successful the HFC firm has competitive advantage *vis-à-vis* the LFC firm. Nevertheless,

Figure 3.3a. Fixed-cost strategy enterprises

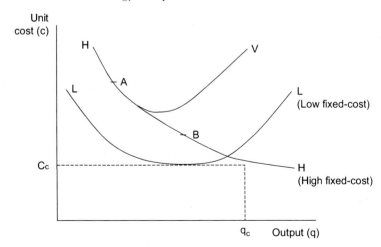

Figure 3.3b. Achieving internal economies of scale by shifting the cost curve of fixed investment in technological and organizational factors

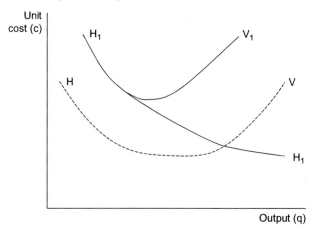

Figure 3.3c. Adaptive strategy

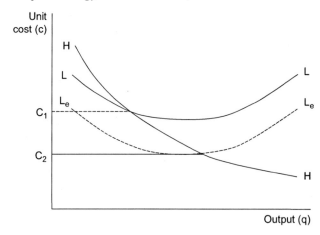

the HFC firm would show high cost at a low level of output during the process of development of its productive resources (e.g. at points A or B in Figure 3.3a).

The outcome of the situation is not known to the HFC enterprise, before the product is developed and sold on a large scale in the market. In case it does not succeed in selling in large volume, the cost curve of the enterprise may look like HV in Figure 3.3a, which implies that it cannot compete with LFC and it will be in a disadvantaged position. In other words, the innovative strategy involves high risks (ibid., chs 3 and 6).

Implications for risks

According to Lazonick (1991, 198–203, 217–21) an investor usually faces two kinds of risks: those related to productive uncertainty and those related to competitive uncertainty. Productive uncertainty is related to the internal operation of the firm; competitive uncertainty is related to the activities of its rivals with their impact on the firm. Each uncertainty in turn is related to the phases of development and utilization of productive resources. During the first phase a firm runs the risks of not developing a new product or process. Nevertheless, even when it does there is a risk it may not be able to achieve a high rate of utilization of its existing resources, both capital and labour. Moreover there are further risks that the firms' rivals may develop superior products and processes and/or utilize their resources more productively. Even more, the extent of product demands may not be known. Lazonick argues that usually an 'innovative firm' runs more risks than an 'adaptive firm' does. An innovative firm tries to 'develop its productive resources in order to produce a superior product at competitive cost (product innovation), a saleable product at lower cost (process innovation)' or both. In contrast, an adaptive firm, being 'factor driven', uses the existing technology to 'produce a saleable product at a competitive cost'.

How can an 'innovating' enterprise reduce the risks involved in an innovating strategy? There is a risk that the enterprise may end up being on the HV curve in Figure 3.3a as stated earlier. At a low level of output diseconomies of scale may prevail because of a decline in material productivity of its resources for technological and/or organizational reasons. The technological reason is related to the decreasing quality of material inputs and labour as their demand increases. The scarcity of high-quality inputs can be remedied by stockpiling, long-term supply contract or in-house development of those factors, through vertical integration. Another possibility is to develop a technology which would save the scarce factor and replace it by more abundant factors (Lazonick 1991, 101–3). Both vertical integration and development of new technology requires further fixed expenditure.

The organizational reason for diseconomies of scale is related to the loss of management control as the throughout expands. Here again further fixed investment is required to improve managerial organization and enhance motivation of employers by providing, for example long-term employment (Lazonick 1991, 104).

In short, by undertaking more fixed-cost investment in technological and organizational issues an innovating enterprise can shift its cost curve H1V1 downward to HV (Figure 3.3b) in order to attain competitive advantage.

The HFC enterprise may also face higher prices for its inputs as a result of an increase in the demand for products produced by the industry. Here again the enterprise may invest in order to provide those inputs internally at a lower cost. Alternatively the government may intervene to generate external economies, e.g. through wage control or provision of infrastructure, etc. (Lazonick 1991, 105–7).

Implication of the adaptive strategy of a developing country firm

An LFC enterprise, for example an enterprise of a developing country, can compete with an innovating HFC enterprise only if it can enjoy some external economies. Following an innovative strategy usually is beyond the capabilities of firms from developing countries at early stages of their development due to their lack of technical knowledge, skills, experience, brand name and access to marketing and distribution network in the international market. As developing countries at early stages of development are usually factor driven, they run less risk related to productive uncertainty. Nevertheless, they run more competitive risks than established firms of developed countries. There is a risk of fallacy of composition and cut-throat price cutting by similar firms from other developing countries. Further, in some cases they are faced with competition from innovative firms of industrialized countries which may develop new products or technology, undermining their competitive position. The risk related to upgrading and innovation is particularly greater for firms of developing countries than those of established firms of developed countries because they have inferior technological capabilities.

The external economies can arise from government investment in education, training, infrastructure, institutions and back-up services (see Chapter 5). It can also arise from collective investment of firms in R&D, marketing, market information, etc., through industry associations, or from collective efficiencies resulting from industrial districts and clustering (see Chapter 5). Another source of external economies is the sheer expansion of an industry or the manufacturing sector as a whole – the Marshallian external economies (Lazonick 1991, 107–8). The external economies can lead to a shift in the cost curve of an adaptive enterprise, from LL to LeLe in Figure 3.3c, provided that the enterprise uses its productive resources to enjoy such economies. Hence if the HFC firm does not drive its cost below C2 the adaptive enterprise will remain competitive. Nevertheless, in reality, the internal economies of large established firms tend to be more important than the external economies which an adaptive firm of a developing country may enjoy. After all, the established firm enjoys external economies not only in its home country but also internationally (see the next section). Even in developed countries HFC enterprises have advantages over LFC enterprises. This is why HFC enterprises have managed to drive many LFC enterprises out of the market either by mergers and acquisition or through their closure and exiting.

Lazonick also refers to the importance of national characters and the role of government policies in contributing to the transformation of the HFC firms from high-cost to low-average-cost producers over time. It can be done through provision of subsidies, equal to C1C2, to the adaptive firm in order to make it competitive in both internal and external markets. The subsidies could be paid either to the factors of production or on the price of the final product. A protective tariff equivalent to C1C2 can also make the adaptive firm competitive in the domestic market but not in the international market, unless exporters are provided with subsidies. Apart from infant industry protection, government may invest in infrastructure, institutions, etc. or intervene through other types of industrial policies as stated before.

We will consider the problems of SME (small and medium-sized enterprises) clusters in Chapter 5. Considering the importance of increasing return to scale in the competitiveness of many modern manufacturing industries, let us explain the issue further here.

Increasing Return to Scale and Competitiveness: Further Explanation[10]

As stated before, the competitive advantage of manufacturing firms is based on two main elements: cost factors and other factors such as the ability to develop and design new

---

10 The following passages are based on Shafaeddin (2005c), ch. 4.

products and processes, product differential, time delivery, etc. Economies of scale at the plant and firm levels (per period) are one source of cost advantage but not the only one; hence per se they may not necessarily provide cost advantage. Cost advantage may also result from patented production methods, entrepreneurship and favourable access to cheap factors of production and inputs. Economies of scope and learning by doing – that is, experience – are another source of cost advantage. If an industry (e.g. a semiconductor industry) is subject to rapid technological change, 'the development of a completely new design often permits an initially handicapped producer to jump to a new learning curve in a position of equality or even superiority' (Scherer and Ross 1990). Product differential can provide a small or medium-sized firm with a market niche, as can location in a particular market.

Nonetheless the established and large firms have, by and large, more advantage in relation to young and small firms of developing countries for different reasons. In contrast to the theory of CA, these firms are not passive; their action affects the price, as well as the nonprice attributes, of their products. Given their factor cost, as they produce more, they can reduce the average cost and thus the market price as stated earlier. Apart from economies of scale, they are often better equipped, for example, to take advantage of product differential and economies of scope. Further, their scale of production contributes to learning by doing over time through accumulated output. Consequently they can create barriers to the entry of new firms and increase the risks of their investment. More recently economies related to globalization, particularly those resulting from networking and strategic alliance, have been providing another source of cost and competitive advantage for established firms. A larger internal market in developed countries and their experience over time have allowed them to achieve internal static and dynamic economies of scale. International trade can allow even further realization of such economies.

In theory a larger international market – thus trade – should help newcomer firms to reap the benefits of internal economies. In this sense trade is important in providing markets as well as greater specialization and division of labour. Nevertheless, new firms of developing countries wishing to enter into the international market face a dilemma because, in order to enter the international market in the first place, they need to become competitive. In fact, according to Krugman, in order to enter the international market developing countries should first protect their industrial firms so as to grow the scale of production large enough to enable them to compete in that market. In other words, for industries characterized by increasing returns import-substitution is a prerequisite to entering the world market; import-substitution can serve as an instrument of export promotion policies (Krugman 1984). According to Krugman this argument is applied no matter whether static economies or dynamic economies prevail. Policy intervention is regarded as justified under imperfect competition; nevertheless it is maintained that providing subsidies is preferred to protection (see also Kierzkowski 1984; Ocampo 1993, 229).[11]

---

11 However, Corden (1974) has argued that the existence of static economies per se cannot provide justification for protection. They provide justification when domestic production involves externalities in two specific cases concerned with investment coordination and R&D. Otherwise, static scale economies necessitate exportation and thus free trade.

Therefore, one implication of increasing return to scale (internal to a firm) is to nullify the recommendation made by proponents of CA to all countries to adopt free trade. The cost which decreases with the scale of production is not the same as that determined by the abundance of resources. Moreover every strategic move made by a firm enjoying economies of scale affects not only the structure of its current costs and prices, but also the structure of its future costs and prices. In addition every decision and action by one firm affects the position of other firms. Contrary to CA doctrine, there is intertemporal interdependence of decisions and interdependence of action among firms. In this sense past or present decisions made by businesses in developed countries will affect the current and/or future competitive position of firms in developing countries. Further, internal economies may involve externalities as well. Any established firm which enjoys increasing return creates additional markets for the products of other firms, thereby contributing to a reduction in their cost through created externalities.

If this is the case, those developed countries which first started the process of industrialization have gained from the increasing return, division of labour and experience, and developed 'competitive advantage', particularly in certain lines of production-manufactured goods. Further, through their know-how and technology they can now reap the benefit of 'competitive advantage'.

What is more often considered in the literature as a basis for free trade is economies of scale *external* to a firm, e.g. scale economies at industrial level when perfect competition prevails, i.e. firms are small. In this case individual firms are still characterized by constant return to scale. Nevertheless, one has to make a distinction between national and international (static) external economies (Ethier 1979, 1982, 1988). In the former case, it has been shown that under certain conditions free trade can be harmful to a country and complete specialization may take place. To explain, assume a developing country – South (S) and a developed country – North (N) are producers of agricultural goods (A) and manufactured products (M). The production of A is characterized by diminishing return to scale and that of M by increasing return to scale arising from the size of the national industry. If free trade prevails, the developed country specializes in M and the developing country in A. Free trade would be detrimental to S because it specializes in the wrong line of production; it increases production at increasing cost (diminishing return) of product (A), and reduces production of the decreasing cost product (M). The cost of production of both goods increases (Ethier 1988, 454–50).

Ethier (1979), however, shows that if the source of economies of scale is division of labour among industries at the international level, *and two countries produce manufactured goods*, one needs to distinguish two different situations. If the two countries are similar in factor endowment, taste and technology, interindustry trade in intermediate goods prevails and the pattern of trade is explained by international scale economies. If, however, the two countries are not similar, interindustry trade takes place and CA explains the pattern of production and trade.

One implication of this theory is that when the source of external scale economies is national, specialization in export is arbitrary; it was a historical accident that the North specialized in manufactured goods and the south in primary commodities; the pattern of specialization cannot be explained by the doctrine of CA. To promote manufactured goods in the south, infant industry support is required. Whether trade policy or other measures are preferred is a secondary question. In contrast, when international (external) economies prevail, free trade is superior because CA explains the pattern of trade and production (Ethier 1979).

Nevertheless, in the latter case it is assumed that developing countries are already producers of manufactured goods, i.e. possess supply capabilities and perfect competition prevails. Even if these conditions prevailed, the theory would not explain how a developing country could achieve upgrading. After all, markets are not competitive, internal and external economies also prevail at the same time, and the distinction between internal and external economies is blurred.[12]

Even if one wrongly assumes the existence of perfect competition, it should be stated that the argument on international external economies has been developed on the basis of Adam Smith's often neglected 'productive theory of international trade' (Myint 1958). There is an interaction between the division of labour and the extent of the market over time – thus the theory is a dynamic one. As the market expands, the division of labour is facilitated and reaping benefit from the economies of scale, at the industry level, is permitted. Thus trade is a dynamic force. By expanding the extent of the market and furthering the division of labour, trade contributes to increasing skills and innovation, and allows a country's enterprises (which may be small) to benefit more from increasing return at the industry level. This point, however, is valid provided a newcomer firm or a country can easily penetrate the international market.

The distinction between internal and external economies of scale is not clear. Large firms often enjoy simultaneously both internal and external economies of scale. Consequently there is interaction between internal and external economies. According to A. R. Young (1928) there are two interrelated aspects of division of labour: one caused by 'roundabout' methods of production owing to the division of a task into small 'occupations' within a firm (Adam Smith's pin factory is an example), the other being the division of labour among industries (external to a firm). However, they interact. A firm 'drives its external economies from such qualitative changes as appearance of new products, new industries'.

Creative destruction is a source of competitive advantage and change. This perception of business – also shared by Schumpeter – would imply that a firm is never in equilibrium and competition takes place not only on price but also on nonprice attributes (Young 1928, 528), as explained earlier. The realization of 'increasing return' is progressive and takes time (Young 1928). It leads to dynamic competition and cumulative causation, in the process of which firms are active and become the driving force in international trade. In this sense the extent of the market is an important element of economic progress over time, as is international trade. Nevertheless, trade is the result of a dynamic process of disequilibria – not a tendency towards a 'competitive equilibrium' (for more details see Streeten 1990). In the language of Porter (1990) it is the result of the 'competitive advantage' of firms.

---

12 Of course some sort of division of labour can take place with the involvement of TNCs, but experience shows, as discussed in Chapter 3, that it would be in assembly operation with little upgrading.

Hence *greater openness to trade and international competitiveness should be the ultimate aim of all countries.* Nevertheless, it is not necessarily the immediate aim of countries at early stages of industrialization. With the presence of increasing return – whether internal, external or a combination of both – the foundation of CA doctrine is shaken. There is a dilemma for a developing country at an early stage of industrialization intending to benefit from the advantages of the extent of the market through international trade as described earlier. While entry into the international market can improve productivity and competitiveness by learning, etc., to enter the market one has to be competitive. To Young (1991) learning is more important than size. Learning takes time, and the process of learning is specific to each industry and activity. Skills are not homogeneous and they have to be developed in each particular industry; one cannot jump from one plateau to another without going through the learning process. Neither CA doctrine nor the theory of division of labour, as introduced by Adam Smith, provides the answer. An alternative approach is required. List's theory of productive power provides a framework for the explanation of the importance of learning and experience in developing the supply capacity and competitiveness.

The Theory of Productive Power of F. List[13]

The basic departure of List from the classical theory of comparative advantage is that competitiveness based on specialization in accordance with static comparative advantage is not desirable as a long-term strategy. What is required is enhancement of 'productive power', which eventually could result in specialization and competitiveness attained through dynamic comparative advantage. In other words, while the classical economists were concerned mainly with interchangeable values (international trade), List was concerned with what he called 'productive power' or, in modern language, development. Trade, thus international competitiveness, are means to development; they are not an objective per se. To repeat, according to the classical theory, specialization of developing countries in accordance with their static comparative advantage would provide them with 'competitive edge' in the international market; if all countries specialize in the production and trade of goods in whose manufacture mainly their abundant factor of production is used intensively, the *world welfare* will be maximized. List, however, argued that nations may have different objectives from maximizing world welfare. A newcomer is interested in attempting to develop its economy in line with what is called in modern language 'dynamic comparative advantage'. As a result, though it may not be currently competitive in the international market in certain lines of production, it may become competitive in the future through 'a policy-based' approach to industrialization and development.

We will briefly discuss three main features of List's theory of productive power: distinction between cosmopolitan [international] economy and national economy or universal association and national objectives; knowledge and experience as the main cause of enhancing productive power and division of labour; and the fact that division of labour and accumulation of (material) capital are results of development.

---

13 The following pages are based on Shafaeddin (2005a).

Cosmopolitan economy and national economy

Let us begin with List's distinction between 'universal association' and national perspective and objective. To List, development is a precondition for universal association, and trade and competitiveness are but means to development. He was not, by any means, against universal association and international trade (List 1856, 70–71) but argued that though 'nature leads nations gradually to the highest degree of association…the association of nations, by means of trade, is even yet very imperfect'. Hence, 'to preserve, to develop, and to improve itself as a nation is consequently, at present, and ever must be, the principal object of a nation's efforts' (List 1856, 70–71). List emphasizes that:

> That insane doctrine ['laissez-faire, laissez-passer'] which sacrifices the interests of agriculture and manufacturing industry to the pretensions of commerce – to the claims of absolute free trade – is the natural offspring of a theory too fully occupied with values and too little with productive power, and which regards the whole world as simply a republic of merchants, one and indivisible. (List 1856, 341)

Thus, considering the nature of human association, at the national and cosmopolitan levels, with different perspectives, List puts forward his 'theory of productive power' (economic development). He proposed this theory for the development of the national economy as against the theory of interchangeable value (international trade) of Adam Smith designed for the cosmopolitan economy. List emphasizes that: 'the objective [of a given nation] is not to increase directly by means of commercial restrictions the sum of exchangeable values in a country, but its productive power' (List 1856, 253). Hence one can interpret that competitiveness would be a relevant concept were it to serve the long-run objective of enhancing productive power. This would be attainable in the long run in line with dynamic comparative advantage which requires learning and acquisition of knowledge.

Thus the theory of productive power goes far beyond international trade. In modern economic terms this theory is similar to the theory of 'capability building' in the context of state-directed economic development (Lall 1991). In fact it is a multidisciplinary theory: the productive power of a nation depends on not only economic factors, but also knowledge and experience, socioeconomic, institutional, intellectual and moral factors, and its national independence and power as a nation.[14]

Knowledge and experience

Knowledge, learning and experience are the backbone of productive power. Interpreting List, Levi-Faur (1997, 157) argues that three kinds of capital contribute to 'productive

---

14 'The productive power of nations is not solely dependent either on the labour, saving, morality and intelligence of individuals or on the possession of natural advantage and material capital; it is also dependent upon social, political and civil institutions and law, but above all on the securities of nations, their independence and their power as nations' (List 1856, 74). Industrial production depends, *inter alia*, on the moral and material association of individuals for a common end (List 1856, 74).

power': natural capital (natural resources), material capital (machinery, equipment, etc.) and mental capital ('human capital'). In contrast to Adam Smith, List believes that 'mental capital' is much more important than material capital in enhancing productive power. Mental capital is acquired through experience, education and training, and is the most important source of wealth. When a country exports manufactured goods in exchange for a (primary) commodity, the exporter country maximizes its productive power because it augments its mental capital (experience) while at the same time putting pressure on the productive power of the commodity exporter. In this sense protection is effectively an educational tax. Protection of some industrial products will eventually enable the primary commodity exporter to exchange mental capital for mental capital, not matter for matter, as it develops its industrial export capabilities (Levi-Fauer 1997, 166). In other words, production of industrial output contributes to learning and experience which is the main contributing factor to productive power and competitiveness.

According to List mental capital is determined by 'social order', meaning a combination of sociopolitical and institutional factors such as a 'high moral culture among individuals, legal security of the citizens in their personal affairs and properties, free exercise of their "moral and physical faculties"' (List 1856, 211). It also involves regulating and facilitating trade, and suppressing all restraints upon industry, liberty, intelligence and morality such as feudal institutions (List 1856, 76). Accumulation of discoveries, inventions and experience is the intellectual capital of a living race of man and a nation (List 1856, 223). He also refers to other sources of productive power such as the importance of science, art (List 1856, 212), liberty of thought and conscience, transparency of judicial decisions, law enforcement, control of government by public (democracy), local administration of towns (decentralization and participation), liberty of press, freedom of association (List 1856, 216–17), government policies (Senghaas 1989), large populations, political power and division of labour (List 1856, 223).

Division of labour, competitiveness and development

List's theory of development is different from that of Smith also on the role of 'division of labour'. According to Smith division of labour and the accumulation of capital are two interrelated factors which are primary *causes* of development: accumulation of capital is a precondition for the division of labour and the division of labour in turn leads to further capital accumulation and economic development. For List, in contrast, the direction of causation is the opposite: division of labour and accumulation of (material) capital are characteristic results of development rather than its causes. Mental capital is the most important cause of development. Therefore, it is the role of the state to develop a system of education to educate and mobilize the masses (Levi-Fauer 1997, 158–60).

List further distinguishes between 'objective' and 'subjective' division of labour. In the objective division of labour a person allocates time to perform different tasks during a day. In the subjective division of labour a number of people work together to produce an object. The division of labour, whether among individuals in a firm or among enterprises within the manufacturing sector in a nation, involves association of (cooperation among) different individuals or enterprises who work in combination, requiring cooperation and coordination (List 1856, 229–31).[15] This is similar to what Hirschman (1958) calls the cooperative function of entrepreneurship. List also discusses the need for associations between sectors of the economy under one political power (List 1856, 232). The national division of labour (for example for agricultural production) requires a sophisticated system of communication, infrastructure and transport to exchange the surplus of each region with those of others.

Therefore, the division of labour should be accompanied by a sense of national unity, independence, common goals and cooperation of productive forces, requiring involvement of the state in the process of development (List 1856, 74). Nevertheless, List warned against overregulation, arguing that when productive forces can 'better regulate themselves [through the market] and can be better promoted by private exertion', the government should avoid interference (Levi-Fauer 1997, 171).

Finally List emphasizes that when an industry reaches near maturity, trade liberalization should be introduced gradually in order to put pressure on the industry to become competitive in the internal and international market. Before reaching that stage the industry should become subject to competition in the internal market to prepare it for international competition.

The theory of productive power of List is an interdisciplinary one where trade and industrial policy is its centrepiece. List's theory, however, lacks a solid micro-foundation, i.e. does not deal with issues at the firm level. The theory of capability building, built on the theory of productive power of List, takes care of this lacuna while it also deals with the question of FDI.

The Theory of Capability Building (TCB)

Being an extension of the infant industry argument of F. List, the theory of capability building (TCB) can be regarded as a theory of industrial policy. After an introductory remark we will define the theory, explain its mechanism and outline its implication for competitiveness. Finally a brief reference will be made to its critics.

A few general points

In addition to the infant industry argument, TCB draws on the evolutionary theory of change,[16] as a micro-foundation for industrial and trade policies (Nelson and Winter 1982), and the new growth theory as its macro-element (Lucas 1988; Romer 1986, 1987). 'The core concern of the evolutionary theory [of capabilities and behaviour of a firm] is with the dynamic process by which firm behaviour patterns and market outcomes are jointly determined over time' (Nelson and Winter 1982, 18–19). While firms are influenced by the market they also respond to changing market conditions. Capabilities

15 '[A] division of the operations, without the association of productive power of a common end, would be very little help in the production. That a favourable result may be obtained it is necessary that the different individuals be united and co-operate in the work intellectually and bodily.' (List 1856, 231).

16 For a pioneering work on the subject, see Nelson and Winter (1982).

are firm specific. Accordingly the firms are diverse and active, and the theory is dynamic. The firms have 'at any given time, certain capabilities and decision rules. Over time their capabilities and rules are modified as a result of both *deliberate* [my italics] problem-solving effort and random events' (Nelson and Winter 1982, 4). Moreover, over time, a sort of 'search and selection' or 'creative destruction' takes place by a process of 'cumulative change' in technology and economic organization, which leads to survival of innovative firms and disappearance of noncompetitive ones. Furthermore the conditions of industry and any action and decision taken in each period influence its condition in the subsequent period. Even more, market and prices are not the only social mechanism for transmitting information. Institutions are also important and the future is uncertain (Nelson and Winter 1982, 19–20). These characteristics obviously contrast with the general equilibrium theory which is the basis of the doctrine of CA.

The new growth theory has a few distinctive characteristics as compared with the traditional neoclassical theory of growth. First it regards knowledge as a factor of production. Learning by doing is an important means of gaining knowledge. Secondly learning by doing involves externalities because it spills over across goods. Thirdly technical progress is endogenous. Fourthly there prevail increasing return (of the Marshallian type) at the industrial level arising from specialization where it is assumed that the market structure remains competitive (see Lucas 1988; Romer 1986, 1987; Prescott and Boyd 1987).[17] When the theory is applied to international trade it is concluded that 'free trade will tend to raise the rate of growth of the DC [developed countries] and lower that of the LDC [less-developed countries]' (Young 1991, 402). In other words, in the presence of learning by doing involving externalities and increasing return to scale some market failure prevails; thus protection is more beneficial to a developing country than free trade at the early stages of industrialization.

The gist of the theory[18]

The advocates of TCB regard technological capabilities (learning), which are prerequisite to successful technology absorption and diffusion, as the backbone of industrialization and international competitiveness (e.g. Teubal 1987). They define technological capabilities in a very broad sense 'as *the information and skills – technical, organizational and institutional – that allow productive enterprises to utilize equipment and information efficiently*' (Lall 1993a, 7). In this sense technological capabilities go well beyond engineering skills and technical know-how and include other activities than production. In other words, it also encompasses all information, knowledge, skills and learning necessary for investment, production, marketing, innovation and the interaction of the firm with the external environment in obtaining inputs, in the sale and marketing of its products and in the innovation of new products and processes, necessary for upgrading, and their transfer to

---

17 These authors also show that government policy can have important effects on the growth rate of GDP.

18 The following passages are based mainly on various writings of S. Lall (1991, 1992, 1993a, 1993b and 2005) who has synthesized and developed the theory. Interested readers may refer to these sources and their references for details.

others. In contrast with the neoclassical theory the proponents of TCB theory argue that technology is not freely available to all countries and firms. Further, the market fails to develop technological capabilities automatically due to reasons of dynamic externalities, uncertainties, risks and missing and malfunctioning markets.[19] Moreover technological learning involves costs and takes time. It does not take place instantaneously because the required learning is a long and evolutionary process. It also requires purposeful efforts by enterprises as well as government and it needs investment in knowledge, human and physical resources, and organizational change. Trade policy, exchange rate and export subsidies alone are not sufficient to promote export and output growth. The failure of infant industries to mature and attain international competitiveness has been attributed, to a large extent, to the lack of, or lack of appropriate, policies to overcome market failures constraining development of technological capabilities (Bell et al. 1984).

The theory of CA attempts to explain the present pattern of trade and international competitiveness. In contrast, TCB tries to analyse how the pattern of comparative advantage could evolve and change over time through acquisition and development of technological capabilities the mechanism of which depends on the demand and supply for capabilities and their interactions.

Mechanism of capability development

The demand for capability development in any firm is determined by incentives facing the firm that operates through market signals and nonmarket factors. Competition, domestic and international, is among the most important incentive/pressure factors. International competition is affected by the trade policy regime of the country concerned as well as other countries. Domestic competition is, *inter alia*, affected by market process and competition policies, i.e. policies to regulate the domestic market. Other incentive factors which influence investment in technological capabilities include the initial need to get into production, the political and macroeconomic environment, prospects for growth of output and sale in the domestic and foreign markets, and the rate of technological progress – including changes in organizational and institutional factors – at the national and international level (Lall 1993a, section IV, 1992).

The supply factors are related to 'capabilities' of the firm to respond to incentives and are, in turn, related to the characteristics of the factor markets prevailing at the national and international levels. The prevalence of market failure in the factor markets, particularly in the markets for skills and knowledge, technical efforts and finance requires government intervention. For example, in the case of skill the market failure may be due to information failure, missing and imperfect markets and externalities involved in learning.

The government's intervention, however, cannot be purely functional to develop and correct the factor markets. In the particular case of skill formation, i.e. development of human capital, selective intervention is required for two main reasons. First some specialized forms of education and training are highly industry specific. As a result they

19 See Shafaeddin (2005a, ch. 4) for the causes of market failure.

require selective policies to address them. Secondly different activities bear different externalities in learning, including learning by doing. Discriminatory support of those with strong externalities will be more beneficial to the industrial sector, or the economy, as a whole.

To remedy the market failures there is a need for institutional supports not only in the forms of rules and regulations governing economic activities, but also in the form of entities to implement the required government policies.

It is emphasized that development of technological capabilities (TCs) requires continuous interactions of the demand and supply factors outlined above. For example it is not enough to provide only 'right incentives' by 'getting prices right' or by protection, subsidies, etc. Government intervention, as a part of coherent industrial strategy, is required for purposeful development of capabilities that contribute to market failure. Otherwise, while provisions of incentive might increase the level of output or exports once and for all, it will not lead to development of technological capabilities, growth, diversification and upgrading of output and export structure. Trade policy needs to be an integral part of such an industrial strategy.

Implications for trade policy and competitiveness

Unlike the theory of CA, TCB theory is essentially concerned with dynamic growth rather than static allocation of resources. Hence trade liberalization per se may not lead to a higher growth rate; it would involve what Lucas (1990, 21) calls 'level effect'. Neither does protection per se lead to long-run development and competitiveness. The nature of technological learning process, requiring intervention in skill markets, provides a case not only for integration of technological learning into trade and industrial strategy but also for intervention in international trade. The learning process is also regarded as a main justification for protection in the infant industry argument. The TCB, while developing on this argument, however, emphasizes the role of 'technological learning' in a broader sense and also refers to the importance of institutional factors and interaction of various demand and supply factors as stated above.

According to Lall TCB has three main implications for the trade and industrial policies and competitiveness of developing countries (Lall 1993a, section IV). First there is a need for government intervention, both functional and particularly selective. Some advocates of 'new growth theory' (e.g. Young 1991) suggest that there are some *'industrial activities that are more conducive to industrial success and trade dynamism than others'* (ibid., 18–19). This is mainly because they provide learning, more than other activities, for the economy as a whole, as mentioned earlier. At the micro-level, while learning and technological development are firm specific, they are also technology specific and activity specific. Furthermore, technologies differ in their tacit features and externalities (Lall 2005). For example 'the learning curve differs across quite similar products such as distinct types of memory chips' (Gruber 1992, 885). At the same time these activities may involve different learning costs and duration because of their differences in complexities. 'The nature of technological learning process…provides the most cogent and irrefutable case for [selective] interventions in free trade' (Lall 1993a, 16). Further, all activities and industries cannot be developed at the same time because of the scarcity of skills and other resources (Shafaeddin 2005b).

Secondly, consequently, even when some industries are selected they should be protected discriminately, i.e. a different rate of protection and phase-out period should be applied to them. Thirdly protection involves risks of inefficiencies because, if it is not handled appropriately, it *reduces* incentives to enter the international market and become competitive. As a countervailing measure the government should put pressure on the protected industries to enter the export market as soon as possible, even before protection is phased out.

The role of FDI

In the age of globalization, government action to enhance a firm's capabilities to achieve competitive advantage becomes more important than before because the minimum entry barriers and skill requirement have become higher and risks involved in entry of firms of developing countries into new activities have increased, as explained in the previous chapter (see also Archibugi and Michie 1997, 121; Shafaeddin 2005c; Lall 2005). FDI may provide certain skills and marketing channels for exports. Further, it is argued that when an economy opens up to trade and FDI an initial period of imitation will lead to a large catch-up opportunity followed by a shift towards innovation 'as the knowledge gap is reduced and the economy's technical maturity rises' (Elkan 1996). However, a test of the impact of FDI on the industrialization of a developing country is its impact on development of local capabilities through spill-over channels of demonstration, training and linkages effects (Paus 2005). Such capabilities can be influenced, *inter alia*, by learning, experience, skill development and the accumulation of knowledge by the labour force of the host country.

Generally speaking the findings of the literature on the spill-over effects of the FDI on the host country is mixed (for a comprehensive review of this literature see Görg and Greenaway 2004). Its spill-over effects and its impact on technological upgrading depends on the level of development as well as social capability and the degree of its management by the authorities of the host country. The capabilities of the host country depend, *inter alia*, on its 'well-educated workforce, effective communication infrastructure, great trust and effective economic [including financial], social and political institutions' (Kemeny 2010, 1550). Moreover in countries where the government has managed FDI and supported R&D, technological development, training, etc. the country has succeeded. Where the government has followed a hands-off policy domestic capabilities have not developed much. The contrasting experiences of Ireland and Costa Rica (Paus 2005) and China and Mexico (Gallagher and Shafaeddin 2010; Shafaeddin and Pizarro 2010) provide good indication in this respect. Both China and Ireland have succeeded in developing impressive domestic technological capabilities because of the active role of their governments, while the success of Costa Rica and Mexico has been very limited because of the passive attitudes of their governments.

The experience of many developing countries with traditional import-substitution also indicate that learning from experience alone is not sufficient for building up necessary technological capabilities; appropriate policies are required to overcome market failures constraining the development of technological capabilities (Bell, Ross-Larson and Westphal 1984).[20] In fact in the case of Asian NICs government policies and close cooperation between the government and the private sector were crucial in promoting technological capabilities for industrialization and upgrading, and for remedying the related obstacles (see e.g. Lall 2005).

Critique of TCB

TCB is one step forward in dealing with the issue of building up competitive industrial capacity and upgrading the industrial structure. Its micro-foundation, i.e. the evolutionary theory of the firm, takes into account the active role of the firm in trade and industrialization, and develops a dynamic theory in explaining the process of growth and 'cost competitiveness'. However, it suffers from three main weaknesses. First it does not sufficiently develop the active role of the firm in 'product', as against cost and price competitiveness, and nonprice strategic behaviour of firms. This is covered in the theory of 'competitive advantage' explained earlier.

Secondly its micro-foundation does not build up on the importance of increasing return to scale in a dynamic process of industrialization and export expansion. Even though it refers to increasing return it is at the level of industry alone and not at the firm level. In other words, its macro-foundation, i.e. the new growth theory, remains in the sphere of competitive market structure. Finally, though the theory refers to the role of firms, government and institutions it does not fully consider the respective role of various elements of the coordination mechanism at each point in time and their changes over the course of industrialization and development, as explained in Chapter 1.

Conclusions

The theoretical literature on competitiveness provides insight into some aspect of the issue. Nevertheless, there is a lacuna for a comprehensive dynamic policy framework to achieve competitiveness at a high level of development, encompassing both macro and micro issues and nonprice factors, in the context of developing countries while envisaging the firm as a social unit with its own unique culture. Porter's theory of competitive advantage is a step forward in taking into account some of these issues. Nevertheless, it does not go far enough to investigate the implication of increasing return at the firm level over time. Further, it does not expound sufficiently on the relative role of government, firms and market, and their changes over the course of development. Lazonick considers the interrelation between increasing return and innovation, outlines the differences between 'innovating' (large) firms and 'adaptive' SMEs, and deals with the role of government to some extent. It lacks a macro-foundation and development perspective, however, and does not consider the firm as a sociocultural unit. Such deficiencies are overcome by the theory of productive power of F. List. While progressive and relevant to the case of developing countries, the List theory lacks a micro-foundation. The proponents of

---

20 For more details see (Shafaeddin and Pizarro 2010).

capability-building theory have developed the List theory and provided a dynamic theory of competitiveness integrating the evolutionary theory and the new growth theory. However, it does not sufficiently develop the active role of a firm in product, as against cost and price competitiveness, and the nonprice strategic behaviour of firms. Moreover, the importance of increasing returns to scale at the firm level is not appreciated as the new growth theory remains in the sphere of competitive market structure. Finally it does not fully consider the respective roles of various elements of the coordination mechanism at each point in time and their changes over the course of industrialization and development in a way that we have explained in the introductory chapter. In the following chapters we will expand on our own framework of analysis presented in the introductory chapter.

4

FIRM STRATEGY AND NEW INDUSTRIAL ORGANIZATION

> History shows that the driving force of
> successful capitalist development is not
> the perfection of the market mechanism
> but the building of organizational
> capabilities [of firms and government].
> (Lazonick 1991, 8)

Introduction

In order to compete in the marketplace the management of a firm should be familiar with the sources of competitiveness, follow a strategy to create value for the customers and thus enhance its revenues. The capabilities are necessary to create supply capacity, operate the firm efficiently and upgrade its activities in order to sustain its competitiveness through relocation of the rent in the value chain. The performance of the firm then would depend on its capabilities, strategies and organization of its activities and the environment in which it operates. The sources of a firm's capabilities are three-fold: its own distinctive resources (human capital and skill, technological capacity, organization, culture and strategies), and external economies. The external economies are related to the general environment in which a firm operates, including government policies and the organization of the industry in which it operates, particularly collective efficiencies involved in an industrial cluster and production sharing.

This chapter is allocated to the discussion of the organization of the firm, interfirm relations and externalities involved including factors influencing cost of production, firm's strategy and organization, and the application of new methods of production such as the flexible manufacturing system (FMS). The discussion of external economies in general and those resulting from clustering and other interfirm relations will be picked up in Chapter 5.

In this chapter we will, more specifically, first discuss mainly the internal sources of competitiveness of firms including both cost/price issues (arising from, factors such as cost, increasing return to scale and economies of scope) and nonprice attributes. Subsequently, the issues related to the firm's strategy, including the mission and vision of the firm, will be explained. The discussion of the new methods of production will be the subject of a separate section before the chapter's conclusion.

Factors in Competitiveness

Cost factors and internal economies

A number of factors influence cost and prices in addition to factor endowment, and thus factor prices. These factors include, e.g. economies of scale, economies of scope, vertical integration, and organizational capabilities of the firm, capacity utilization, X-efficiency and economies of speed.

In a simple model of a firm, price is determined by prime cost plus a mark-up. The prime cost is equal to the cost of material input and labour cost (Kalecki 1971), while the mark-up depends on the degree of monopoly of the firm in the market. The prime cost per unit of output is influenced by economies of scale (increasing return to scale), economies of scope and economies in transaction costs. The scale economies imply that as production volume increases, average cost (cost per unit of output) declines. The sources of economies of scale are internal to the firm, external economies or a combination of both. Internal economies may arise at the plant level or at the firm level (Scherer and Ross 1990). In industries in which technology of production and the volume of capital investment dictate a minimum efficient scale of production, scale economies are very important. In labour-intensive industries the scale of production is not as important, at least at the plant level. The sources of internal economies of scale at the plant level include:

- *Production engineering*: as the volume of production increases, average cost declines; e.g. cost of harvesting depends on surface but output depends on the volume of the product obtained affecting the cost per unit of output;
- *Technical indivisibilities*: some plants have minimum size, e.g. still furnace, or require a minimum size in order to be efficient;
- *Specialization and division of labour*: specialization and division of task in a factory requires large volume of production;
- *Stochastic economies of scale*: these depend on the level of inventory and the number of spare parts required to be kept for repairs;
- *Learning and experience*: these depend on the accumulated amount of output, length of time involved in the operation, scale of production and the rate of growth of output (Scherer and Ross 1990).

Internal economies at the firm level arise not only from economies of scale, but also from economies of scope and economies in transaction costs (Chandler 1990, 8). Economies of scale at the firm level result from the bulk purchase of input, production, marketing, distribution, R&D, management and economies of globalization (in cases where a firm operates in different countries) and agglomeration and reputation (see Chapter 6). Economies of scope (or economies of joint production) arise from producing a number of related, or unrelated, products by the same firm, thus spreading the overhead cost of production, marketing and distribution among various products. The degree of economies of scale and scope in an industry depends not only on the technology of production and distribution, but also on the size and the location of the market (Chandler 1990, 18).

'Transaction costs are those involved in the transfer of goods and services from one operating unit to another' (Chandler 1990, 17). The operating units can be firms or individuals. 'The costs of transactions are reduced by a more efficient exchange of goods and services *between* units, whereas economies of scale and scope are closely tied to more efficient use of facilities and skills *within* such units' (Chandler 1990, 17). Transport, communication and telecommunications infrastructure contribute to lowering the cost of transactions. So do long-term interfirm relations with suppliers and distributors, etc. The use of the internet has also contributed to the decline in the transaction cost in more recent years.

According to Chandler (1990, 8–9) 'three pronged investment' in production, distribution and management has created competitive advantage to the first enterprises which undertook such investment. Such 'first movers' and 'a few challengers that entered the industry, no longer compete primarily on the basis of price. Instead, they compete for market share and profits through functional and strategic effectiveness' (Chandler 1990, 8). The functional and strategic effectiveness, in turn, depend on organizational capabilities of the firm which are also the source of its growth. At the firm level the economies of scale are also present in R&D, distribution and procurement of inputs. Thus economies of scale provide sources of comparative advantage. Nevertheless, this is because the cost which decreases with the scale of production is different from the cost determined by the abundance of resources, as stated earlier. The decreasing return to scale nullifies the implications of the theory of static comparative cost by which universal free trade is recommended (A. R. Young 1928; Streeten 1990). It provides a source of competitive advantage which is independent of factor prices.[1]

Chandler also distinguishes potential as against actual economies of scale and scope. The potential economies of scale and scope are the physical capacity of production. The actual economies depend on the way the capacity is utilized (see X-efficiency below) and the amount actually processed within a specific period of time, referred to as 'throughput', or the intensity by which the capacity is used, i.e. economies of speed. The actual economies depend on organizational factors which, in turn, depend on 'knowledge, skill, experience, and teamwork – on the organized human capabilities essential to exploit the potential of technological processes' (Chandler 1990, 24). The economies of speed of course depend not only on capabilities of the firm but also on the in-time availability of quality input and delivery of output to the distributors. Thus the relations between suppliers and distributors are important as well as the availability of transport and a communication network.

The 'three-pronged investment in manufacturing, marketing and management [by the first movers] created powerful barriers to entry' (Chandler 1990, 598). The first movers have not, however, remained without challengers (Chandler 1990, 597–605). Occasionally challengers have succeeded partly because of the mistake made by the first mover and partly for other reasons. For example after World War I the Ford automobile company made the mistake of weakening its capabilities by driving out nearly all its experienced and qualified managers. This paved the way for the

---

1 For more details, see Shafaeddin (2005c, ch. 5, particularly 125–32).

challengers to invest and develop the organizational capabilities to capture the market share from Ford.

More importantly government action was an important factor in creating successful challengers. Government action took place through providing finance, imposing tariffs, paying subsidies, introducing patent regulations (e.g. antitrust in the USA). In some cases it took the form of direct government investment or government procurements (e.g. purchase of steel by government-owned railway and telegraph system). Development of new sources of supply and market (e.g. in the oil industry) and growth of markets was among opportunities for challengers to enter into the market (Chandler 1990, 599–601; Shafaeddin 2005c, ch. 7).

Currently the challenging of an established firm by newcomer firms from developing countries is more difficult and risky than in the past for the reasons stated in Chapter 2.

Other cost drive factors

A number of other factors may influence the cost of production. They include, e.g. the degree of vertical integration through which a firm internalizes activities in upstream or downstream operations, linkages and interrelations with other firms through supply contracts, timing of procurement, capacity utilization and X-efficiency (see below pages 83–4). Through choosing the timing of procurement of inputs and inventory policies a firm may be able to procure inputs more cheaply than others. This can be done, for example, by moving earlier than others to the market for a product the price of which is expected to rise or by not jumping into the market when there is panic buying where the inventory would allow.

Geographical location is another factor which may contribute to low cost. For example it may allow access to cheap labour and/or raw materials, or it may involve low taxes, favourable government policies on tariffs and local contents, availability of infrastructure, institutional factors and other national environment factors. One reason why TNCs move production, or assembly plants, to developing countries is geographical location that may also provide easy access to a market.

Product attributes and other nonprice factors

Product attributes and nonprice factors contribute to competitiveness of a firm for reasons other than cost of production. Product attributes include: high-quality and differentiated product, product variety and diversity (producing a range of products to satisfy varied demand), design, packaging, styling and labelling, in-time delivery, dependability and reliability, after-sale services and guarantee that the product will always work (The International Business Machines Corporation (IBM) is an example of a reliable firm). Among other nonprice factors one may mention uniqueness of product and services, advertising and sale promotion, expanded marketing and distribution network, accessibility of the distribution channel, product and process innovation to upgrade or develop new variety or new products, and time competition. Time competition and X-efficiency require some explanation. Sony is an example in this respect (Hayes and Wheelwright 1984, 40, cited in Fleury 1995, 75).

Time competition

Time competition takes three forms: response time, process time and delivery time. Response time is the time it takes to respond to new and emerging opportunities in existing or new markets and to change in consumer requirements. This requires designing a new product and implementing it, which may involve new technology, production method or marketing and distribution channel. Here speed is more important than the cost of production as the new opportunities provide some sort of rent for the first mover. Process time is the time it takes to process material inputs into finished products. Finally delivery time is also important because even when a product is produced quickly, if it does not reach the buyers or consumers fast or on time it may deter the customers (Best 1990, 14). In other words, both on-time delivery and the speed of delivery are important.

X-efficiency

In technical terms a firm/economy is X-efficient if it produces on a production possibility curve (B in Figure 4.1) rather than inside it (e.g. at point A). Efficient allocation of resources (allocative efficiency) is accompanied by a move on the production possibility curve. In contrast, an improvement in X-efficiency leads to growth through movement from point A towards points on curve B. A movement from point B on the curves towards the horizontal access indicates changes in the allocation of resources from good B to good A. Technical progress or expansion of resources (creative efficiency) will lead to growth through movement from curve B to curve C. As mentioned before, allocative efficiency is the concern of the theory of static comparative advantage while creative efficiency is in the realm of dynamic comparative advantage.

Figure 4.1. Production possibility curves

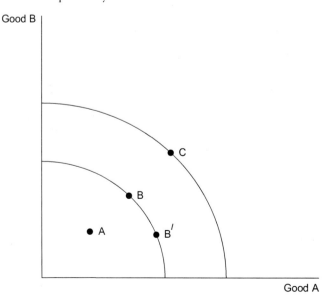

The utilization of existing inputs by a firm takes place outside the market mechanism, i.e. within firms, and is affected, *inter alia*, by both organizational factors within the firm and institutional factors outside the firm (Leibenstein 1980, 1989). Moreover an improvement in X-efficiency may involve dynamic externalities. We shall refer to externalities involved in learning effects of entrepreneurship in the following chapter. There is, however, another source of externality which requires explanation here. According to Arndt (1955) dynamic externalities related to increasing return and complementarity of various lumpy activities may be due to either the construction of new equipment (investment) or the fuller utilization of existing equipment (which is a type of X-efficiency). X-efficiency may not only spill over to other firms (through the learning effect), but also, if it takes place in a number of firms/industries, it would involve dynamic pecuniary externalities (see Chapter 5). Institutional factors also act similarly to infrastructure; in a sense one may refer to them as socio-economic infrastructure. Hence they involve similar externalities. The organizational and institutional factors affect performance of an economy at both the macro- and micro-levels. Economic growth at the macro-level and profits of a firm at micro-level both depend on the availability and efficient use of resources once allocated, i.e. X-efficiency. Institutional and organizational deficiencies result in X-inefficiency.

In Figure 4.1, to move rapidly from point A to curve B in order to improve competitiveness, or from curve B to curve C to expand production capacity or to upgrade the production structure the development of capacity in nonprice factors of the economy is required. In practice developing countries are characterized by underdeveloped organizational and institutional frameworks and other nonprice factors, particularly for production and exports of manufactured goods. The market mechanism would not function well if nonprice factors are constraints and the nonprice factors will not be developed by themselves. If the development of nonprice factors were left to the market and the private sector, it would take a long time. Moreover, since this development involves externalities and is often lumpy, underinvestment would prevail. Hence the government ought to intervene in institutional build-up, organizational development and provision of other nonprice factors.[2]

Strategy

As defined in the introductory chapter, strategy is about the direction of the firm to guide business over a long time period. We have also stressed that the emphasis should be placed on the reallocation of rent in the value chain in order to improve income at the firm and national levels continuously. Within this perspective we will explain issues related to drawing a strategy at the firm level. The discussion of the strategy at the national level is postponed to Chapter 8.

A strategy is not a short-term functional activity. Neither is it concerned with just selling more at any price. Strategy is therefore different from tactics which are concerned

---

2 While government might be able to improve some of the institutional and organizational deficiencies, it will not be able to improve all market deficiencies since some of the problems facing the government are similar to those facing the market, such as imperfect knowledge, information and insight (Stiglitz 1989).

with shorter-term issues. Whether a strategy should be designed through a top-down or bottom-up approach is controversial. In the top-down approach a strategy is designed and decided by the management and is implemented by the employees of an enterprise. In contrast, the bottom-up approach relies on the views of customers to improve the enterprise system. In practice a combination of both is desirable. A bottom-up approach alone cannot lead to competitive advantage as it ignores the role of changes in technology and innovation, and future development of the market. A top-down approach alone may miss the taste and preference of the consumers and the market situation.

A strategy requires that the firm has mission and vision. Through its creative function an entrepreneur develops a vision and a mission for the firm in cooperation with its employees. As the environment in which a firm operates is related to its interaction not only with other firms but also with its customers, employees, suppliers, government, institutions, etc. in implementation of its strategy, an entrepreneur also has to rely on its cooperative function.

Mission and vision

A company's mission and vision are indications of its character and personality. They are concerned with the company's purpose, strategy, value (what the management believes in) and behaviour standards (policies which guide how thecompany operates) (Davies et al. 2003, 189). A vision statement provides 'the company's views of itself into the future'. A mission statement 'defines the purpose of the organization' (Davies et al. 2003, 29). According to these authors vision and mission statements should have the following attributes:

• Imaginable: conveys the picture of the company in the future;
• Desirable: takes into account the interest of the stakeholders (customers, employees, shareholders, etc.);
• Feasible: goals should be realistic and attainable;
• Focused: provides clear guidance in decision making;
• Flexible: possibility of response to changing conditions in the future;
• Communicable: easy to explain within a few minutes.

One should distinguish corporate strategy from business and functional strategy. A business strategy is about how to compete in a market for a product or products. In other words, business strategy is concerned with positioning within an industry and therefore it deals with the market and competition within an industry. Functional strategy is concerned with various activities within a business, for example marketing strategy, production strategy, etc. A corporate strategy is about the business a firm would like to be in (Davies et al. 2003). Hence a corporate strategy may be defined as making choices among various industries or businesses. In other words, for a new firm, it is related to the question: what industry would a firm like to be in and in which market would it wish to operate? For an established firm the question is: how to allocate resources of the firm between existing and new products and/or existing and new markets? In both cases, i.e. business and corporate strategy, anticipating change is important as the firm needs to prepare itself for changing environment, market structure and the competitive position of its rivals, as well as changes in consumer demand and taste. There is a controversy about the importance of anticipating change for choosing a corporate strategy and characteristics of the market for a business strategy. The first step in anticipating change is to know what is going on in the global economy and what the tendencies are. Similarly one should know the structure of the market and the behaviours and strategies of the rivals. The degree-of-demand dynamism of products, changes in technology, market structure and strategies of rival firms are among the factors to be considered.

Porter's definition of strategy[3]

Porter's conception of competitive strategy is different. He is concerned with creating a unique position to deliver greater value to consumers than its rivals or comparable values at a lower cost or both (Porter 1996, 2–3). First of all he distinguishes operational effectiveness from a strategy the combination of which provides necessary and sufficient conditions for achieving competitive advantage. Operational effectiveness is concerned with such management tools as productivity improvement (productivity in its traditional sense), total quality control (TQC), quality improvement, speed, benchmarking, outsourcing, etc. Operational effectiveness enhances efficiency and better utilization of inputs for higher quality, faster delivery, etc. These elements of operational effectiveness are necessary but not sufficient as they cannot replace strategy (Porter 1996, 2). Operational effectiveness is subject to the 'fallacy of composition'. If one company applies management techniques of operational effectiveness it can win over its rivals through cost and/or product competitiveness. Nevertheless, the management techniques can be easily defused and applied by rivals of a firm. Benchmarking is about comparing the performance of a firm with the best practices in the industry in which a firm operates. The gap analysis is about the gap between the performance of a firm and where it would like to be in the future (Davies et al. 2003, 5). Here again, unless the firm also takes into account the performance of its competitors and aims at a superior situation to their own, the exercise can be futile. Therefore, while the absolute position of all firms improves, their relative position in the market may remain the same. As a result, for example, productivity improvement and cost competitiveness would result in lower profits for the firms involved in the industry. Further, there is a limit to cost reduction when companies achieve best practice. Similarly improvement in quality, delivery time, etc. can be also imitated, leaving the relative position of firms unchanged.

The essence of a strategy is creating a unique position for the purposes described above. A unique position implies that the position cannot easily be copied by others. 'Delivering greater value [to consumers] allows a company to charge higher average unit prices; greater efficiency results in lower average costs' (Davies et al. 2003, 3). Thus, according to Porter, a sustainable competitive advantage has the following characteristics: it provides unique competitive position for the company; activities of the firm are arranged in a way

---

3 The following pages are entirely a summary of Porter (1996).

that they are tailored to the strategy of the firm; it involves trade-offs and requires 'fit' across activities: various activities of the firm are parts of an integrated whole; it involves continuous operational effectiveness. Let us explain each briefly.

Activities of the firm are the basic units of competitive advantage. To provide a unique competitive position a firm should choose 'a different set of activities [from its rivals] to deliver a unique mix of values' or perform activities differently from its rivals (Davies et al. 2003, 6). Not only is it important that each individual activity is tailored to the overall strategy, but it is also necessary that it is consistent with other activities of the firm in a way that they make a unique set. In choosing its activities *the strategic position* of a firm can have three sources:

- Variety-based: producing a subset of products or services in an industry, e.g. tyres for automobiles.
- Needs-based: producing all needs of a group of customers, e.g. IKEA's production of house furniture is geared to the needs of youth.
- Access-based: providing customers in special geographical areas. Raffaisen Bank in Germany and Switzerland is an example; it provides services mainly in rural areas as its services are oriented towards the needs of small customers.

Trade-offs: in choosing its activities a firm should also avoid activities which are incompatible with each other. It has to choose not only what to do but also what not to do. For example, if a company chooses to produce a differentiated product for the special need of customers which creates high value for them and cannot be imitated easily, it should not go for mass production of similar products with low prices which other firms produce. Otherwise it will get what Porter calls 'stuck in the middle'. There are three reasons to avoid incompatible positions. The first is that getting involved in incompatible activities will lead to inconsistencies in the image and reputation of the firm. Images and reputations are created over the long term, as stated before, requiring extensive investment in time and money. Entering into a new incompatible activity therefore not only would not result in creating a new image, but also might damage the established image of the firm. Secondly, as different positions and activities require different set-ups in management, production, marketing and distribution, the related costs may increase more proportionately.

Thirdly, when a company tries to do everything for all customers a clear framework would be lacking as there is often a limit on the ability for internal coordination and control.

Fit across activities: operational effectiveness concerns achieving efficiencies in individual activities. A strategy is about combining a set of activities as a system and not just as a collection of activities. The idea behind a system of activities is to create a situation which would not be easily imitated by others. Three factors contribute to 'fit' across activities: consistency between each activity and overall strategy; reinforcing of activities by each other; and optimization of efforts of the firm. For example, GAP's strategy emphasizes product availability. It therefore restocks its main products on a daily basis.

By creating a system which includes the above-stated factors it would be more difficult for the competitors of a firm to imitate the company's competitive strategy. Further, fit provides incentive and pressure for enhancing operational effectiveness.

Of course the organizational structure should also be strategy specific to provide continuity and to reinforce identity (culture) of the firm. An effective organizational strategy requires leadership, discipline and communication. Misconception of competition – by mistaking it for operational effectiveness – and organizational failure both contribute to strategy failure. The leadership should opt for continuous improvement in operational effectiveness, intensify and strengthen its fit and extend its uniqueness. If there is a major structural change in the industry, a company may have to change its strategy.

Some managers think that by expanding the activities of their firm, e.g. through merger with another company, they can contribute to the growth of their firm even if its activities and products are not compatible with the activities and products of their own company. Such expansion may contribute to higher sales but not to a higher profit per share.

In short 'The operational agenda involves continual improvement everywhere, there are no trade-offs. Failure to do this creates vulnerability even for companies with a good strategy. The operational agenda is the proper place for constant change, flexibility, and relentless efforts to achieve best practices. In contrast, the strategic agenda is the right place for defending a unique position, making clear trade-offs, and tightening fit. It involves the continual search for ways to reinforce and exert the company's position. The strategic agenda demands disciplines and continuity; its enemies are destructions and compromise' (Davies et al. 2003, 24).

Formulating and implementing a strategy[4]

Formulating and implementing a strategy is an ongoing dynamic process as depicted in Figure 4.2. After clarifying the strategic vision of the firm and setting its objectives the process involves three phases: formulation, implementation and control, and revision and modification of the strategy. While profitability is the main objective of the firm it may also have other managerial objectives such as gaining market shares, social responsibility, etc. In setting the objective usually short-run goals are distinguished from long-term objectives; thus distinctions are also to be made between tactics and strategy.

SWOT analysis

There are different methods for appraising the internal situations of the firm and the external conditions prevailing in the market. One technique is comparison of strengths, weakness, opportunities and threats (SWOT). The capabilities of the firm are identified in different areas of its 'production and distribution chain' and supporting services, and are compared with the requirements of the market. In order to appraise the external situation, i.e. opportunities provided by the market and threats of rivalry, one may apply Porter's five-force structural analysis. Further, consideration should be given to the possible future changes in the market, including changes in the world economic situation, demand, technology and

---

4 This section is based mainly on Davies (1991, ch. 11).

Figure 4.2. The process of formulation and implementation of a strategy

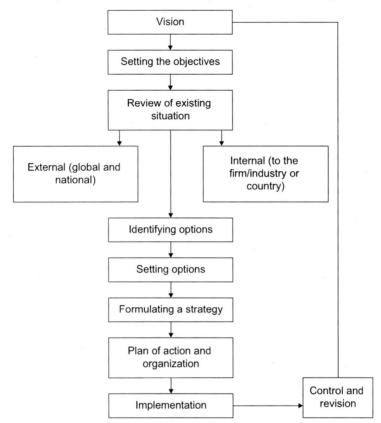

Source: Expanded from figure in Davies (1991).

the sociopolitical situation in the countries which are the main market for the products. The SWOT method is to some extent subjective as it depends on the knowledge and experience of the managers and others who are involved in the appraisal of the situation. Further, one missing element is the appraisal of changes in the legal framework in which internal and international trade takes place. This includes the trading system, regionalism and other factors related to the context in which competition takes place, as discussed in Chapter 2. Another missing factor is the analysis of the degree of 'demand dynamism' of a product in the internal and international market and its changes. This deficiency is overcome in 'portfolio analysis' techniques.

Portfolio analysis

There are different versions of the portfolio analysis techniques including Boston Consulting Group (BCG) growth/share matrix, the General Electric (GE) business screen and Hofer and Schendel's (H&S) product/market evolution matrix. The common features of these techniques are that they allow for the degree of dynamism of the products as well as the relative market share, or competitive position, of the firm.

In BCG one classifies products as high- and low-growth groups and the market share of the firm in each product as high and low. Accordingly the products produced by a firm would include four categories: 'stars' (high growth, high market share); 'dogs' (low growth, low market share); 'cash cows' (low growth, but high market share); and 'question marks' (high growth, but low market share). Accordingly the firm can dispose of dogs which provide low profit with little prospects but expand stars by using resources provided by cash cows. Question marks have good prospects, but require allocation of more resources to their production in order to benefit from market opportunities.

The GE business screen provides more details on the attractiveness of the industry and the competitive position of the firm (including its capabilities). After the classification of the products the firm puts emphasis on the production of goods with a high and medium degree of attractiveness and the high and average competitive position of the firms (four groups). In contrast, it divests those products with a low degree of industrial attractiveness and weak, or average, competitive position of the firm (four groups). Three groups with weak competitive position/high growth, low attractiveness/strong competitive position and medium attractiveness/average competitive position will be given low priorities.

The H&S product/market evolution matrix is similar to GE's business screen method with the difference that the stages of evolution of a product over its life cycle are taken as the degree of attractiveness of the related industry. The stages considered include: development, growth, shake-out, maturity and saturation, and decline.

Various methods explained above have their own advantages and disadvantages. For example, BCG is simple but very subjective while the other two methods are more sophisticated but at the same time are more complex as the degree of attractiveness of products is not easy to measure or the different stages in a market's development cannot be distinguished easily. What is important, however, is that a firm should make some objective appraisal of the internal and external situation before identifying and setting its strategic option.

Having set its strategic option, a firm should formulate a detailed strategy for implementation together with development of a plan of action and organizational set-up for its implementation. Over time, the achievements and shortcomings of the strategy should be reviewed in order to provide feedback for the revision of the strategy (see Figure 4.2).

The Flexible Manufacturing System (FMS) and Japanese Techniques

Industries in which the technology of production has potential for extensive economies of scale are organized through what Chandler calls managerial capitalism or 'Fordism', as explained above. In this system SMEs are in a disadvantaged competitive position *vis-à-vis* large firms. During recent decades another organizational system has been developed which is also applied to SMEs and labour-intensive industries. It is called the flexible manufacturing system the main characteristic of which is not only to compete on price but also on the ability to move quickly with changing demand for different but related products. In contrast to the managerial capitalism system which requires function-specific and product-specific skills, both at the shop-floor and management, in FMS multifunctional skills are required. In this section we will first define the system and refer to its origin and the characteristics of its organization of production. Subsequently the experience and problems of its implementation in developing countries will be explained. Finally the role of government will be outlined.

Definition

According to Best (1990) FMS is 'about seeking a competitive advantage by continuously upgrading product, process and organization...a business organization that pursues a strategy of continuous improvement by integrating thinking and doing' through problem solving and innovation (Best 1990, 144). According to Piore and Sable (1984) 'flexible specialization is a strategy of permanent innovation: accommodation to ceaseless change, rather than an effort to control it. This strategy is based on flexible-multi-use equipment; skilled workers; and the creation, through politics, of an industrial community that restricts the form of competition to those favouring innovation' (Piore and Sable 1984, 17). To grasp the detailed characteristics of this method of production let us describe its origin.

The origin of FMS

The idea of flexible specialization is sometimes attributed to Japan where its development goes back to the late 1930s (Fleury 1995) but the system in fact has its origin in France and the UK, going back as far as the early nineteenth century. The Japanese introduced it in their industries in the 1930s and further developed and applied it in the 1970s.[5] Hence it is referred to as a Japanese technique in the literature.

The origin of FMS is the craft form of production and its revival and development emerged first among silk weavers in the industrial districts of Lyons, in France between 1800 and 1820. Later on it spread to metalworking and some other industries in Birmingham and Sheffield (UK) (Piore and Sable 1984, 31–2). The development of flexible specialization was somewhat entwined with industrial districts – or *fabriques collective*. The industrial districts of the time had three main characteristics: production of a range of products and rapid alteration of the goods produced; flexible use of technology; and the creation of regional institutions to balance competition and cooperation to encourage innovation (Piore and Sable 1984, 29–30). In order to produce varieties of new goods firms, however, were discouraged from competing on wage and price reduction as opposed to 'competition through the innovation of products and processes' (Piore and Sable 1984, 30). Vertical specialization and subcontracting were also some characteristics of industrial districts of the time. Therefore, almost a century before Schumpeter wrote about a 'new method of competition', it was to some extent being practised by industrial districts of the time.

The use of FMS by Japanese firms was in the development of the old system of craft production (Piore and Sable 1984, 30). The development of Japanese firms during the postwar period till recent years has been based on three pillars: competitive

---

5 For a brief evolution of the need for new methods of competition see Fleury (1995).

strategy, organization and culture (Best 1990, 138). Further, the Japanese government played an important role in the development of Japanese enterprises and evolution of FMS.

Strategy

To understand development in the competitive strategy of Japanese firms we should first explain Porter's concept of 'value chain' in order not to confuse it with 'value chain' as explained earlier; we have called the former supply chain (production and distribution chain) (Gereffi and Memedovic 2003). As is explained in Box 4.1 the concept of value chain has evolved over time with slightly different meanings).

Box 4.1. Evolution of the concept of value chain

The concept of value chain is given different meanings by different scholars. M. Porter (1990) uses it in its wide sense: a chain of activities for a firm operating in a specific industry. It includes all the activities of a firm, both 'primary and supportive activities' (see Figure 4.1).

The way the concept has been used by other authors has gone through some evolution. Initially a value-added chain was defined as a 'process by which technology is combined with material and labour inputs, and then processed inputs are assembled, marketed, and distributed' (Kogut 1985, cited in Gereffi et al. 2005, 79). This is more or less the same as 'supply chain'.

Gereffi (1994) used the concept of 'commodity value chain' which tied the concept of value-added chain to the global organization of industries by distinguishing a 'buyer-driven' from a 'producer-driven' value chain. He emphasized the important role of buyer firms (particularly retailers) and their relation with producers. Buyer firms were added to the 'supply chain'. Such definition, on the supply side, is also clear in the subsequent writing of (Kaplinsky and Morris 2000): 'The *value chain* describes the full range of activities which are required to bring a product or service from conception, through the different phases of production (involving a combination of physical transformation and input of various producer services), delivery to final consumers, and final disposal after use' (Kaplinsky and Morris 2000, 4). These authors do not include buyer firms in the chain.

Subsequently production for the global markets was emphasized by introducing the concept of 'global value chain'. 'Global value chain research and policy work examine the different ways in which global production and distribution systems are integrated...' (Gereffi et al. 2005, 79). It 'focusses on the nature and content of the inter-firm linkages, and the power that regulates value chain coordination, mainly between buyers and the first few tiers of suppliers' (Gereffi et al. 2005, 98). In this sense the providers of inputs are also included in the chain.

Other authors also discussed differences in various types of global value chain depending on the 'characteristics of specific products and process and the

Box 4.1. *Continued*

[firm-specific] routines and regulations that prevail in particular industries' (Stugeon and Memedovic 2011, iv). The complexity of transactions, the ability to codify transactions and the capabilities in the supply-base as well as the role of outsourcing by producers are among important determinants of the type of value chain. The technological complexity of intermediate products is, inter alia, a particularly important factor in determining those variables (Gereffi et al. 2005, 98). For example it is shown that electronic, automotive, and apparel and footwear are, in order of importance, four industries with complex and dynamic division of labour and a high degree of fragmentation and global integration, i.e. a value chain which is spread across various countries (Stugeon and Memedovic 2011, particularly 22, fig. 4). Global trade in intermediate goods, particularly in electronic goods, has been expanded a lot faster than final products (Stugeon and Memedovic 2011, 8) particularly in developing countries (Stugeon and Memedovic 2011, 14, table 1). Among developing countries China, Hong Kong SAR, Singapore, Republic of Korea, Mexico and Malaysia show, in order of importance, the highest share in total global trade in manufactured intermediate goods (Stugeon and Memedovic 2011, 16, table 2).

Following M. Porter (1990) the production and distribution chain (see Figure 4.3) consists of primary and supportive activities. Primary activities include those activities which are directly involved in production, marketing, sales and after-sale services. Supportive activities provide back-up services for primary activities. Primary activities include:

- *Inbound logistic*: activities related to receiving, storing and handling inputs. They include, e.g., data collection, transport, material storage and customer access;
- *Operations*: activities related to manufacturing including component moulding, machining, assembly, branch operation, testing and maintenance;
- *Outbound logistic*: activities concerned with the stage between operations and sales consisting of, e.g., storage of the products within the firm, warehousing, order processing and scheduling, report preparation, etc.;
- *Marketing and sales*: activities related to promotion and sale of products; they include advertisement, trade shows, offers, tendering, sales management, relation with distribution channels;
- *After-sale services*: activities provided by the firm for installation, maintenance and use of the product; e.g. installation, repair, customer support and training, upgrading.

Support activities consist of:

- *Firm infrastructure*: planning, finance, investment relation, accounting, legal services, quality management and general management;
- *Human resource management*: recruitment, training, appraisal, promotion, development and compensation of the staff;

Figure 4.3. The value chain

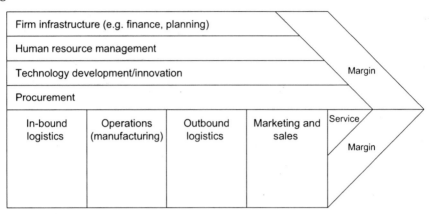

Source: Porter (1990, 41).

- *Technology development*: activities related to R&D such as product and process design, testing, market research, material research, information technology and telecommunications;
- *Procurement*: all activities related to purchase of material and service inputs, equipment, spare parts, office tools and machinery, etc.

All labour and workforce involved in primary activities are regarded as direct labour because they contribute directly to the production and distribution process: in contrast, those engaged in support activities are regarded as indirect labour because their contribution is indirect.

Although Japanese enterprises have had their own strategy it is not easy to separate their strategy from that of the national strategy pursued by the Japanese government, particularly at early stages of industrial development after World War II. At the early stages of its post–World War II industrialization the policy of the country was factor driven. Initially Japan concentrated on the development of labour-intensive industries as wages were low and technological capacities were limited. This phase was followed by the production of intermediate goods followed by the development of some capital-intensive industries with large economies of scale, such as steel, ship building, petrochemicals, electronics, transport equipment, etc. and this process is referred to as a flying geese model in the literature (Akamatsu 1961). Cost and price competitiveness was the strategy in the first two phases, which were factor driven.

The factor-driven phase was subsequently followed with what may be called an organization-driven phase, which started with 'focused production' and was followed by flexible production. The focused production phase continued to be geared to cost competitiveness, whereas flexible production involved other considerations as well. While in mass production the emphasis is on cost reduction in production, i.e. in cost of direct labour; in focus production the emphasis is on reducing indirect labour cost. This is done by focusing on the production of a fewer number of high-volume products to enjoy economies of scale, avoiding diseconomies of scope and scale on products which are not sold in large volume and thus reducing overhead cost. In the focused production system the organization of production had to be different from that applied at earlier stages. While quantity consciousness was a characteristic of the scale economies as well as of focused production and flexible production strategies, the flexible production system went beyond it and required a totally different organization of production.

Organization of firms in FMS

FMS is different from the mass production system (Fordist system) in the existence of a pool of multiskilled workers and multifunctional machinery, teamwork and loose division of labour, a flattened supervisory hierarchy, just-in-time (JIT) delivery, in-process quality control instead of end-of-the-line inspection, and participation of the workers in improvement of quality and performance through their consultation (Ozawa 2003, 9–10).

More specifically FMS has a number of organizational characteristics which distinguishes it from the Fordist system (Best 1990, 144; Capecchi 1992, 20–21). First, in the Fordist system of mass production a number of standardized products are produced sequentially over time. In contrast, in the FMS the production plant is provided with flexibility to produce a range of small batches of different products on the same production line without extra indirect labour costs. While in the mass production system it would take some time to change over from one production to another, in FMS the changeover time is extremely short. Mass production requires big factories; FMS is based on many SMEs which may be organized into a cluster of firms or networking.

Secondly therefore just-in-time (JIT) production is an element of FMS but not the only one. While the mass production concentrates on reducing the cost of production at each stage of primary or support activities, JIT production concentrates on reducing the time spent at each stage by elimination of wasteful practices. As a result not only will the time spent on the whole production process be shorter, but also the product will be produced in time to match demand. What is important is not only JIT production of an item, but also producing a range of products economically with a short changeover time. One example is shifting production from children's clothes to clothes for adults or from production of clothes to production of shoes in a few minutes. This may require more tools and machines but the cost of extra tools and equipments is overcompensated by the benefits of reduction in inventories and value created for buyers.

Thirdly, while in mass production the decision on production of various products is made ex ante by forecasting demand, the decision on production under FMS is made when the order is received. The idea here is not merely to reduce or eliminate inventories of input and output, but also to produce products on time and during the same period. For example, summer clothes are manufactured in summer when an order is given and not in the previous season in expectation of orders.

A fourth element is total quality control (TQC). Accordingly inspection for quality control is undertaken at each stage of production rather than at the end of the production process. Quality control would be built in to all jobs; thus everybody would undertake quality control at each stage of production and distribution chain. For this purpose, in the

Japanese technique of production, machines were made in such a way that manufacture would stop automatically when the system detected abnormality. As a result each worker could work with a few machines instead of one. Further, when a problem emerges the workers can solve it rather than simply minding the machines. They also contribute to the improvement and upgrading of the production process. TQC would not only contribute to cost reduction as repeating some jobs and rejection of some products would be minimized if not eliminated, but also would contribute to the reputation of the enterprise. Such reputation in turn would enhance the value to the buyers.

Fifthly in the Fordist system there is a clear separation between white collar workers and the rest of the employees. In FMS, TQC requires integration of planning and operation on the shop floor; thus there will be a close interrelation between the management and the workers as there will be consultative relations with suppliers and distributors. The aforementioned characteristics and interrelations imply that there is a need for teamwork and close cooperation both at horizontal level, i.e. among employees, and vertical level, i.e. between the employees and management at different hierarchical levels and between various employees and their supplier and distributor. Such an interrelation requires a different enterprise culture (see section on 'Culture of firms in FMS').

Sixthly FMS involves considerable indirect labour cost savings. The savings result from concentration on operational efficiency rather than process efficiency. Operational efficiency is about the time spent on the 'operation' in the production chain, referred to as productive time. Process efficiency is concerned not only with productive time but also with unproductive time – the time spent on nonoperational activities in the first three stages of the primary activities in the production chain. In this case one may distinguish the operational throughput efficiency as against process throughput efficiency. The latter is the ratio of time spent in transformation of a product at the stage of operation to the time spent in the production system as a whole. In other words it is the period between the time when inputs arrive at the firm and the time they leave the production plant,i.e. when it reaches the stage of marketing and sales in the supply chain. If one regards the inventory of inputs necessary for production as work-in-progress (WIP) the ratio of annual sale to WIP will be WIP turn, i.e. the number of times inputs turn over to produce a given amount or volume of sales. (For Toyota WIP turn was 300 as against 10–25 for western automobile companies.)

Finally the system is a dynamic and continuous process with the capacity to change and adapt to the environment in which it operates, with continuous learning of all involved in the production process. People from various activities in the production chain would cooperate with each other as a team to develop and upgrade product quality and production methods. For development and application of new technologies people who are involved in operations can also contribute to the planning and design due to their experience and knowledge.

In the case of Japan, where SMEs acted as a supplier to large firms, they have had close consultative relations directly and through the association of suppliers of part makers – which was created, *inter alia*, for this purpose. Often the design and development of parts were undertaken by the suppliers with the consultation of the parent companies. The cooperation between parent firms and suppliers, and the teamwork within an enterprise requires a culture – referred to as the culture of collective capitalism by Lazonick (1991).

Generally speaking, Fordism is based on central production planning with a strict hierarchical system of management. In FMS the output level of an operational unit is dictated by the level of demand. JIT and stockless production, high quality and productivity are its main characteristics. Further, to ensure secure operation, the workers are encouraged to make their own decisions on minor modifications during the production process. In other words they subject themselves to self-management. Teamwork and collective action are two other characteristics of the system (Gjerding 1992, 103–4 and 109).

Mass production (Fordism) and FMS have only two common features. In both cases market characteristics are identified and a competitive strategy is accordingly established. Further, on the basis of the strategy drawn, productive resources are organized. The Japanese technique of FMS in addition involves two extra features: a great emphasis on learning and continuous improvement, and a better and clearer recognition of a firm's relative competitiveness in targeted markets (Fleury 1995, 74). In other words, in FMS the organizational practices of a firm are based on a dynamic approach, which is a feature of the system by definition, while that of Fordism was predefined.

Culture of firms in FMS

As stated in the introductory chapter, a company's culture can be defined as a set of principles and practices that the firm follows, which provides it with a collective identity. To have a collective identity requires teamwork, cooperation among the workforce and between the management and the workforce, or what Hirschman calls 'group-focussed image of change' (Hirschman 1958). Further there is a need for commitment and trust from all parties. For example, commitment to quality products becomes a part of the enterprise's culture. As each firm has a different set of strategies and principles, culture is firm specific. For example, lifetime employment together with the seniority rule and enterprise unionism was part of the enterprise culture in Japan. They were a vehicle for cultivating motivation, commitment and trust in the Japanese enterprise culture (Odigari 1992, ch. 3). In particular the idea of life-long employment was based on the perception of the knowledge of Japanese managers. It was believed that knowledge has three main features: it is embodied in individual workers; it is to a large extent firm specific and worker specific; and it is human capital which can be accumulated through education, training and experience. Therefore, the loss of a worker was regarded as a loss of knowledge to the firm particularly as it was also believed, *à la* F. List (see Chapter 3), that human capital was more important to the growth and competitiveness of firms than financial and material resources (Odigari 1992, 1–2). Hence 'only by continuously working in the same firm can a worker fully utilize his knowledge and be motivated to accumulate it' (Odigari 1992, 1–2, 2). Therefore, lifetime employment was regarded as important in the realization of productivity. In fact a better productivity performance of Japan, as compared with other industrial countries, during 1950–1995 is attributed to a large extent to lifetime employment provided to workers in exchange for loyalty and productivity (Griffiths 2000). Nevertheless, lifetime employment did not imply that a worker would not be laid off; all it meant was that it was a norm (ibid., 2 and 21). Competition among workers for promotion was also an incentive for performance.

Relation with suppliers and subcontractors

Long-term relation with their suppliers is regarded as an important factor in the success of JIT production in Japanese FMS. Over 90 per cent of a sample survey of about 100 large Japanese firms in the early 1990s indicated that they had continuous business relations over the previous five years (Odigari 1992, 151). Nevertheless, the suppliers were subject to competitive pressure despite their long-term relations with the purchasers of their products. In fact the relation between the two was not confined to sale and purchase of the products. The suppliers and the assembler would also cooperate in design, technological development and R&D. Unless the inputs were standardized products, the detailed specification of the input would be prepared by the assembler and given to the supplier. Alternatively the supplier would prepare the specification and get approval from the buyer firm. In the process of production the supplier would also try to improve productivity. The supplier would be subject to performance requirement and sanction and/or rewards. At the end of the contract period the supplier would be evaluated. In case of more than satisfactory performance the supplier would be promoted to a higher rank and would be provided with more orders in the future. Further, it would be allowed to increase its mark-up in order to get encouragement for further effort. In the case of unsatisfactory performance the supplier would be punished; while discussing the problem the buyer firm would reduce the agreed mark-up and its order in the following contract. If the unsatisfactory performance continued its contract would not be renewed subsequently. Throughout the period of the contract rapid adjustability of quantity of production is facilitated in order to guarantee JIT delivery. The existence of trust between the supplier and the buyer was a feature of their long-term relationship. The system of reward and punishment together with collaboration in R&D encouraged innovation by the supplier which also was often provided with financial and technical support by the buyer (Odigari 1992, 151–60; Fleury 1995, 74).

The role of government

The success of Japanese competitive strategies is owed partly, but not entirely, to government policies in providing supporting institutions, pursuing macroeconomic policies conducive to industrialization, establishing close government–business relations, and encouraging and facilitating interfirm cooperation (see Best 1990, ch. 6; Lazonick 1991; Porter 1990; Odigari 1992, ch. 11; Akamatsu 1961).

Industrial policy was used by the Japanese government as a tool for shaping markets to enhance the international competitiveness of Japanese firms (Best 1990, ch. 6). M. Best argues that in Japan the government tried to use market as a means of growth (for creative efficiency) rather than as a pure instrument of allocative efficiency. In fact the criterion for enterprise success was strategic advantage; continuous upgrading and reallocation towards a higher value-added production process was a reason for success (Best 1990, 168). Nevertheless, the government pursued a dynamic approach in its intervention. While pursuing industrial policy and technology policies throughout the period of industrialization, the relative role of market and government changed over time. As the firms and market institutions developed, the government introduced antimonopoly policies in the domestic market to encourage competition. Further, over time the relative role of the government *vis-à-vis* market and firms was reduced. More importantly, Odigari argues, the government policies alone were not effective if the firms were not prepared to follow what he calls 'the growth pursuing behaviour of firms'. The firms were keen to use the opportunities provided to them to their advantage and the government policies were geared to intensifying competition and market forces. The government provided administrative guidelines but the firms themselves were the main actors even in R&D (Odigari 1992, 25 and ch. 11). Moreover there was also close interrelation between government and the private sector (see Chapter 6).

Applicability of Japanese Techniques in Other Countries

The success of Japanese techniques of FMS is sometimes attributed to Japanese culture. It is argued that imitation of this system by other countries might run into problems because of cultural differences (e.g. Gjerding 1992). There is, however, some evidence that a number of western companies have applied some elements of the Japanese technique or even the entire system with some success. For example, IBM had a lifetime employment policy and Marks and Spencer has applied strict quality control independently of Japanese influence with success (Odigari 1992, 317–18). Similarly some Japanese firms have applied these techniques in other industrial countries with some satisfactory results (Odigari 1992, 318–22; Oliver and Wilkinson 1992). Further, a number of firms in other developed countries, both in Europe and the USA, also practise some elements of the Japanese techniques with favourable outcomes. Nevertheless, in two respects they could not match the best Japanese practices: 'continuous improvement' and an effective relation with their suppliers and customers (Kaplinsky 1995, 61).

The experience of developing countries

Therefore, a question remains whether or not the Japanese techniques can be successfully applied by firms in developing countries. The short answer to this question is that the results obtained in a number of case studies on the whole are positive, albeit they vary from one case to another. An earlier successful case of the application of the FMS is that of the Sunny Face Garments Company in Cyprus (see Box 4.2). A number of enterprises in Latin America, Asia and Africa have also tried to adopt some elements of the Japanese techniques but not FMS as a system. The results are mixed as firms have tried to adapt the technique to local conditions (see Humphrey 1995b for a summary and the sources of country studies). In the case of Latin America studies of Brazilian industry by Fleury (1995), Meyer-Stamer (1995) and Humphrey (1995b) conclude that there has been some awareness on the part of the Brazilian industry of the need to enhance competitiveness as a result of trade liberalization, particularly since the early 1990s. Further, there was also some improvement in lean time, throughput time and quality. Nevertheless, they were achieved more due to utilization of traditional rationalization than intentional application of new methods (Fleury 1995, 80). Yet their gap with international standards was still wide (Meyer-Stamer 1995).

Box 4.2. Application of FMS to Sunny Face in Cyprus

Sunny Face started in 1974 as a small family business specializing in high-quality children's clothing as a handicraft production. However, it converted to mass production in 1975. Between 1974 and 1987 its turnover increased by 35 times reaching £736,000. Then diseconomies of scale, which had been felt since 1985, started to bite seriously and the company started transmission to FMS. Accordingly the management introduced three main changes:

- Small batch production – a cellular layout instead of functional layout;
- Reorganization of production line;
- A computerized information processing system;
- The integration of marketing and production.

The cellular layout would imply that each worker would perform three to four different tasks with two to three different machines requiring a multiskilled workforce. Further, each worker was responsible for quality at source in order that no faulty goods would be handed over to the next worker in the cell. Despite some problems at the beginning the results were initially very promising. For example, WIP vanished; quality improved; lead time and throughput time decrease was measurable; the process became more manageable.

In the process, however, a number of problems arose mainly related to the reluctance of the partners and some workforce members to accept changes in the system; there was a tendency to return to the old mass production system. The response of the manager who initiated the application of FMS was to discuss, to coach and arrange training of the workforce, particularly in the areas of data management, computerization of the information system and control management. In particular, the computerized database was developed, with the help of software which customized menus, as an integrated one to include data on the characteristics of the orders including input requirements; scheduling the tasks and cutting materials into the requisite shapes; production and progress of the work; delivery and checking the data against the order schedule.

The data collected were utilized for management decisions, production scheduling and ordering of material supplies. Further, it helped the analyses of the market situation and sales of various products, and the reduction of inventories of inputs as well as output.

Box 4.2. *Continued*

By linking production to orders (by introducing a demand-pulled system of make-to-order-named just-in-time production) contributed not only to the reduction of inventory costs but also to rapid response to changes in demand. The improvement in its designing and opening a number of retail shops provided the company with better ability to satisfy the demands of buyers and changes in their tastes.

The reorganization involved some costs in terms of equipment, software, management time, lost production and occasional mistakes in purchases of excess raw materials. Nevertheless, the overall benefits of reorganization far exceeded its costs, some of which cannot be quantified. It also improved the competitive advantage of the company substantially in Cyprus and abroad by reducing overall costs, halving the lead time (time to meet customer orders) and enhancing flexibility.

Source: Based on Kaplinsky and Posthuma (1994).

In Mexico Ford applied the American version of the JIT technique with a Californian system of labour relations in three automobile plants in different parts of Mexico. In cases where the labour was motivated, the results were more satisfactory than in other cases. Education was more important in plants where high technology was used. In other plants, while training was essential, education was not that important. Where labour relations were tense there were difficulties in applying the technique. In higher-technology plants some success was noticed even though labour relations were not good. In the old plant, in particular, the labour was not cooperative and the level of education and training was lower than in newly established plants.

Problems of application and implementation

Although a few firms of developing countries have managed to make radical changes to their production system successfully, overall there is little evidence that the system as a whole has been applied (Kaplinsky 1995, 62). Some of the techniques used in FMS, such as JIT, TQC and efforts for 'continuous improvement', have been used in different developing countries, but the application and sustainability of the FMS as a whole has been difficult because of the low levels of education and training, poor management–labour relations, lack of motivation by labour, the lack of managerial capabilities for rapid decision making, macroeconomic instability, inhibiting habits and practices inherited from the import-substitution era and sudden exposure to foreign competition as a result of trade liberalization (Humphrey 1995b; Fleury 1995). Kaplinsky (1995) has identified a number of obstacles to the application of the system to developing countries. One problem is the lack of commitment from the top management; but there is also resistance to change from workers and middle managers, even when the leadership intends to introduce the new methods. Another is the lack of awareness about the change in the nature of competition imposed on developing countries through trade liberalization, the requirements of the market and involvement of the TNCs in the value chain in production and international marketing (Kaplinsky 1995, 61–2). There has also been weakness in human resource development due to the lack of formal education and training which are particularly necessary for activities requiring the use of high techniques. Nevertheless, this problem has been less serious in labour-intensive activities (Kaplinsky 1995, 63–4). Weak management, poor management–labour relations and weak interfirm cooperation have been another important factor collectively. It is often difficult to encourage suppliers to upgrade their performance in the production process and collaborate in innovation. The lack of trust and availability of unreliable supplies has been an important obstacle, requiring vertical integration (Kaplinsky 1995, 65). Often there is a need for government to take specific measures in tackling weaknesses, e.g. in infrastructure, transport and communications systems in developing countries.

The sudden trade liberalization in particular made managers give priority to cost reduction before embarking on quality, delivery time, etc. (Fleury 1995). In fact Meyer-Stamer (1995, 147) argues that the experience of Brazil indicates that applying a new technique would not necessarily lead to competitiveness if firms were to start from a low level of efficiency and quality.

An important conclusion of the studies undertaken so far is that there is a need for government support in providing education, health, infrastructure and housing in addition to providing stable and predictable economic policies, including industrial policy (Fleury 1995, 84; Meyer-Stamer 1995, 147; Kaplinsky 1995). Further, while there is a different path to competitiveness, there is a need for approaching the issue of competitiveness in a systemic way, i.e. designing policies at various levels: firms, industry, sectoral and national (Meyer-Stamer 1995, 148).

One problem in the implementation of the FMS is shortcomings in the managers' perception of a firm and misconception of their function. These shortcomings in their perception are related to their lack of understanding that a firm is a social unit. As a result some managers concentrate on their creative function by introducing the Japanese techniques without paying enough attention to the cooperative function, i.e. management–labour relations and other social relations. In the FMS labour is an asset of the firm, not an element of its costs. For example, in the case of Zimbabwe the application of new techniques by a few firms led to improvement in their performance indicators, particularly where attention was paid to training. Nevertheless, two main factors constrained the progress and sustainability of those improvements. One was the lack of management's commitment to change and their lack of participation throughout the process. Another factor was the absence of sufficient resources necessary, particularly for training (Posthuma 1995). 'In general, management was not aware of [the] relationship between technical and social innovation [creative and cooperative functions of entrepreneurs] and how they sustain each other' (ibid., 112). Another problem was related to the way workers were treated. They did not participate in the restructuring programme of the firms as they were not provided with financial incentives, motivation and a sense of involvement in the process of reform. Low levels of education and the failure to pay attention to training also affected enthusiasm for change in Zimbabwe (Posthuma 1995).

In contrast, in the case of a few Indonesian automobile companies, the limited application of Japanese techniques was relatively successful because of close attention to social relations, the important role of labour in the reform process, and training. The Japanese labour institutions and personnel policies of Japanese firms were not, however, replicated. They created their own corporate culture and initiated many of the Japanese social practices (such as teamworking, sense of unity and cooperation, disciplines, seniority system of pay). These changes were made possible despite differences in the two cultures (Harriss 1995).

The question of lack of awareness is more of a general problem. Often managers are not aware of the relative importance of product attributes and nonprice factors in competitiveness and of the requirements of the market or the existence of new methods of competition and organization. Such lack of awareness became clear, for example, in the case of managers of some firms in the Dominican Republic in a training exercise undertaken by the government with the cooperation of UNDP (Bessant and Kaplinsky 1995). In fact in this case, when a few pilot plants were chosen to demonstrate the positive impact of the application of FMS, the participants were impressed by the effectiveness of this manufacturing strategy. The results of implementation of such a strategy included the following. First there was a reduction in waste (anything which adds to cost without adding to value) and the time and space necessary for production. In a fruit processing factory waste included overproduction, e.g. having produced when there was no demand for a product; waiting time, e.g. waiting on the table for peeling; waste in transport, e. g. transport to a scale and to store; processing waste; inventory, piling up input and output; poor quality; unnecessary motions due to the dispersed layout of machines instead of a cellular manufacturing technique; unfulfilled orders, due to sequential production.

Secondly there was reduction in inventories which had been too high due to piling up of output as well as inputs, long WIP and stock of worthless inputs and finished products.

Thirdly machine downtime and changeover time were reduced. Machine downtime is the time a machine is down, i.e. it remains idle, because of the need to wait for the arrival of material input or for the clearance of output by the manager. The changeover time is the time needed for changeover from production of one product to another or production of the same products in response to a different order.

The strategy of FMS also requires changes in the social relations of production and teamwork, e.g. change in the payment system based on yield and productivity rather than output of individual workers. A number of teams are required to work with each cell, referred to as cellular layout. Nevertheless, workers should be assured that the reduction in waste and increases in productivity will not lead to their redundancy (Bessant and Kaplinsky 1995).

Further, the JIT cannot be implemented the same way in different parts of the same country (Carrillo 1995). In fact the JIT model is useful as a starting point the core principle of which can be applied in other institutional contexts. Nevertheless, to apply it to a specific company in a specific country the particular situation of the country, the industry and the dynamics of transformation during the process of change within the firm should be taken into account (Humphrey 1995c). Further, the system as a whole may be difficult to apply at once and one may adapt and adopt its various elements gradually. There are also different ways of organizing FMS (Pior and Sabel 1984, 265–8): regional conglomeration which requires community ties (ethnic, political or religious) for success; federated enterprises (networking); solar firms (producers–suppliers relationship) and workshop factories. Which method is applied also depends on the specific characteristics of individual countries.

Overall, according to Pior and Sabel (1984), to be successful the application of FMS requires a few characteristics. These include flexibility in production by reshaping the productive process specialized in a set of products; flexibility of the labour force in terms of its skills related to the needs of the production of a range of products; a sense of community; the encouragement of competition among the labour force (such as competition for promotion in the case of Japan), but not in such a way as to distract innovation (Pior and Sabel 1984, 268–72). Further, government policies for innovation are essential as the firms in FMS are small and have limited capacity to innovate unless they make arrangements with other firms through interfirm cooperation, discussed in the following chapter.

Conclusions

We have explained in this chapter that factor cost and product prices are not the only determinant factors in competitiveness. The international market is not competitive and increasing return to scale in production, marketing and distribution, economies of scope and X-efficiencies of large established firms influence not only their cost of production but also 'nonprice attributes' of the products they supply; the products they produce are not necessarily homogeneous. Further, in contrast to the neoclassical assumption, the large established firms are not passive; through their 'three pronged investment' in manufacturing, marketing and management, control of technology, strategic behaviour and 'creative destruction' they create barriers to entry to newcomer firms. Therefore, newcomer firms of developing countries are in a disadvantageous position *vis-à-vis* established firms of industrialized countries. In addition to developing efficient supply capabilities, newcomer firms also ought eventually to have their own strategy for creating a unique position in order to develop value for the consumer to enjoy rent. Such a strategy requires upgrading of product, process and organization of production.

Regarding the organization of production, some developing countries have applied the FMS, which had been developed in Japan, for continuous improvement by integrating 'thinking and doing'. This system requires more than advantage in factor cost. It also has major differences with the system of mass production which is based on advanced planning on production, production of a number of products sequentially and increasing return to scale. In the FMS the system is dynamic, decision on production is made when an order is received and thus planning and operation are integrated and the production is flexible. It requires, *inter alia*, a multiskilled workforce, a multifunctional machine, a culture of teamwork, a 'group-focussed image of change' and close interrelations among the management, the shop floor, and the suppliers and distributors for TQC, problem solving and JIT delivery.

Developing countries which have applied the FMS, or some elements of it, have experienced some success but many countries have also faced a number of obstacles.

The most important problems in its implementation in developing countries include: the lack of perception by the management about change in the nature of competition in the global economy, or the lack of the necessary commitment by the management and misconception of their function; resistance to change by workers and middle managers; low levels of education and training; the lack of teamwork culture; and weak labour–management and weak interfirm relations. An important finding of the country cases studied is that the complexity of the system required support from the government in providing institutional set-up, infrastructure, education and training in addition to conducive macroeconomics and industrial policies, and a close government–business relationship. The lack of an industrial structure and environment to provide external economies and interfirm relations has led some countries to embark on initiating 'clustering' for the development of interfirm relations in order to enjoy external economies in the form of 'collective efficiency'. We will consider issues related to external economies and interfirm relations in the next chapter.

5

EXTERNAL ECONOMIES: ORGANIZATION OF INTERFIRM RELATIONS

> [E]xecutives must extend their thinking beyond what goes on inside their own organizations and within their own industries. Strategy must also address what goes outside. (Porter 1998, 86–7)

Introduction

External economies contribute to the competitive advantage of a firm. The sources of external economies may be at the industrial level, national level or international level. At the industry level the previous existence of other industrial firms and their experience will provide newcomers with external economies; these firms may be suppliers or engaged in distribution or other downstream activities. The large size of the market is the most important source of external economies because it not only allows for the specialization and division of labour at the industry level, but is also necessary for the materialization of internal economies. External economies may also arise from agglomeration: collective efficiency through clustering, industrial districts and production sharing and, further, from learning and experience at the industry level. At the national level, the existence of developed infrastructure, efficient institutions and availability of back-up services is beneficial to a firm through their dampening influence on production and distribution costs. Thus government policies which aim at provision of these facilities contribute to external economies indirectly. Further, a favourable national reputation (e.g. the Japanese reputation in electronics) allows a firm to engage in mass production and thus increase returns. Ethier (1982) argues that the source of external economies can also be international: in the age of globalization economies resulting from agglomeration, production sharing among various countries, etc.

To proceed we will first provide general comments on these sources of external economies. Although interfirm relations take various forms, we will subsequently concentrate on explaining externalities arising from clustering because clustering is the main source of external economies provided through 'collective efficiency' As SMEs are in an unfavourable competitive position *vis-à-vis* large firms because of their small size, clustering is regarded as a means of improving their competitiveness, particularly in developing countries where the size of firms is often small. In the age of globalization the international dimension of cluster dynamism is also important. Hence, before concluding the chapter, we will examine the externalities provided through production sharing, which is arranged mainly by TNCs who operate across countries.

External Economies: General Issues[1]

In the neoclassical theory of the firm there are no external economies. Firms are independent of each other in their costs/benefits of production at any period and over time. Moreover, in the neoclassical theory within a firm current/future costs/benefits do not depend on past/current costs/benefits. In practice, however, they do. And where there is interdependence of cost and benefits among firms, complementarities and externalities exist. In order to analyse externalities a few conceptual distinctions should be made here for clarity. The first is between internal and external economies. Internal economies are confined to a plant or firm, one example being internal economies of scale, i.e. size of the plant or the firm. Externalities to an economic *unit* prevail when its activities influence others – producers or consumers – whether positively or negatively. The economic unit here may be a plant, a firm, an industry, a sector or the whole national economy *vis-à-vis* the global economy. The second distinction is between static economies and dynamic economies. Static economies result when increasing return (decreasing cost) prevails at any point in time, e.g. due to the scale of production (size of the firm or plant). Dynamic economies prevail when there is a negative relation between the unit cost of production and time or between the unit cost and cumulative production over time, even if the scale of production remains unchanged. In the literature this is often referred to as dynamic economies of learning and experience. Such an intertemporal relationship between present and future cost (benefit) is ignored in the neoclassical theory.

Hence one can distinguish the terms 'static internal economies', 'dynamic internal economies', 'static external economies' and 'dynamic external economies'. To avoid confusion in the use of the term 'externality', one should distinguish four economic units: firm, industry, manufacturing sector and the national economy. For example, certain economies may be external to a firm but internal to an industry or external to an industry/sector and internal to the sector/national economy. Unless specified, our economic unit will be a firm throughout this chapter. The sources of external economies include investment decisions, dynamic externalities of learning, attitude towards work and atmosphere creation, economies of trust and reputation, and the social user cost of production and exports of exhaustible resources or products based on exhaustible resources. These issues will be discussed in this chapter except external economies of trust and reputation, which are the subject of the next chapter.

Investment Coordination

The price mechanism fails to stimulate the socially optimum level of investment mainly because of the existence of externalities related to investment coordination. These include pecuniary external economies and technological external economies. Pecuniary

---

1 The following passages are based on Shafaeddin (2005c).

externalities are the result of the influences of activities of an economic agent on (an)other agent(s) through prices. Technological externalities influence other agents directly.

According to Scitovsky (1954) *pecuniary external economies* may exist for a number of reasons and include both static and dynamic economies. One reason is related to the lumpiness of large investments. In neoclassical economics investments made by firms are marginal, perfectly divisible and reversible. In reality interdependence of profit opportunities may exist among various firms or industries undertaking lumpy investment. As a result the social net benefits of investment may exceed its private net benefits. An important source of such interdependence is enlargement of the market in general due to the complementarities of demand. Achieving the benefits of increasing return to scale in a plant or firm is feasible if availability of demand (size of the market) will allow the growth of the size of the firm (Young 1928). Investment in a firm, or industry A, would create demand for products of firms/industry B, and the investment by B adds demand for products of A. As a consequence the average cost of production will decline in both industries. The extent of demand creation in each case would depend on the income elasticity of demand. Hence if a number of investments take place simultaneously, the risk of finding markets would be reduced.

One may argue that foreign markets also provide markets for a country's products; hence the limitation of domestic market should not pose a serious obstacle to the expansion of supply capacities. Nevertheless, during the early stages of industrialization, penetration into the foreign market is not easy (Shafaeddin 2005c, ch. 5). At any rate domestic markets usually constitute the main market at the early stages of a firm's operation in any country. Moreover, even if exportation were easily possible, simultaneous development of a number of export activities would help to sustain any one of them since they require development of common institutions and infrastructure (Murphy et al. 1989). It also reduces the possibility of underinvestment. Nevertheless, the market mechanism fails to coordinate investment decisions. Hence another coordination mechanism might be necessary. When the number of agents involved is small, the coordination may take place through negotiation or integration of agents into a single unit in order to internalize externalities (Stewart and Ghani 1991, 571). Otherwise state intervention is required to coordinate investment decisions.

Market failure in coordination may also arise due to the existence of strategic dependence among oligopolistic firms leading to the risk of underinvestment or overinvestment. When a large fixed investment in specific assets is required in an industry characterized by significant scale economies, under certain conditions there is a risk of a price war (Fellner 1949; H. Chang 1994, 65–7). These conditions are related to the unfavourable demand situation or shortfall in demand beyond expectations due to external shocks, etc. The rigidity of the fixed asset structure, i.e. the installed equipment, and thus the inability of the entrepreneurs to recover fixed costs may tempt firms to engage in a price war. If entry is not restricted, i.e. contestability prevails, the fear of a price war may result in underinvestment. If entry is restricted or there is expectation of a limited number of entries, overinvestment may result because firms may attempt to install as much capacity as possible to reduce their unit cost (Chang 1994, 66). In these situations the market mechanism is incapable of the necessary coordination.

Overhead capital is one example of lumpy investment involving externality because it provides opportunities in investment in other economic activities (Rosenstein-Rodan 1984). It involves the crowd, in effect. The market mechanism alone does not lead, or it does not lead sufficiently, to investment in social overhead because the private net benefit of such investment diverges from its social net benefit. The failure of the private sector to invest in infrastructure in Mexico and Brazil and some other Latin American countries during recent decades is mainly due to this issue (Shafaeddin 2005c, ch. 3).

There are also other pecuniary external economies related to a lumpy investment: provision of inputs for other industries; provision of demand for intermediate products produced by other industries; provision of demand for products which are complementary to, or substitute for, goods produced by it (Scitovsky 1954). In all these cases, investment in one industry creates opportunities for investment and profit in other industries. Such interdependence among various industries provides a form of production and consumption linkages (Hirschman 1958). To the extent that the entire benefits of an investment cannot be appropriated by an investor, it would involve externality.

Dynamic External Economies of Learning

Professional experience and investment in human capital involves dynamic external economies in many respects because, even when learning is activity specific and firm specific, the benefits of learning spread beyond the individual or the firm which undertakes such an investment. Moreover, as learning accumulates over time the unit cost of production declines. Learning improves not only the skill of the labour engaged in the process of production, marketing and distribution, but also the quality of entrepreneurship and the capacity of the firm for innovation. Learning consists of the acquisition and diffusion of knowledge (know-why) and technology (know-how). It takes place through education, formal training, learning by doing, learning by accumulating experience, learning to learn, learning by trial and error, leaning by using and learning by adapting and imitating.

The market for knowledge and know-how, like the market for information, is imperfect. In fact knowledge/know-how is a public good, the return to which cannot be appropriated by a firm which invests in it, except in cases where the result can be patented. When appropriateness is incomplete there will be underinvestment. When patenting is possible the diffusion of knowledge will be imperfect; hence underutilization will result, i.e. the social benefits of the investment will not materialize entirely (Stiglitz 1989).

Technological learning is the most important example of learning in the LDCs and it is particularly important for upgrading the product structure. During the early stages of development, technological learning takes the form of learning to apply existing technology for the first time, even if it has been used before, elsewhere. It would require the ability to install, operate and maintain machines. It involves borrowing, adapting and improving upon a foreign design to make it appropriate for the local situation (Stiglitz 1988; Amsden 1989). In other words, to a large extent in most developing countries at early stages of development technological learning involves imitation rather than innovation. In its pure sense of the term innovation requires heavy expenditure on R&D (see Chapter 7). Nevertheless, in any imitation there is also an element of learning and innovation.

Technological learning requires learning by doing and training which involves costs. The results of learning by a firm may be transferred to other firms through mobility of labour, specialized journals or interaction between a firm and its suppliers of input or purchasers of its output (Lall 1993a; Stewart and Ghani 1991, 574).

Attitude to Work and Atmosphere Creation

Corden (1974, 264) regards creation of attitudes to work and 'atmosphere', discipline, sense of collective responsibility and teamwork as important sources of dynamic externality. Such attitudes, resulting from the training of workers in a firm, may leap from worker to worker not only within the same firm but may also spill over to other firms even if workers do not move from one firm to another. Thus experience in industrialization itself contributes to the attitude towards work. In developing countries at early stages of industrialization the workers who are engaged in industrial activities, including rural workers, have to adapt to new working conditions and gain confidence in the new way of life and new attitudes.

Atmosphere creation is not, however, confined to workers. It is also, and in our view more importantly, relevant to entrepreneurship. Entrepreneurship has two vital components: cooperative and creative. We have already referred to the creative component. According to Hirschman (1958, 17):

> ...the cooperative components...involve the ability to engineer agreement among all interested parties, such as the inventor of the process, the partners, the capitalists, the supplier of parts and services, the distributors, etc., the ability...to enlist cooperation of official agencies in such matters as customs duties, permits, exchange control regulation, etc.; the ability to bring and hold together able staff, to delegate authority, to inspire loyalty, to handle successfully relations with labour and the public, and a host of other managerial talents.

Hence the cooperative components of entrepreneurship contribute to the destruction of an 'ego-focused image of change' and to the creation of a 'group-focused image of change' within a firm which will also spread to the industry or the economy as a whole. The group-focused image of change is essential for the process of economic change and development. Japanese long-life employment (Odigari 1992) is a good example of atmosphere creation among workers and the attempt by the Republic of Korea to link incentive provided to firms to their performance (Amsden 1989) is another example of atmosphere creation in entrepreneurship.

External Economies of Reputation

We will explain the issues related to external economies of reputation in more detail in the following chapter. At this stage let us state that such reputation may arise in countries which are already industrialized. If reputation has been acquired by a firm of a country, consumers may lump goods produced by other firms of the country together in terms of quality of goods (Stiglitz 1989), reliability of after-sales services, etc. As a result other firms may benefit from external economies of reputation, reduction in the cost of establishing themselves in the new market or in a market for a new product. Japan has built up its reputation for electronic products with Sony and for its automobile industry with Toyota. In contrast, exports of low-quality goods by some Indian firms in the early stages of their attempts to expand exports of manufactured goods in the 1960s did not create a favourable reputation for either those firms involved or the whole manufacturing sector of the country.

For a firm of a developing country wishing to enter international markets for manufactured products, marketing barriers to entry are an important obstacle (see Chapter 2). Such barriers to entry are related to the lack of marketing channels and the lack of information about consumers' taste and requirements for quality. Nevertheless, even if a firm can produce high-quality goods, consumers in the importing countries may lack information about or confidence in the quality of goods produced. The supply of high-quality goods and provision of information to consumers (as well as collection of market information) or other marketing activities are all costly and involve dynamic externalities because they cannot be perfectly appropriated by a firm (Lall 1991).

Clustering for Collective Efficiency

> The main problem for small firms is not being small but being lonely. (Pyke and Sengenberger 1992, 11)

What is clustering? What is its historical background? What is its economic rationale for the competitiveness of firms from developing countries? How is it organized? What are its advantages and requirements? What is the experience of developing countries in clustering? The purpose of this section is to shed some light on these questions. Before proceeding, let us mention a few points about the competitive position of SMEs in developing countries.

As discussed in Chapter 4, the newcomer firms of developing countries are often small and are in a poor position to compete with large established firms which benefit from the 'dynamic interaction among economy of scale, experience, innovation and organization'. Nevertheless, though SMEs suffer from some weakness, they do, in principle, have some advantages for business as well as for economic development. SMEs do not benefit from division of labour and increasing return to scale in production, R&D, marketing and distribution channels and other activities which contribute to cost reduction and product attributes. They have less creditworthiness than large firms. They also suffer from barriers to entry because of their small size. In other words, they lack the capabilities to take strategic action to gain or maintain competitiveness (Pyke et al. 1992, 11). On the other hand SMEs can be more flexible than large firms. They also generate more employment than large firms do. The question is how they could be organized to be able to compete. In other words, how could they organize themselves to compete at a high level of development? One channel has been to link themselves to large TNCs through supply contract, outsourcing and production sharing. While such a strategy may provide them with market and scale economies in production of parts and components, it does not per se provide their country with the opportunity to consolidate its industrial structure. Further, the firm involved still needs to compete on the basis of factor cost, in Porter's language, or 'low road' to competitiveness in the language of (Pyke et al. 1992, 12). A low road to competitiveness is short-lived and makes little contribution to economic development as it involves competition based on factor costs. Competitiveness at a high level of development requires a 'high road' to competitiveness. For this purpose SMEs need to organize themselves in such a way that they can also benefit from the advantages of large scale. Clustering has been regarded as a solution. How effective are clusters?

Historical background and definitions

The idea of clustering was first introduced by Alfred Marshall (1920, ch. 10) in the context of the industrialization of Great Britain, although he used the concept of 'industrial district'; rather than 'cluster'. His argument was based on the benefits of the division of labour and the external economies involved in industrial districts, which he regarded as a collection of firms engaged in the same industry in a geographical location. During recent decades there have been different definitions of cluster. According to Schmitz and Nadvi (1999, 1) a cluster is a 'sectoral *and special* concentration of firms'. In a similar manner Porter (1998) regards cluster as the manifestation of 'diamond' at work (see Chapter 3) and gives it the following definition: 'Clusters are [a] geographical concentration of interconnected companies and institutions in a particular field' (Porter 1998, 78). He continues:

> Clusters encompass [an] array of linked industries and other entities important to competition. They include, for example, suppliers of specialized inputs such as components, machinery, and services, and providers of specialized infrastructure. Clusters also often extend downstream [activities] to distribution channels and customers and laterally to manufacturers of complementary products and to companies in industries related by skills, technologies, or common inputs. Finally, many clusters include governmental and other institutions – such as universities, standards-setting agencies, think thanks, vocational training providers, and trade associations-that provide specialized training, education, information, research, and technical support. (Porter 1998, 78)

The Competitiveness Institute distinguishes between different terms used in the literature on the concepts related to clusters:

- An industrial cluster is a set of industries related through buyer–supplier and supplier–buyer relationships, or by common technologies, common buyers or distribution channels, or common labour pools.
- A regional cluster is an industrial cluster [in the same or closely related activities] in which member firms are in close geographical proximity to each other.

- Industrial districts are concentration of firms involved in interdependent production processes, often in the same industry or industry segment that are embedded in the local community and delimited by daily travel to work distances.
- A business network consists of several firms that have ongoing communication and interaction, and might have a certain level of interdependence, but that need not operate in related industries or be geographically concentrated in space (www.competetiveness.org/article/articleview, based on Enright 1996).

The above-stated definitions miss an important point which is the way clusters are actually organized; clusters are to be distinguished from industrial estates or industrial zones which are collection of firms, whether large or small, in a geographical area.

Organization of a cluster

According to Pyke et al. (1992) an important feature of a cluster is its organization, which contributes to its productivity; thus clusters are a group of 'firms of a district which are organized together according to a definite principle' (Pyke and Sengenberger 1992, 4). The competitive advantage of a cluster is based more on its economic and social organization than its access to low factor cost stressed in the static theory of comparatives cost advantage (Pyke et al. 1992, 4–6; Porter 1998). Pyke et al. emphasize that, while geographical location may contribute to the success of a cluster because of availability of a pool of skilled labour and infrastructure, the operation of a *group* of firms in a limited geographical area per se is not sufficient unless the firms are organized in a way that benefits from externalities provided by the cluster. First of all the firms involved should divide the work required for the production of a good (or goods), as well as its (their) related upstream and downstream activities and services, into a number of tasks in which each firm will specialize. The cluster of firms then operates like a vertically integrated firm while each firm retains its independence but collaborates with other firms. If the cluster as a whole grows and succeeds in becoming efficient, each member firm will also succeed.

Secondly the geographical proximity of firms and their employees may contribute to their efficiency not only because of reduction in transaction costs of the member firms, but also because of the possibility of interchange of information, knowledge and technology, and their sense of collective interests. Nevertheless, exploiting such potentials necessitates coordination, cooperation and trust (see Chapter 6). It should be noted, however, that as far as social networking and exchange of information is concerned learning can also be derived from firms at a distance due to the advance in information technology (Stanley and Helper 2003).

Thirdly there is a need for entrepreneurial dynamism and the ability to compete not only on prices but more importantly on a range of 'nonprice attributes' of their products.

Finally flexibility is an important feature of a successful cluster as it is a key factor in competitiveness. Flexibility requires entrepreneurship and a trained and adaptable workforce to be able to respond to the needs of the market and innovation for upgrading (ibid., 4–6). For this purpose labour should not be regarded as cost – as is the case in the neoclassical theories of trade and growth – but an important 'input of varying quality and varying effectiveness'. Thus good rewards, working conditions, fair treatment of employees and the existence of trust are among the important factors in the successful performance of a cluster. The government also has an important role to play (Pyke and Sengenberger 1992, 14–27).

Advantages of clustering

According to Alfred Marshall (1920), by increasing the division of labour, clustering can contribute to competitiveness through easy access to suppliers, labour pooling and dissemination of information and knowledge. But, depending on the form of cooperation among the firms involved, there are also other advantages in clustering such as easier access to finance, common training, R&D, etc. Although the forms of cooperation among firms in a cluster may vary from one kind of cluster to another, the common advantage of all forms of cooperation among firms is attaining 'collective efficiency'. Collective efficiency is a form of external economy. It accrues to the member firms not only as a result of the emergence of unplanned external economies, particularly when firms are located in proximity to each other, but also more importantly through their intentional joint actions. Thus collective efficiency is defined as 'the competitive advantage derived from local external economies and joint action' (Schmitz 1995, 536). Collective efficiency allows each member to enjoy economies of scale without being large. In other words, the external economies of scale replace internal economies in each firm (Schmitz and Nadvi 1999, 1505). 'Organizational proximity' allows coordination of dispersed activities (Justo 2003, 12). Accordingly clustering, or localized agglomeration, provides a pooled market for skilled labour and facilitates and encourages the development of specialized skills, leads to division of labour in production and supply of material and service inputs, and facilitates technological spill-overs – all of which in turn contribute to economies of scale external to individual firms, i.e. at the industry level. Of course the presence of demand, or the size of the market, is an important factor in the realization of the external economies of agglomeration (see also Young 1928; Stigler 1951).

According to M. Porter the quality of local business environment affects the ability to compete, and cluster can contribute to competitiveness of firms by increasing productivity, enhancing innovation and stimulating the formation of new businesses in these area which, in turn, 'expands and strengthens the cluster itself' (Porter 1998, 80). Better access to the labour force, suppliers, specialized information and complementarities arising from marketing and familiarity with customers' needs are among the factors contributing to productivity. Better information about the market in turn puts pressure on the companies to innovate and provides them with the capacity and flexibility to do so (Porter 1998, 82–3). Entrepreneurs are the key to innovation and opportunities for entrepreneurial discovery are promoted in agglomeration centres. According to Marshall this is so because of the contribution of the division of labour, development of specialized inputs and services, creation of a proliferation of related industries and specialized routines. Such proliferation in turn increases the opportunities for innovation and creation of a 'new combination of related routines' (Oxley and Yeung 1998a, xix).

Thus the small firms involved can benefit, for example, from division of labour and specialization, economies of scale, scope and speed provided by suppliers of input machinery, repair facilities and the emergence of a pool of skills necessary in the process of production and distribution. They may also take action to develop new products and new technologies or arrange for joint marketing, transport and distribution of their output. They may further take joint action to cope with new competitive pressure and to upgrade (Schmitz and Nadvi 1999, 1505; Schmitz 1995, particularly 533–6; Pyke et al. 1992). Further, they may join forces in the form of business association for lobbying and bargaining with the government or foreign companies.

While firms involved in a cluster take joint action to tackle some common problems, they at the same time compete in the market for their final products – where they are involved in production of the same, or similar, products. What is important in their collaboration effort is cooperation and trust.

Implications for the member firms

Clusters have three implications for the strategy of a firm: the choice of locations, upgrading and the contribution of the cluster to the common goal of its member firms. To begin with, locating an industry should not be based on factor costs alone; productivity is more important. So is the role of innovation. For home-based activities of a member firm the location of the clusters is important. These activities include, e.g. strategy formulation and R&D. Such activities should be based where the environment is conducive, while the labour-intensive portion may be located in another place or even another country. Secondly the cluster and its member firms can be upgraded with the help of suppliers, government and buyers for enhancing marketing and improving input quality and skill. Japanese firms have undertaken this task efficiently. Thirdly personal relationship and a sense of common interest are important in benefiting from a cluster. So companies should be present and involved locally. Finally, while companies involved in a cluster may compete in the final market for output they have an interest in collaborating with each other in such issues as marketing, R&D, skill development and training, etc. (Schmitz 1995, 87–9; Porter 1988, 97 and 534;). They may also join forces in the form of a business association for lobbying and bargaining with government or with foreign companies. Thus the small firms involved can enjoy, for example, division of labour and specialization as well as economies of scale and speed provided by suppliers of inputs, machinery and repair facilities. They can also benefit from the emergence of a pool of skills necessary in the process of production and distribution. Further, they may take action to develop a new product or a new technology, or arrange for joint marketing, transport and distribution of their output (Schmitz 1995, particularly 533–6). What is important in the interrelation among the firms involved is cooperation and trust. Firms may be close to each other physically but if they mistrust each other they will not cooperate with each other (see Chapter 6).

Experience in clustering

Setting aside handicraft workshops, the first experience of modern clustering is the industrial districts in England mentioned earlier. The Manchester industrial zone which specialized in production of textiles is a good example. More recent experience of clustering is the Italian industrial districts which started in the late 1970s (Piore and Sabel 1984), the example of which spread to other European countries. The main characteristics of the Italian and other industrial districts of the industrialized countries were geographical proximity; sectoral specialization; dominance of SMEs; interfirm collaboration; sociocultural identity which contributes to trust; competition among the firms; support by regional and local governments (ibid., 537).

A number of developing countries in Asia, Latin America and Africa have also tried clustering (see Strojer et al. 2003; Rabellotti 1995; Schmitz 1995; Piore and Sabel 1984). While the experience is mixed in both developed and developing countries, a few general observations can be made. First the initial (static) collective efficiency befits of clustering have been noticed in both developed and developing countries, though to a varying degree. For example, clustering has borne fruit in both Italy and Northern Ireland. In the case of the Italian shoe industry clustering increased the value of production by over 10 times between 1970 and 1985, far exceeding its volume expansion and implying the ability of the cluster to have increased value for consumers. Similarly clusters of information technology firms in Silicon Valley and the Boston area in the United States, and in Northern Ireland have shown significant initial gains in competitive advantage. For example, the Silicon Valley area accommodates about 120 main technology companies, including Intel, Microsoft, IBM, EMC. Further, there are 26 universities in the region which provide research and education facilities.

Secondly the competitive advantage gained varies in the form of static and dynamic gains. For example, the Italian clusters concentrated on design, fashion and other product attributes and thus continuously enhanced their capabilities for upgrading and the sustainability of competitive advantage. The above-described USA clusters were also dynamic in innovation, organizational flexibility and skill development and thus have maintained their competitive advantage. In contrast, the Northern Ireland technology cluster could not sufficiently build on its initial gains mainly because of the lack of development of the innovative and organizational capabilities of firms (Best 2001, ch. 7). Similarly some firms in the Italian clusters suffered because they did not pay attention to the need for functional upgrading (Morrison et al. 2008). On the whole, other empirical studies also indicate that firms in clusters show superior performance. For example, a study of a cluster of component manufacturing industries in the USA indicated that firms in the cluster have shown superior performance in general, particularly in their ability to compete with foreign companies (Stanley and Helper 2003). Similarly a study of industrial clustering in Denmark shows higher productivity, particularly in the textile industries, than in other firms (Madsen et al. 2010). Studies of clusters in the USA indicate a positive impact of clustering on entrepreneurship, employment, wages, technological development growth and transaction costs (Delgado et al. 2010, 2011). Similarly a study of a children's garment cluster (Zhili Township) and furniture clusters shows the positive impact of clustering on upgrading quality, enhancing total factor productivity (Fleisher et al. 2009) and encouraging innovation, diffusion of new ideas and specialization (Shao et al. 2008).

Upgrading

The sustainability of competitive advantage has been more difficult in clusters of developing countries. This is mainly because they have mostly concentrated only on the stage of production in the value chain, relied on factor cost advantages and price competition and did not develop firm capabilities or what Best calls cluster dynamics. For example, the contrast between the Penang electronics cluster in Malaysia and the Bangalore cluster in India is telling. The study of the Malaysian (Penang) cluster by Best (2001) indicates that it showed significant success in growth of output but mostly in assembly operations. The value added was low. Low value added implies small contribution to per capita income. Moreover, as similar plants were installed in other countries of the region, particularly in China, Malaysia suffered from a decline in product prices. In other words, the cluster failed to command higher return over time. The failure was mainly due to the lack of capacity to move from assembly operation to production of components and technology-intensive products where barriers to entry were higher. In M. Porter's language it was the failure to upgrade from factor-driven activities to technology-driven activities. The main shortcomings included the lack of engineering skills and innovation capabilities for product and process upgrading, and the lack of 'packaging and integration activities' necessary for functional upgrading (see also Best 2001, ch. 6). The experience of Malaysia contrasted with that of China where some scientific parks were created and firms, universities, research institutes and governments cooperated to enhance technological capabilities (see Boxes 5.1, 5.3 and Chapter 9).

In contrast, the Bangalore software industry cluster in India[2] has benefited from upgrading. The number of companies in the region increased from a few to nearly 1 200 within eight years between 1991 and 2003. Although initially the firms got involved in simple activities such as data entry and low-level programming, they have become involved in more sophisticated R&D activities. The success of the Bangalore cluster is sometimes attributed mainly to ethnic and cultural factors (Taeube 2003). Nevertheless, in our view, the development of capabilities of the firms involved is a major factor in their ability to upgrade. The development of their capabilities was facilitated by three main factors. First the region benefited from the availability of large numbers of educated manpower, particularly engineers, and university establishments (ibid., 11–12, tables 1 and 2).

Secondly the earlier immigration of a considerable number of Indians to Silicon Valley and their engagement in management and entrepreneurship provided substantial

---

2 As of 4 October 2011, there were 101 industrial clusters in India in various industries (Business Development: http://www.nif.org.in/bd/list_industrial_clusters).

Box 5.1. Experience of Malaysia in clustering

The Malaysian Penang cluster of high-tech industries is an example of the low ability of firms to innovate. The country has managed to increase output successfully through assembling, IT and total quality management (TQM), followed by production sharing (see the following section). The value added has been low in assembly operation despite the fact that Penang had better technological and management capabilities than other regional concentrations of production, partly due to the nurturing by regional government authorities (Best 2001, 171–90, particularly 181). There have been weaknesses in skill formation and what Best (2001) calls cluster dynamics necessary for innovation and upgrading, for which entrepreneurial firms and government support are needed. While some firms of this kind were developed, they were not enough and those which were developed lacked sufficient networking and technological differentiations to be able to develop capabilities in the region (Best 2001, 173–9). The lack of skill formation capabilities was the main shortcoming in innovation, which was also constrained by the lack of engineers. The Penang Skill Development Centre offered some courses for training shop-floor employees with the help of the government but qualified teachers were lacking (Best 2001, 179). The production of parts and components has expanded in Malaysia in more recent years through TNCs. Nevertheless, the country has not been able to upgrade the technological capabilities of its domestic firms sufficiently to increase value added to the same extent as China. Further, the rapid development of production sharing has also made the country vulnerable to changes in the external environment, including the world market and policies of China. Demand for parts and components from China, which exports finished products to third countries, is particularly important as the country is the main importer of parts and components (P&T) of IT products from Malaysia.

Source: Based on Shafaeddin (2008).

impetus to the success of Bangalore firms in two ways. One was the return of some experienced entrepreneurs to India. Another was their contact with Indian managers in Silicon Valley who outsourced 'a large part of activities in the global value chain to their home country' (ibid., 7).

The third factor in the relative success of the Banglore cluster was the nature and the type of the industry in which the firms were involved. For example, the activities of the Malaysian Penang cluster consisted mainly of assembly of hardware data processing and other electronic equipment and their production of simple P&C mainly by TNCs. The manpower involved gained little experience in the production of components, which requires high technology controlled by the mother company and to which the barriers to entry are high. In contrast, the Bangalore firms have been involved in the software industry the nature of which is such that the workers learn by doing. The barriers to entry to production are low in the software industry. There are, in contrast, high barriers to entry into the international market for hardware products because of the brand name and the lack of the necessary marketing channels, unless one relies on TNCs. The local manpower managed to engage in the stage of production but the firms involved lacked resources to develop their own marketing networks and design. Further, they were too suspicious of each other to cooperate in marketing and share market information (Holmström 1994).

In fact there is further evidence that the type of industry characteristics do matter in the upgrading of clusters integrated in global value chains. A study of 39 Latin American clusters engaged in various industries by Giuliani et al. (2003) on the influence on upgrading of collective efficiency, firms–buyers relations in the global value chain and other factors led to the following conclusions. First collective efficiency is more pronounced in the case of natural resource-based and specialized supplier industries (namely software industries) where there is low appropriability of knowledge and low barriers to entry resulting from both external economies and joint actions. These industries enjoy the highest efficiency due to passive external economies and joint actions. Joint action is the lowest in cases where it is most needed, i.e. in complex product system industries, where there are large economies of scale, high barriers to entry and medium appropriability of knowledge. In all industries the impact of passive external economies on collective efficiency is more than the impact of joint action.

Secondly with respect to upgrading, the impact of local firms on upgrading is also less noticeable in the case of complex product industries and more so in the case of natural-based and software industries. In the case of traditional industries (light industries) local firms influence product upgrading but not process and functional upgrading as both are controlled basically by technology suppliers and designers.

Thirdly the global buyers not only did not contribute to functional upgrading in any industry group, but also their contribution was often negative as they did not want to create new competitors. In the case of natural resource-based products, they contributed to product and process upgrading but only in a passive way. In other words, they set the target and provided market outlets but normally did not engage in supporting initiatives. In the case of complex industries their contribution to product and process upgrading – if any – has been indirect by providing incentives (ibid., 7–15).

Functional upgrading is crucial in increasing value added; it is important that the firms upgrade their industries by enhancing their own capabilities. The study described above indicates that the local value chain could better contribute to upgrading, particularly functional upgrading, than to the international value chain though it takes a long time. The relation between the manufacturing firms in a cluster and the buyers are different in the case of the local value chain as against foreign value chains. In the case of global buyers the relationship is mostly of quasi-hierarchy type (except in the software industry, which is of market/network type), whereas in the case of local buyers it is mainly of market/network type. To explain, Humphrey and Schmitz (2000) refer to three types of governance: (1) quasi-hierarchy, which is the relationship between independent firms where the leader (the buyer) defines the rules which the subordinates (manufacturers) have to comply with; (2) hierarchy, where a manufacturing firm is owned by another firm; (3) network, through which the firms of more or less equal power cooperate with each other within the value chain by sharing their capabilities. To continue, in the case of market/network type, the manufacturers are dictated by the buyers who control the design and/or technology and distribution channel. If the manufacturer attempts to upgrade functionally it could be penalized by the buyers who impose barriers to entry and collect the rents. In contrast, when market/network prevails, manufacturers are free to develop their own capabilities.

As the internal governance of the value chain is important in upgrading, joint action needs to be encouraged by creating the necessary institutional mechanism, creation of trust, public support to joint action, creation of industrial associations, research centres, cooperation with universities and existing research institutions (Giuliani et al. 2003, 9–10). The efficiency of internal governance of the cluster is influenced by the willingness to cooperate in undertaking a dynamic approach to clustering, which requires changes in the attitudes of entrepreneurs and employees in a liberalizing and globalizing world economy. An important obstacle to upgrading competitiveness is what Hirschman calls 'resistance to change' as indicated by the case of some clusters in Santa Catarina, Brazil (see Box 5.2).

Experiences in different types of clustering

Surveying the literature on the experience of clustering in developing countries, based on a number of studies published in a special issue of *World Development*, Schmitz and Nadvi (1999) concluded first of all that while there have been a large number of clusters in developing countries, their growth experience varies. The artisan clusters have shown little signs of dynamism, innovation or growth. At the other extreme there are clusters which have managed to deepen their division of labour and succeeded to enter into the international market and improve their competitiveness. In between there are many intermediate cases.

Secondly in matured clusters some medium and large firms have emerged and played 'an important role in the governance of these clusters' (Schmitz and Nadvi 1999, 1504).

Thirdly in analysing success and failure of clusters, one needs to distinguish between 'incipient and advance stages of industrialization' (Schmitz and Nadvi 1999, 1505). In the case of incipient clusters it became clear that the realization of collective efficiency is possible where there are trade networks and trust. In the case of African clusters where the external distribution network and linkages are often poor, clusters have had poor growth performance. In the case of Africa trust among members also was lacking because of the sociocultural problems related to ethnic issues, e.g. the sociocultural divide between African and Asian business communities. In contrast, in the case of Indonesia, where trade networks are well developed, clusters performed better and sociocultural factors also had positive impact (Schmitz and Nadvi 1999, 1506).

Box 5.2. Upgrading and trade liberalization in Santa Catarina clusters, Brazil

The Santa Catarina clusters experienced little cooperation among their members during the import-substitution era, even though they were located in the same geographical area. During that era the firms were used to easy business as they were geared to the protected domestic market and felt little competitive pressure to cooperate with each other to benefit from collective efficiency. They had done well in the protected market by undertaking some R&D, training, etc. The lack of suppliers and supporting institutions as well as the lack of awareness of advantages of cooperation had also made them internalize many activities. When trade liberalization was introduced the individualistic business culture inhibited change in the attitude of many clusters for cooperation to innovate and introduce new methods of production and organization despite the fact that firms felt the competitive pressure.

Nevertheless, feeling the competitive pressure of trade liberalization, a minority of clusters did manage to introduce some reforms even without any help from the government. Their business associations became more active to provide support, e.g. by seeking alternative sources of supply abroad and lobbying. Further, the Association of Commerce and Industry initiated exchange of business-related information among firms. In the case of the tile industry, replicating the practices of Italian ceramic clusters, new management techniques were applied, training was intensified, a technical school was established and contact with a local university was initiated. As a result of all these initiatives the competitive position of member firms improved. An interesting aspect of the reforming clusters was their attitude towards the state. They saw business and state as totally different spheres. In fact they were not seeking any assistance from the state as they regarded them resistant to change! And the state was not active in supporting the reform process either.

Source: Based on Meyer-Stamer (1998).

Fourthly the competitive pressure from trade liberalization and globalization led to the closures of many firms which were members of more matured clusters, particularly in Mexico and India, in cases where they had concentrated on the domestic market. Those that survived were those which managed to do so by upgrading their competitive strategy. The most important factor which helped their competitiveness was interfirm cooperation for joint action. However, while vertical cooperation, e.g. between manufacturers and their suppliers, was significant, horizontal cooperation was poor. This implies that the sense of rivalry among them has been stronger than the need for collaboration.

Government policy towards clusters

Schmitz and Nadvi (1999) show that joint action alone was not sufficient in many clusters; government intervention or mediation was also required. Thus they explained that a cluster may not succeed without support from the government. The national and local governments should do all they could to contribute to productivity at the firm level by providing external economies in areas where the members of the cluster cannot act on their own. The provision of external economies may take place through a number of 'IN's (see Chapter 1) to the clusters, including assistance for the initiative to build on local sources of uniqueness rather than imitating other clusters (Porter 1998, 89); the government may also provide inputs to skill formation and education; infrastructure; intellectual property protection; innovation-oriented incentives and institutions; institutions of back-up services. There is also a need for a mechanism for a public–private relationship to exchange information, coordinate and remove constraints and/or enforce contracts (see Chapter 6).

Porter (1998) advocates that the government's intervention should be confined to support and development of existing clusters and should not initiate new ones. Nevertheless, the context which he has in mind must be that of developed countries as in a developing country, particularly at the early stages of industrialization, no cluster may exist. Therefore, government action and intervention are also needed to set-up clusters as required.

The need for government intervention arises, for example, to attain or improve the capacity for innovation, provide common service or collect and disseminate market information (Brusco 1990). In large firms the management deals with the question of innovation. In a cluster where a decision-making body at the level of the cluster is lacking, the government or the local authorities may provide the necessary back-up services to create the necessary institution. The evolution of industrial cluster in Italy is an indication of the need for government intervention in the new era. In Italy clusters started with the traditional artisan model applying labour-intensive techniques and engaging in subcontracting (often around the vicinity of a large firm). In the mid 1970s they transformed into the *Mark I model* of clusters, where the firms involved utilized the same technology used by large firms. In this model of vertically integrated clusters a great deal of innovation was possible. It took place through learning by interaction among skilled workers of member firms and entrepreneurs of the firm which produced the final goods. The government was not involved. In around the early 1980s it became clear that the *Mark I model* clusters suffered from the lack of proactive policies to innovate and to adapt their products to the requirements of the market. Hence there was a need for what Brusco calls *Mark II clusters* to boost innovation and upgrade competitiveness with support from the government (Brusco 1990, 17).

It is true that in the cases of Silicon Valley, the Cambridge Region (UK) and Third Italy the government was not involved in the creation of clusters. Nevertheless, it is similarly true that when they were established the role of the local government was important; the government was involved in either developing a new organizational strategy in the 1990s in the case of Silicon Valley or in the regional policy coordination of their operation, in the case of both Silicon Valley and Third Italy. In Germany the Federal Government got involved in government-driven policies in, e.g. Bio Region. Often subsidies were also provided by the federal government through local authorities (Tayanagi and Colovic-Lamotte 2003, 5–6).

The experience of Japan

Contrary to the recommendation by Porter that government should not initiate clusters, the Japanese government has been very active not only in nurturing but also in initiating and transforming the cluster structure. Generally speaking the evolution of Japanese clusters has a number of features (Ozawa 2003, 5–17). The first is dynamism. The structure and nature of the clusters and the role of the government changed in different stages of industrialization. Initially clusters were of traditional community-based (*jiba sangyo*) within cottage-based industrial organization. At this stage the government had no role. Before the war the government established clusters (*konbinato*) along coasts in order to handle and process imported bulky inputs for use in heavy and chemical industries. These clusters resembled export processing zones. They turned out to be efficient with the support of the government and provision of funds by main banks which belonged to mainstream Japanese industrial groups such as Mitsui, Mitsubishi and Fuji, etc. In the late 1960s 'just-in-time delivery clusters' were created by the government in assembly-based electronic industries (*keiretsu*) which obtained their necessary parts and components through vertically integrated firms. The automobile industry, particularly Toyota town, was the best example, consisting of the assemblers at the top and about 30,000 SMEs at the bottom of the pyramidal structure of production. The Toyota cluster also invented the flexible manufacturing system and just-in-time delivery (see Chapter 4). This cluster is similar to the production sharing system with the difference that firms involved in a cluster are in the same country and location.

In the early 1980s the government initiated, through MITI (the Ministry of International Trade and Industry which was transformed into METI, the Ministry of Economics, Trade and Industry, in 2001) and local governments, R&D clusters and set up about 20 'technolopolises' throughout the country to make the regional economies more research-oriented. The technolopolises were supplemented by regional research core clusters in 1986 to nurture new industrial knowledge established by the government. In the meantime the private sector also created its own research centres, individually and through strategic alliance, both at home and abroad (e.g. in the UK, Ireland, USA) and created links with the universities, local officers, business consultants, etc. (Tayanagi and Colovic-Lamotte 2003, 7). In the late 1990s new clusters were created by the government in IT industries to provide knowledge-based hardware to the industry and the related laws were revised. Then two industrial cluster plans were designed and started implementation in the early 2000s, one by the METI and the other by MEXT (the Ministry of Education, Culture, Sport, Science and Technology). The main objectives of the plans were to encourage technological development and innovation to improve regional and national competitiveness, particularly in high-tech industries. The METI created 55 regional platforms in 1999 and 19 projects started in 2002. An important change in the organization of METI during this period is direct contact with local SMEs through the SME Agency (a department of METI) in addition to its indirect relation through regional governments. The MEXT's Intellectual Cluster Plan broadened the industry–university–government relationship aiming at encouraging advanced research and technological organization. Some coordination was organized between METI and MEXT subsequently (Tayanagi and Colovic-Lamotte 2003, 8–9).

An empirical study of the cluster plans based on three clusters shows great success in two of them (Hitachi City and Ota Industrial Network, which had around 6,000 SMEs as its members). Nevertheless, some shortcomings were noticed in the relations between the university and industry in the case of the Hiashi Osaka Satellite Project. In all cases government support was continuous (Tayanagi and Colovic-Lamotte 2003, 13–14).

Furthermore another feature of the cluster policy of the Japanese government was upgrading the structure of clusters by creating clusters in new industries/activities, as is evident in the preceding paragraphs.

The third feature was internationalization of clusters by creating clusters in East Asia through FDI, linking them with the national clusters after the Plaza Agreement when the Japanese yen appreciated (Ozawa 2003, 5–17).

Let us comment aside that the Italian clusters also tried somewhat to create relations with clusters in other countries through FDI or cooperation agreements to improve technological and organizational deficiencies in the Mexican shoe cluster in Leon and the Guadalajara region. The aim of the Italian cluster was access to the Mexican market and thus the nature of the internationalization effort was different (Primavera and Pezzetti 2003).

One could comment that the evolution of clusters in Japan followed the pattern of 'flying geese' industrialization at the national level, which eventually spread to the East Asian countries through a combination of government policies and change in the strategies of the large Japanese companies after the Plaza Accord (Shafaeddin 2008). As the industrial structure of Japan was upgraded from factor-based competitive advantage to investment-driven, *à la* Porter (see Chapter 3), the government cluster policy was also adapted and upgraded to achieve in turn the upgrading of the country's competitive advantage. Globalization has also brought the international dimension of clusters into focus, to which we will return shortly. The importance of Japanese large industrial groups is well known in the literature. What is less known is the role of SMEs and their relations with each other and with large firms. In 1999, 550 industrial districts and 4,837,000 SMEs were active in Japan (Tayanagi and Colovic-Lamotte 2003, based on MITI).

In developing countries where the necessary institutions are lacking the government should not only provide support to clusters when they are established, but it should also initiate their establishment. For example, the success of the Chinese Puyuan cashmere sweater industrial cluster is mainly due to close and intensive government support (Box 5.3). Government support was also important for achieving quality improvement and employee safety in the case of the Zhili children's garment cluster in China (Fleisher et al. 2009). It should be noted, however, that the experience of Africa shows there are limitations in the transfer of best practices of successful cases to other countries. One may draw on the experience of others but specific national and local conditions of each country should be taken into account in designing government policies (Oyelaran-Oyeyinka and McCormick 2007).

Schmitz and Nadvi (1999) explain that government intervention should follow a 'triple C approach'. It should be customer-oriented; collective and cumulative. 'Collective' means that support should be provided to all enterprises; 'cumulative' implies that support should be provided for generating the capacity to upgrade continuously. The authors state, however, that in applying this approach one should distinguish among three different types of clusters: survival SMEs, advance clusters, which are mass producers of differentiated products, and clusters of TNCs and their suppliers. As preservation

Box 5.3. Experience of the Puyuan cashmere sweater industrial cluster (China)

The local government played a crucial role in the success of the Puyuan cashmere sweater industrial cluster, located in Zhejiang Province near Shanghai. It produced 500 million sweaters of sweaters in 2004. It grew out of the activities of a silk producer 'collectively owned enterprise' (a form of cooperative) and it started producing cashmere sweaters in 1976 using weaving machines. The success of this enterprise led to emulation by others, who set up similar workshops. Initially the products produced were sold along the main road in the region. Then the local authorities intervened by raising finance for establishing a cashmere sweater marketplace which attracted the merchants. The marketplace functioned as a catalyst in deepening the division of labour. After receiving market orders merchants 'put-out production to different workshops'. By raising further finance the local government created 11 more marketplaces with more than 3,000 shops between 1992 and 1994. In 1995 the local government organized 27 private logistic and transport companies with the participation of the government as the main shareholder. This arrangement led to a reduction in the shipping cost. In 1997 the local government introduced quality-control measures in response to the deterioration in the quality. In 2000 the government created a large industrial park to attract well-established companies with their brand names from other parts of China, and provided security and other public services for the park.

By 2004 a total of 3,900 enterprises and workshops and 6,000 shops were engaged in the production and sale of sweaters, respectively engaging 50,000 people who accounted for 65 per cent of the labour force of the region. The market transaction exceeded 10 billion yuan, with the production of 500 million pieces of sweaters as compared with 28,000 yuan in 1976.

An important characteristic of the cluster was its reliance on other (informal) sources of finance than the banks for their starting and working capital. The cluster lowered the capital barrier to entry. The banks played virtually no role in financing smaller workshops and dealers while larger factories and logistic companies received some credits from the state-owned banks – mainly through the local government. Founders of firms, their relatives and a flexible payment system for purchase of inputs were the main sources of financing. The clustering itself facilitated raising finance through these sources because of the way it was organized. The production and procurement of inputs was divided into 10 different stages for each of which a number of enterprises were involved. The small size of the vertically related enterprises made obtaining their capital requirements through informal sources easier.

The experience of the Puyuan cluster was not unique in China. The footwear cluster in Wenzou shares many similarities with Puyuan.

Source: Based on Huang, Zhang and Zhu (2008).

of employment is important in the first category of clusters, government intervention should help in fostering networks for cooperation to improve efficiency. The clusters with better market channels have more chances of success. In more advanced clusters policy measures should aim at upgrading, particularly through technological development, innovation and learning from best practices. In this respect Dosi et al. (2008) emphasize the importance of knowledge accumulation. In such clusters usually the emergence of significant differences among members of clusters may tend to increase conflict, the resolution of which may need government intervention (ibid., 1507–10). Nevertheless, while government intervention is particularly needed in such enterprises, empirical studies of early attempts in clustering in developing countries indicates that when organic links between bureaucratic state institutions and the cluster were lacking, state support programmes were not effective (Nadvi 1992).

In particular, as the size of some firms in the cluster increases, it may create conflicts among members inhibiting cooperation. For example, in the case of a Brazilian cluster leading enterprises developed their alliance with a large global buyer at the cost of cooperation with local firm members of the cluster needed for upgrading (Schmitz 1999). Similarly in Italy some organizational change took place in the larger firms which allowed them to gain organizational autonomy, helping their export expansion, and thus they undermined cooperation with other firms (Basile and Giuta 2003).

International dimension of cluster dynamism

Globalization has implications for the functioning and competitiveness of clusters both in internal and international markets as they become more exposed to competition on price, quality and other nonprice attributes. Further, member firms can have established linkages with external firms for procurement of imports and for establishing market channels; they can also learn from foreign firms through their interaction, flow of knowledge and cross-national network and cooperation (Justo 2003). When buyers are TNCs the strategies of clusters and their member firms as well as their interrelation with their buyers is governed by TNCs (ibid., 11). Foreign firms can have a positive effect on the competitiveness of a local firm through quality improvement. For example it has been shown that the stringent quality demanded by foreign clients and firms forced some Asian manufacturers to upgrade their products and services (Gereffi and Tam 1999). Of course the failure to do so could result in firm closure, as has been the case of many domestic firms in Latin America after trade liberalization. Demanding consumers induce the firm to improve the quality of their products and services to upgrade their competitiveness (see Chapter 3). Failure to do so would result in loss of market for them.

An important obstacle to the entry of clusters into the international market is the lack of marketing channels. A study of 876 firms in Ireland, India and Israel in the software industry showed that technological capabilities were necessary for producing for the international market, but they were not sufficient. Technological activities and agglomeration effects were important in the survival and growth of firms (Giarratana and Torrisi 2003), but links with TNCs will provide them with the necessary marketing and distribution channels.

Networking with domestic or foreign firms, and production sharing have also become important factors in some cases. Thus the question of functional integration and coordination, and governance of dispersed activities in a 'global production chain' across countries becomes relevant. We will turn to these issues in the following sections.

Production Sharing

Interfirm relations takes different forms ranging from networking and supply relations to production sharing. Networking and supply relations can take place among various national and/or international firms; production sharing often takes place through subsidiaries of a TNC located in different countries. As production sharing is the newest and the most common practice we will explain its impact on the competitiveness of developing countries. It will be argued that although production sharing contributes to the competitiveness of the host developing countries, its contribution to growth of income of the host country and upgrading of production is limited. After defining production sharing and explaining its mechanism of operation we will discuss its growing importance in international trade in manufactured goods and its impact on domestic value added in developing countries. Subsequently reference will be made to the vulnerability to external factors of developing countries involved in production sharing.

Definition and mechanism

As defined in the introductory chapter, production sharing is a form of intraindustry trade and industrial collaboration whereby the process of production is fragmented into various parts and components that are produced in different countries, crossing borders to another country for assembly. Such a vertical production chain is facilitated by liberalization of international trade and FDI, and a reduction of transaction costs due to reduced costs of transportation and communication (Arndt 2002). In the traditional trade theory intraindustry trade consisted of trade in differentiated products in final form. In his dynamic theory of specialization Rayment (1983) introduced trade in intermediate goods as an element of intraindustry trade. Thus production sharing contributes to the division of labour and specialization within, or between, industries in the production of parts and components, allowing economies of scale and leading to what Casson calls 'economies of simplification' (Casson 1995., 5). Note that although the concept of production sharing is relatively new, as late as 1964 Prebisch mentioned that the 'peripheries' (developing countries) should explore possibilities for subcontracting production of certain types of components and intermediate goods for their use in industries of developed countries (Prebisch, in UN 1964).

The emergence of offshore processing and assembly operation in developing countries contributes to the dispersion of activities among developed and developing countries. Although, in principle, production sharing can take place among various firms through networking, supply contract and outsourcing, the bulk of production sharing among various countries takes place through intrafirm operations of TNCs which locate plants in different countries. Machinery and transport equipment, particularly electrical and electronic products, automotive products, textiles and clothing, rubber and chemicals are among the main industries subject to product sharing (Ng and Yeats 2003; Inomata 2008). In Latin America product sharing has been facilitated in the region due to the regional trade agreement (North American Free Trade Agreement (NAFTA) in the case of Mexico) or bilateral free trade agreements (FTAs) in other cases. In the Asia-Pacific region China has played an important role in promoting production sharing with the involvement of TNCs (Shafaeddin 2008, 2010b).

FTAs also play an important role in the determination of the direction of trade in production sharing arrangements by TNCs and their affiliates. For example, sales of US affiliates in the NAFTA region (Mexico and Canada) to the USA accounts for 34 (in the case of Canada) to 54 (in the case of *maquiladoras* in Mexico). In contrast, the corresponding figures for European and Japanese affiliates of the US companies are 4 per cent to 6 per cent. More importantly exports through production sharing constitute a significant share of the total exports of Canada (47 per cent) and Maquiladora (55 per cent) as against 17 per cent and 2 per cent in the case of Europe and Japan (Burstein et al. 2008, table 1). Almost similar tendencies are noticed in the EU, exemplified by the case of affiliates of Germany and Austria in the Czech Republic, Hungary, Poland and Slovakia in their trade relations with their parent companies and home country (Tesar 2006, cited in Burstein et al. 2008, 6).

Taking trade in P&C as an indicator of production sharing, the rate of growth of such trade has been increasing faster than the total trade in manufactured goods. For example, during 1981–90 the annual average growth rate of exports of P&C was 12.1 per cent – 1.5 per cent greater than that of manufactured goods as a whole (10.6). During the 1990s the differential rate increased to 2.4 per cent (the corresponding rates were 9.6 per cent and 7.2 per cent, respectively) (World Bank 2003, 55). As a result the share of P&C in total world exports increased from 13.2 in the 1980s to 18.5 in the 1990s and 20.7 per cent in 2004 (World Bank 2003; Aminian et al. 2007, table 4). This trend continued. Asia under the influence of East Asia, particularly China, has shown faster expansion of production sharing than other regions (see Chapter 9 and also Oikawa 2008; Lall et al. 2004). The involvement of TNCs has been crucial in the expansion of production sharing in East Asia (Aminian et al. 2007) and China has been playing the role of a hub (Shafaeddin 2008). While Japanese TNCs were initially more active in investment and production sharing in the region, US firms have also become increasingly involved, particularly in China, to the extent that China is the biggest recipient of exports of P&C from the US (see Athukorala and Yamashita 2008, table 3).

Impact of production sharing

While production sharing contributes to competitiveness for the expansion of exports, the real test of this method of production is its contribution to value added and upgrading. Further, the impact on the vulnerability of the country engaged in production sharing to external factors needs consideration.

As stated earlier, production sharing through TNCs and their affiliates is a sort of vertical integration of economic activities across borders. Hence it increases the market power of the companies involved (Fan et al. 2009). The increase in their market power would imply that they can decide not only on the division of labour among various countries, but also on the division of value added between the home and the host countries. Hence, while the capabilities of companies involved in each stage in the value chain is important in the creation of value added, the corporate power of the TNC is critical in the organization of the value chain and thus the value added created in the home and host countries. In particular, when domestic firms have low technological capabilities, the value added in the host country will be small. In fact the results of empirical studies undertaken on the electronic and automotive industries in East Asia, where production sharing is more widespread than in other regions, are telling:

> ...our results clearly show rather unsuccessful performance of TNC-led industrialization pursued in ASEAN economies. The industrialization policy has largely allowed TNCs to decide how much value added would remain in the host economy. An extreme case is Malaysia which could retain only less than 40% of total value-added of the country's electronic sectors created in 2000, and the rest has been flown-out externally. Moreover, such value outflows have been exaggerated as time goes. A similar tendency is reported in other ASEAN economies. Thus this study concludes that a larger value loss is one of the economic consequences of TNC dependence. (Oikawa 2008, 18)

The reason for low value added in the host country was that '...the largest value-added nodes remain within the US home and less profitable segments were outsourced externally. The study clearly shows that the US increasingly reaps the benefits from the East Asian production networks' (Oikawa 2008, 18). The share of the US in value created in the East Asian region has increased from 41.4 per cent in 1990 to 42.6 per cent in 2000 in the case of electronic and electrical industries, and from 32.4 per cent to 53.5 per cent in the case of the automobile industry (Oikawa 2008, tables 5-1 and 5-2).

The TNCs basically purchase their parts and components from their own affiliates and outsource to the local firms has been small (Aminian et al. 2007). For example, the evidence provided by activities of Japanese multinationals engaged in electronic industry abroad indicates that they also purchase their input mainly from their own affiliates rather than from local suppliers; local content regulation had little effect on their procurement policies. However, the quality of infrastructure and the size and capabilities of local suppliers had positive impact on backward linkages of Japanese firms with local suppliers. So did joint ventures and acquisition of local firms by TNCs (Belderbos et al. 2001).

Further, all developing countries in the East Asian region have not gained equally from the creation of value added through production sharing arrangements in the region. In the electronics industry, where technology is more sophisticated and changes rapidly, there appears to be a close association between domestic technological capabilities and the gain in the share of value added in the region. Thus Taiwan, Republic of Korea and Singapore seem to be the main gainers. Among other countries of the region the performance of

China seems an exception. For example, the country's share in the regional value added in the electronics industry increased colossally from 2.1 per cent in 1990 to 12.5 per cent, seconded in 2000 by Republic of Korea (4.9 per cent). Such explosion requires close examination. China's performance in the automobile industry has also been better than that of other countries but not as spectacular as that of the electrical and electronics industries; its share in the regional value added increased from 2.2 per cent in 1990 to 4.8 per cent in 2000 (ibid., table 5.2). More recent development is explained in Chapter 9.

Data on value added in the processing industries of China are not available. The available data, however, indicate significant increase in the share of domestic production in exports. For example, while the percentage share of net exports (exports minus imports) to exports was negative during the whole of the 1980s, it became positive in the early 1990s and increased to about 21 in 1995, nearly 33 in 2000 and over 34 in 2005 (Shafaeddin and Pizarro 2010). The share of P&C in exports of SITC 7 (machinery and equipment) increased from 5.3 in 1992/93 to 13.2 in 2004/5 (Shafaeddin 2008, table 13). Although the data on the share of P&C in production of manufactured goods was not available, the combination of the two sets of data mentioned indicates that China's achievement in increasing domestic value added is considerable. The experience of China contrasts with that of Mexico. The share of processing trade in exports was more or less equal for the two countries. Nevertheless, the ratio of net exports to total exports of Mexico has, unlike China, declined over time, from 30.5 in 1980 to 22.2 in 2005 (Shafaeddin and Pizarro 2010).

Of course, China's performance may be partly due to the large size of the country which makes it attractive to TNCs; thus TNCs try to accommodate the wishes of the host country for increasing domestic value added. Nevertheless, the size alone cannot explain the country's exceptional performance in the region. Indonesia, the second largest country in the region, suffered from the decline in its hare in the regional value added of the electronics industries, which decreased from 1.2 in 1990 to 0.9 in 2000 (ibid., table 5-1). It should be noted, however, that the value added created in each country consists of those resulting not only from activities of TNCs, but also from activities of local firms. Thus a question arises as to what extent the capabilities of the local firms have been developed in order to upgrade their technological capacity to increase value added and why China has succeeded better than other countries in this respect? Has the government policies played a role in this respect? We will return to these questions in Chapter 9.

Regarding the role of the government, there are striking differences between China and Mexico; both of them have been heavily involved in production sharing but the Chinese government, unlike the Mexican government, has taken an active role in the development of capabilities of domestic firms. We will return to this issue in Chapter 9. Let us mention here that there is also other evidence on the importance of the role of the government in development of capabilities of domestic firms. In cases where the government has taken measures for the development of technological capabilities of the domestic enterprises, value added in assembly operations has increased substantially. In contrast, in cases where the government has taken a passive attitude, production sharing has not contributed much to growth in domestic value added and upgrading of the industrial structure of the country beyond assembly operations (see, e.g., Paus 2005 for a comparative study of Costa Rica and Ireland). We will return to this issue where we will examine the contrasting cases of China and Mexico.

Vulnerability to external factors

Production sharing increases the vulnerability of the host country to the international business cycle because during the economic recession the TNCs attempted to replace home products with imported inputs more proportionately than in the absence of production sharing (Burstein et al. 2008). The correlation of trend growth rate of Asian developing countries with world trade and US trade is 0.62 and 0.54 for 1987–91; but both have increased at the same pace to 0.96 and 0.83 in 2002–07, respectively (Brooks and Hua 2008, 3). Further, the correlation of business cycles between economies across the Asian region increased over time as of the early 1980s (Zebregs 2004).

More than 70 per cent of intra-Asian trade consists of intermediate goods, out of which half is driven by final demand outside Asia (Burstein et al. 2008, 30). In the case of East Asia, while in 2005/6 intraregional exports account for 40 per cent of total exports of manufactured goods, the share of intraregional exports of P&C in total exports of components was 60 per cent (ibid., 30). China functions as a hub in the Asian production sharing system. The increased interdependence of the countries in East Asia and the dependence of China on the third markets for finished products (US and Europe) is a source of risk. The countries of the region are vulnerable to the risk of the transmission of boom-and-bust cycles, particularly through a large trading partner such as China. Such risk has been increasing not only because of the increase in the interdependence of the countries of the region, but also because of the increase in the frequency and intensity of boom-and-bust cycles in the world economy over the recent decades (Akyüz 2008). The unprecedented economic crisis of 2008–9 following the economic boom of the previous years since the Great Depression is an indication of the severity of the boom-and-bust cycles. Although the GDP of China started accelerating again in 2010/11 due to the fiscal stimulus package introduced by the government to increase domestic demand, the risk of dependence on the external markets, particularly that of developed countries, has not been reduced much. Yet another problem is the risk of development of protectionism in the USA due to its growing trade deficits, particularly imbalance in its trade with China.

I have shown elsewhere (Shafaeddin 2008, ch. 5) that the interdependence of the East Asian economies could also entail a number of other risks. These include development of shocks in the economy, or bottleneck in production, in one country and their transmission to others. Furthermore, trade and industrial policies, macroeconomic and exchange rate policies as well as changes in the currency and exchange rate system pursued by one country, particularly large ones such as China, have important effects on the economies of other countries.

Conclusions

In this chapter we have explained the impact of external economies on competitiveness of enterprises in general and examined external economies arising from interfirm relations through clustering and production sharing. We have shown that in contrast with the assumption made in the neoclassical theory of the firm external economies prevail and play an important role in the competitiveness and development of firms and the national economy. The price mechanism fails to stimulate a socially optimum level of investment mainly because of the existence of externalities related to investment coordination which take the forms of pecuniary externalities and technological externalities. When the number of agents is large, state intervention is required to coordinate investment decisions. Professional experience and investment in skill development also involves dynamic external economies. As the market for knowledge, know-how and technological learning is imperfect, again there is a need for government intervention in the market. There are yet other forms of externalities including attitude to work, atmosphere creation and reputation which can be firm specific but would also become country specific when a number of incumbent firms are the source of those types of externalities as exemplified by the electrical and electronics firms of Japan.

We have also explained the externalities involved in interfirm relations in the form of clustering to achieve economies of scale and 'collective efficiency' (which is derived from local externalities and joint action), and from production sharing which enhances division of labour and economies of scales through vertical integration of production. The main advantage of clustering for SMEs, in particular, derives not only from proximity of firms, access to the sources of supply of inputs and skills, labour pooling and exchange of information, knowledge and experience, but also and more importantly it derives from joint action in organizing the operation of the firms 'according to a definite principle' for reaping external economies. Clustering can also contribute to enhancing productivity and competing on 'nonprice attributes' of products produced by the firms involved.

A number of both developed and developing countries have been involved in clustering. While the experience is mixed, a few general observations can be made. First the initial static collective efficiencies have been made through clustering, particularly in developed countries. Secondly on the whole firms involved in clustering have shown superior performance in competitiveness compared with other firms by pursuing dynamic policies for upgrading. Thirdly, nevertheless, the sustainability of competitive advantage has been more difficult in clusters of developing countries as they have taken a less dynamic approach than clusters of developed countries. Fourthly skill development has been an important factor in the success of clusters. Fifthly the clusters of developing countries have shown better success in resource-based and similar industries where there is low appropriation of knowledge and low barriers to entry than in technologically complex industries.

Sixthly the existence of trade networks and trust among member firms has been important in the success of clusters, as has been the role of government through provision of assistance in innovation and upgrading, common services, and through dissemination of information as highlighted by the experience of Japan.

Seventhly the global buyers have contributed little to functional upgrading but when clusters are linked to TNCs, foreign firms can have a positive effect on the competitiveness of local firms through provision of marketing channels and quality improvement required by demanding foreign clients.

Another contribution of foreign firms to competitiveness is through production sharing, which is a vertical division of labour among firms of different countries leading to assembly operations. Production sharing has, however, contributed to the enhancement of domestic value added when the host government has been active to develop the capabilities of the domestic firms, as indicated by the comparison of the cases of China with Mexico and Ireland with Costa Rica. One downside of production sharing is vulnerability to external factors when the final products are exported to the third market, i.e. developed countries.

6

REPUTATION AND TRUST: A FIRM'S RELATIONS WITH STAKEHOLDERS AND OTHERS

> Trust is…seen as an economic lubricant, reducing the cost of transactions, enabling new forms of cooperation and generally furthering business activities, employment and prosperity. (Fukuyama 1996)

Introduction

This chapter will briefly analyse the role of reputation in competitiveness and its main contributory factors. A firm can develop reputation by providing value to the buyers of its products. If a firm in a particular industry of a country develops a favourable reputation it will be beneficial to the whole industry and country because it involves dynamic external economies of reputation, contributing to the competitiveness of not only a firm but also the related country, as described in Chapter 5. The quality of products and after-sale services are important factors in creating and maintaining a favourable reputation.

The reputation of a firm is made by a combination of 'image' and 'identity'. The way a firm is viewed and identified by customers, stakeholders and its employees is an important factor in its competitiveness. Such perceptions are influenced, to a large extent, by the development of trust between the firm and these customers, stakeholders and employees and thus there is an interrelation between trust as social capital and reputation (Chang et al. 2006). Trust among employees themselves and between the firm and government authorities is also important to reputation and sociopolitical and cultural factors play a significant part in the development of trust among various actors and agencies involved in the interrelations of firms with others, particularly in their relations with government authorities.

To proceed we will first explain the concept of reputation and its contributory factors. Subsequently we will outline factors which explain trust between a firm, its stakeholders, other firms and government authorities. The importance of cultural and sociopolitical factors in developing trust in public–private partnerships in particular will be illustrated.

External Economies of Reputation

Reputation is an important contributing factor to competitiveness at all levels, i.e. country, industry and firms. If a firm in a particular industry of a country develops a favourable reputation it will help the whole industry in the field concerned. Nevertheless, a country and an industry cannot develop a favourable reputation without the main firms involved. The Swiss reputation in the watch industry is not an abstract notion. Nor is the Japanese reputation in the electronics industry. It is the firms, or the main firms, involved in a related industry in these countries which have developed the reputation for both the industry and the country. Therefore, the key to the creation of reputation is the performance of the firms involved in an industry and resident in a country. In other words, reputation at the firm level creates external economies.

For a developing country wishing to enter international markets for a manufactured product, marketing barriers to entry are an important obstacle, as explained in Chapter 2. Such barriers to entry are related to the lack of marketing channels and lack of information about consumers' tastes and requirements for quality. Even if a firm can produce high-quality goods, consumers in the importing countries may lack information or confidence in the quality of the goods produced. The supply of high-quality goods and provision of information to consumers (as well as collection of market information) or other marketing activities are all costly and involve dynamic externalities because it cannot be perfectly appropriated by a firm (Lall 1991). If a reputation has been acquired by a particular firm, consumers may lump goods produced by other firms from the same country together in terms of quality of goods supplied (Stiglitz 1989), reliability of after-sale services, etc. As a result other firms may benefit from external economies of reputation and the reduction in their cost of establishing themselves in the new market or in a market for a new product.

Requirements of reputation

If the ability to create value for the buyers is an important element of competitive advantage, the consumers would give the firm a favourable reputation – a reputation that the firm is 'unique' in providing 'value' to the buyers of its products. In other words, those consumers should believe that the firm could provide them with value. If they get satisfaction, they remain loyal. To develop such a reputation is a prerequisite for competitive advantage. Nevertheless, since a firm, as a social organ, has cooperative relations with others in order to be able to create a reputation for providing value to the consumers, it should also be able to create a favourable reputation in the minds of others with whom it has a relationship. These are suppliers, investors, shareholders and, last but not least, its own employees. In fact it is argued that 'the external image of many organizations is driven by the way customer facing employees perceive the organization' (Davies et al. 2003, 31). In order for employees to perceive the enterprise favourably they should also get satisfaction, which will be influenced by their motivation and retention (Davies et al. 2003, 70). Therefore, according to Davies et al., reputation requires two interrelated elements:

- Image: the view of the company held by external stakeholders, particularly customers;
- Identity: the view of the company held by its own employees.

The interaction of the two contributes to building up a reputation; in particular, identity influences image (Davies et al. 2003, 61). But the reputation of a firm will not be made overnight, nor even over the long term unless the enterprise behaves consistently and predictably (Davies et al. 2003, ch. 5, particularly 74).

Advertising is sometimes regarded as a means of creating an image. Nevertheless, unless advertisement is in conformity with the reality of the situation experienced by customers and employees, it will be counterproductive (Davies et al. 2003, 61). According to these authors, 'having employees who are fanatical about their corporate brand is not enough. What they value about their organization should harmonize with what the most important stakeholder group, customers, value in the corporate brand' (Davies et al. 2003, 1). The experience about the reality of various aspects of the performance of the firm is, of course, to be developed over a long period.

Management of reputation therefore involves management of image and identity, and harmonization of the two aspects in order to provide objective and subjective (rationale and emotional) links in what is referred to as reputation chain (Davies et al. 2003, ch. 3, particularly 75–8). The emotional aspect of reputation is related not only to the brand name of the company concerned, but also to the 'country' and 'industry' effects, which are related to the external economies of reputation.

Reputation is made over the long term but it can also be easily destroyed in a short time (Davies et al. 2003, chs 2 and 5). Even a company with a good reputation may face a crisis as the result of a mistake and publicity by pressure groups and the media. In this situation contact with the pressure group and the media for listening, and providing them with information and explanation on controversial issues will help. Ignoring them may make things worse.

As internal identity is a key factor in reputation, one way to manage external image is to focus on internal identity (Davies et al. 2003). The fortune magazine publishes the list of the best and most admirable companies to work for every year. To draw this list, of course, the employees' perception of the firm's internal identity is taken into consideration.

Contributing factors to reputation

In a survey of 15 organizations by Davies et al. (2003) the main dimensions of enterprise personality which contributed to the satisfaction of customers and employees was revealed to be, in order of their importance, as follows:

- Agreeableness: it provided significant satisfaction to both customers and employees by warmth (friendly, pleasant, open and straightforward attitudes); empathy (being concerned, reassuring, supportive, and agreeable); integrity (honesty, sincerity, trustworthiness, social reasonability).
- Competence: it provided significant satisfaction to both customers (particularly for department stores) and employees. The element of competence includes conscientiousness (reliability, security, hard work); drive (being ambitious and achievement-oriented); technical capabilities.
- Human personality: factors contributing to human personality consist of modernity (being cool, trendy and young); adventurousness (being imaginative, up-to-date,

exciting and innovative); boldness (being extravert and daring). Human personalities made some contribution to customer satisfaction.

- Chic: it was important particularly to the customers of fashion retailers. Its elements include elegance (charming, stylish); prestige (being influential, exclusive and refined); snobbery (snobby, elitist). Nevertheless, the last element did not add significantly to staff satisfaction.

- Informality: it requires being casual, simple and easy going. It had minor influences on customer satisfaction.

- Ruthlessness: ruthlessness means being egoistic (arrogant, aggressive, selfish) and dominant (inward-looking, authoritarian, controlling). Ruthlessness had a negative impact on customers.

Developing reputation is also related to the development of the relation of trust between the firm and its stakeholders. In this sense reputation is 'a strategic matter' (Davies et al. 2003, 2) influencing competitiveness.

Trust

Trust is the mutual confidence that the parties involved in an exchange, cooperation or joint action will remain loyal to the agreed terms, avoiding exploitation of the other's vulnerability in their own self-interest. In the absence of trust no one would risk moving first, and thus all would sacrifice the benefits of cooperation to the pursuit of their self-interests even if it were less remunerative. Trust is 'widely regarded as a precondition for competitive success' (Sable 1992, 215).

Trust is regarded as a social capital which makes social life predictable, creates a sense of community and makes it easier for people to work together (Misztal 1996).

Trust is important at both the micro-economic and macro-political levels. For example, Arrow (1972, 357) has argued that without trust, markets cannot function nor deliver their efficiency gains. At the macro-level there is also a positive correlation between trust and economic performance. Tu and Bulte (2010) have gone further by arguing that economic backwardness can be explained, to a large extent, by the lack of mutual confidence; and greater trust results in greater market participation. Easterly (2005) attributes the failure of market reform and liberalization in many developing countries to the absence of sufficient trust at the bottom (see Tu and Bulte 2010 for a survey).

At the micro-level, when firms are afraid to take action because of the fear that others may act opportunistically, it would lead to the lack of dynamism for joint action which is essential for competitiveness. Trust would reduce or remove such risk (Pyke and Sengenberger 1992, 19).

As a firm has various interrelations with its stakeholders and the government, the concept of trust takes various dimensions: trust between a firm and its buyers (consumers and other firms) or franchisers of its products, suppliers of its inputs, its shareholders and its employees. Further, teamwork within the firm is essential; there is a need for mutual trust among the employees. Similarly trust between the private sector and the government is a crucial factor in the growth performance and competitiveness of the firm.

The services provided to customers, particularly after-sale services, are more important than the product itself, especially when the customer is an enterprise, mainly because of the importance of time delivery and the quality of products and services provided. Customers should have trust in the company and its after-sale services. The quality of the goods and its after-sale services are equally important. A company may first aim to achieve a reputation for the quality of its products and its after-sale services. The reputation for quality, in turn, would lead to increases in sales and help to gain economies of scale, thus lowering average cost and higher profits. Any default in a product would involve two types of losses: the losses resulting from the lack of the use of the product and the service it provides; the loss of the user's time during the waiting period while getting it repaired or replaced. Therefore, the delivery time of goods and after-sale services is extremely important. Nevertheless, the delivery time is not the only factor. Zeithaml et al. (1990) distinguish two sets of services: the delivery process and its outcome. Factors important in the delivery process include: responsiveness, i.e. the speed of response of the staff to customers; their competence, their knowledge and skill; their skill in communication, illustration and explanation of the service involved; courtesy, their politeness. Factors important in the 'outcome' of services consist of: access to and the ease of obtaining the service; credibility and the trustworthiness of the company; knowledge about and understanding of the problem by the staff involved; reliability, dependability and consistency of the service provided; security of the service, i.e. the lack of risks related to the service provided.

The issue of trust is important for teamwork among employees and cooperation between the managers and stakeholders for enhancing not only the operational efficiency of a firm, but also its dynamic efficiency (Deakin and Wilkinson 1995, 4). Operational efficiency is concerned with making the existing production system efficient. Dynamic efficiency is related to the capacity of the firm to adapt to changing conditions and taking up new opportunities such as globalization, trade liberalization, changes in technology, market conditions, tastes, emergence of new competitors, etc.

As already stated, trust cannot be created over night. Stakeholders should be able to believe over time that the claims made by a firm or party are justified and correct. Further, the key to mutual trust in the workplace among the employees is the existence of trust between the managers and the employees. If the employees were to believe that all of them are treated by their managers in accordance with known, fair and transparent criteria, they would trust not only their managers but also each other.

The question of trust arises in two different contexts – although they are in some cases interrelated. One is trust between a firm and others when a transaction is involved, for example trust between a firm and its suppliers of inputs or buyers of its products. Another context is trust between a firm and its stakeholders even though no transaction may be involved. The interrelation between the management of a firm and its shareholders is an example. Similarly trust may also be needed for the sake of cooperation, for example between the firm and its employees, between the firm and the government and among the employees. Another example is when cooperation is needed for a joint action by a number of firms. Such is the case in the initiative to take joint actions in a cluster, as will be shortly explained.

When transactions are involved, trust can be built up through three mechanisms: the existence of long-term personal ties and experience involving knowledge about the other party (Dwivedi and Varman 2003) and reputation; sociocultural and moral factors; and the creation of private and public institutions (Platteau 1994). In traditional small societies, sociocultural factors and attitudes help cooperation among members. As members know each other and interact with each other closely they are more interested in their long-term reputation and refrain from acting dishonestly (Platteau 1994, 548). Such personal ties and sociocultural factors are important in establishing trust as they contribute to group cohesion and solidarity; so are the levels of education of those involved (Kristiansen 2004). Nevertheless, their effectiveness is limited, particularly when joint actions are required, as is indicated by the experience of some clusters.

Trust among Firms and in a Cluster, Network and Strategic Alliance

Trust is important in both explicit and implicit contracts among firms, but implicit contracts (gentlemen's agreements) require a higher degree of trust than formal (explicit) contracts (Casson 1995, 110).When there are long-term supply contracts between firms transactions take place through 'social co-ordination', facilitated by trust among the parties involved rather than through the market (Casson 1995, 10–14).

In the case of interfirm relations in a cluster or network the relations between firms are of two kinds: vertical, the relation of the firm with its suppliers and buyers; and horizontal, the relation among rivals. In the former case transactions are the dominant activities of the firms involved. In the second case cooperation dimension is the dominant feature as there may be no or few transactions. In such cases the situation is more complicated as some sort of 'prisoner's dilemma' prevails. For example, the firms involved in a cluster engaged in horizontal activities, i.e. producing the same or similar products, have two different interests: common and individual self-interest. They have some common (long-term) interests to cooperate with their rivals in various activities such as R&D, training, market information, product development, quality improvement, etc., as stated before. At the same time they have some individual short-term interests which may provide them with incentives not to cooperate or to cheat. There is some evidence that sociocultural identity and ties have helped the creation of trust for cooperation among members of clusters, for example in the Sinos Valley shoe cluster in Brazil (Schmitz 1995, 552) or in Bangalore's IT cluster (Holmström 1994). Sociocultural values and norms (informal rules of conduct) also sometimes help the existence of trust among member firms. For example, in the Indian Kanpur saddlery cluster the collective activities of firms wer based to a large extent on norms rather than formal institutions or contracts. Norms therefore operate irrespective of the personal ties (Dwivedi and Varman 2003) which we may call a sort of accepted gentlemen's agreement contributing to trust.

However, there is a limit to the use of reputation and sociocultural factors, particularly when the size of societies/firms becomes larger and the division of labour goes beyond a certain stage. This has been the case, for example, in the Sinos Valley cluster in Brazil (Schmitz 1995).

Therefore, some formal private and/or public institutions, such as business associations or labour associations, are required for cooperation among members, or the government should intervene. Often the role of private institutions in self-regulation and voluntary cooperation is limited (Hoesch 1996). Hence the self-interest of individuals cannot necessarily guarantee social order; social rules or norms should constrain individual behaviour (Platteau 1994, 542). Hence the state needs to play an important role. For example, the government needs to establish institutions for property rights, contract enforcement, bankruptcy law and the freedom to choose occupation and trade (Platteau 1994, 534). The role of the state is more important at the early stage of development when the necessary institutions are lacking. Let us comment here that in all early industrialized (developed) countries the state in fact was active in laying the necessary legal and institutional foundations (Hoesch 1996). This was the case in Japan and other East Asian countries (Wade 1990; 1995).

The intervention by the government may help through awareness raising and/or contract enforcement. Awareness raising is particularly important in cases where the member firms are ignorant of the long-term benefits of cooperation. For example, the lack of awareness about the need for product quality and safety requirements was a problem among the member firms of Pune, an Indian food processing cluster. When the United Nations Industrial Development Organization (UNIDO) acted as an intermediary to raise awareness of the need for food safety, it became clear that the lack of testing facilities in the region was also a constraint requiring government assistance (UNIDO 2001, 10). On the other hand there is also some evidence that sociocultural problems may hinder cooperation among member firms because they may be suspicious of each other, as is indicated by the case of the Bagru cluster of artisans, the members of which failed to cooperate for 20 years before UNIDO intervened as an intermediary (UNIDO 2001, 11).

Cultural factors influence trust between economic agents. For example, Japanese society is characterized by a higher degree of trust among economic agents than in US society (Casson 1995, 118–24). The feudal culture of attachment of individuals to family and village is transformed and extended into the attachment of the individual to the employer, particularly when that individual and family reputation, and its preservation, plays an important role in Japanese society (Casson 1995, 119).

A high degree of trust has a positive impact on competitiveness because, *inter alia*, it reduces transaction cost by relying on implicit rather than formal contracts (Casson 1995, 109). The existence of trust has also allowed Japanese firms to establish relations with other firms for supply of inputs, marketing, etc. In contrast, US firms try to internalize economic activities through vertical integration, which requires strict hierarchical control. Hence one could add that to the extent that horizontal interfirm relations, such as production sharing, allow a higher degree of specialization and division of labour, it could contribute to efficiency and cost reduction unless transport cost overcompensates the gain due to specialization. Also when a high degree of trust prevails within the firm, there is no need for constant supervision and control (Casson 1995, 112). In the absence of trust, the lack of control and supervision affect the performance of the firm negatively and the necessary control and supervision will contribute to increases in costs. Sociopolitical and cultural factors also contribute to the trust between the private sector and the government.

Public–Private Partnership (PPP)

Activities of firms are affected by government directly, through its coordination function and allocation of resources, and indirectly through government policies (see Chapter 8). Government activities and policies may also provide external economies or diseconomies, depending on their nature. At the same time the performance of firms and their competitiveness affect various variables at the national level including, income, employment, foreign exchange earnings, imports, etc. Therefore, public–private partnership (PPP) can be beneficial at both the micro- and macro-levels particularly if it is arranged efficiently. More precisely in this respect one needs to provide answers to the following questions: why is there a need for effective PPP? What is its objective? How can it be arranged? We will provide some answers briefly in the following paragraphs.

Some regard the PPP as a search for 'discovery', i.e. the discovery of obstacles to the performance of firms, and thus taking action for its removal (Rodrik 2004). But the issue is far more complicated. The government formulates policies, regulates markets and the private sector, and also provides information and guidance to the private sector. Policies and guidance need to be implemented, evaluated and modified over time, as necessary, depending on the change in circumstances. The participation of the private sector in the process of policy has two main advantages in formulation: implementation and modification of those measures. First the private sector will provide policy makers with first-hand information regarding the operation of the firms and their needs – referred to as 'discovery' by Rodrik. Secondly the participation of the private sector in policy formulation and the transparency involved create a sense of ownership. The sense of ownership in turn will contribute to better implementation by the private sector of the policies formulated. Thirdly, after their implementation, the private sector can provide feedback on the results and discuss necessary modifications, particularly if the market situation changes.

An effective PPP mechanism is the realm of political economy depending on the nature of the government and its relation with its citizen. A democratic government by nature has to give weight to the views of its citizens, including the representative of the private sector. In contrast, one cannot expect a totalitarian regime to allow the participation of the representative of the private sector in decision making and policy formulation. Of course the private firms in each industry can participate in the PPP mechanism through their industry association, which involves less cost than each firm having its own representative.

To continue, similarly the private sector will not trust a totalitarian government. In such circumstances any dialogue between the two, even if it is arranged, would be a talking shop rather than a serious attempt at partnership. For example, during the administration of General Rawlings in Ghana, an attempt to create a consultative mechanism for dialogue between government officials and representatives of the private sector did not succeed due to the prevalence of the atmosphere of mistrust (Herzberger and Wright 2005, 11).

Even where democracy prevails when PPP is initiated for the first time there is a need for confidence building and the creation of mutual trust (Herzberger and Wright 2005).

The very nature of dialogue, participation and transparency contributes to the creation of trust credibility.

There is no one-size-fits-all argument for the type of institutional set-up required for public–private dialogue. Much depends on the specific situation of each country but as a general rule the partnership should be arranged in a way that 'enables it to be reactive to change and reaching out to a range of stakeholders' (Herzberger and Wright 2005, 37). This would imply that the representatives of both large firms and SMEs should be involved through their association. In some countries the representatives of the labour unions and academic community are also involved. For example, in Malaysia representatives of government, industry and labour are members of the business council created in 1991 and chaired by the prime minister (UNCTAD 1997, 10). While consultative councils or steering committees are set up at the high level, this could be complemented by working groups with the involvement of technicians and the shop floor. The dialogue between the public and private sector should not be confined to the capital city; it is vital that local governments should also have dialogue with the representatives of firms in their vicinity (Herzberger and Wright 2005).

Perhaps the most efficient case of PPP is the Japanese experience of the postwar period. As there is a more widespread sense of trust in the Japanese culture than in many other countries, the PPP was very effective, as was interfirm cooperation (see Chapter 5). In this case the partnership also covered areas such as R&D and technological development.

While we have discussed the role of firms, we should also refer to the special case of cooperative firms. Producer cooperatives of course can be represented in PPP mechanisms through representatives on their board.

Conclusions

In this chapter we have briefly analysed the relations of a firm with its stakeholders and the role of reputation and trust and their influence on competitiveness. We have explained that a firm can develop reputation by providing value to the buyers of its products. By developing a favourable reputation, a firm creates dynamic external economies of reputation which are beneficial to the whole industry and country. The quality of products and after-sale services are, *inter alia*, two important contributory factors in creating and maintaining a favourable reputation for a firm. Further, a combination of 'image' and 'identity' is regarded as the way a firm is perceived by its customers and employers. Image is the view of the company held by its stakeholders, and identity is the views of its employees. Both are important elements of the reputation of a firm. Such views are influenced, to a large extent, by the development of trust between a firm and its customers, stakeholders and employees. Trust is also important among employees themselves and between the firm and government authorities. We have shown that sociopolitical and cultural factors are important in the development of trust among various actors and agencies involved in business relations. It is particularly important in the relationship between the private sector and government authorities for public–private cooperation in the process of development and attaining competitiveness.

7

INNOVATION AND UPGRADING

> [T]he real opposition to *techno-nationalism* is not, as so often *suggested techno-globalism* but rather *techno-liberalism*. It is not, therefore, no surprise that the literature on national systems generally advocate a stronger role of government to foster innovation. (Archibugi and Michie 1997, 134)

> The real competitive problem is laggards versus challengers, incumbents versus innovators, inertial and the imitative versus the imaginative. (Hamel and Prahalad 1994, 17)

Introduction

As explained in Chapter 3, it is widely agreed that competitiveness based on low factor cost is short-lived; and the competitive advantage of a nation arises, in the long run, from firm-level capabilities to innovate. Innovation is required, *inter alia*, to upgrade firms and industrial activities in order to achieve and maintain competitiveness. Further, there is a close correlation between innovation and development (Fagerberg et al. 2009, 40–42). As we have mentioned in the introductory chapter, firms are the centrepiece of economic activities of a country. Upgrading and innovation are not an exception to this general statement; they have to be carried out by the firms, and any related government support and policies should eventually be targeted at the firms.

The literature on innovation is geared basically to the case of established firms of advanced industrial countries. Newcomer firms of developing countries, particularly countries which are at the early stages of development, are not at the same stage of industrialization. Hence innovation takes on a different meaning in the context of these countries. Nevertheless, it is important to explain how established firms in developed countries innovate for two reasons. First firms of developing countries, whether newcomer or incumbent, have to compete with the established firms of developed countries not only in the international market, but also in their own internal market. Hence it is necessary for the firms of developing countries to get familiar with the rules of the competitive game played by those firms. Secondly, though their upgrading initially requires catching up with the established firms as followers, the firms of developing countries eventually have to pursue similar strategies practised by 'technological leaders'.

Therefore, in the first part of the chapter, we will explain, in general terms, issues in innovation and upgrading as discussed in the literature. Subsequently we will devote the second part of the chapter to the explanation of elements and characteristics of innovation in 'follower' firms, i.e. firms of developing countries. The national strategy for innovation and upgrading is discussed in Chapter 8.

I. UPGRADING AND INNOVATION: GENERAL ISSUES

In the following pages we will first define the concepts of upgrading and innovation and the interrelation between the two; subsequently the features of innovation and its impact on competitiveness ad growth will be explained. The discussion of the national systems of innovation and the subsequent literature will be followed by the influence of globalization.

Concepts

Upgrading can be defined as any change in a firm's activities which would contribute to value added in any of the following manners: reducing the operational cost of the firm; enhancing productivity; increasing the value to the buyers; or increasing barriers to entry; or by any combination of the above-stated measures. Hence upgrading can take four forms. The first is product upgrading, which means improving existing product, i.e. making the same product more efficient for use by final consumers/users. An example is the production of more efficient or higher-quality computer chips of the same capacity by Intel. It can also take the form of developing new product (e.g. development of new chips for mobile telephones). The second is process upgrading, which means improving efficiency by applying new technology or new methods of production and organization, or changing and improving other activities in the production chain (e.g. reducing inventory or introducing on-time delivery). The third type of upgrading is functional upgrading, i.e. changing the mix of activities in the production chain to increase value added by taking up new activities. The function of designing in the garment industry is an example. Outsourcing some activities in order to improve quality and/or reduce cost (e.g. outsourcing of marketing) is another example. Finally chain upgrading, or intersectoral upgrading (diversification), involves moving to a new value chain or chains (e.g. Nokia has moved from the production of satellite receivers to mobile phones). Chain upgrading may also include liquidation of an activity to concentrate on a product, or products, for which the firm has 'core competence' (Giuliani et al. 2003, 5; Kaplinsky et al. 2002, 38). One may add to the list the enforcement of higher entry barriers to maintain the profit margin. Generally speaking what is important in upgrading is that the change or innovation introduced by the upgrading firm should be faster than those introduced by its competitors (Kaplinsky and Morris 2002, 37; see also Gereffi and Tam 1999, and the literature on the value chain referred to earlier).

Innovation and upgrading

Upgrading involves change and often requires innovation. Innovation is defined as doing things differently – new things – in a way that creates value for buyers and contributes to value added for the producing firm. Baumol (2002) defines innovation as 'the recognition of opportunities for profitable change and the pursuit of those opportunities all the way through to their adoption in practice' (Baumol 2002, 52). As stated before, innovation entails 'creative destruction', which according to Schumpeter implies combining existing resources in a new way or with new resources; elimination of old combinations (of doing things) and habits. In this sense according to Dosi, 'innovation concerns the search for, and discovery, experimentation, development, imitation and adoption of new products, new production processes and new organizational set-up' (Dosi 1988, 222, cited in Carlsson and Stankiewicz 1991, 228).

Following Schumpeter (1934) we may include the following items in the list of innovation types related to the types of upgrading outlined above.

Product innovation: the introduction of new goods, or a new (higher) quality of existing products.

Process innovation: making things better, in contrast to product innovation which is making better things. Process innovation may take place through introduction of new methods and techniques of production by applying new technology, e.g. the use of robots in production or the internet in communications. It can also be undertaken by the introduction of a new way of handling a product commercially. For example, contrasting with the usual practices of other airlines, Easy Jet introduced a new method of sale of air tickets by selling tickets cheaply at first but then increasing the price as the date of departure approaches; Amazon and Dell introduced sale of their product through the internet.

Organizational innovation: the introduction of new methods of organization and management of an industry or firm. Examples include flexible specialization, production sharing, vertical integration, outsourcing or concentration on the production of core products.

Market innovation: that is, conquest of an existing market previously unexploited by the firm, or entering a new market which was closed previously.

Innovation in procurement: the access to a new source of supply of inputs (raw materials and semimanufactured goods) by creation of a new source of supply (e.g. a fuel cell); access to a newly created source of supply; or even access to a source of supply already in existence but not previously used by the firm.

Product-service innovation: the introduction of new ways of providing after-sale and/or before-sale services; or the introduction of innovation in a combination of the above-listed activities, e.g. production, distribution, organization, etc. For example, Dell introduced not only new ways of selling its products but also new methods of after-sale services. Similarly, IKEA introduced off-the-shelf sales of unassembled cheap products supplied mainly for the taste of a particular group: the young.

Intensity of innovation

Regarding the intensity of innovation, Freeman and Perez (1988) distinguish four types of innovations. The first is incremental innovations, which are continuous but marginal improvement in products and techniques of production mainly through learning by doing and learning by using within the firms. The second is radical innovation, or technological development, which is the development of new production technology in the form of new machinery or new products. It is based on R&D. Thirdly new technological systems are a combination of interrelated radical and incremental innovations such as the development of synthetic materials and petrochemical innovation. Finally change in the techno-economic paradigm is another type of innovation which is the appearance of many sets of incremental and radical innovation that may result in a wide range of changes in products and processes, and may embody technological systems affecting various branches of industry. The introduction of steam power, electricity and information technology gives a few examples. The techno-economic paradigm is the concern of the national system of innovation.

Adoption of innovation means imitating innovations made and used by others, e.g. the use of new machinery or new production processes such as flexible specialization. Adaptation implies the modification of existing technology to local conditions or for producing goods for local taste.

Embodied and disembodied technology

Knowledge is the source of technology which is either embodied in machines and equipment or disembodied. Disembodied technologies are of two types: codified and intangible. Codified knowledge or formal knowledge is the scientific or engineering knowledge available in books and learned through the educational system and training. Tacit, or intangible, knowledge is embodied in the mind of a skilled workforce, called 'mental capital' by F. List and referred to as human capital in the literature.

Knowledge/technology spill-over means the 'knowledge developed by one firm becoming potentially available to others. Absorptive capacity refers to the ability of [the] firm to learn to use technology developed elsewhere through a process that involves substantial investment, particularly of an intangible nature' (OECD 1992, 7). Learning by doing is one source of knowledge; R&D is another. 'R&D…both develops new products and enhances the capability of firms to learn to anticipate and follow future development' (OECD 1992, 47).

Features and Characteristics of Innovation

Innovation is a *cumulative, collective learning and a social process* which involves uncertainty and thus risks because of the lack of full information and related techno-economic problems as well as its outcome. As stated before, it involves *change*, i.e. 'creative destruction', to break old habits (or combination) and replace them with a new combination. Hence it requires cultural change to be effected not only by employers and entrepreneurs but also by the employees. It is also a complex phenomenon requiring formal organization; it relies increasingly on advances in scientific knowledge; it is an experimental exercise requiring learning by doing and learning by using (Dosi 1998, 222–3, cited in Carlsson and Stankiewicz 1991, 227). In fact the competitiveness of a firm is related to the process of learning which affects both production and process innovation. Thus learning is a basic factor influencing innovation and depends on the type of work organization and the management system which guides the organization of the work (Gjerding 1992). These characteristics require a national system for cooperation of various people not only within firms, but also among firms and various agents such as universities, research institutes, users/consumers and suppliers as well as governments (OECD 1992, 67).

Innovation breeds innovation. In other word, innovation is a cumulative process which 'leads to economic developments that, in turn, stimulate and facilitate the innovation process' (Baumol 2002, 284–5).[1] Innovation is a cumulative process because one idea leads to another. For example, the computer gave rise to the need for a mouse (Baumol 2002, 285). According to Baumol competition among firms leads to innovation, innovation stimulates competition further and both stimulate, and are stimulated by, foreign trade. Innovation also extends the supply of natural resources by savings arising from the method of production and use of resources (Baumol 2002, 286–8).

The *collective* nature of innovation is related to the collective nature of capabilities and skill formation, which in turn are related to the collective nature of the firm as a cultural and social unit, *à la* Penrose, as explained in the introductory chapter. 'Firms are coalitions of thinking, information-processing individuals each with their own life experiences and accumulated stock of knowledge' (Carlsson and Stankiewicz 1991, 100). The collective nature of firms and the tacit and specific content of technological knowledge imply that there is a need for cooperation of all workforces and the management. Not only is the cooperative function of the entrepreneur important in this respect, but also the motivation of the workforce is crucial. Such motivation is crucial because the experience of the workforce over time contributes to the uniqueness of the capabilities of the firm. The workforce should be motivated to develop a sense of belonging to the firm and to cooperate with each other and with the management. Therefore, the culture of the firm as a social organ and its collective nature play an important role in the development and sustainability of core competences. It is also important in its cooperation with other firms in the supply chain.

Culture of change

Upgrading in general, particularly upgrading of the strategy and organizational structure, involves changes in past habits. Often change is difficult not only for employees, but also for managers and stakeholders (see FMS in Chapter 4). As stated earlier, Hirschman regards resistance to change as one of the main obstacles to innovation and efficiency. 'Institutional factors through their inertia and rigidity retard the dynamic of technical change. Institutions are regarded as inflexible, and institutional change is supposed to be lagging behind technical change', restricting the full realization of potentials of new technologies (Jonson 1992, 23–4).

Impact of Innovation

In the neoclassical theory of the firm, technical progress, innovation and entrepreneurship have no place because firms are assumed to be in a perfect competitive position. Technological progress is exogenous to the firm; it is 'manna from heaven'. In our

---

1 See also Nelson (1996).

Schumpeterian model of competitiveness, innovation, entrepreneurship and technological development play an important role. According to Baumol (2002) in a *capitalist economy* innovation plays a more important role than price in the competitiveness of firms. In fact the results of a study on the main developed countries indicate that 90 per cent of growth in the main industrial countries (USA, Japan, Germany, France and UK) derive from innovation (Oxley and Yeung 1998a, xix, and sources therein). In some industries, innovation replaces price as the 'name of the game'. Following Schumpeter, Baumol argues that free market and competitive pressure forces firms into 'a continuing process of innovation because it becomes a matter of life and death for many of them' (Oxley and Yeung 1998a, 2). He continues:

> [I]n a key part of the economy the prime weapon of competition is not price but innovation. As a result, firms cannot afford to leave innovation to chance. Rather managers are forced by market pressure to support innovative activity systematically and substantially, and success of the efforts of any business firm forces its rivals to step up their own efforts. (Oxley and Yeung 1998a, 3)

Baumol considers innovation to be a driving force of growth of not only firms, but also a country and he argues that productive entrepreneurial activities are contributing factors to innovation and growth. Hence he suggests that the best way to stimulate productive entrepreneurial activity is to 'reduce the rewards to unproductive or destructive rent-seeking' (Oxley and Yeung 1998a, 2). According to Archibugi and Michie (1998) innovation has a positive impact on international competitiveness in three ways: process innovation reduces production costs; minor product innovation contributes to quality improvement; major product innovation creates temporary monopolistic position and thus helps bring monopoly rent (Archibugi and Michie 1998, 322–3). In the long run 'innovative nations will have two main advantages: improved terms of trade; the ability to specialize in whatever proves to be most rewarding industries. Both of these could prove crucial factors in allowing a nation to achieve higher growth rates' (Archibugi and Michie 1998, 323). In contrast, in the long run, specialization based on static comparative advantage, i.e. low wages, will not lead to the industries that can be highly rewarding to the factors of production employed.

To explain further, by putting more people to work the firm can increase value added, but it has a limit and involves no rent, and it is vulnerable to shifting of plants to other countries where labour is cheaper. One may start with it but should move up in the value chain as otherwise 'immiserizing growth' will be the result. Innovation can contribute to competitiveness if it creates value for the buyers by providing them with a lower price or higher quality or new products, and so on. For example, a product innovation which involves new product contributes to profit by creating a temporary monopolistic market condition and the resulting 'entrepreneurs rent'. Similarly a product innovation involving new quality of goods contributes to market share and thus profits. Process innovation may contribute *ceteris paribus* to cost reduction, on-time delivery, shortening of the production process and/or simplification of the distribution process – all of these will contribute to improving market share. Further, if cost is decreased substantially it allows limit pricing and thus deterring competitors. Limit pricing is the highest price which a firm can charge without inducing a new entry in the industry. Product-service innovation may also contribute to increasing market share and developing a reputation for reliability.

Competitive advantage is the source of economic rent stemming from proprietary technology and superior business strategy but both technology and strategy can be imitated (see Casson 1995, ch. 4). However, business strategies which are concerned with coordination among different functions in production and both down- and upstream activities are less likely to be imitated as they are embedded in a 'complex institutional arrangement' (Casson 1995, 87). Otherwise continuous innovation in technology and business strategy contributes to the competitiveness of a firm in the long run (Casson 1995, 87).

Innovation and Export Competitiveness

Innovation is important in export expansion, and competitive pressure induces innovation in developing countries. As stated earlier in this chapter, Baumol regards market forces as the major determinants of innovation. He argues that the competitive pressures provide incentives for 'rapid dissemination and exchange of improved technology throughout the economy' (Baumol 2002, 9). He outlines the following preconditions for the existence of a workable free market economy under imperfect competition: oligopolistic competition in large firms with increasing return; utilization of innovation in ordinary decision process and activities of firms; productive entrepreneurship, encouraged by incentives for entrepreneurs to follow productive innovation; rules of law for enforcing and respecting contracts; dissemination of innovation through voluntary selling and trading of technology through licensing (Baumol 2002, ch. 1).

A survey of nearly 3,000 SMEs in Vietnam in 2005 showed that product and process innovation played an important role in the export activities of the firms of the country (Nguyen et al. 2008).

The increase in innovation activities of the textile and clothing industry of Sri Lanka after the ending of the Multi-Fibre Agreement is an example of the impact of competitive pressure on innovation. Competition in the USA market induced the Sri Lankan firms, as well as foreign firms located in the country, to take various measures in introducing process and production innovation with support from the government and with positive impact on their exports (Wijayasiri and Dissanayake 2008a). At what stage of development of an industry competitive pressure should be introduced through creating domestic rivalry or trade liberalization, and whether the introduction of domestic rivalry should precede subjecting a firm to foreign completion are issues requiring detailed discussion, to which we will return in Chapter 8.

The National System of Innovation (NSI)

Innovation is a complex phenomenon which proceeds through the interaction of many players, and is influenced by a number of factors many of which are country specific.

The complexity and country specificity of innovation has led some to introduce the concept of a 'national system' of innovation in recent decades. Others have introduced other concepts such as Mod 1, Mod 2 and Triple Helix to explain the role of innovation and technological change. Nevertheless, the literature on NSI is still the most relevant, to which we will devote the following pages and subsequently refer to the new literature in Box 7.3.

The origin of the idea of the systemic nature of innovation goes back to F. List (1856) in his book *The National System of Political Economy*. The terminology used by List was, however, different. As mentioned in the introductory chapter, List regarded mental capital (knowledge), rather than material capital, as the main source of productive power, and productive power as the main source of comparative advantage. Knowledge is acquired through education, science, training, discoveries, inventions, experience and division of labour, and application of experience of other countries. It is determined by 'social order' and requires government intervention (see Chapter 1; Shafaeddin 2005a; Freeman 1995). As can be seen, according to List acquiring knowledge is a 'systemic issue' which also depends on 'social order'. As explained below, in the recent literature the terminologies used consist of 'National System of Innovation', instead of 'National Political Economy', 'Social System' instead of 'social order' and 'intangible assets' instead of 'mental capital'.

The misinterpretation of List's ideas led to the neglect of his pioneering contribution to competitive advantage in the literature until very recently. He has been subject to attack by neoclassical economists, who misinterpreted his infant industry argument, which was only a part of his theory of 'productive power' for achieving development and acquiring comparative advantage in an international market. But, on the basis of his ideas, Germany developed 'one of the best technical education and training systems in the world' and managed not only to catch up with the UK but forge ahead (Shafaeddin 2005a).

Before the concept of 'National System of Innovation' was introduced by Lundvall in 1992, a number of economists referred to the role of national domestic market and 'nation-specific' factors in competitiveness and innovation. For example, the role of the national market in the development of competitive advantage was emphasized by (e.g. Linder 1961; Krugman 1984; Porter 1990). Porter's view on the role of demanding domestic consumers and users and the national environment within which a firm operates is emphasized despite the growing role of globalization. Later on others have established the role of 'users' and nation-specific issues in promoting innovation within the context of a national system of innovation (e.g. Lundvall 1992; Freeman 1995; Fagerberg 1995).[2]

Lundvall (1992) introduced the concept of national system of innovation. Accordingly invention and innovation takes place within or outside a firm, i.e. in other firms or in universities and research institutes or in any combination of these depending on the national system of innovation of a country. According to him:

> [A] system of innovation is constituted by elements and relationships which interact in the production, diffusion and use of new, and economically useful, knowledge

---

2 For more details and references see Archibugi and Michie (1998, 324–5).

and that a national system encompasses elements and relationships, either located within or rooted inside the borders of a nation state. (Lundvall 1992, 2)

He adds:

[A]ll parts and aspects of economic structure and institutional set-up affecting learning as well as searching and exploring – the production system, the marketing system and the system of finance – present themselves as subsystems in which learning takes place. (Lundvall 1992, 12)

NSI and the technological system

The national system of innovation has certain elements in common with the 'technological system' but the latter is broader in its scope. A technological system is:

[A] network of agents interacting in a specific *economic / industrial area* under a particular *institutional infrastructure* or set of infrastructures and involved in the generation, diffusion, and utilization of technology. Technological systems are defined in terms of knowledge/competence flows rather than flows of ordinary goods and services. They consist of dynamic *knowledge and competence networks*. (Carlsson and Stankiewicz 1991, 111)

According to these authors there are two main differences between the two systems. First the boundaries of technological systems are not necessary national boundaries; it could be national, regional or international. Secondly the national system of innovation is concerned with generation and distribution of knowledge. In contrast, in the technological system the emphasis is put on the adoption and utilization of technology by stressing economic competence and knowledge networks rather than institutional infrastructure (Carlsson and Stankiewicz 1991, 112). However, the relevance of the second distinction depends on the definition of innovation. In the context of developing countries we define innovation as the application of the existing technology, which may already have been used for the first time elsewhere, rather than generation of new knowledge, i.e. frontier technology.

Features and elements of NSI

As so defined above, the national system of innovation has a few main characteristics as follows. It is a social order involving learning and it is sector- and country specific. Further, a number of factors are important in the NSI, including entrepreneurship, R&D, knowledge and intangible capital (intellectual or mental capital), human resources, and strategy.

Accumulation of technological competence is sector specific (Archibugi and Michie 1998, 323) and, more importantly, country specific. Examples are pharmaceutical industries in Switzerland and Germany. Innovation and technological change involve learning and skill formation which are firm- and activity specific. NSI is a 'social system' requiring interaction between people; learning, searching; exploring and enhancing knowledge is its main activity requiring an institutional set-up for the activities of scientists, engineers and technicians. Learning takes place at various levels: individual, enterprise and national; it also requires, firm and government strategy for, *inter alia*, cooperation, creativity and competition. Learning may be in the form of learning by doing, learning by using; learning by interacting; learning by experience; learning by visiting and learning by imitating. Learning is a dynamic, gradual, continuous and cumulative *process* and it is mainly nation specific despite globalization (Archibugi and Michie 2003, 2–3 and 8–9).

Lazonick (2004) also correctly argues that there are strategic differences in the national system of skill formation in different countries due to structural differences in the social organization of nations. Further, the nature and requirements of skill formation are different in different industries. As a result different countries develop different capabilities necessary for gaining competitive advantages in different industries. For example, in the pharmaceutical and chemical industries, innovation and organizational learning take place mainly through close relationship between the industry and universities. In contrast, in machine-based industries both product and process innovation are important: product innovation for development of new products and process innovation for reducing costs and improving quality.

The Japanese system of skill formation includes an integrated system whereby skill formation within the managerial system and the involvement of managers, shop floor workers and suppliers in process innovation contribute to product innovation. As stated earlier, in Chapter 4, in the case of FMS in Japan workers at the shop floor level are multiskilled: they are trained to undertake a number of tasks to give them flexibility and enable them to solve problems as they arise. In contrast, in the USA there has been a strategy of substituting machinery and materials for the skills of workers at the shop floor level. As a result the Japanese enterprises succeeded well in competing with the USA's enterprises in industries such as consumer electronics, automobile and steel through cost reduction and quality improvement. In contrast, they were unable to compete effectively with the American and German pharmaceutical and chemical industries. In the USA and Germany there has been a long tradition of industry–university relationships which has been absent in Japan (Lazonick and O'Sullivan 1994). One implication of the dominant system of skill formation in the USA, as well as Europe, has been to put pressure on workers to demand more effort from them, to restrain wage increases or to downsize the firm. The aim has been to control cost rather than invest in the national system of skill formation. Expenditure on human resource development is considered an operating expenditure rather than productive investment (Lazonick and O'Sullivan 1994, 38).

Nations are also different in their internal organization of firms, interfirm relationship, role of public sector, institutional set-up, their financial sector, R&D organizations – all of which are important for innovation. One implication of the nation specifity of the system of innovation is that although developing countries should apply and adapt imported technology, development of competitive advantage in the long term depends on capabilities developed by their own national firms. In fact Casson (1995) does not deny the role of national factors despite his more general concept of 'technological system'. Indeed he goes so far as to argue that it is the entrepreneurship culture which has led to the development of economic dynamism in industrialized countries (Casson 1995, ch. 6). In his view three main factors contribute to economic development: geography (access to sea), a scientific outlook and a commitment to a voluntary method of social and economic coordination (Casson 1995, ch. 6). There are other factors as well, of course.

Entrepreneurship

In traditional economic theory entrepreneur and innovation have no place. In the Schumpeterian theory of firm and development entrepreneur plays an important role – although it is defined differently by different scholars. To Schumpeter the entrepreneur is an innovator because he leads the process of carrying out change and the creation of the 'new combination'. Some regard the entrepreneur as a risk taker. Casson (1995, 46–7) defines it as: 'someone who specializes in taking a certain type of decision' for handling complicated situations. Decisions about innovation and about an uncertain situation are of this kind, requiring the use of judgement (Casson 1995, 47). Thus, according to him, entrepreneurship may be defined as a capacity for successfully taking judgement decisions – that is for solving problems in highly complex situations (Casson 1995, 89).

Schumpeter's definition of entrepreneurship is in fact, the most relevant one. Expanding on this definition, Baumol adds that an entrepreneur is:

> [T]he bold and imaginative deviator from established business pattern and practices, who constantly seeks the opportunity to introduce new products and new procedures, to invade new markets, and to create new organizational forms. In short, the entrepreneur is the independent innovator, in the broadest sense, meaning that the activities of this individual include, but go considerably beyond, technical inventions and their utilization. (Baumol 2002, 91)

As mentioned earlier entrepreneurs have two main functions: creative and cooperative. Creation of a 'new combination' requires the destruction of the 'old combination'; its constructive part requires the cooperative function of the entrepreneur, i.e. organization, to create the new combination and manage innovation in a way that creates value for the buyers. To bear fruit from the creative aspect of *production* innovation also requires an efficient organization. It may require reaping the benefit of the economies of scale depending on the industry involved. It is the interaction of innovation and organization which contributes to competitiveness (see Lazonick's theory in Chapter 3 of the present volume).

The creative activities of the firm cannot be, however, attributed to the creative function of the manger alone. Casson argues that it stems from the 'cooperative creativity of the individuals within it' which is in turn influenced, *inter alia*, by cultural factors (Casson 1995, 45). National cultural factors are important in both innovation and growth; high norms to raise standards of living and demand for high quality are important (Casson 1995, ch. 3). While Casson calls it high norm, Porter calls it demanding users and consumers as mentioned before. Similarly entrepreneur culture is a source of comparative advantage (Casson 1995, ch. 4). Casson adds that, while cultural factors are important, the culture of TNCs may hinder rather than help the process of development of the host country (Casson 1995, 127).

Further, there is a need for national dialogue, consultation and cooperation among the stakeholders and nongovernment actors on needs and opportunities regarding science and technology policies and programmes, i.e. between economic and social policy makers and science and technology professionals (OECD 1992, 280).

R&D

An NSI requires a system of research and development. Problem solving should start from the shop floor where problems and bottlenecks arise. While entrepreneurs should be prepared for organizational change, the workers on the shop floor should also be prepared to not only accept change, but also participate in problem solving. When problems cannot be resolved at the shop floor level they should be referred to the R&D unit of the company. The nature of R&D, however, is different in the case of technology followers at early stages of development, from that of technology leaders. Followers initially should concentrate on building up the absorptive capacity to use and apply technology which has been applied efficiently elsewhere. While process problems may be easier to resolve in the company, product innovation may need external help, particularly at the early stages of industrialization. It should be noted, however, that at the early stages of development adaptation and 'development' of technology are needed rather than spending money on research at the frontier of science.

R&D is an important contributory factor to innovation but, as far as the contribution of R&D expenditures to competitiveness is concerned, with the nature of R&D expenditure and the involvement of agents of innovation (public institutions and firms) a number of qualifications are necessary.

Changes in the technological paradigm and leading-edge technologies require scientific research and the heavy involvement and interaction of public sector and business. Other types of technological development are more dependent, at least in developed countries, on investment on innovation by firms (see, e.g., Archibugi and Michie 1998, 324). Generally speaking the experience of both developed and developing countries indicates that at the early stages of development the state has to play a more significant role in R&D in relation to the private sector because of the underdevelopment of the private sector. Nevertheless, the share of the private sector in R&D expenditure should increase as the country develops.

In fact the experience of developed countries indicates that in-house R&D by firms is the driving engine of invention and innovation. One example is in-house R&D expenditure by German chemical and pharmaceutical industries introduced in 1870 which has intensified since 1959. It made German companies leaders in these industries (Freeman 1995, 8–10; Chandler 2005; Boldrin and Levine 2008, ch. 9). For example, BASF is the largest global chemical industry (McCoy et al. 2006). Further evidence also indicates that efficient diffusion rather than being first in the world of innovation contributes more to the rate of technical change and economic growth, and that the success of innovation and diffusion also depends on other factors such as interaction with users and suppliers in addition to R&D (ibid., 10).

Further, the sheer data on R&D expenditure alone do not guarantee improvement in competitiveness, as is evident by comparison of the national systems of innovation in the USSR and Japan in the 1970s as well as those of East Asia and Latin America in the 1980s. For example, while in the 1970s the ratio of gross expenditure on R&D to GDP of Japan was less than two-thirds of that of the USSR (4 per cent – the highest in the world), the NSI of Japan was geared to and targeted at industrial production for commercial use; enterprises accounted for over two-thirds of total R&D; there were interactions between producers, suppliers and users and the managers and employees were provided with a strong incentive to innovate. In contrast, the USSR system was geared mainly to military R&D, government accounted for 90 per cent of R&D; R&D was separate from industrial production with few linkages between marketing, production and procurement, and there was little incentive and little pressure from international competition (Freeman 1995, 11–13). The result for the international competitiveness of the two countries is well known in the literature and need not be explained.

Similarly the success of East Asia in the international market in the 1980s contrasted with the case of Latin America to a large extent because of difference in NSI, particularly in the way R&D was allocated. East Asian countries invested heavily in universal education with emphasis on tertiary technical education. They used imported technology, mainly through Japanese TNCs, while at the same time they took initiative in domestic capability building and increased public R&D mainly for industrial purposes through heavy concentration in government laboratories and providing support to the research activities of state-owned enterprises (SOEs). They initiated linkages among universities, research institutes and firms, increased investment in IT and promoted the electronics industries. Public R&D has been important in East Asian countries where the government established many laboratories and also undertook R&D through SOEs (OECD 1992, 265–7). In contrast, in the case of Latin America the educational system, particularly technical education, deteriorated; significant transfer of technology from the USA took place but there was little effort in building up domestic capabilities in most countries and industries (one exception was the Brazilian automobile and aerospace industry – see Shafaeddin 2005c); industrial R&D was low; science-technology infrastructure and its linkages with industry were poor; and modern telecommunications expanded slowly (Freeman 1986, 12–14; OECD 1992, 265–7).

More recent evidence also indicates the importance of in-house R&D in the competitive performance of China and other East Asian countries. We have explained the case of China extensively in Chapter 9. Accordingly the country not only increased R&D rapidly, but also the share of its enterprises in total R&D expenditure increased fast, and there was a close interrelation between national firms, universities and research institutes and TNCs. Most of all, the government followed a clear strategy and proactive role in technology and industrial development.

The Role of the Firm and Other Institutions in R&D

There are different notions and levels of cover of institutions in the literature. Normally institutions are regarded as rules of the game including norms, culture, rules, laws and regulations as well as traditions which influence and shape patterns of behaviour. For example, attitude to change, patent legislation, and regulations related to labour relations and the financial system are among factors which influence the diffusion, development and application of technology. Some scholars refer to the organizations involved in technology issues, such as universities, laboratories, training and research institutes, etc. and their interactions, as institutions of technological development and innovation (Nelson 1993, 50–53). Others include both as institutions. Yet others also regard R&D and government policies as elements of institutions of innovation and technological development (Edquist 1997, 26–8).

In this study we distinguish institutions from organizations and policies from factors. For example, norms are institutions, universities are organizations, R&D is a factor or activity and government policies are obviously policies. However, the educational system or R&D system is part of the institutional infrastructure.

It is sometimes argued that large firms are more endowed with their own resources for R&D and thus they are more active in innovation (see, e.g., Corsino et al. 2008 for the case of the semiconductor industry). A Survey of empirical investigations indicates, however, that large size is not always necessarily accompanied by R&D spending unless certain conditions are met. These include 'high sunk cost per individual project, economies of scale and scope, in the production of innovation rents' as well as technological characteristics (e.g. the average cost of an R&D project), demand and institutional framework (Symeonidis 1996, 2, 33–4). According to another study large firms are more innovative than smaller ones, but the smaller firms tend to report relatively higher proportion of sales of innovative products (Fagerberg et al. 2009, 44). Generally speaking firms with more well-developed technological capabilities are more innovative.

Small firms have an advantage over large ones for radical innovation because they enjoy lower agency cost, but they lack financial resources. Thus TNCs and smaller start-up firms can complement each other in innovation activities (Oxley and Yeung 1998a, xvi).[3] In fact TNCs often outsource research for technological development to small start-up firms. Nevertheless, the receivers of such outsourcing are firms of developed, not developing, countries. In developing countries, SMEs which are the main agents of production, particularly in small countries, require assistance from the government, universities and research institutes. Therefore, collaboration between these institutions and SMEs in particular are essential in developing countries, where SMEs normally play a more important rol, than large firms do in industrial activities.

There is some empirical evidence that the main contribution of universities and R&D centres to innovation has been indirect. For example, the government of Hong Kong pursues an active policy to promote innovation by establishing R&D centres and facilitate their cooperation with the private sector, particularly the electronics industries. A survey of electronics SMEs in Hong Kong indicates that 'the main way through which universities and R&D centres support HK [Hong Kong] electronics SMEs innovation

---

3 For further references see ibid.

activities seems to be the provision of a highly-qualified labour-force transmitting academic knowledge to companies' (Liu 2008, 1).

An empirical survey of firms in Zhongguancu (Beijing) shows that the collaboration between SMEs and research institutes has been effective when they were located near each other. In contrast, geographical proximity was not important in collaboration between those institutes and a large firm (Nobuaki and Yoshihiro 2008).

Although TNCs are locating some of their activities in developing countries, such relocation is still small. Their R&D activities are located mainly in their home country. Furthermore their relocation of R&D activities to developing countries depends on infrastructure facilities, tangible and intangible assets, and other capabilities of the host country (Archibugi and Michie 1995; Lall 1993b; OECD 1992). As exemplified by the case of China (see Chapter 9), development of indigenous capabilities are important not only to attract FDI in general, and their R&D activities in particular, but also for enhancing the technological capacities of domestic firms for competition in the international market. Acquisition of knowledge as an intangible asset is an important element of endogenous capability and a national system of innovation, as will be explained below.

Intangible Capital as an Important Element of NSI

Intellectual capital (knowledge), or mental capital in the language of F. List, is regarded as an important determinant of economic performance and competitiveness to the extent that one talks of a 'knowledge society' or 'learning society'. The importance of intangible capital in total capital stock and its contribution to GDP has been increasing rapidly during recent decades. Its share in the stock of capital has increased, e.g. from about 35 per cent in 1929 to 53.5 per cent in 1990; it took over the share of tangible capital in the 1970s (Mortensen 2000, 8, table 1.1). Although intangible capital is not quantifiable, the author's emphasis on its role, à la List, is not deniable. The contribution of intangible assets has been increasing even faster since the early 1990s partly due to the development of information and communications technology (ICT). Differences in productivity levels in various countries are also largely explained by the accumulation of knowledge (Mortensen 2000, 11). One difference between knowledge and physical capital is that knowledge is not subject to diminishing return; it also involves externalities (Mortensen 2000, 12).

Penrose (1959) argued, inter alia, that resources possessed by the firms in an industry determine the industry's structure. There is no general agreement on the definition, nature and coverage of resources (see Bounfour 2000, 21–3) but it is generally agreed that intangible resources are the main firm-specific, nontradable and nonimitable resource. Corporate strategy is to a large extent influenced by the stock of resources and the capabilities (or core competence of the firm) in combining them. Together they are the basis for competitive advantage (Bounfour 2000, 22).

Intangible resources (assets) are regarded as a lever for competitive advantage. This approach is close to the capability-building theory, though the capability-building theory (TCB) is more general. The stock of capital of a firm includes both intangible capital and tangible (fixed) assets such as plants and equipment. The International Federation of Accountants provides a list of intellectual (intangible) capital as shown in Box 7.1. A somewhat similar list is provided by Forbes and Wield (2002) as shown in Box 7.2. According to the OECD (1992, 113) intangible assets are augmented by intangible investments, which can be divided into four groups:

1. Intangible investment in technology (R&D including software R&D, technology acquisition, design, engineering, and scanning and search activities);
2. Enabling intangible investments; investment in human resources, organization and information structure; these are not easy to measure and analyse due to the lack of data;
3 Market exploration and market organization; market exploration is important at periods of shortening product cycles and greater competition;
4. Software, including software integrated into equipment (software-intensive computer-controlled manufacturing processes.

Corporate strategies and organization are being built on greater inputs of intangible investments and the balance between tangible and intangible assets and necessary complementarities between them is important.

Box 7.1. Elements of intellectual capital

1. Human capital	*2. Customer (relational) capital*
– Know-how	– Brand
– Education	– Customers
– Vocational qualification	– Customers loyalty
– Work-related knowledge	– Company name (brand)
– Occupational assessments	– Backlog order
– Psychometric assessments	– Distribution channel
– Work related competencies	– Business collaboration
– Entrepreneurial plan, innovation,	– Licensing agreement
proactive and reactive abilities,	– Favourable contracts
changeability	– Franchising agreement
Organizational (structural) capital:	
3. Intellectual property	*4. Infrastructural assets*
– Patents	– Management philosophy
– Copyright	– Corporate culture
– Design right	– Management process
– Trade secrets	– Information system
– Trademarks	– Networking system
– Service mark	– Financial relations

Source: Reproduced from (Bounfour 2000, 25), based on International Federation of Accountants sources.

Box 7.2. List of intangible assets

- Technological assets include assets that can be protected with intellectual property rights, but also the tacit knowledge that determines a firm's competencies.
- Complementary assets cover many non-technical functional areas and include brand, marketing, after-sales system and financial institutions.
- Institutional assets, including the public policy environment within which the firm operates, and national innovation system within which it innovates.
- Locational assets, such as proximity to attractive markets and being part of dynamic industrial cluster.
- Prepositional assets, the image that others hold about a firm which is a key to how it is seen in the outside world.

Source: Forbes and Wield (2002, 183).

Upgrading of human capital

Acquiring intangible knowledge necessary for innovation and upgrading requires the upgrading of human capital. Generally speaking, as far as the interrelation between human resources, innovation and competitive performance of firms is concerned, a number of points are worth mentioning. First innovation is a necessary condition for upgrading but is not sufficient.

There is some evidence that reliance on technology or innovation alone would lead to increases in cost without necessarily increasing the value added (Lundvall 2004). What is required is a combination of innovation, organizational change and competence (capability) building. Both organizational change and competence building, however, require the upgrading of human resources and managerial capabilities which in turn involves a process of skill formation and learning through education and training. As stated in the introductory chapter, human resources (employees of a firm) are its critical assets necessary for the development of competitiveness.

In a survey of 4,000 Danish firms over the period 1992–7 two groups were differentiated: dynamic and static. Dynamic firms were defined as those in which their organizational change and activities were geared to development of both products and markets, and static firms as those which did not meet either of those demands. The dynamic firms were those for which:

- skilled workers occupied a higher proportion of their workforce than unskilled workers;
- growth in the number of skilled workers was faster than the growth in the number of unskilled workers;
- when faced with competition, the number of their skilled workers also increased after a temporary decline. In contrast, the unskilled workers suffered from high redundancy levels, particularly when competition was severe;
- the total size of the workforce employed by the dynamic firms increased continuously;

- while the employment in static firms suffered significantly, the increase in employment in the dynamic firms overcompensated the decline in the static firms;
- the dynamic firms created more stable jobs as the core labour force was bigger (Lundvall 2004, 6–9).

An important implication of these findings is that there is a need for upgrading human resources and promoting organizational change. Therefore, expenditure on human resource development, or what List called 'mental capital', and organizational change should be regarded as productive investment rather than current or operational expenditure. Unfortunately, however, this is not the case in the USA and Europe, as will be explained shortly.

Upgrading the competitive strategy

As competitiveness involves creative destruction, upgrading should include the upgrading of the competitive strategy of the firm itself in order to create new and *unique* advantages which cannot be easily copied by others. It is not enough to try to copy what the competitors do in order to catch up with best practices and benchmarks (Hamel and Prahad 1994, 275–6). In fact, when barriers to entry are high it is not even easy to catch up with the competitors. In such a situation what is needed is to 'redraw industry boundaries so that what is now attractive lies outside the former barriers' (Hamel and Prahad 1994, 275). To do so there is a need for a vision about the future in order to follow a future-oriented corporate strategy for creating and dominating emerging opportunities and to become a leader in the field (Hamel and Prahad 1994, 22, 280, 288). The future-oriented strategy is therefore different from copying best practices or from strategic planning which is a series of tactical moves. Strategic planning is relevant to the situation where information about the market, the rivals and customers is known and remains unchanged. It involves marginal improvement in market share and the enterprise's position in the market (Hamel and Prahad 1994, 281–3).

In contrast, future-oriented strategy involves vision about the future and transformation of the industry to create new competitive advantage. Particularly where there are barriers to entry in an industry there is a need to reinvent the industry and transform its structure with new boundaries. The enterprise should gain the capacity to become different-*unique*: to do things that other companies find it difficult to do (Hamel and Prahad 1994, 33). To achieve this Hamel and Prahad (1994) argue that there is a need for the company to have unique 'core competence' in order not only to react to changes, but also to generate opportunities.

Core competences

A core competence is a more precise definition of economic competence. 'The economic competence of a firm is the sum total of its ability to generate and take advantage of business opportunities. It includes the firm's competence in all areas of its activity, whether defined by function…product, or market' (Carlsson and Stankiewitz 1991, 101). 'A core competence is a bundle of skills and technologies that enables a company [not a business unit] to provide a *particular* [our italic] benefit [value] to the consumers' (Carlsson and Stankiewitz 1991, 199) by becoming a leader in a range of products and services (Carlsson and Stankiewitz 1991, 197).Through its core competence a firm can contribute to the competitiveness of a range of products not only within the existing market, but also more importantly in new markets to be created by new opportunities in the future (Carlsson and Stankiewitz 1991, 201–2). To explain further, core competences are:

> Management's ability to consolidate corporate-wide technologies and production skills into competencies that empower individual businesses to adapt quickly to changing opportunities... Core competencies are the collective learning in the organization, especially how to coordinate diverse production skills and integrate multiple streams of technologies. (Parahald and Hamel 1990, 81–2, cited in Carlsson and Stankiewitz 1991, 101)

Competences 'are also about the organization of work and delivery of value... [They] are glue that binds existing businesses. They are also the engine for new business development. Patterns of diversification and market entry may be guided by them, not just by attractiveness of markets' (Carlsson and Stankiewitz 1991, 101). For example, miniaturization as a focus of business strategy is the core competence of Sony and optics, imaging and microprocessor controls are the core competences of the Cannon electronics company (Carlsson and Stankiewitz 1991, 101).

Hence a core competence is an intangible asset; it is a set of capabilities which are developed over a long period of time and it has a number of characteristics. It is the result of collective effort and it is firm specific and industry specific. Further, as development of capabilities and skills are based on education and research, they are also country specific, continuous, cumulative and more importantly a collective process, as explained before (see also Lazonick and O'Sullivan 1994).

Globalization and NSI

A view has been expressed that globalization has reduced the role of the national system of innovation and nation state in innovation, calling into question the 'technonationalism'. It is true that today, to a great extent, firms face a similar market situation in the domestic and international markets because of liberalization of trade and FDI. Nevertheless, while there are similarities, there are also differences in the NSI of different countries. Countries are different in their size, natural and other resource endowment, level of development, historical, cultural, political and socioeconomic structures. They are also different in their educational, training and R&D institutions, public infrastructure, concerns for national security, and the role of government in the economy and its objectives, policies and activities – all of which affect development of technological capabilities (see, e.g., Nelson 1993, ch. 16). In fact proponents of capability-building theory, as well as M. Porter (1990), have argued that intensification of global competition has made the role of home nation and national system of innovation more important not less (Porter 1990; Freeman 1995; Archibugi and Michie 1995, 1997, 1998; Nelson 1993).

Therefore, although the interaction of the NSI with TNCs is increasing, 'national policies for catching-up in technology remain of fundamental importance' (Freeman 1995, 57) and 'government action to enhance firms' competitive advantage becomes more important not less' (Archibugi and Michie 1997, 137). According to Porter 'competitive advantage is created and sustained through a highly localized process' (1990, 19). Similarly:

> [W]hether or not FDI and other international knowledge sources contribute to the performance of the local firms in developing countries, depends on local circumstances and capabilities of the firms on the 'receiving end', and when TNCs are not technologically active in the host country, knowledge transfer is not significant. (Fagerberg et al. 2009, 54–7)

In particular the emergence of new technologies and development in existing technologies has increased the importance of the systemic aspect of innovation and the need for government policies (ibid., 11). Thus globalization does not negate location entirely for yet another reason, that is, the importance of 'knowledge hubs' in competitiveness. An empirical study of East Asian countries shows:

> [T]he growth of knowledge societies will increase rather than decrease the relevance of location by creating knowledge cluster and knowledge hubs. A knowledge cluster is a local innovation system organized around universities, research institutes and firms which intend to drive innovation and create new industries… Countries and regions form an epistemic landscape of knowledge assets, structured by knowledge hubs, knowledge gaps and areas of high or low knowledge intensity… Knowledge hubs… and clustering takes place despite globalization and the growth of ICT… Knowledge hubs have…dynamics related to externalities produced from knowledge sharing and research and development output. (Evers 2008, 4)

The literature on the direct impact of globalization on innovation is scanty. There is some empirical work on the impact of trade liberalization and FDI on productivity of domestic firms and their entry and exit as well as the spill-overs of technology to domestic firms by TNCs. For example, a study of 11,500 firms in 27 Central European and countries from the Commonwealth of Independent States (CIS) has led to two main findings. The first concerns the negative impact of product competition (through trade liberalization) on innovation by domestic firms, particularly for firms further away from efficiency frontier. The second finding is that the 'supply chain of multinational enterprises and international trade [vertical relationship with TNCs] are important channels for domestic firms' innovation', and firms which have market power innovate more (Gorodnichenko et al. 2008, 194–226).[4] The first finding is not unexpected as the evidence on Latin American

---

4 In the case of the US and UK, a study of 23,000 firms indicated that entry by foreign firms had a positive effect on the productivity of firms which were close to the frontier of efficiency through its 'complementarity effects', but negative impact on the productivity of those at a distance from the frontier through its 'competition effect' (see Aghion et al. 2006).

countries is also in conformity with it (Shafaeddin 2005c). What is not clear, however, in the above-stated study, and in the literature in general, is the extent to which firms which are away from the frontier are among those which are in the early stages of infancy or among firms which have been established a long time ago but have remained inefficient. With respect to the second finding, the role played by the government in encouraging indigenous firm in their innovation effort as well as assistance provided by the EU authorities is not

Box 7.3. The literature on Triple Helix

The literature on NSI has been followed up by the discussion of three other models of innovation, that is, Mode 1, Mode 2 and Triple Helix. Despite some difference, they all emphasize the enhanced role of knowledge in the economy and society. Nevertheless, the nature of research and its organization, in different models, has also been the subject of some discussion. Mode 1 and Mode 2 deal mainly with the nature of research. In Mode 1, knowledge production is academic, investigator and disciplined based. In other words, it concerns 'basic scientific research' (Limoges 1996). Mode 2 is context driven, problem focused and interdisciplinary. In other words, it is concerned with applied research; a multidisciplinary team engages in research for a short period of time on an ad hoc basis (Gibbons et al. 1994).

There are some controversies on the empirical validity, conceptual strength and political value of Mode 2 and its usefulness (Hessels and Van Lente 2008; Etzkowitz and Leydesdroff 2000). Furthermore there are even some objections to the 'Modist' view of the nature and history of science (Feuller 2000).

Thus some scholars have introduced the concept of Triple Helix thesis (Triple Helix of university–industry–government). The Triple Helix model provides the social structure for the explanation of Mode 2 and its relation with Mode 1 (Etzkowitz and Leydesdroff 2000). This model is close to the NSI but with an important difference. In the NSI approach, firms play a leading role in innovation. In contrast, according to the Triple Helix thesis the universities play an enhanced role in increasingly knowledge-based societies not only as a provider of trained personnel but also as a source of technological development (Etzkowitz and Leydesdroff 2000). In the Triple Helix case,[5] there is an interaction among various players in the NSI through communications, network and other inter-organizational relationships, and the system is dynamic. The roles of the players are not fixed and each institution can assume the role of the other and the internal organization of each player also changes (Etzkowitz and Leydesdroff 2000).[6]

---

5 In fact Triple Helix (TH) configurations also envisage three models. In TH1 the state directs relations between industry and academic institutions (e.g. the Soviet Union). In TH2 the interrelation among the three players is loose (laissez-faire model, e.g. the USA); TH3 is the one where there is some overlapping among the three players and the system is dynamic. Usually when mention is made of TH it is usually TH3 that the authors have in mind as most countries are trying to attain some form of it.

6 For an extended discussion of the TH model see also Etzkowitz and Leydesdroff (1997).

taken into account. In the particular case of China, where both indigenous innovation and TNC involvement have been ample, basically government policies and measures as well as efforts of the domestic firms have been crucial to innovation (see Chapter 9).

Before ending this section let us refer to two points: the new literature on technology and innovation; and the possibilities of regional South–South cooperation by developing countries. The first issue is discussed in Box 7.3 and it does not nullify our analysis of NSI. Regarding the regional cooperation, as R&D for technological development is costly and developing countries lack the necessary financial resources, knowledge and skills, regional cooperation through division of labour and specialization in R&D and development of skills will be helpful. An example is attempt by the Association of South East Asian Nations (ASEAN) and China to cooperate in research on ICT activities for which they have envisaged the establishment of an R&D centre for telecommunications equipment (Shafaeddin 2010b).

II. INNOVATION BY FOLLOWERS AND LEADERS[7]

If we accept Schumpeter's definition of innovation, which implies 'elimination of old combination' and creation of a new one, we can distinguish two types of innovation: adaptive and proactive. Proactive innovation is the domain of leaders in technology development and adaptive innovation is the domain of their followers.

Adaptive innovation also involves elimination of the old combination practised by a firm. Such elimination would involve application of a new combination which may already have been practised by others. For example, the application of a new machine for the first time in a firm of a developing country and the process of learning to work with it should be considered as innovation even though the machine may have been used elsewhere previously. Similarly breaking with old habits, or the use of such methods of production as FMS by a firm of a developing country for the first time, may be regarded as a process and organizational innovation. Broadly speaking in developing countries innovation is defined as 'a process by which firms master and get into the practice of product design and manufacturing processes that are new to them, if not to the universe or even to the nation' (Nelson and Rosenberg 1993, 4). Thus, at the early stages of development, innovation is not geared to the behaviour of the firm at the forefront of world technology – although eventually they have to adopt proactive innovation at the forefront. '[L]earning of foreign technology, its diffusion, and perhaps its adaptation to local circumstances of demand or production' constitute the bulk of technological innovation at the firm level (Nelson and Rosenberg 1993, 509). In the context of developing countries anything new to the firm is innovation (OECD 2005). Thus the adaptive innovation can also take place in low-tech industries (von Tunzelmann and Acha 2004).

The proactive innovation entails the introduction of totally new methods, or combination, or what is referred to as 'frontier technology' in the literature. Nevertheless, even in this case one should distinguish between 'invention' and 'innovation' as far as

---

7 The following pages are based mainly on Forbes and Wield (2002).

product and process innovation are concerned. Invention is in the realm of science, or 'know-why', involving a new discovery. In contrast, innovation is in the realm of 'know-how', or the application of a new discovery or existing method for the first time. In other words, in business by 'proactive innovation' a firm applies the new discovery commercially to create value for buyers.

'Technology-leader countries are those which collectively define the technological frontier at any point in time and move forward... Technology follower countries (and firms within them) may be far, near, or even at the technology frontier for particular industries or sub-sectors, but are generally not involved in pushing it forward' (ibid., 14–15). The innovation task of a follower is to learn how to use an existing technology or to produce a product efficiently. Developing countries at early stages of development start with being efficient followers but they should eventually aim to join the leaders (Forbes and Wield 2002).

Being a follower does not mean, however, that its innovation task is easy or is confined to the adaptation of technology to local conditions. Access to all available technology may not be feasible as it is often controlled by proprietary holders. Even when the technology embodied in equipment is transferred the tacit part of the related technology may not be transferred, requiring development of local knowledge. As technology changes rapidly, catching up with the leaders requires that the indigenous technological capability (ITC) is developed at a faster pace than changes in frontier technology. The sheer adaptation and modification of technology requires local effort. Further, a follower cannot stop making the existing products more efficiently but needs eventually to develop new products to move up the international value chain.

Myths and Realities

The literature on innovation basically deals with the innovation by leaders. As a result Forbes and Wield (2002) argue that there is a lot of myth, confusion and misunderstanding about technological innovation in the context of developing countries. In their book *From Followers to Leaders* they provide a rare source of analysis of innovation in the context of developing countries as well as the necessary guideline, which is worth referring to at length. This section is mainly based on the content of that book.

According to Forbes and Wield (2002) the myths include: technology is the same as applied science; technological self-reliance is key to breaking away from technological dependence; more technology is always good and one should focus on R&D spending; high tech is the best tech, thus high-tech champions are funded; attention is focused on blueprint and learning, while adaptation and tacit knowledge are ignored or underplayed; the focus is on R&D, particularly R, rather than industrial innovation (Forbes and Wield 2002, ch. 1, particularly 8–9). Accordingly distinguishing between science, which is the realm of theoretical knowledge, and technology, which is the realm of production of technique to expand 'practical human possibility', the authors explain the question of innovation and technological development in the context of developing countries. They maintain that 'the aim of ITC building is to grow value-added' (Forbes and Wield 2002, 11) and that 'ITC is really about the ability of a particular firm or nation to be competitive by continuously increasing firm or national value-added' (Forbes and Wield 2002, 10). Subsequently the authors explain the forms of technology that have been built up, outline the dynamic of the interaction of factors in such development and apply the concept of 'process–product–proprietary grid' to explain the process of innovation over time (Forbes and Wield 2002, 184).

To explain, technological capability building in a follower firm initially requires ability in problem solving on the shop floor, reverse engineering, drawing, redesigning and improving products. Tacit and local knowledge is important in innovation but tacit knowledge is experimental, firm specific, activity specific, continuous and thus cumulative, as stated before. The competitiveness of a firm in a developing country at the early stages of development depends more on tacit competence than proprietary knowledge.

The ITC (indigenous technological capability) of a firm is influenced by the interplay of the following factors: transfer of technology from other firms/countries; endowment, i.e. education, entrepreneurship and culture; efforts in learning through learning by doing, learning by analysis (e.g. reverse engineering, or breaking up a process into its components and analysing each step), learning by explicit action (e.g. training) and R&D and learning to be internationally competitive; and finally government policies (Forbes and Wield 2002, 11–14). It is argued that effective technology transfer also requires some degree of ITC in order to be able to apply, adapt and adopt the technology to local conditions. The question is how firms organize themselves to undertake incremental innovation at the shop floor and how to upgrade further. Moreover in order to upgrade they need a vision of the future for which there is a need for technology strategy for innovation, which in turn requires investment in firms' resources and capabilities. How can that strategy be designed and what is the role of the government? We will return to this issue shortly.

Process–Product–Proprietary Grid

The process–product–proprietary grid shows the firm's current position and the path it follows to get there (Forbes and Wield 2002, 184). 'At any point in time the sum total of a firm's assets [resources] and capabilities defines its position' (Forbes and Wield 2002, 184). A firm in a developing country at the early stages of industrialization starts the dynamic process of innovation with building capabilities in process innovation on the shop floor by incremental innovation; then it moves to product innovation to compete on what we called 'nonprice attributes' and eventually it develops its own design followed by development of a proprietary product (patents, trademarks, copyright, own brand)/ process innovation. To achieve proprietary capacity requires distinctive knowledge, including tacit knowledge, management capacity and other competences. In all cases the firm aims at increasing value added per worker (Forbes and Wield 2002, 15 and ch. 9).

To explain, for a follower firm at early stages of development incremental innovation, particularly through process innovation, is to be given priority. Here upgrading means producing the existing goods more efficiently to reduce cost or quality through reorganization of the production chain, etc. In Figure 7.1 process innovation is shown moving upward in the South-West quadrant of the diagram. The technology applied could be a generic one (nonproprietary) transferred from abroad. Thus the transfer

Figure 7.1. The process of upgrading through innovation

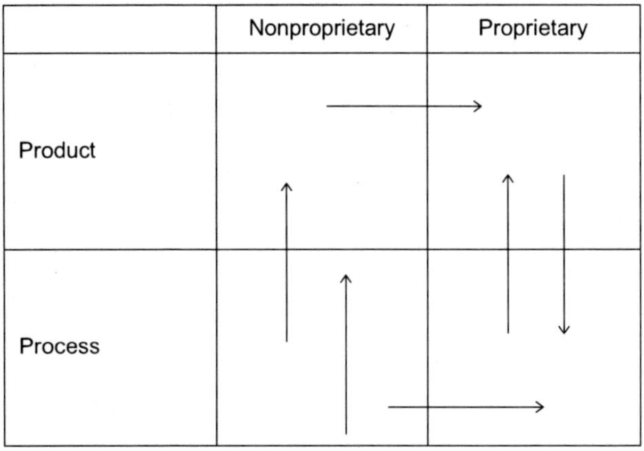

	Nonproprietary	Proprietary
Product		
Process		

Source: Adapted from the contents and illustration contained in Forbes and Wield (2002, 173–81).

and application of the technology itself is new to the firm and it is in a sense a major innovation. What sort of process a firm chooses depends on the nature of the industry, the environment in which it operates and its resources and capabilities for changes at the shop floor. Some of the methods of organization of production we have explained earlier, such as TQC, JIT and FMS, and eliminating waste and inventory management, are among some of techniques which can be tried, but they are not the only ones. One may also refer to changes in the relationship with suppliers of inputs, capital equipment, repair agencies and customers as well as efficiencies in transaction by using IT and software, etc. The efficient use of technology also requires not only learning by using, but also incremental innovation to improve on the technology (ibid., ch. 4).

It should be noted that to strengthen their internal capabilities firms need to combine foreign technology with their own experience and knowledge, which requires learning. The experience of successful industrializers, including NICs, indicates that the dynamics of learning at the firm level progresses through 'learning to produce [developing supply capacity], learning to produce efficiency [reducing production cost], learning to improve production [improving technique and organization of production], learning to improve products [quality improvement and design] and finally…learning to develop new products' (Forbes and Wield 2002, 81) through production innovation.

Thus the firm cannot stop at process innovation. As it develops, it also needs to upgrade further through product and proprietary innovation; to move from the South-West quadrant in Figure 7.1 to the North-West and eventually to the North East. The Mexican *maquiladoras* are example of firms which have been competing on the basis of low wages since the early 1970s without much attempt at product and proprietary innovations. As a result they have lost to the Chinese as TNCs relocated their plants to China, which at the same time has developed its own products and brands as discussed in Chapter 9.

Product/proprietary technology provides the opportunity to exploit rent. Product innovation allows production of a new product, but can be followed by incremental innovation to improve the product. One example is the development of the cine camera over time. Heavy cameras with a separate and heavy battery were the first generation of the kind introduced over forty years ago. Over time the camera has been developed first by integrating the battery into the camera, then replacing tapes with CD-ROM and more recently with hard disks and memory sticks. Meanwhile development has taken place for the use of smaller, light, replaceable batteries and miniaturizing of the cameras. Such product innovation, however, took place partly due to the product and process innovation in subtechnologies, i.e. parts and components such as software, batteries, etc. This process indicates the complexities of innovation systems and the relation and coordination of producers and suppliers which have been a norm, e.g. in Japan.

Further upgrading of proprietary innovation requires developing one's own design and brand. The design of a product need to match not only new technology in use, but also the taste of the consumers in a way that creates value for the consumer, thus contributing to the value added of the firm and country (Forbes and Wield 2002, 112–99). A new design may require both process and product innovation in order to capture the high end of the market segment where the income elasticity is high and price elasticity of the product is low.

Product innovation requires entrepreneurship, will, investment in assets (resources) and capabilities. A firm may start production of a new product by developing ideas for a new design followed by developing a totally new product of its own brand (proprietary product).

In an age of rapid technological change when established firms have monopoly power over technology through IPR, a firm cannot apply the nonproprietary (generic) technology, which is often low and old technology, forever. It has to upgrade further by developing its own technology. This does not imply, however, that initially it has to come up with a totally new technology or product. All it needs to do initially through reverse engineering and R&D is to make its own brand of an existing proprietary product monopolized by others. Fabricating chips for computers or mobile phones by China is an example (see Chapter 9).

Finally proprietary technology should follow process innovation until the firm can become a leader in innovation by innovating at frontier technology. The experience of Japan, Taiwan and the Republic of Korea provides good examples of firms which started being a follower by building around process innovation and incremental product innovation and eventually became leaders by acquiring proprietary capabilities. The process they went through was from OEM (original equipment manufacturer) to ODM (original design manufacturer) and eventually to OBM (original brand manufacturer). Acer, the Taiwanese computer firm, is also an example in this respect (Forbes and Wield 2002, ch. 5).

For leaders innovation includes a leap to new technological paradigm. Nevertheless, subsequently incremental innovation is necessary and important. The creation of hard disks for use in personal computers was in a sense a new technological paradigm. However, initially the capacity of the hard disk was small and had to be increased in order to allow more efficient use of computers.

In a follower firm thus the focus of investment in R&D activities should be initially on activities which contribute to catching up with rather than advancing the frontier technology. The R&D unit of the firm should be its learning unit, with access to external knowledge for sharing internally and working closely with people engaged on the shop floor. It works not only on building up product development capacity, but also on such issues as design and packaging. The advantage of introducing new design is that it needs little change in technology but it can contribute to value added. Value can be added by improving the 'product attributes' through targeting taste and 'emotional appeals – such as craftsmanship, elegance, symbolism and human fit' (Forbes and Wield 2002, 180). Market research and needs finding will be helpful in introducing ideas for changing design. R&D obviously requires employing qualified staff and entrepreneurship to act as agents of learning and change (Forbes and Wield 2002, ch. 6).

The Culture of a Firm

As innovation involves change, it also requires a culture of learning and change in the firm, as stated before. Learning through benchmarking and trial and error, reverse engineering, re-engineering and research are some of the avenues for change and building innovation competence. Sometimes the national culture may be an impediment to change but it is not unsurmountable. What is important is the will for upgrading and moving up the value chain and confidence in the internal capabilities of the firm. In developing countries usually the 'inferiority complex' and 'foreign is better' mentality are impediments to change. Self-confidence should replace the sense of backwardness, which calls for cultural confidence (Forbes and Wield 2002, 17, 94). If the attitude is that 'it is not invented here' [in the domestic economy] and 'foreign [made] is better', little effort would be spared to adapt the imported technology or come up with a new product or, eventually, new technology. Copying is not enough; creativity is required and should be rewarded. Thus the culture of both exploiting the existing knowledge and exploration, i.e. creative search for new solutions, is essential for innovative activities. The application of TQM is an example of exploitation for process innovation; R&D to improve existing products is an example of exploitation for product innovation. Building an international brand is an example of exploration for product innovation. The balance between exploitation and exploration depends on the stage of the development and position of the firm (Forbes and Wield 2002, ch. 8).

Strategy for Innovation

Catching up and forging ahead in technology and innovation also require government vision, and a firm's strategy and will. It is particularly necessary that the government has a clear vision of the future and the firms' will and the strategy to attain and maintain competitiveness. Upgrading requires an innovation strategy to move up the value chain by gradual improvement followed by proprietary innovation. To achieve this the firm has to build up its specific and unique assets (resources), particularly its intangible assets and its capabilities and core competences in utilizing those assets effectively, in order to differentiate it from other firms, i.e. to develop competitive advantage. The firm has to make a choice regarding its strategy for the future. What the firm will achieve depends on what it wants to achieve as well as its past and current position. For example, in its marketing would it prefer to follow, in the language of Porter, a cost-focused or a differentiation strategy? Would it concentrate first on developing its own design or its own product? Would the firm continue producing goods within the same industry or diversify to other industries? (Forbes and Wield 2002, ch. 9).

While the government has a role to play, in the end innovation takes place in the firm even if inventions take place elsewhere. Hence government policies should basically target the firms. In a sense one function of the government is to create and make winners by assisting selected firms and industries to build up their assets and capabilities. Of course concentrating on firm-level issues alone is not sufficient to create competitive firms. There is also a need for complementary policies such as industrial and trade policies (see also Chapter 8). Regarding firm-level issues, the government can create positive externalities for firms through provisions of market institutions, general and technical educational, training, back-up services, provision of technical and market information, as well as information about best practices elsewhere. It can also reduce transactional cost by investing in transport and communications systems and a reliable judiciary system for preserving IPR, etc. It can further provide facilities for R&D or get involved directly, particularly in basic research through universities and research institutes (see also Forbes and Wield 2002, ch. 9). Furthermore, as there is a need for selectivity in promoting competitiveness, there is a need for industrial policy. We will return to this issue in the following chapter.

Conclusions

In this chapter we have analysed the relation between innovation and upgrading of the industrial structure in order to achieve and maintain international competitiveness and at the same time enhance development. We have discussed general issues relating to innovation for countries which are at the frontier of technology (technology leaders) before analysing innovation in developing countries, i.e. the technology followers who need to join the leaders eventually. We have made distinction among product upgrading, process upgrading and functional upgrading. Accordingly, following Schumpeter, we have referred to various types of innovation required for upgrading including product innovation, process innovation, market innovation, product-service innovation and innovation in procurement. In each case innovation can be incremental, radical or systemic, i.e. a combination of incremental and radical- and techno-economic paradigms, that is, a set of incremental and radical innovations. Technology can be embodied in machine and equipment or may be tacit, which can be obtained by various types of learning and spill-over from one firm to another. Learning is a social process which is cumulative and collective, and is influenced, *inter alia*, by cultural factors.

We have explained that in contrast to the neoclassical theory, innovation plays a more important role than price in the competitiveness of firms and it is a driving force behind the growth of not only firms, but also a country. We have also shown that specialization and competitiveness based on static comparative advantage will be short lived and will not lead to industries with high rewards to factors of production. For this purpose continuous upgrading is required for which innovation in its broad sense of the term is essential. In this context we have referred to the systemic nature of innovation as implied in the national system of innovation (NSI), which is a development on List's ideas in *The National System of Political Economy*. NSI is concerned with generation and distribution of knowledge; it is a social order involving learning and skill formation and it is sector- and country specific. We have also explained that one implication of NSI is that, as it is country specific, the development of competitive advantage in a country depends on the development of the capabilities of its national firms. Such capabilities, we have shown, include, *inter alia*, entrepreneurship, R&D institutional build-up and, most of all, 'intangible assets' or what List calls 'mental capital', government policies and a firm's strategy for upgrading. Mental capital itself is a complex issue affected by a number of factors in addition to the technological capabilities and 'core competences' of a firm.

We have highlighted views expressed by Forbes and Wield (2002) regarding myths surrounding technology issues in the context of developing countries. At the early stage of industrialization, firms in developing countries may act as a technological 'follower' by undertaking adaptive innovation. In doing so they apply for the first time a method of production, process or organization that may already have been practised by others. Nevertheless, they have to join the technology leaders eventually. In other words, they need to develop their own technological capacity that eventually adopts proactive innovation at the frontier of technology. A firm in a developing country would start with capabilities in process innovation by incremental innovation, then it would move to product innovation and eventually it would develop its own design followed by the development of a proprietary product and its upgrading. The important point is that as innovation involves change, it also requires a culture of learning and adaptability, government vision and the firm's strategy.

Trade and FDI may, under certain conditions, make a contribution to the technological development and competitiveness of a country. Nevertheless, we have argued that M. Porter was correct to believe that intensification of globalization and global competition has made the role of home nation and national system of innovation more important, not less. The speed of technological change and the lengthening of the period of learning necessitate the nurturing of firms and industries in a developing country. Hence the role of government strategy on technological development, innovation, trade industrialization and FDI is important. We will turn to these issues in the following chapter.

8

GOVERNMENT POLICIES

The market mechanism will not allocate
the right amount of support to innovation
activity not least because of peculiarities of
knowledge as an economic commodity…
there is a divergence between private
incentives and social incentives which
government can correct. (Metcalf
1997, 411)

At no time, therefore, has the building of
indigenous technological capabilities in
developing countries assumed as much
urgency as it has today. (OECD 1992,
2759)

Introduction

Industrialization in developing countries requires catching up with industrialized countries
by building up and accelerating supply capacity, making the supply capacity efficient and
competitive in the internal and external markets, and moving up the value added ladder
and value chain by upgrading the industrial structure. The upgrading of the industrial
structure requires, *inter alia*, enhancing the technological capabilities of the country in
order to increase value added per worker. The implication of the neoclassical theory of
industrialization and growth is that developing countries will catch up automatically as
long as market forces are allowed to operate. In other words, in the long run GDP per
capita will grow at the same rate in all countries.

Do catch-up and technological upgrading take place automatically as suggested by
the proponents of neoclassical theory? The new growth theorists argue that differences in
economic development across countries are due to the differences in endogenous knowledge
(Romer 1986). As shown in Chapter 3, according to the proponents of capability building
industrial development requires development of endogenous capabilities.

We will argue in this chapter that a developing country wishing to develop competitive
supply capabilities in production and/or exports of manufactured goods and catch up with
industrial countries has to go through three phases: acceleration of the supply capacity, *efficient*
use of the *installed capacity*, and *upgrading* of its industrial structure. As we have noted earlier, the
market mechanism alone is incapable of achieving any of these objectives. An oligopolistic

international market structure, where large and strategically active firms enjoy competitive advantages *vis-à-vis* newcomers, with internal market failure and market inadequacies, with the existence of risks in investment in new activities, etc., all these necessitate government intervention in the process of industrialization, export expansion, upgrading and international competition. Nevertheless, the extent and the type of intervention may change over time as industrialization proceeds and the emphasis put on different policies alters as development proceeds.[1] At the early stages of industrialization policies should be geared mainly to the acceleration of supply capabilities. Subsequently the efficiency of the installed capacity requires the attention of policy makers before attempts are made for upgrading which requires, *inter alia*, technological policies. Such a process necessitates a dynamic and flexible industrial strategy by both government and enterprises.

To pursue our analysis we will first present, for analytical purposes, a typology of developing countries in the following section. Considering the importance of the supply capacity we will first review various theories of supply expansion where the role of market and government in general is discussed. Thus, after a brief review of neoclassical ideas, we will explain the catch-up and divergence theories, and present a Kaleckian approach to the acceleration of industrial capacity and development. Subsequently the need for trade and industrial strategy, and its modalities, for supply expansion, achieving efficiencies, competitiveness and upgrading, will be explained. Because of its importance, we will discuss technological policies for upgrading in a separate section. In dealing with government policies we will first outline the government policies that are necessary for the expansion of competitive industrial supply capabilities under an ideal situation, assuming that there is no external regulatory constraint on developing countries. Subsequently we will explain to what extent their implementation is feasible and to what extent they are limited by external constraints which limit their policy space. Such constraints are imposed by international regulations and the practices of international financial institutions, WTO and bilateral donors. Thus, before concluding the chapter, we will outline changes necessary in international rules to make them conducive to the development of a competitive industrial structure and its upgrading in a way that entails raising the standard of living of the population.

Typology of Countries

There is no such thing as a 'typical developing country'. The conditions of each country vary from the others in economic, social, political, historical, cultural and structural terms. So do their objectives and levels of development. For the purposes of our analysis, however, at any time we may distinguish three groups of developing countries. The first group includes countries with little or no industrial base. These countries are also most often characterized by low levels of development, poor infrastructure, both physical and institutional, and low levels of productivity in general. Further, in these countries goods and factor markets are underdeveloped or even missing. With the exception of

---

1 The need for government intervention is further intensified if governments of importing counties interfere in the free flow of trade or the established firms in the industrial countries are also supported by their government.

plantations and some mineral activities, often dominated by foreign firms, these countries also mostly lack modern enterprises. This group consists of most of the least developed countries, the majority of whom are located in Africa, and a number of other low-income countries. The key issue facing these countries is to develop their supply capacity rapidly while avoiding inflation. Hence for them the *acceleration* of the pace of supply capabilities, beyond what is achievable through market forces, is a challenging task.

The second group includes countries which have developed some industrial base previously through import substitution but whose industrial structure is not efficient and have often delayed the transition to export promotion of their import-substituting industries. Their across-the-board and rapid trade liberalization during recent decades has led them to deindustrialization or stagnation of their industrialization process (Shafaeddin 2006a). These countries also often enjoy higher levels of development in relation to the first group in terms of infrastructure, quality of human resources and enterprise capabilities. Moreover their market and the necessary institutional set-up are also more developed than in the first group. The second group consists of most Latin American countries, Middle Eastern states and some Asian and a few African countries. The principal problem for these countries is to make their existing industries efficient and competitive in both the internal and international markets and to deepen their process of industrialization.

The third group consists of countries which have already developed some export supply capabilities and penetrated into the international market for exports of their manufactured product. They have an established and relatively diversified industrial structure. Moreover they possess, relatively speaking, developed enterprises capable of developing and modifying their production, trade and investment, including foreign investment, strategies. This group is composed of a handful of developing countries (NIEs and second-tier NIEs) located mainly in East Asia. The key issue for these countries is to sustain or improve their competitiveness in international trade through continuous upgrading, innovation, productivity improvement and diversification of their production and export structure.

There are two points worth emphasizing at this stage. First a country may not necessarily be placed exactly in any of these categories, but close to it. Nevertheless, such a categorization is useful for the purposes of analysis. Secondly, although we have referred to a cross-section of countries at a point in time, any specific country, or to be precise any industry within a country, may go through the three above-listed phases over time during the course of its industrialization, export expansion and development. As already stated, these phases comprise the expansion of supply capacities, making the installed capacity efficient to prepare for the competition in the national and internal markets, and upgrading the industrial structure. Hence, instead of dealing with different countries in our analysis in this chapter we will concentrate on issues relating to different phases.

Theories of Supply Expansion

There are two main strands of theories which deal with the question of development of industrial supply capacities in developing countries: neoclassical (market-oriented) theories, and those which also allow for an important role for government policies. To proceed we will first briefly explain the neoclassical theory followed by theories of catch-up and divergence developed by Gerchenkron and Abramovitz. Subsequently the Kaleckian approach to the political economy of acceleration of industrialization and development will be presented.

Neoclassical theory

To the neoliberals, including proponents of the 'Washington Consensus', all that is necessary for rapid growth is the allocation of resources in accordance with the principle of static comparative advantage. Indigenous technological development has no place as technology and technological progress is 'manna from heaven' and higher productivity is the result of increasing capital per worker. In the language of the World Bank, as long as 'basics are put right' the economy will flourish. In other words, in addition to free operation of market forces, the accumulation of physical and human capital, stable macroeconomic conditions and rapid technological catch-up are important (World Bank 1993a; J. Williamson 1990). While technological catch-up and accumulation are regarded as important, it is not made clear how rapid technological catch-up can be achieved.[2] All that is implied is that the market forces will take care of the issue. Otherwise the role of the state should be confined to providing an enabling environment for the private sector and a regulatory framework for the operation of the free market and civil society (World Bank 1997; 2001). Accordingly, even if selective government intervention is theoretically justified it is not advocated because of the practical problems of implementation and the low capabilities of government machinery in developing countries (World Bank 1993a).

Theories of catch-up

Veblen (1915) initiated the discussion on catch-up. According to him, before machinery was invented technology was tacit, i.e. embedded in persons. So the transfer of technology to other countries required migration. With the invention of machinery, technology also became embodied in machinery, he argued. So it can be easily transferred to other countries which can purchase it. Therefore, the countries which purchase the machinery can catch up with others without having to develop the technology themselves (see also Fagerberg et al. 2009, 130–49). The Veblen view was adopted by neoclassical economists in their market-oriented approach to industrialization and development. Subsequently Gerschenkron (1962) and Abramovitz (particularly 1986 and 1994) developed the theory of catch-up with a different orientation. The first emphasized the role of government and the second the role of market forces.

Gerschenkron's theory

Gerschenkron's theory of catch-up is based on two main pillars: the dominant role of technology in industrialization and development, and the need for active government policies. Drawing on the experience of Europe during the nineteenth and early twentieth centuries, Gerchenkron (1962) referred to the implication of a significant difference between early

---

2 More recently the Bank implicitly has recognized the need for government policies on technological development.

industrializers and the latecomers for the economic development of the latter. In the case of early industrializers development of knowledge and technology took place slowly. In the case of the latecomers the availability of the stock of technology and knowledge, developed by early industrializers, provides an opportunity for rapid development. He argued, *inter alia*, that the more backward a developing country is (the wider its gap with advanced countries is), the greater the chance for rapidly catching up with advanced countries. This is because, he argued, the more backward a country is, the greater its possibilities for importing borrowed technology from more advanced countries will be. According to him to benefit from modern technology and economies of scale, the establishment of large firms is a requirement of rapid catch-up. The more backward a country's economy is, the greater the technology gap will be and thus the need to establish large plants and enterprises. Further, the expansion of interdependent industries and supporting infrastructure would provide synergies and markets necessary for sustainable growth – a proposition similar to the views of proponents of the theory of balanced growth. Such an expansion requires a proactive role from the financial system to facilitate investment.

Nevertheless, Gerchenkron also argued that backwardness could work somewhat as a double-edged sword; it could create obstacles to rapid development due to shortages of skilled labour and other complementary factors of production. It was also constrained, he argued, by the absence of risk-taking capabilities among private investors due to the prevailing social environment of the country. Therefore, he recommended activist government policies for directing resources to leading industries in order to provide industrial entrepreneurs with guidance and to develop the necessary infrastructure. The more backward a country, the larger will be its technology gap from the 'leaders' and thus the greater the need for government intervention in the economy. Although it is not explicitly mentioned, it is assumed that technology is readily available and costless.

Abramovitz and 'social capability'

Developing on and modifying Gerchenkron's views, Abramovitz (1986) introduced the concept of 'social capability' into the theory of catch-up. His starting point is that 'productivity growth rates tend to vary inversely with productivity levels' (Abramovitz 1986, 385); thus 'being backward in level of productivity carries a *potential* for rapid advance' (Abramovitz 1986, 386). Like Gerchenkron he states that the backwardness of a country provides an opportunity for rapid growth in productivity based on the use of borrowed technology: 'the larger the technological and, therefore, the productivity gap between leaders and followers, the stronger the follower's potential for growth in productivity' and output (Abramovitz 1986, 387). In contrast with Gerchenkron, however, Abramovitz stresses the role of market rather than government policies. In his 1986 article Abromovitz clearly argues that the free operation of market forces tends to guarantee the conditions necessary for the allocation of resources for the effective introduction of technology. In his view the realization of the effective potential growth of productivity depends on the ability of the country to realize its potential. The degree of realization of the effective potential in turn depends, according to him, on the degree of integration with the world economy, including policies to encourage FDI for the diffusion of technology, flexible labour market and suitable environment for investment through favourable macroeconomic conditions and social attitudes. Technological opportunity, in particular, encourages rapid growth of capital accumulation and enhances productivity and thus output. Further, both embodied and disembodied technology carry opportunities for modernization by efficient allocation of unemployed and underemployed workers in farming and petty trade (Abramovitz 1986, 387).

Like Gerchenkron, Abramovitz argues that social backwardness inhibits taking advantage of availability of the stock of technology for achieving rapid growth. Therefore for him, while the application of the available technology is a necessary condition for growth of supply capacity, 'social capability' is the sufficient condition. For him social capability is identified with technical competence and the level and quality of educational system, experience in management, organization and operation of large-scale enterprises, developed political and social characteristics that influence the risks, the incentive and personal rewards. Social capability is also identified with commercial, industrial and financial institutions for financing and operating large-scale business and a competitive market structure (Abramovitz 1986, 386–7; Abramovitz 1994, 25). Thus social capability includes not only educational levels and research laboratories, but also the socio-political process affecting educational system, infrastructure and the legal and regulatory apparatus of the government (Abramovitch 1962). Social capabilities should be 'sufficiently developed to permit successful exploitation of technologies already employed by technological leaders' (ibid., 390). Further, there are cumulative forces created by an interaction between technological development and social capabilities (Abramovitz 1994, 25). The lack of social capabilities can limit catch-up potentials (Abramovitz 1994, 38, 47).

Critique of Abramovitz

Abromovitz's formulation of the catch-up theory in fact implies that a backward country should already be developed to be able to exploit the technology 'employed by technology leaders'. To explain, looking at the factors included in his definition of social capabilities leads one to conclude that a backward country cannot in fact have the required social capabilities. Such characteristics are those which prevail in more advanced countries rather than a country which is at the early stages of industrialization and development. Developing countries at early stages of development particularly suffer from the lack of market institutions and entrepreneurs, and from market failure. In fact Abramovitz himself admits that 'the institutional and human capital components of social capability develop only slowly as education and organization respond to the requirements of technological opportunities and to experience in exploiting it' (ibid., 405–6). One may also add that markets develop gradually. If so, government action is required to remedy these shortcomings at the early stages of development.

In fact, in his 1994 article, drawing on the experience of Japan without undermining the role of the market Abramowitz gives some weight to the 'stability and effectiveness of government' regarding it as an element of social capability (1994, 35). Accordingly, in Japan as well as some other advanced countries, government not only facilitated technology diffusion and has provided support for investment, but also invested directly in the economic activities. For example, the Japanese government invested not only in the socioeconomic infrastructure, but also in the industrial sector, particularly heavy industries, provided guidance to the private sector and upheld the tradition of regulation and protection (Abramowitz 1994, 43–4). 'It was government that provided much of early impetus, and this was carried forward only later by the rising confidence of private business' (Abramowitz 1994, 44).

The modern version of the catch-up theory emphasizes the role of technological spill-overs to developing countries mainly through the operation of market forces. The role of government policies is considered important by Gerchenkron, the founder of catch-up theory. In contrast, technological spill-overs are regarded basically as a passive process by the modern version of the catch-up theory – although the role of the government is not totally ignored.

Another problem with Abramovitz's catch-up theory is that he implicitly assumes that technology of all kinds is freely available and there is no cost in its acquisition; that the world economic conditions, international market, operation of TNCs and policies of advanced countries have no negative bearings on the growth of a backward country.

The catch-up theory is based on the experience of Europe in the nineteen and early twentieth centuries as well as the assumption of free operation of market forces, availability of free and costless technology and its free diffusion as well as automatic spill-overs. Currently the international situation is different from that of the earlier period. The technological gap between the leaders and followers is greater, technology changes more rapidly, technology is under the monopoly of technological leaders, i.e. industrial countries, through patents and IPR, and the market is concentrated in favour of TNCs that own modern technology. Generally speaking the control of technology by its owners has increased over time. It is true that during the seventeenth-century to nineteenth-century period Britain often exercised its monopoly power on technology. It did so, for example, by prohibiting by law the exporting of machinery to colonies between the end of the seventeenth century and 1843, and by preventing the installation of the woollen industry in Ireland in 1699 (Reinert 1994). Imports of technology to the USA notwithstanding could took place (Fagerberg 1994, 12). Today technology transfer is governed by IPR, the transfer of which is either not possible, in certain cases, or is highly costly.

In order to catch up all early comers exercised industrial policies as well as commercial policies, though to a varying degree, for selective development of the industrial sector (Shafaeddin 2005b). Further, even today industrial countries justify protectionism when they consider free trade does not fit their interests, for example for the development of new technology and agriculture. Yet they preach free trade where they are dominant players in the international market (Fagerberg et al. 1994b, 14; Shafaeddin 2010c).

As explained by capability-building theorists, reported in Chapter 3, the latecomers can benefit only to a limited extent from technological spill-overs, and need to undertake serious efforts to develop their own capabilities, including technological and innovation capabilities as well as managerial and administrative capabilities of the government.

In short, acceleration of growth for catching up cannot take place automatically through the operation of market forces and a passive government role, particularly in countries which are at early stages of industrialization and development. One implicit assumption of catch-up theories is that technology is a public good and firms can choose different available technologies. In practice, while generic technology is available, mastering a technology is an 'organization-specific' investment and subject of learning. If so, 'there is nothing automatic about convergence', i.e. catching up (Nelson and Ewright 1992, 961). In fact in reality the economy of developing countries may diverge from those of advanced economies under the operation of market forces.

Economic divergences

In contrast to the catch-up theory which predicts convergence of productivity and economic growth among countries, a number of economists, including Myrdal (1957) and Kaldor (1981), argued that the market forces may result in widening the technology gap and thus divergence in productivity and growth against developing countries.[3] Myrdal argued that capital accumulation and growth in advanced countries, which involves positive cumulative causation for them, might encourage technical progress in these countries which in turn leads to further capital formation. In contrast, less-developed countries may be caught in the 'backwash' as capital and technology flows to advanced countries increase.

Assuming technical progress to be an endogenous factor, Kaldor argues that technical progress is a function of capital accumulation per worker because investment and learning were interrelated; that the manufacturing sector involves more learning than other sectors; that there is a positive relation between the rate of growth of productivity and the rate of growth of output of the manufacturing sector; hence exports of manufactured goods will allow increasing learning, growth of productivity and output and the competitiveness of the country (ibid., 7). Thus industries characterized by increasing return involve a higher degree of learning and cumulative causation (Kaldor 1981). Of course the implicit assumption made by Kaldor is that supply capabilities for entering the international market already exist or have to be developed.

Acceleration of Supply Capacity: Kaleckian Approach

Kalecki initiated a comprehensive theory of acceleration of growth as early as 1955, in which he envisaged an important role for international trade and government. He developed it further over time. In this section we will develop on his ideas, considering changes in the global economy during recent decades. To proceed, first we assume that the economy is closed. Subsequently we will introduce the role of foreign trade, foreign credit and FDI, and change in the terms of trade. Then we will briefly refer to the limitations of policy space by such external factors as conditions imposed on developing countries by IFIs and international trade rules.

Assuming that the objective of the government in a developing country is to accelerate the rate of growth of production capacity without inflationary pressure, there is a need, *inter alia*, for the acceleration of investment outlays and thus investment/income (I/Y) ratio. To do so the government needs to intervene in the economy to raise the propensity to save given the possibility of external financing. Nevertheless, even if investment funds

---

3 For a review see Fagerberg et al. (1994).

are available, the capacity to invest may be limited by the supply of physical resources, the supply of human resources and by institutional and political factors. Physical resources include infrastructure, capital goods, intermediate goods and raw materials, and consumer goods. Infrastructure is complementary to other resources. Even if other resources are available, the lack of infrastructure limits their use. Consumer goods may be divided into necessities (basic needs) and nonessentials (luxury). The increase in investment raises the demand for necessities (including food) because of the rise in employment and income. Human resources include both skilled and unskilled labour. Institutions may create, or fail to remove, constraints on growth, as we shall explain shortly.

The supply of capital goods is limited in a developing country, particularly at early stages of development. This is mainly because of inflexibility in the production capacity of investment goods due to the scarcity of investment resources and technological know-how. The possibility of expansion of raw materials and some necessities, namely foods, is limited because they are among 'supply-determined industries'. Supply-determined industries are those activities whose long-run rate of growth is limited by technical and organizational and/or institutional barriers, 'so that even a considerable increase in capital outlays will not help to raise their output at a high rate' (Kalecki 1963).[4] Raw materials are 'supply determined' largely owing to natural, physical, technical and organizational barriers. These barriers consist of limited natural resources (land, mines, water resources, etc.), the time necessary for adaptation of new technology, difficulties in training and recruiting skilled manpower, and long gestation periods.

Food is supply determined mostly because of institutional obstacles to development of agriculture. These obstacles are the feudal or semifeudal pattern of land ownership, where land reform is not implemented, and the lack of infrastructure, back-up services and other facilities even where land reform is undertaken. Such facilities include provision of finance, technical services, transport network and, above all, marketing channels.

Even assuming that there are some reserves in the production capacity of capital goods industries, the extent to which increased investment outlays can contribute to the acceleration of growth of industrial production without causing inflation is limited. It is limited by the ceiling on the rate of growth of skilled labour, necessities and other supply-determined industries. Increased investment outlays beyond that limit would cause a rise in the price of food and other necessities. Inflationary pressure would be felt. Unless wages follow suit, the result will be lower real wages, forced savings and redistribution of income in favour of the upper classes. If wages do increase, an inflationary spiral will become inevitable which will also adversely affect the competitiveness of domestically produced goods in the internal and international markets.

Such analysis indicates the importance of three factors in the acceleration of industrial supply capacity. The first is the need for foreign exchange for importing capital goods because of the limited capacity for production of these goods as well as that of raw materials and intermediate goods. The second is the importance of the development

---

4 In contrast, demand-determined industries are supply elastic and their output can be increased in the short and medium run more easily than that of the supply-determined industries (Fagerberg et al. 1994).

of agriculture and early development of industrial wage goods (necessities). The third is the important role of skilled labour and institutional factors. Let us briefly describe the role of international trade and external financing in remedying these factors in order to facilitate industrialization and growth.

The role of international trade

Foreign trade eases the ceiling on the rate of growth of supply-determined products through enhancing possibilities for importation. Kalecki regards trade as the 'joker' of growth: 'all the tensions and bottlenecks of such an economy [a developing country] can be translated into additional demand for imports' (Kalecki 1966, 1967). Consequently a higher rate of growth of industrial production and GDP will become attainable as a result of increase in the rate of growth of exports provided the necessary infrastructure and institutional framework for trade expansion are available. A 'favourable trade' will particularly facilitate the import of necessities and this will allow a higher rate of growth easing *inflationary pressure* (Kalecki 1970, 1966). The higher the rate of growth in investment, the more rapidly does the demand for imports of capital goods, raw materials and semimanufactured intermediate goods increase. So does the demand for necessities. In other words, the marginal propensity to import is an increasing function of growth of GDP; it will tend to unity as the objective rate of growth increases.

A favourable growth in export earnings will allow bridging of the gap between the rate of growth in the demand for necessities and industrial inputs and the rate of growth of their domestic supply. Therefore, rapid transition of the industries, established through infant industry protection and import-substitution, to the export market is important (see the following section) in order to increase foreign exchange earnings, given the limited possibilities of external financing. Nevertheless, the contribution of imports to growth is limited. First of all, for a given growth in export earnings it becomes progressively more difficult to increase imports of necessities because of growing demand for imports other than necessities. Secondly the growth of foods and some other agricultural products are affected adversely by the agricultural policies of developed countries as well as trade liberalization by the developing countries. Governments of those countries subsidize their exports of agricultural products heavily.

Thirdly the contribution of imports to growth of industrial capacity and GDP depends on complementary factors such as infrastructure, skilled labour, supply of nontraded supply-determined goods (e.g. utilities) and services, and institutional factors.

Fourthly the willingness of the public sector, or the private sector motivated by incentive, to invest is not sufficient for achieving the expansion of supply capacity. Willingness and/or incentive should be complemented by other physical and institutional factors described above.

The role of external financing and improvements in the terms of trade

We have already stated that the expansion of investment outlays requires increases in savings/income ratios given the availability of external financing. The increase in the propensity to save can be achieved, in theory, by the government through taxation of the well-to-do by imposing taxes and import duties on luxury goods. The availability of external sources of finance would, however, tend to reduce, *pro tanto*, the need for taxation of the well-to-do. A radical expansion of taxes is usually difficult in a developing country for institutional reasons: the required legislation is prevented by the vested interests concerned and even when tax laws are passed, collection is not easy and tax evasion is rampant. Under such conditions our earlier assumption of financing the acceleration of development through taxation of the well-to-do does not seem in many cases to be realistic. Hence external sources of finance could play an important role in financing development.

At early stages of development, i.e. until the infant industries become mature for transition into export promotion, external financial resources in the form of foreign credit and foreign grants take on crucial importance. An improvement in the terms of trade has an even more beneficial impact as it is achieved at no extra production cost. External sources of finance and an improvement in the terms of trade have two aspects: supply effects and financial effects. Not only do they increase the supply of necessities and other commodities, but they also add to the financial resources, i.e. economic surplus, available to the country for a given volume of output. Let us call the latter aspect the financial effect. Foreign grants, unlike foreign credits, do not involve repayments and debt services, but they may carry some political and economic obligations as a result of the conditions attached. An improvement in the terms of trade is more advantageous than foreign credits and grants because it does not involve repayments and conditions and yet it adds to the availability of foreign exchange. In practice most developing countries have been losing on their terms of trade in the long run until recently because of their dependence on exports of primary commodities. Even prices of traditional light manufactured goods exported by developing countries have shown signs of weakness in relation to prices of manufactured goods imported from developed countries. Thus the continuation of industrialization based on labour-intensive light manufactured goods is not a solution to the terms of trade problem of developing countries. There is a need for upgrading their industrial structure.

Let us also say a few words about the role of FDI, which also involves both supply effects and financial effects. The net financial effects of the inflow of FDI over time depends on the amount of inflows minus the remittance of the profits. Further, the TNCs can act as a channel for exports as they have the market knowledge and distribution network. As discussed before, the spill-over effects of FDI to the national economy depend on the capabilities of domestic firms.

Negative impact of external financing

While contributing positively to the acceleration of growth of supply capacity, reliance on external sources of financing, both borrowing and grants, beyond a limit have also some detrimental impact on the process of supply capacity building. The dependence on the external borrowings involves the accumulation of debts which have to be repaid through the expansion of exports. If infant industries are not rapidly transformed into export promotion and grants are not abundant, debt repayments will become a problem as the commercial banks do not continue to provide sufficient sources of finance. Consequently the government may rely on loans from international financial institutions i.e. the International Bank for Reconstruction and Development (IBRD) and the IMF and/or further grants from donors. Such sources of finance involve some conditions including currency devaluation, uniform (across-the-board, i.e. indiscriminate) trade liberalization, expenditure cuts, etc. These conditions are imposed through Structural Adjustment Programs (SAPs) of the World Bank and/or the Stabilization Program (SP) of the IMF or by bilateral donors. Such universal conditions might not necessarily be suitable to specific situations of individual developing countries at early phases of industrial development. The external sources of finance provided by the IBRD and IMF are used partly on repayment of debts and contribute partly to the reduction of the need for the taxation of the well-to-do. Hence the rich continue to benefit demand for and consumption of luxury goods, imported or home-produced, and luxury housing. At the same time across-the-board trade liberalization would contribute to a change in the structure of domestic prices in favour of imports of luxury goods and against domestically produced goods. The resultant increase in imports of luxury and other goods involves diseconomies impinging on infant (and other) industries. Each dollar spent on such goods deprives infant industries of the equal amount of imported inputs necessary for industrial expansion (Shafaeddin 1991, 1994). Failure to ensure that industries with large externalities could secure sufficient foreign exchange contributes to underutilization of the existing capacity and to slowing down of supply capacity building.

Impact of devaluation[5]

Of course a compensatory devaluation of the local currency could, in theory, re-establish the incentive for production of tradable goods, particularly exports. Nevertheless, in practice it would be ineffective per se to stimulate production and exports of manufactured goods for a number of reasons. First the impact of devaluation on production costs in the manufacturing sector, particularly for exports, is greater than for other sectors and industries because of its higher import intensity, which reaches over 60 per cent in certain cases (Shafaeddin 2009c, table 1).

Secondly devaluation results in uniform price changes over the whole range of tradable goods rather than for selected products. Supply response to prices is much lower when all the outputs of a sector are equally affected; it is stronger when relative prices increase only for one good or for a few goods (Streeten 1987). Even in industrialized countries there is some evidence that reallocation of resources from nontradable to tradable sectors, and within tradable from importable to exportable (and in the latter from traditional to new products), might be more responsive to targeted incentives such as subsidies than to exchange rate adjustment (Schydlowsky 1982, cited in Fontaine 1992).

Thirdly devaluation, as well as import liberalization, tends to turn the domestic terms of trade in favour of primary commodities and against manufacturing goods because of differences in the nature of price determination in the two sectors. Prices of primary

---

5 The following pages are based mainly on Shafaeddin (2005b).

commodities are demand determined in the international markets. As a result devaluation does not change their international prices – at least if the producing country is small – but increases domestic prices. In contrast, the prices of manufactured goods are cost-determined.[6] Hence devaluation decreases their international price but does not change their domestic price, except for the contribution of increased cost of imports, which can result in pressure on their profit margin (Shafaeddin 1991). In many developing countries devaluation remedies, to some extent, the previous bias against the agricultural sector; thus it can have a welcome positive effect on food production. It would seem, however, that cash crops benefit more than foods in many developing countries applying devaluation through Structural Adjustment Programs (Stewart et al. 1992).

Fourthly, at early stages of development the industrial base is small and the supply structure is rigid. Hence, while trade liberalization puts competitive pressure on the manufacturing sector, the compensatory devaluation cannot stimulate expansion of production capacity. The combination of import shortages, higher cost of imported inputs, reduced effective demand, as a result of contractionary macroeconomic management, could lead to a decline in productivity. While in the short run devaluation might increase exports by diverting domestic sales, it is unlikely to lead to the expansion of investment in the industrial sector (Shafaeddin 1992).

Fifthly devaluation could, for the reasons stated above, lead to serious inflation, reducing the prospect for real devaluation. In fact it has been estimated that for every 10 per cent nominal devaluation during the period 1980–87, in countries with per capita income of less than 400, there was only about 3 per cent decline in the real effective exchange rate (Shafaeddin 1993).

Sixthly, as inflation accelerates and the money income of the well-to-do is not taxed away, the availability of liquidity contributes to speculative hoarding and property speculation or a tendency for capital flight abroad. In contrast, the uncertainty created due to the lack of success in the liberalization process, import shortages, increases in the prices of capital and intermediate goods, inflationary pressure and the reduced effective demand are inimical to incentives for expanding investment in the manufacturing sector.

Finally currency devaluation by a large number of countries producing the same commodity, though it may lead to a higher output of the commodity, results in terms-of-trade losses due to the 'fallacy of composition' (UNCTAD, *TDR*, 2002), as exemplified by the case of tea and other commodities which constitute the major exports of LDCs (Bhaskar 1989; Gilbert 1988; Maizels 1988; Wattleworth 1988). It should be noted further that a large number of developing countries produce and export the same light manufactured goods. Hence, as they do, these products will also suffer, like primary commodities, from the 'fallacy of composition'; their international price will fall and the exporting countries will suffer from terms-of-trade losses even without devaluation (UNCTAD, *TDR*, 2002, ch. 4).

The failure of SAP/SP (particularly across-the-board trade liberalization and devaluation) to enhance manufacturing supply capabilities in low-income countries,

---

6 When the country is a producer of standard manufactured goods, the price of such goods in the international market may also behave like the price of primary commodities.

together with the expansion of production of primary commodities, will leave the countries concerned locked into production and exports of primary commodities. Terms-of-trade losses together with deindustrialization have detrimental effects on the prospects for acceleration of growth of industrial capacity and economic development of the country.

Inimical role of political and institutional factors

While there may be a pressure for implementing alternative reform programmes, the government of a developing country is not often in a position to do so for two main reasons: the dependence on external sources of finance and the lack of policy space and capacity to formulate those programmes rather than accepting a recipe from outside. Moreover, while producers have vested interests in opposing universal and uniform liberalization, there are also some strong vested interests to go along with it. These include some government officials, traders, etc. who benefit from trade in imported products and/or external financial resources in one way or another.

We have already mentioned the role of institutional and organizational factors in inhibiting the growth of agriculture and taxation of the well-to-do. Other institutional factors which prevent the operation of market forces and reallocation of resources include lack of education and training facilities, lack of credit market and marketing facilities, etc. The point to be stressed here is that universal and uniform trade liberalization efforts will fail not only because of their irrelevance in design, but also because of the inhibiting role of institutional obstacles. Moreover they may in fact also slow down the development of institutions by the government as the philosophy behind SAPs and SPs advocates the diminishing role of the government in the economy in general.

We have concentrated so far on the theory of acceleration of growth and described the inhibiting role of universal and uniform trade liberalization on the development of supply capacity because most developing countries are at the early stage of their development. It is not, however, enough to expand supply capacity; the industrial sector should also become efficient and competitive in the international and internal markets and be upgraded. Furthermore the fact that investment capacity is limited in low-income countries implies that all attempts should be made to ensure that the installed capacity be utilized efficiently. For the development of competitive supply capabilities and upgrading of the industrial structure there is a need for a different development strategy, particularly trade, industrial and technological policies. We will turn to these issues in the following sections.

The Need for and Modalities of Trade and Industrial Strategies

The need

As mentioned in Chapter 2 the international market structure dominated by large firms creates barriers to entry for firms of developing countries. Such barriers in turn create obstacles to the attainment of objectives of industrialization and development of a developing country over various phases of its industrialization and development; that is, expansion of supply, entry into the world market and upgrading. Generally speaking we have already explained that the barriers to entry related to the existence and strategic behaviour of established firms may involve two types of disadvantages for newcomers: relative cost and uncertainty. With respect to the cost it should be stressed that internal economies of scale, both static and dynamic, particularly the 'learning effects' at the firm level, provide an additional reason for disadvantages of a developing country *vis-à-vis* established firms on top of other disadvantages related to the domestic market structure and underdevelopment.

Uncertainty involves risk. So risks related to barriers to entry add to other risks facing a developing country firm. Even if a new firm manages to overcome cost-related barriers to entry, there is no guarantee that it could penetrate into the international market.

As we have already stated, the process of industrialization embraces three phases. At the first phase, when development of the production capacity is the main objective, a developing country firm may enjoy advantages in terms of wages and cost of natural resources. Yet even for sale in the domestic market it could face production cost/price-related barriers to entry when free trade prevails. This is because of other cost factors, low productivity and price and nonprice strategic behaviour of established firms, particularly if they practise transfer pricing and price discrimination. At the second phase, when achieving efficiency and entry into the international market is the main challenge, barriers to entry are mainly in the form of marketing and advertisement costs, the lack of experience in the international market, the lack of marketing channels and, more importantly, existence of product differentials caused by quality, time delivery, etc. – let alone protectionist policies of the importing countries. Finally, at the third phase when upgrading the industrial structure is the main concern, patented technology and technological learning, i.e. the learning cost of innovation, is the main barrier.

In fact, generally speaking the 'learning effect' is a common phenomenon at all stages so it is not related to only the first phase; it is crucially important in other phases as well. Moreover, not only does it affect the cost of production and sale price, but it also influences nonprice factors such as quality, delivery, product differentiation, etc. The experience of Republic of Korea, Taiwan and other East Asian countries, including China (see Chapter 9) indicates that capital accumulation alone is not enough; learning is crucially important but is not automatic. Learning in general and learning by doing and experience (through cumulative production) contributes to decline in a firm's unit cost of production (Dasgupta and Stiglitz 1985).

To overcome the barriers to entry at each stage a developing country firm should be compensated for the risks involved at that stage. The absence of perfect competition in the international market, caused by entry barriers, would require a second-best policy of intervention in trade and industrialization by the government of a developing country. In other words, faced with the existence and strategic behaviour of the established foreign firms, a developing country should also have a dynamic strategy at both firm and industry levels.

The compensation for risk provides an additional argument to cost-related reasons for infant industry protection. Thus we may speak of three layers, or phases, of infancy over the course of development of an industry, which could be referred to, for the sake of simplicity, as production infancy, export infancy and technological (or innovation) infancy.

The modalities[7]

In the neoclassical theory of competitiveness, trade and industrial policies have no place. The assumptions of perfect competition and full efficient market imply that the optimal allocation of resources takes place through the operation of market forces. Competitiveness is determined by the factor endowment of the country. Nevertheless, in practice there is a need for trade and industrial policies, as stated above. We will first outline the framework for trade and industrial strategy assuming that there is no external constraint on its implementations. Subsequently we will consider the limitations and possibilities of its implementation, taking into account international rules and regulations, particularly trade rules.

We have explained the elements of flexible and dynamic trade and industrial policies in detail elsewhere (Shafaeddin 2005b; 2009c). Here we will briefly review its main ingredients. To begin with, for the following reasons the process of industrialization should proceed on a selective basis at various phases of its development until the industrial structure is consolidated: scarcity of resources, including the government decision capabilities; activity specificity and firm specificity of skills and learning and other capabilities; existence of different learning and linkages effects; and different levels of externalities in different industries. Furthermore, if it is accepted that industrialization requires pursuing the principle of dynamic comparative advantage, the need for selectivity follows. Dynamic comparative advantage has to be created; hence one cannot by definition develop comparative advantage in all fields and industries. Even if development in all fields were desired, it would not be possible. Above all, based on past experience of both industrialized and developing countries, particularly in recent decades, it would be naïve to believe that across-the-board, rapid and premature liberalization, operation of market forces and competitive pressure and macroeconomic environment per se will induce firms to become efficient and competitive in the international market in such a way that they could raise the standard of living of their population rapidly (Shafaeddin 2005c, 2006b).

Thus development of supply capacity should begin with some consumer goods most commonly demanded in the internal market the production of which will also involve significant 'learning effects'. At this stage the government may even directly embark on investing in areas where the amount of investment and its related risks are too high for the private investors but the production process involves important external economies of learning and experience. The government also has to build up the necessary institution and infrastructure, and provide education and training to assist in enterprise creation. In particular, as it is more likely at this stage that the country has to rely on its factor advantages, investment in human resources in the form of education and training is crucial.

---

7 The following pages are mainly based on Shafaeddin (2005b) and (2009c).

Further, development of the agricultural sector is essential, where feasible, in order to provide wage goods, ease the pressure on the balance of payments and prevent inflationary pressure.

While the final products of selected industries are protected, import of inputs to these industries should be free of duties. Provision of protection to the selected industries should not, however, be provided without conditions and without a time limit. While some firms might be allowed to be established with no, or limited competition, the government should insist on performance in exchange for incentive, and sanction firms in cases where their performance is not satisfactory. Moreover, gradually, as firms develop their production capacity, the government should introduce or increase competitive pressure first by allowing new entrants to the field followed by gradual trade liberalization. In cases where economies of scale are important, particularly for entering the international market, however, the competitive pressure should not be introduced too early as it would be at the cost of production at an inefficient scale. One criterion for performance should be cost reduction and quality improvement.

As domestic capacity is developed in an industry, all measures should be taken for the entry of the firm into foreign markets rapidly in order to make the industry efficient and competitive in the international market. There is also a need for cost reduction and quality improvement. On the demand side there is a need for providing assistance to firms for obtaining market information and marketing channels. The pressure for improved efficiency should also take the form of gradual liberalization of imports of final goods. Nevertheless, as far as sale in the domestic market is concerned, the enterprises should know in advance that infant industry protection is temporary.

While the first group of industries go through the second infancy phase, i.e. for entering the international market, attempts should be made to use their export proceeds for parallel development of a second group of industries, again on a selective basis. These industries may include some other consumer goods and/or intermediate goods needed for the first group of industries. As the second group of industries matures in the production process and enters the international market, as appropriate, some sophisticated and durable consumer goods and some inputs to the second group of industries might also be added to the list for infant production.

As can be seen, after a while import replacement and export promotion go hand in hand but in different industries. This process could continue until an industrial base is established and some export capabilities are developed. During such a process, for each industry while government intervention in the production process is reduced, the role of the market is augmented and the responsibilities of firms are increased. Interfirm relations, through trade and industrial association, could be developed to help undertake such responsibilities. However, government intervention should be targeted at the second layer of infancy, i.e. at the stage of penetration into the international market. At this stage the related firms need to improve efficiency and quality to compete in the internal and international markets; but the cost disadvantage, external economies in marketing, lack of experience in exporting and marketing and risks related to entry barriers require what we call 'infant export protection' through export subsidy, tax holiday and/or any other fiscal incentives. Once again incentive should be provided in exchange for performance. One policy practised by Japan and some other East Asian countries has been, for example, to allocate more foreign exchange for importation of inputs to firms which perform well. A close government–business relationship for drawing and implementing the related rules and guidelines would facilitate such a process.

Obviously, infant-export protection should also take place on a selective basis at each period and, as the firm matures in exportation, the degree of protection should decline. Subsequently selected industries in the second group should be candidates for export expansion and lessening of protection at the production level.

Ultimately some heavy industries and capital goods may be chosen for expansion and eventual export promotion. The choice of machines may be influenced by the size of the country and type of existing industries.

To provide an example, if textiles are chosen as a first group of industries for industrial development in the first phase, textiles should be provided with some support and supplied with a free flow of yarns and machines. In the second phase the support for the production of the final goods should be gradually reduced, but assistance and incentive should be provided for promotion of exports of textiles. In this phase expansion of export of textiles can be accompanied by support for production of yarns. Ultimately assistance to exports of textiles should be reduced to zero as the industry penetrates into the international market. In the meantime textile machines can be developed domestically and possibly exported later on.[8]

It should be emphasized that not all industries which are selected for expansion could be necessarily candidates for export expansion. Nevertheless, this should not imply that providing assistance to an industry should continue forever; it should be made efficient enough that it could at least compete in the domestic market. As the industrial base widens, the expansion of investment in production and export capacity takes on more importance. The expansion of such capacity for production and exports of standard consumer goods is essential for initiating the process of industrialization. Nevertheless, this process should not be limited to production and exports of these commodities as otherwise the country would not be able to sustain its competitiveness in the international market. Further, it might suffer from terms-of-trade losses if a large number of other countries follow the same policy at the same time.

To avoid this industrial deepening should follow industrial widening. Industrial deepening requires the upgrading of products and the production process, and the introduction of new products and new varieties of the same products. This process would require technological innovation. At any rate, at the third phase of industrialization innovation requires the development of new technologies. At this stage R&D is essential and technological development also requires 'infant' protection or support because of barriers to entry and the existence of dynamic internal and external economies of learning and scale. We will turn to these issues in the following pages.

---

8 When a number of industries are developed in this manner over time, the related process is said to resemble 'flying geese'.

Technological and Upgrading Policies[9]

Because most economists were trained in neoclassical welfare economics, many are unwilling to accept that some micro-economic policy decisions depend on a significant amount of subjective judgement rather than solely on scientific analysis (Lipsey and Carlaw 1998, 438).

In this section we will analyse technological policies for upgrading the industrial structure in developing countries. After explaining the need for technology policy, a few conceptual issues will be described. Subsequently the impact of various types of technological policies on upgrading will be discussed.

The need for technology policy

The literature on technological development has focused on upgrading at the firm level in the context of developed countries. Except for upgrading the value chain, upgrading takes place mainly on the existing product or product category – although new products also come to the market every now and then. Even the upgrading of the value chain also takes place often in activities related to the same product.

As far as developing countries are concerned, upgrading takes a different form at the national level. In this case the upgrading of the production structure is a feature of the Schumpeterian approach to competition which implies mobility, that is, movement of factors of production from low occupation to high reward ones or upgrading from low-value uses towards high-value uses (see Chapter 3). In the language of Porter (1990) it is a shift from 'dog industries' to 'star industries'. As noted in the introductory chapter, Reinert (1995) regards upgrading as a shift from low-quality to high-quality activities. Although the jargon used is different the essence of Porter and Reinert's argument is the same: upgrading means entering into, or shifting from, activities which involve low rewards for factors of production (value added) to activities with high rewards.

In the neoclassical theory of competitiveness all activities are similar. In contrast, in the Schumpeterian approach different activities bear different rewards for factors of production and have different impacts on the national income. In the language of Schumpeter the neoclassical economics provides a 'simple' answer to the complicated question of economic development; that is, it recommends specialization in accordance with the static comparative advantage of the country. This means lethargy and lack of action by the government: let market forces operate and allocate resources in accordance with the factor endowment of the country. Nevertheless, the neoclassical answer to the question of long-run economic development of a developing country is not a 'useful' one. The continuation of specialization in accordance with the static comparative advantage, though it is initially inevitable, will involve 'competitiveness at a low level of development' if a country stops at such a stage. For catching up to high-quality activities there is a need for the creation of activities in accordance with the principle of dynamic comparative advantage in the long run, as stated before. As all activities are not of a

---

9 This section is based mainly on Hanson (1996b).

high-quality type, the country needs a strategy to allocate resources to 'specific' activities selectively, as discussed earlier in this chapter. In other words, development is an 'activity-specific' process (Reinert 1994, 1995); but to develop competitiveness at specific high-quality activities a reliance on market forces alone is not sufficient. There is a need not only for dynamic and flexible trade and industrial strategies as explained in the previous pages, but also for a dynamic and innovation driven, technological strategy as well as institutional and organizational strategies. Such strategies are irrelevant in the world of static comparative advantage and perfect competition. Before explaining policies for upgrading the industrial structure, let us clarify a few general issues regarding upgrading at the national level.

A few general comments[10]

According to Lipsey and Carlaw (1998, 422) 'the process of diffusion and innovation are intertwined'; most new technologies are improved and changed when applied at the firm and industry level. Government policies can change the pace of technological development through the provision of incentives or by altering the degree of concentration in an industry, the location of firms, policies on FDI and education and training (Lipsey and Carlaw 1998, 1). The government can also influence technological development and innovation through its industrial, trade and financial policies or through direct involvement in R&D. The evolutionary theory of technological development argues in favour of both functional and selective intervention, as explained in Chapter 3. It also distinguishes among three types of policies (Lipsey and Carlaw 1998): framework policies, focused policies and blanket policies. The first 'provides general support for one specific activity across all of the economy' (Lipsey and Carlaw 1998, 423). In other words, it is a sort of functional intervention applied to technology issues; patent protection and provision of subsidies and tax credit are two examples. Focused policies include those to support development of a specific technology for a specific activity, e.g. nuclear power. So it is a targeted policy. Blanket policies are a mixture of the two; they provide support to some specific activities such as R&D to viable firms or to projects with a chance of success (Lipsey and Carlaw 1998, 423). Blanket policies may have some advantage over focused and framework policies for a number of reasons. First, unlike framework policies, blanket policies may use multiple instruments, such as taxes, subsidies, credits, etc., to achieve a policy objective. Secondly blanket policies are context specific and can be made conditional. Blanket policies can be applied to change the element of the facilitating structure (e.g. public labs) used by firms for a specific activity such as R&D or by changing the internal structure of firms to alter the attitude of employees towards the use of new technology (Lipsey and Carlaw 1998, 443–50).

Any programme goes through stages of design, implementation and performance. Unlike the neoclassical model, technological change and competition are processes; technology is endogenous – not 'manna from heaven'. Thus technological development has a few characteristics: technology is largely embodied in a complex set of interrelated capital goods (including their components); there is no equilibrium in the technology market as

---

10 The following pages are based mainly on Lipsey and Carlaw (1998).

technology is changing constantly; interfirm competition prevails; both informal (within the firm and at the shop floor) and formal R&D are relevant; complementarities among related activities prevail, implying that technological change in capital good induces redesigning or reorganization of some of the other activities. Thus it involves externalities; there prevails bounded rationality[11] rather than maximizing assumption; technological development responds to incentives and economic signals (Lipsey and Carlaw 1998, 424–30).

The Impact of Technological Policies

Technological change (both product and process technology) requires and induces change in the 'facilitating structure' to make it fully operational; both technological change and the facilitating structure are influenced by government policies. 'The facilitating structure is the embodiment of technological and organizational knowledge' (Lipsey and Carlaw 1998, 430). It includes physical capital, human capital (intangible assets), the organization of production facilities including labour practices, the management and financial organization of the firms, the physical location of industries, industrial concentration, infrastructure, private financial institutions, and financial instruments (Lipsey and Carlaw 1998, 430). These factors influence the NSI either directly or indirectly. The realization of government policies depends on the capabilities of the government machinery embodied in the public sector institutions and the related government employees.

There are fundamental differences between the neoclassical theory and that of the evolutionary theory regarding technological development. In the neoclassical theory a generalized R&D subsidy may be justified if the social return of R&D exceeds its private return due to the existence of externalities which are assumed to be uniform across all lines of R&D. Therefore, only framework policies are considered optimal. In contrast, in the evolutionary theory, because of the existence of uncertainty, judgement rather than maximization behaviour is crucial in decisions to encourage technological development beyond what is achieved through market operations. There is a case for encouraging R&D beyond the level provided by free market operation. R&D and innovation are risky activities whose social benefits diverge from their private benefits. So government intervention is required to create the appropriate institutions and invest directly in R&D when it is necessary. However, there is no optimal level of R&D, innovation and technological change as technology changes under conditions of uncertainty. Hence subjective judgement is important (ibid., 16–18). There is also no optimal policy to allocate resources to innovation and diffusion of technology (ibid., 21). If this is the case, 'the potential pay-off from re-allocating resources to increased R&D exceeds any potential losses from socially misallocating resources' (Lipsey and Carlaw 1998, 438).

In the evolutionary theory the market fails to achieve a desired and attainable state, i.e. the unique optimal equilibrium considered by the neoclassical economists. Such market failure is regarded as another justification for government intervention. In this theory the

---

11 Bounded rationality is the property of an economic agent (e.g. consumer or producer) that behaves in a manner which is nearly optimal with respect to its goals as far as its resources will allow.

spill-overs are also very complex. There are spill-overs between technology, facilitating structure and economic performance, within technology, and within the facilitating structure (Lipsey and Carlaw 1998, 439). Hence such complex interlinkages and externalities have a few implications for government policies. First technology policy is linked to industrial policy, trade policy, institutional and organizational policies. Secondly selectivity in technology policy is important. Thirdly, in addition to the need for coordination and consistencies in government policies there is a need for a government–private sector relationship for consultation in the process of decision making.

Government policies may aim at changing the facilitating and policy structure to accommodate changes in technology. An example of the policy structure is change in the regulations of the educational system or infrastructure to facilitate the adoption of new technology. Changes in facilitating structure may also indirectly induce technological change. For example, integration and coordination of research activities of universities, public and private institutions and encouragement of the private sector to develop research facilities can contribute to technological development (ibid., 21). Nevertheless, successful implementation of any policy requires institutional competence of the government machinery.

Comparative advantages of framework policies, focused policies and blanket policies

Public policy assistance should be allocated among various activities and agents according to the externalities their innovation creates, even though such externalities are not measurable quantitatively. As externalities differ among various activities, a framework policy is less superior to focused (targeted) and blanket policy, except for generic technologies. Nevertheless, technological policy should not rely exclusively on focused policies because of some of the practical problems involved in such policies. These problems range from the lack of information, requirement of sophisticated administrative machinery and their cost, influence of the self-interest of politicians and the risk of conflicts with WTO rules (ibid., 444). Nevertheless, when these problems can be avoided or minimized, focused policies could complement framework and blanket policies in cases where specific need and externalities are identified (ibid., 445).

Lessons of experience suggest that the likelihood of success of focused policies is increased first of all when incremental technological changes should be given importance; in fact most technological changes at the firm level are incremental. Secondly policy for each type of technological change (incremental, catch-up or radical) requires changes (small, medium or large) in the existing facilitating structure. For example, a large leap in technology to achieve leading-edge developments in technology in the Japanese automobile industry required large changes in the facilitating structure. In contrast, incremental changes to catch-up in processing technology in an Indian trading company, or incremental changes in a leading-edge technology in the production of boats in the same country, required small changes in the facilitating structure (ibid., 446, table 1, 32).

The successful implementation of policies depends on whether the policy resulted in development or diffusion of a new product or process. Even if a policy fails, it might be regarded as worth having tried provided the failure was recognized in 'timely fashion' (ibid., 446). Then the failure could be followed by an alternative policy as part of a trial-and-error process in an uncertain world of innovation.

In order to increase the chances of success of focused policies a number of issues should be taken into account. First, as the outcome of innovation is uncertain and risky, ways should be found to reduce uncertainty and risk – although it cannot be eliminated. Usually large leaps (radical technological changes), focused policies and changes in technological paradigm are dangerous and very risky. Policies which require large leaps in both technology and facilitating structure are extremely risky. In contrast, incremental policies are less uncertain and less risky. In an uncertain world the process of trial and error requires flexibility to correct policies in cases of failure, and diversity in experiment is necessary. Further, 'exposure to uncertainty and risk can be reduced by exploiting the interrelation between users and producers' (ibid., 445). As indicated by the Japanese experience, the users can provide the producers with information on market demand and problems with the existing technology.

Secondly, in designing a technology policy multiple objectives should be avoided in focused policies. In more complex policies multiple objectives may be pursued if they are clearly prioritized and separate policy tools can be assigned to each objective. The design of a technology policy should be judged by its commercial viability rather than national prestige; the prestige is an outcome and not a primary objective. Further, policies and programmes should not be influenced by the vested interest of a political group or individuals. National interest is the key.

Thirdly, as changes in technology and facilitating structure are interlinked, policy makers should target both as they affect performance and outcome of policy measures. In order to reduce costs of innovation, policies and programmes should induce coordination and joint conduction of precommercial R&D, such as collecting technical information. Further, as different technologies involve different externalities, policies should be designed such that they maximize externalities by choosing technologies which have complementarities with the subtechnology of the main technology.

Finally the role of the market and commercial signals in innovation should not be ignored. In designing and developing policies the expertise and experience of the private sector should be utilized whenever and wherever available. The technology chosen should also be commercially viable. This of course requires public–private consultation (see Chapter 6). The balance between the role of market, enterprises and government is to be changed over time as explained in the introductory chapter. Interfirm competition should be induced. The government machinery for development of technological policies obviously requires reliance on expertise and in-house development. The government should always provide technical information and knowledge on best practices and disseminate them. The example of MITI/METI in collecting information on technology and providing it to the private sector is an example.

Possibilities and Constraints

The proposed policies explained in this chapter are relevant in an ideal situation where developing countries have the necessary policy space. As we have explained in Chapter 2,

Figure 8.1. The neoclassical approach versus the structuralist/evolutionary approach in technology development

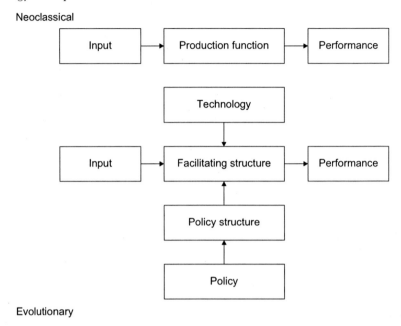

Source: Lipsey and Carlaw (1998, 453), reproduced with permission from the Public Works and Government Services Canada, Government of Canada.

in practice they are faced with constraints imposed on them through WTO rules, IFIs and bilateral donors. In this section we will first outline the remaining policy space available to developing countries. Subsequently we will emphasize that developing countries should resist further loss in their policy space whether through WTO, EPA or bilateral trade agreements. A few words will be also devoted to the need for information and knowledge about the remaining policy space as well as the perception of the government authorities regarding trade, industrial and technological policies needed for industrialization and also their political will to formulate and implement policies. Finally we will describe the need for the changes in WTO rules and practices of IFIs and bilateral donors to make them development friendly. Such changes are required in order to enable developing countries to develop their industrial base in accordance with the principle of dynamic comparative advantage and to be able to compete in international markets on that basis.

Before going further we make distinction between the minority of countries which are not yet members of WTO and those which are. Further, the member countries can also be classified into two groups: those with per capita income of less than $1,000 as well as least developed and other countries.

For a limited number of developing countries (fewer than 30 in early January 2011) which have not yet acceded to WTO what is important is not to submit to the pressure of member countries when they intend to impose WTO plus conditions on the acceding countries during the negotiation for accession. As stated before, WTO plus clauses or conditions are those which impose certain obligations on the acceding countries beyond what is contained in the WTO rules. Further, they should insist on long transitory period for the implementation of those obligations which they do accept.

Although WTO rules limit the policy space of member developing countries, they still allow them, particularly low-income and LDCs, some room for manoeuvring. In all cases the bound tariff rates are higher than the actual tariff rates. Therefore, they can change tariff rates on individual items within the range of the actual rate and bound tariff rate for specific products.

According to the Agreement on Subsidies and Countervailing Measures (ASCM) the least developed countries and countries with per capita income of less than $1,000 are allowed to use targeted subsidies, including subsidies linked to export performance. For other developing countries the payments of subsidies 'upon export performance' and 'upon the use of domestic over imported goods' to specific enterprises is prohibited, as explained in Chapter 2. Nevertheless, production subsidy to all enterprises in the same industry is not prohibited if they are not linked to export performance.

Member countries may also, under certain conditions, take some temporary trade measures under 'balance of payments' and 'safeguard' clauses. Under the balance of payments clause a country can impose temporary restrictions on imports in general if the surge in imports destabilizes its balance of payments (WTO Agreement, article XVIII). Similarly a country can take safeguard measures if import surge threatens a specific industry (WTO Agreement, article XIX).

Furthermore there are a number of other measures the member countries can take to support export and supply capability building or to upgrade their industrial structure. For example, fiscal measures such as cheap loans and tax incentives to specific sectors or industries are allowed and are being used by a number of developing countries (Rodrik 2007). Nevertheless, the fiscal incentives have been mostly used to 'increase production efficiency and thus [gain] the world market shares of existing sectors [e.g. in export processing zones] rather than entry into new sectors or markets' (Di Maio 2008, 26). The People's Republic of China is a rare exception (see Chapter 9). Similarly financing the promotion of science and technology modernization and provision of nonfinancial services to producers and exporters, encouragement for enlarging the scale of production in industries which are characterized by economies of scale, and support to SMEs are among other measures which can be, and in some cases are being, used (Di Maio 2008, 27–30).

In general the government can embark directly on activities which provide externalities to various or even specific industries. In this respect Lall (2004, 27) refers to supports for skill formation, technological development and innovation, infrastructural development for information technology and subsidies not linked to export performance. For example, there is no restriction on the direct involvement of the government in functional or targeted promotion of skills of the workforce through investment in education, training, knowledge development and in R&D activities. Such possibilities are especially helpful for countries which intend to upgrade their industrial structure, as indicated by the successful case of China (see Chapter 9).

Nevertheless, two points should be stressed. First, to utilize the available policy space not only is there a need for information on the availability of remaining policy space, and the political will and capabilities to formulate and implement policies, but more importantly there is a need for knowledge about the limitations of the so-called market-oriented industrialization. Secondly, drawing on the experience of successful industrializers, the existing policy space may not be sufficient for development based on the principle of dynamic comparative advantage and upgrading of the industrial structure. Thus there is a need for change in international trade rules, and the practices of IFIs and bilateral donors. We will briefly return to these issues shortly.

Political Constraints

The success in the formulation and implementations of policies for building up competitive industrial capacity is, to a large extent, the domain of political economy; that is, it depends to a large extent on the political will and the capacity of the government. Both the interventionists and neoclassical economists make extreme assumptions about the 'will' and 'capacity' of the government. The interventionists assume that the government is benevolent and competent. The neoclassical economists assume that the government group looks after its own interests, not the interests of the public at large, and that the government is inefficient. In reality the situation is more complicated. The political will of the government is the subject of political economy, for which a theory of the state is required. Unfortunately a satisfactory one is still not available. We wish, however, to stress that it is not possible to achieve an economic goal effectively without a suitable political environment (Meier 1993); that the political will of the government for industrialization, export expansion and upgrading depends *inter alia* on its structure and the vested interest of the dominant governmental group. The interests of the government might not necessarily coincide with the interests of the public at large. For example, the rate-of-time discount of politicians may tend to be higher than that of the community (i.e. they give more weight and preference to current expenditure than savings and investment). In this context one may differentiate the government 'indifference decision curves' from the communities' indifference curves (Kalecki 1971).

If political will exists, however, the information, knowledge and perception about the need for appropriate government intervention in the economy is required to correct, develop and complement the market on a trial-and-error basis. Further, the degree of government success would depend on its ability to analyse, formulate and implement policies and correct them over time. The successful experience of China is an example of a case where the combination of political will and development of the capabilities of government machinery and domestic enterprises has, *inter alia*, contributed to industrialization and international competitiveness before and after the accession to WTO. We will return to this issue in Chapter 9.

The Need for Changes in WTO Rules and Practices of IFIs and Donors

The experience of successful early and late industrializers indicates that the policy space currently available to developing countries is not sufficient. Therefore, the international rules and practices of IFIs and bilateral donors should change in order to become development friendly and allow them to compete in the international market in accordance with the principle of dynamic comparative advantage.

As stated earlier the economic philosophy behind WTO rules and practices of IFIs and bilateral donors is the theory of static comparative advantage. Accordingly universal and across-the-board trade liberalization imposed on developing countries forces them to compete in the international and internal market for products for which they have static comparative advantage. However, any market access gained for these products would be at the cost of their lack of diversification and development of their capabilities to upgrade their industrial structure in order to compete at the high level of development in the international market. Such capabilities will be necessary in order to enhance the level of income of their population beyond what is allowed by specialization, based on static comparative advantage in primary commodities, and resource-based traditional manufactured goods and/or assembly operations.

As long as this philosophy is not changed and the asymmetries and contradiction in the WTO rules are not dealt with, one cannot have much hope for achieving such objectives. What is needed first of all is that developing countries should have a clear concept of their industrial development strategy and trade policy. This is a necessary condition. However, it should be emphasized that any intervention might not serve the purpose of diversification and upgrading. The decision-making capacity of the governments of developing countries should improve to enhance the efficiency of the government machinery for policy formulation and implementation. While a country may learn from the experience of others, it cannot copy them; each country has its own characteristics which may be different from others to some extent. In other words, while some general principles may be common to various countries, development and industrial strategies are country specific.

The sufficient condition is that the rules of the world trading system should be changed in a way that would allow dynamic and flexible trade, industrial and technological policies with dimensions of space and time according to which the trade rules would:[12]

- Accommodate countries with different levels of industrialization and development at each point in time, therefore allowing 'Special and Differential Treatment' as a rule and not as an exception;
- Therefore, the concept of 'less than full reciprocity' should be taken more seriously as countries are at different levels of development and have different needs;
- Allow change of trade policy in each country as the country develops; hence a country should be allowed the necessary policy space for both selective infant industry protection and gradual and selective liberalization, when an industry reaches near maturity;
- For liberalization of the tariff structure, flexibility would dictate that only average tariffs (which may be even higher than the current average rate) are to be bound with significant dispersion (Akyüz 2005);

---

12 For details see Shafaeddin (2005b, 2010c) and Wade (2006, 10–13).

- Permit the use of export performance requirements by developing countries in TRIMS;
- Allow easier transfer of technology to developing countries by changing the TRIPs Agreement and revising the Agreement on Subsidies and Countervailing Measures and GATS to provide more policy space for developing countries;
- The member countries should not impose 'WTO plus' conditions on the acceding countries during negotiation for their accession.

Of course, such a reconceptualization of the trading system will not take place over night, but it eventually needs to happen. The problem at the moment according to C. Barshefsky, the former US trade representative, is that 'the developing world is not hearing what we are saying and we're not hearing what [the] developing world is saying. We are passing [each other] like ships in the night' (2007). Such an attitude is noticeable in the negotiation in the WTO during the Doha Round, particularly in the case of nonagricultural market access (NAMA) negotiation and regional bilateral trade agreements between developed and developing countries and the EPA. The proposals made on NAMA by developed countries, if accepted by developing countries, will further erode the policy space of developing countries for industrialization and development (Shafaeddin 2010c).

Practices of IFIs and bilateral donors

The change in WTO rules alone is not enough as often conditions are imposed on developing countries through the SAP and/or SP of IFIs or bilateral trade agreements and financial arrangements in which 'WTO plus' conditions are imposed on developing countries. Such practices should stop. In order to reduce their dependence on IFIs, developing countries may establish South Bank at the regional and international levels. The Latin American countries have already initiated such an idea and the establishment of their regional South Bank is in progress (Shafaeddin 2008).

Economic Partnership Agreement (EPA)

EU authorities attempt to impose trade and economic liberalization on African, Caribbean and Pacific (ACP) countries (mostly least developed and low income ones) on a reciprocal basis through the EPA. Developing countries should resist the pressure and avoid signing such agreements (some countries have already initiated the agreement in principle). Otherwise such agreements will be at the cost of the loss of their remaining policy space and thus deindustrialization, specialization based on static comparative advantage and low level of development. They will be locked into production and exports of primary commodities and, at best, some labour-intensive industries and assembly operation. To explain, generally speaking EU authorities are trying to impose a 'reciprocal' free trade agreement on ACP countries, which are by no means at the same level of industrialization and development of EU countries. Yet not only will ACP countries not gain in market access in the EU, but in fact they will also lose whatever preference market access they have in five to ten years. More importantly they will lose their policy space in a number of ways. First 80 per cent of their tariff lines will be subject to zero tariffs within 15 years. The remaining 20 per cent cover sensitive products, mainly agricultural goods, which are subject to severe competition from imports from EU countries which enjoy considerable production and export subsidies. Secondly during these 15 years tariffs will be bound; there will be no possibility for their increase or exchange with other tariff lines or imposition of new custom duties except for the sensitive products. At the end of this period tariffs will be bound at zero rates. Thirdly there will be 'standstill' clauses not only on import taxes, but also on export taxes. The latter will be also fixed and imposition of taxes on any new item should be negotiated with the EU. In other words, this clause also undermines the sovereignty of the ACP countries in policy making. Of course the loss of revenues due to removal of tariffs and reduction of taxes on exports will have a detrimental impact on government revenues and public investment. Fourthly the EU is putting pressure on ACP countries to accept WTO plus conditions and the so-called 'Singapore issues'. These include liberalization of financial and other services, capital flows, i.e. free inflows and outflows of funds, liberalization of FDI, restriction on government procurement for granting preference to domestically produced goods, and market access for EU firms for investment and procurement and competition policy. Fifthly, although some temporary infant industry support will be allowed for 15 years it is subject to very restrictive conditions. It is allowed only as a safeguard measure which is an ex post measure that can be taken when there is injury or a threat of injury to an industry. Further, to take the necessary safeguard measure, there will be a need for consultation with the EU! Even if it is agreed, it can be implemented for only two years. Such a measure cannot in fact be regarded as an infant industry support. Moreover it is in contrast with the EU's right to increase tariffs beyond the Uruguay Round rate in case of severe competition of imports with its domestic products due to the decline in import prices. Finally, the EU tries to impose most-favoured-nation (MFN) clauses on ACP countries. Such a clause will be detrimental to the expansion of regional trade and South–South trade. For example, any preference given to a member of a regional agreement or to any other country will be automatically applied to EU countries.

Anyhow, if such conditions are accepted by ACP countries they will lead them not only to deindustrialization and specialization at low-level development, i.e. specialization in production and exports of primary commodities and some resource-based industries, and, at best, simple labour-intensive industries and/assembly operations – it will also lead to further deterioration in their trade and balance of payments. Unless they resist signing the agreement, according to an African trade minister during a meeting on EPAs in Kigali in autumn 2010, the EPA places 'African countries in the mouth of a lion, in a repeat of the colonial experience' (*South–North Development Monitor* (SUNS) 24 November 2010).

There are some suggestions that there could be an alternative to the EPA with two main features: use of a development benchmark pegged to trade liberalization schedules and a 'goods-only bare bones EPA'. The first feature would imply that liberalization would take place gradually over time. After a period when the countries concerned attain the equivalent of a certain percentage of per capita income and per capita manufacture value added (MVA) of the EU and a certain degree of export diversification, they would eliminate tariffs on X per cent of their tariff lines. As they develop further and attain yet higher levels of income, MVA and diversification, the percentage of tariff lines subject to tariff elimination would increase. The process can be repeated with the same logic until full liberalization is achieved.

The second feature ('goods-only bare bones') EPA would imply that the liberalization agreement should cover only goods but without the inclusion of standstill and MFN clauses and the clauses on freezing import and export taxes. Further, it should include a more proactive infant industry clause and more favourable safeguards as well as a number of other less restrictive conditions (see South Centre 2009, 2010a, 2010b).

Two points are worth emphasizing regarding the above-stated suggestions. First the decision on the type of dynamic and flexible trade policy suggested above, in fact any type of trade policy, is the sovereign right of the governments of ACP countries. Therefore, negotiating with the EU on this issue does not make sense unless the ACP courtiers concerned will get, in exchange, provisions which would help their industrialization and development. Secondly, as far as preferential market access to the EU is concerned, if they were to agree with the current proposals made by the EU they would lose such preferential access in five to ten years anyway. Thus the question is whether keeping a few points in preferential tariff rate for five to ten years is worth trading off their policy space permanently. The average final bound tariff rate and trade-weighted average tariff rate of the EU on nonagricultural goods are 3.9 per cent and 2.4 per cent respectively. For products of interest to low-income countries the average is slightly higher. For example, the average rates for textiles and clothing are 6.5 per cent and 11.5 per cent, respectively and the maximum rates for both are 12 per cent (WTO, IT and UN 2008, tables A.1 and A.2). Low-income countries benefit from preferential market access schemes such as the General System of Preferences (GSP). Nevertheless, they have a supply problem and cannot even use this privilege to the full. For example, in 2001 five preference-receiving LDCs accounted for 98 per cent of total GSP exports to EU markets – out of which Bangladesh accounted for 81 per cent, Cambodia for 8 per cent and Nepal, LAO PDR and Yemen for the remaining 9 per cent (UNCTAD 2005, table 1). To develop their supply capacity some sort of support is required for their infant industries.

Moreover, even if the EU agrees that they keep the current preferential market access to it forever, losing their policy space for developing their industrial base is not worth such an insignificant preferential market access for a few years. This is because tariff preferentials in the importing countries are useful when the countries have some supply capabilities or they can develop such capacities. The proposed liberalization of trade, investment, etc. will cause problems not only in the way of ACP countries advancing their industrialization and development, but also will lead to their deindustrialization. If they lose their capabilities in production and exports of manufactured goods further, the availability of preferential market access can hardly benefit their industrialization and development. Already the Everything But Arms of the EU and the African Trade Act of the USA have had little beneficial impact on exports of the low-income countries because of their low-supply capabilities and the negative impacts of premature trade liberalization on their process of industrialization (Shafaeddin 2006b). In a nutshell the ACP countries should totally reject the EPA and those which have initiated it should not ratify it.

Of course achieving changes in international rules and attitudes and practices of IFIs and bilateral donors and the EU authorities is not particularly easy. Neither is it easy for the low-income countries to resist them. It should be noted, however, that the alternative is persistence in specialization based on static comparative advantage, i.e. competition in the international market at a low level of development. It would lock developing countries with low industrial capacity into production and exports of primary commodities, resource-based and traditional industries and, at best, assembly operation, and prevent upgrading of the industrial structure of those with some industrial capacity.

Conclusions

We have discussed the role of government in the process of building up competitive industrial capacity in developing countries, its constraints imposed by the trading system, IFIs and bilateral donors, and outlined the changes necessary in these respects. We have also explained that the process of developing a competitive industrial base in developing countries and catching up with industrialized countries requires building up and accelerating the supply capacity, making it efficient and competitive in the internal and external markets, and moving up the value-added ladder and value chain by upgrading the industrial structure.

Contrasting the neoclassical theory, we have argued that none of the ingredients of such a process, i.e. acceleration of the supply capacity, *efficient* use of the *installed capacity* and *upgrading* of the industrial structure, could take place automatically through the operation of market forces alone. The process of learning and development of endogenous capabilities necessitate government intervention in the processes of both production and exportation. Government policies should encompass, *inter alia*, dynamic and flexible trade and industrial policies as well as technological strategies complemented by strategic actions at the enterprise level. Accordingly we have presented a typology of developing countries according to their position in the above-stated three phases of industrialization. At early stages of industrialization policies should be geared mainly to the acceleration of supply capabilities. Subsequently the efficiency of the installed capacity requires the attention of policy makers before attempts are made for upgrading, which requires, *inter alia*, technological policies. Having reviewed various related theoretical arguments, we have explained what sort of policies are required at each phase of industrialization in order to achieve competitiveness at a high level of development in an ideal situation assuming there were no external regulatory constraints.

Subsequently we have explained to what extent the implementation of such policies is feasible and to what extent they are constrained by external regulatory issues imposed by WTO rules and by the conditions of IFIs and bilateral donors, which limit their policy space. We have further outlined necessary changes in international rules and practices of IFIs and bilateral donors to make them conducive to the development of a competitive industrial structure and its upgrading in a way that raises the standard of living of the population. The alternative is specialization in accordance with the principle of static comparative advantage and competition in the international market at the low level of development.

9

THE EXPERIENCES OF CHINA
AND MEXICO[1]

> The traditional role of the nation state is
> to support learning. (Lundvall 1992)

Introduction

China is on the road to competitiveness at a high level of development; Mexico is not. Why? To answer this question in this chapter we will briefly analyse the economic performance of the two countries before explaining the reason, which is related to the differences in policies they have implemented. We will show that China's economic performance in growth of GDP, MVA and competitiveness in the international market for manufactured goods has been unique during the last quarter-century or so. The country has managed not only to expand its exports of manufactured goods rapidly during the 1980s and 1990s before joining the WTO, but also to accelerate it after acceding to this organization. Upon acceding to the WTO, China relaxed protection of its manufacturing sector and subsidy of its exports. To do so, contrasting with Mexico, it has also managed to continue upgrading its industrial structure by enhancing the capabilities of its domestic firms while using FDI. The capabilities of domestic firms have been developed through active government policies despite China's commitments to the WTO for trade liberalization. While various government policies contributed to the competitiveness and upgrading of its industrial structure, technological and industrial policies played a major role. In the case of Mexico the country's performance in MVA has not been satisfactory despite its rapid growth of exports of manufactured goods until recent years. It has also managed little in upgrading its industrial structure. Further, the expansion of its exports of manufactured goods has also slowed down considerably during the last decade. It slowed down, *inter alia*, because it could not beat the competition from China in the international market despite its privileged access to the USA market through NAFTA and bilateral trade agreements with the EU, Japan, etc.

While Mexico followed the path recommended by the 'Washington Consensus' and neoliberals, China's industrial and development strategy has been close to what is regarded as 'neodevelopmentalism' in the literature. China was open not only to trade and FDI, but also to foreign knowledge and was willing and able to tap international technology through the engagement of TNCs. More importantly the government tried to develop the capabilities of its endogenous firms in technological development and

---

1 In drafting this chapter we have benefited from and, to some extent, drawn on Shafaeddin and Pizarro (2010) and Gallagher and Shafaeddin (2010).

innovation, aiming at competitiveness at a high level of development. Mexico in contrast was open only to trade and FDI; the in-house product and technological development were not a priority of the government. Thus the competitive environment, through trade and FDI liberalization, was not sufficient to move the economy up the value chain, accelerate the MVA and enhance its ability to compete in the international market at higher levels of development.

To continue we will first review the comparative economic performance of China and Mexico in terms of exports, MVA, GDP and their achievements in competitiveness in exports and production of manufactured goods. Subsequently the government strategy and policies of the two countries on upgrading and competitiveness will be compared. In particular the policies on technological development, R&D, human resource and training, and building up capabilities of national enterprises will be analysed. The role of FDI will be also considered.

The Comparative Economic Performance of the Two Countries

China and Mexico's process of industrialization and export expansion has shown similarities in a number of ways since the early 1980s. Both countries started economic reform, trade liberalization and transition from import-substitution to export promotion strategies around the early 1980s. Mexico acceded to the WTO in 1995 and China in 2000. Both then became open to and encouraged FDI, which engaged in assembly operation and export processing in manufactured goods, particularly high-technology products such as information technology IT and telecommunications products. Both countries have expanded the export of manufactured goods rapidly, particularly in high-technology products. Yet their economic performance is different in a number of ways, particularly in their growth of MVA and GDP, the upgrading of their industrial structure and their international competitiveness.

Table 9.1 shows selected indicators of the economic performance of the two countries for 1980–2009. Accordingly, first of all, both countries, particularly Mexico, experienced a high rate of growth of exports of manufactured goods during the 1980s and 1990s. In both cases the share of manufactured goods in total exports has increased considerably. In the case of Mexico the increase in the ratio of manufactured exports to total exports is more noticeable when exports of petroleum are excluded from the total.

Secondly, unlike China, the high rate of growth in Mexico's exports of manufactured goods was not accompanied by a high rate of growth of MVA and GDP (see also Figure 9.1). Moreover in the case of Mexico the growth in exports of manufactured goods slowed in 2000–2008, i.e. even before the emergence of the global economic crisis. In contrast, over the same period China managed to accelerate the rate of growth of its exports and continued its high rate of growth of MVA and GDP despite its increased exposure to competition from imports as a result of its accession to the WTO in 2000. The objective of the Chinese government in the current development plan is to achieve an annual average GDP growth rate of 7 per cent during 2010–15.

Table 9.1. Comparative economic performance of China and Mexico (1980–2009)

Growth rates:	China					Mexico				
	1980–90	1990–2000	2000–2008	2008	2009	1980–90	1990–2000	2000–2008	2008	2009
MVA	10.8	12.7	11.6	6.5	10.8	1.5	4.3	1.8	2.2	–9.8
GDP	10.3	10.6	10.4	9.6	8.7	1.1	3.1	2.7	1.5	–6.5
GFCF	9.5	14.1	712.1	10.4	23.1	–2.7	4.1	1.4	4.4	–10
Total exports	12.8	14.5	21.8	17.2	–15.5	5.9	16.1	7.2	7.3	–21.3
Exports of man.	17.4	16.7	24.4	17.3	–15.4	24.3	19.8	7.3	10.3	–11.5
Ratios	1980	1990	2000	2008	2009	1980	1990	2000	2008	2009
MVA/GDP	40	35.3	40.7	42.8	41.1	22	20.4	21.3	18.8	17.9
GFCF/GDP	35	34.9	35.3	49	43.8	27	25.8	26.3	26.3	21.7
FDI/GDP	0.17	0.66	3.34	1.51	2.62	1	0.91	3.04	2.24	1.44
Xman./total exports	9	71.9	88.2	92.7	93.5	11	43.3	83.4	72.9	76.5
Xman./total non-oil exports	–	–	–	–	–	(33.6)	(63.3)	(92.3)	(88.04)	(86.6)
Xman./world Xman.	0.8[b]	1.83	4.72	12.72	13.4	0.18[b]	0.47	2.97	2.04	2.06
MVA/world MVA	2.6[b]	2.97	8.33	17.01	17.7	0.24[b]	1.12	2.02	1.63	1.86
(Xman.–Mman.)/Xman.(%)[a]	40.8	4.7	35.1	45.1	40.1	–603	–128	–19.1	–12.1	–9.27

Notes: [a]Beginning of the period. [b]Average 1980–81.
Sources: Based on World Bank, World Development Indicators online, http://data.worldbank.org/data-catalog/world-development-indicators (accessed 10 July 2012); UNCTAD, *Handbook of Statistics*, http://unctadstat.unctad.org/ReportFolders/reportFolders.aspx?sCS_referer=&sCS_ChosenLang=en; ECLAC online (2010), http://www.eclac.org/cgi-bin/getProd.asp?xml=/prensa/noticias/comunicados/3/42233/P42233.xml&xsl=/prensa/tpl-i/ (accessed 10 July 2012).

Figure 9.1. Mexico's GDP and exports 1950–2010

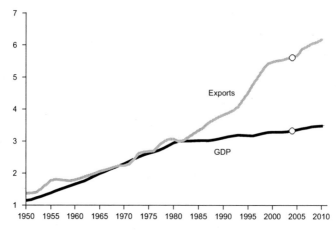

Note: The vertical axis is in log scale and the variables are in three-year moving averages.
Source: Palma (2003, 7) and updated for 2000–2010 by courtesy of G. Palma of Cambridge University.

Thirdly, in the case of Mexico although the balance of trade in manufactured goods, indicated by the ratio (Xman.-Mman.)/Xman, has improved over time it still remains considerably negative. In contrast, the corresponding ratio for China has expanded rapidly from 4.7 in 1990 to over 45.1 in 2008 before declining in 2009 as a result of the global recession. Such a difference in the two countries' trade balance is, to a large extent, due to the superior performance of China in increasing the domestic value added in exports of manufactured goods through the expansion of domestic production of parts and components used in assembly operations, as will be explained shortly. Consequently China has become not only a major player in the exporting of manufactured goods, but also occupies a significant place in global value added in manufactured goods. It is the second largest global economy in terms of GDP and exports, and its MVA reached nearly 18 per cent of world MVA in 2009.

Fourthly foreign direct investment, as a proportion of GDP, was on average greater for Mexico as compared with China, but, unlike the case of China, FDI crowded out national investment (Shafaeddin 2005c). The national gross fixed capital formation as a percentage of GDP declined over 1980–2008, let alone 2009, despite the rapid expansion of FDI. Thus the domestic investment/GDP ratio (FCF/GDP-FDI/GDP) declined from 26 per cent in 1980 to about 24 per cent in 2008 and over 20 per cent in 2009. In contrast, in the case of China it increased from over 34 per cent to about 47.5 per cent during the same period. The reason for such a differential in investment performance was partly due to the cut in public investment in the case of Mexico, which exercised Structural Adjustment and Stabilization Programs in the early 1980s and since then has followed economic liberalization à la the Washington Consensus (Shafaeddin 2006c, 2006a). However, this is not the only reason. Negative rate of growth in investment in the 1980s and its slow growth in the 1990s and during the last two decades (see Table 9.1) was also due to the lack of incentive of the local private sector to invest in productive activities due to competitive pressure from imports

(Shafaeddin 2006c). In the case of China not only did the government pay attention to public investment, but it also provided incentives to private investors and support for developing the capabilities of domestic firms. It has done so by undertaking policies which have led to the expansion of supply capabilities of domestic firms and to the upgrading of exports and the industrial structure of the country.

Outward orientation has made both countries vulnerable to changes in the world economic situation; in 2008 the X/GDP ratios for China and Mexico were 37.8 per cent and 28.5 per cent, respectively. Yet Mexico is more vulnerable to external factors than China because of its greater dependence on one country, the USA, for its exports. In 2008 over 80 per cent of Mexican exports were destined for the USA as against 18.4 per cent in the case of China (UNCTAD, *Handbook of Statistics*, 2010, table 2.1). As a result of a sharp drop in exports the MVA and GDP of Mexico declined by 8.8 per cent and 6.2 per cent respectively in the last quarter of 2008 as compared with the previous quarter and by 9.8 per cent and 6.5 per cent respectively in 2009. In the case of China, although exports have also declined and about 20 million workers were laid off in 2008, the country still showed positive MVA and GDP growth rates of about 11 per cent and 8.7 per cent respectively in 2009 (Table 9.1; J.P. Morgan, *Research Outlook*, 13 February 2009 and 25 February 2011).

More importantly Mexico has a lasting problem as it seems to have been losing competitiveness in the international market *vis-à-vis* China during the last decade. Its rate of growth of exports of manufactured goods had slowed down considerably, from 19.8 per cent in the 1990s to 7.3 per cent during 2000–2008, i.e. before the development of the recent global economic crisis. In contrast, that of China accelerated from 16.7 per cent to 24.4 per cent during the same periods. Moreover, unlike Mexico, the country managed to resume its high rate of export growth again in 2010.

The Development in Comparative Advantage of China and Mexico

In order to analyse the evolution of competitiveness of China and Mexico in the international market during recent years we will use the indicators of revealed comparative advantage (RCA). When applied to exports the RCA formula would be: $Rx = [Xij/Xj]$: $[Xwi/Xw]$. Accordingly, R, i, j, w, x stand for RCA, product, country, world and exports respectively. R is the ratio of the market share of a country (e.g. here Mexico or China) in an item to the market share of the country in total world exports.

- If R is greater than unity it implies that the country has *revealed* comparative advantage (CA) in exportation of the product.
- CR, i.e. change in R over a period (shown as the ratio of R for a period divided by R for the previous period) indicates whether the country is gaining CA in exports (when CR is greater than unity) or losing CA (when CR is less than unity).

One shortcoming of the RCA indicator is the aggregation problem, particularly when the indicators are applied at higher SITC digit levels. Intraindustry trade in differentiated goods and in parts and components are added up and not all their elements may show revealed comparative advantage in exports and/or production. Unfortunately the necessary comprehensive data beyond three digits are not readily available. Nevertheless, even at three-digit level the analysis would indicate the overall tendencies, particularly when data are compared for the two countries.

Tables 9.2a and 9.2b show the indicators of RCA for exports of China and Mexico for the export items of the countries concerned, which account for at least 1 per cent of total exports of each country in 2008/9. We have used the averages of the figures for two years to minimize the impact of the recession, which affects income elastic products such as IT items more than other products. The changes in RCA are also calculated for the period 1992/3–2008/9 and 2000/2001–2008/2009 in order to gauge the evolution of RCA.

According to Table 9.2a in 2008–9, first of all, China shows significant RCA in all manufactured items included in the table, mostly electrics and electrical products, except for (SITC 776 and 784). Even in these cases the country has improved its comparative advantage continuously and significantly during 1992/3–2008/9 as indicated by the value of CR.

Over two-thirds of the items included in the table are among capital- and technology-intensive (K/T) items, which enter in large volume in international trade. China is a major global exporter of the items shown in the table, particularly the first six (K/T) items. Further, most of these items are among demand dynamic products, i.e. products whose average annual growth rate of world exports exceeds that of the average growth rate of world exports for manufactured goods as a whole (which was 10.32 per cent during 2000–2008). Nine items, out of 29, are labour-intensive and one (petroleum products) is resource-based and capital/technology intensive.

Secondly China has improved its RCA in exports of all K/T items shown in the table during the 1992–3/2008–9 period, except for SITC 775 for the 2000–2001/2008–2009 period. In contrast, CR is less than one for all labour-intensive items for the 1992–2009 period (with the exception of two clothing items (SITC 846 and 843).

In the case of Mexico Table 9.2b shows that in 2008–9 the country also had significant RCA in exports of (K/T)-intensive electrical and electronic items listed in the table, most of which are also among dynamic products. Only one labour-intensive product (SITC 821) figures among the items with the RCA indicator greater than unity in 2008–9. Even in this case CR is less than one for 2000–2001/2008–9, implying that the RCA of the country deteriorated in the more recent period. Moreover the country lost some advantage in 6 items (out of 16) of its main K/T export products (SITC 778, 773, 699, 772, 713, 716) during 1992–3/2008–9. Further, SITC 781, 752, 782 are added to the list of export products for which the country lost RCA during the 2000–2001/2008–2009 period.

Some Qualifications: Comparative Advantage in Production

RCA in exports of finished manufactured goods discussed above does not necessarily imply that the country also has competitive advantage in its production; that the export item concerned involves significant value added; that the country has technological capabilities in production of the necessary parts and components. In fact the export of

Table 9.2a. RCA indicators for main export items of China (1992–3/2008–9): value $1,000

Products	VAL3 (000 US$) average 2008–9	Share in country 2008–2009	Share in world 2008–9	RCA 2008–9	Rank on RAC 2008–9	CR: 2008–9/ 1992–3	CR: 2008–9/ 2000–2001
752 Automatic data processing machines and units thereof	117,309,147	9.036	2.328	3.881	11	18.244	2.575
764 Telecommunications equipment, and parts	112,215,318	8.644	3.426	2.523	30	2.917	1.635
776 Thermionic, cold and photo-cathode valves, tubes, and parts	41,907,063	3.228	3.522	0.917	89	5.779	2.048
845 Outergarments and other articles, knitted	39,396,550	3.035	0.973	3.120	19	0.769	0.703
759 Parts of and accessories suitable for 751, 752	35,251,879	2.715	1.605	1.692	50	3.739	1.496
894 Baby carriages and toys	31,516,095	2.428	0.758	3.201	16	0.650	0.635
821 Furniture and parts thereof	31,220,048	2.405	1.036	2.321	35	1.967	1.246
778 Electrical machinery and apparatus, n.e.s.	30,403,000	2.342	1.455	1.609	55	1.931	1.028
851 Footwear	27,343,584	2.106	0.704	2.991	22	0.524	0.545
793 Ships, boats and floating structures	23,967,502	1.846	1.169	1.580	56	3.088	1.545
843 Outergarments, women's, of textile fabrics	23,931,391	1.843	0.188	9.805	2	1.608	2.321
775 Household type, electrical and non-electrical equipment	23,565,757	1.815	0.659	2.755	27	1.499	0.918
871 Optical instruments and apparatus	22,320,064	1.719	0.631	2.723	28	2.061	1.569
763 Gramophones, dictating and sound recorders	22,148,851	1.706	0.520	3.280	15	3.889	1.068
772 Electrical apparatus such as switches, relays, fuses and plugs	21,483,126	1.655	1.490	1.110	75	1.799	1.221
761 Television receivers	17,256,501	1.329	0.723	1.840	43	1.078	1.531
842 Outergarments, men's, of textile fabrics	16,813,776	1.295	0.600	2.159	38	0.330	0.463

(Continued)

Table 9.2a. *Continued*

Products	VAL3 (000 US$) average 2008-9	Share in country 2008-2009	Share in world 2008-9	RCA 2008-9	Rank on RAC 2008-9	CR: 2008-9/ 1992-3	CR: 2008-9/ CR: 2000-2001
749 Nonelectric accessories of machinery	16,671,018	1.284	0.213	6.025	9	14.842	7.221
658 Made-up articles, wholly or chiefly of textile materials	16,651,154	1.283	0.330	3.891	10	0.555	0.785
893 Articles of materials described in division 58	16,088,320	1.239	0.884	1.402	60	0.886	0.665
846 Undergarments, knitted or crocheted	16,007,984	1.233	0.185	6.652	6	1.606	2.223
771 Electric power machinery; and parts thereof	15,689,029	1.208	0.606	1.995	39	1.226	0.815
699 Manufactures of base metal, n.e.s.	14,990,187	1.155	1.014	1.138	72	0.952	0.874
674 Universals, plates and sheets, of iron or steel	14,704,841	1.133	0.387	2.924	24	33.763	13.439
751 Office machines	14,518,867	1.118	0.372	3.010	21	3.092	1.071
831 Travel goods, handbags, briefcases, purses and sheaths	13,562,320	1.045	0.289	3.616	13	0.579	0.633
741 Heating and cooling equipment, and parts	13,495,048	1.039	0.824	1.261	66	12.754	1.487
784 Parts and accessories of 722, 781, 782, 783	13,342,549	1.028	2.226	0.462	123	6.288	2.165
334 Petroleum products, refined	13,215,189	1.018	5.026	0.203	162	0.533	0.642
Total above	**816,986,158**	**62.930**					

Note: CR = Ratio of RCA for a period to RCA for a previous period.

Sources: Based on the UN COMTRADE database.

Table 9.2b. RCA of main export items of Mexico (1992–3/2008–9)

	VAL (000 US$) average 2008–9	Share in country 2008–9	Share in world 2008–9	RCA 2008–9	CR: 2008–9/ 1992–3	CR: 2008–9/ 2000–2001	Rank on RAC: 2008–9
333 Crude petroleum	34,517,528	13.384	9.903	1.351	0.459	0.931	40
761 Television receivers	20,203,655	7.834	0.723	10.842	1.679	1.371	2
764 Telecommunications equipment, and parts	19,180,875	7.437	3.426	2.171	1.368	1.104	16
781 Passenger motor cars, for transport of passengers and goods	18,226,216	7.067	4.403	1.605	1.048	0.813	29
784 Parts and accessories of 722, 781, 782, 783	10,574,761	4.100	2.226	1.842	1.169	1.189	24
752 Automatic data processing machines and units thereof	7,924,523	3.073	2.328	1.320	2.337	0.745	42
782 Motor vehicles for transport of goods materials	7,066,880	2.740	0.896	3.058	2.448	0.810	8
778 Electrical machinery and apparatus, n.e.s.	6,697,688	2.597	1.455	1.784	0.636	0.777	26
773 Equipment for distributing electricity	6,131,441	2.377	0.729	3.262	0.344	0.521	7
772 Electrical apparatus such as switches, relays, fuses and plugs	5,615,344	2.177	1.490	1.461	0.598	0.724	34
334 Petroleum products, refined	5,371,260	2.083	5.026	0.414	0.812	1.873	115
713 Internal combustion piston engines, and parts	4,190,442	1.625	1.075	1.512	0.508	0.787	31

(Continued)

Table 9.2b. *Continued*

	VAL (000 US$) average 2008–9	Share in country 2008–9	Share in world 2008–9	RCA 2008–9	CR: 2008–9/ 1992–3	CR: 2008–9/ 2000–2001	Rank on RAC: 2008–9
872 Medical instruments and appliances	3,998,882	1.550	0.601	2.580	1.403	1.298	13
054 Vegetables, fresh, chilled, frozen or simply preserved; roots, tubers	3,796,653	1.472	0.393	3.743	0.826	0.993	5
775 Household type, electrical and nonelectrical equipment	3,720,649	1.443	0.659	2.190	1.509	1.279	14
821 Furniture and parts thereof	3,683,393	1.428	1.036	1.378	1.101	0.681	37
971	3,404,725	1.320	0.938	1.408	6.881	11.607	36
699 Manufactures of base metal, n.e.s.	3,101,957	1.203	1.014	1.186	0.550	0.652	48
874 Measuring, checking, analysing instruments	3,044,434	1.180	1.123	1.051	1.666	1.058	56
716 Rotating electric plant and parts	2,593,601	1.006	0.652	1.541	0.658	0.661	30
749 Nonelectric accessories of machinery	2,590,486	1.004	0.213	4.713	5.240	4.428	3
743 Pumps, compressors, fans and blowers	2,586,176	1.003	0.810	1.239	1.489	1.375	45
Total above	**178,221,570**	**69.102**					

Source: Based on the UN COMTRADE database.

Table 9.3a. RCA indicators for main import items of China (1992–3/2008–9)

	VAL3 (000 US$) average 2008–9	Share in country 2008–9	Share in world 2008–9	RCA3 2008–9	Change in RCA, 2008–9/ 1992–93	Change in RCA, 2008–9/ 2000–2001	Rank on RAC3 2008–9
776 Thermionic, cold and photo-cathode valves, tubes, and parts	122,845,441	12.720	4.035	3.152	3.682	1.510	18
333 Crude petroleum	109,293,260	11.317	9.977	1.134	2.589	1.157	46
281 Iron ore and concentrates	55,424,930	5.739	0.756	7.587	2.310	1.659	4
871 Optical instruments and apparatus	35,826,357	3.710	0.573	6.469	12.129	2.385	6
583 Polymerization and copolymerization products	30,037,886	3.110	0.038	82.169	28.465	24.564	1
287 Ores and concentrates of base metals, n.e.s.	24,682,297	2.556	0.240	10.659	8.226	4.177	3
334 Petroleum products, refined	24,409,749	2.528	4.722	0.535	0.497	0.778	107
222 Oil-seeds and oleaginous fruit, whole or broken (excluding flours and meals)	21,715,938	2.249	0.446	5.039	45.865	0.962	8
772 Electrical apparatus such as switches, relays, fuses and plugs	20,585,141	2.132	1.490	1.431	1.538	0.829	36
682 Copper	20,206,915	2.092	0.829	2.524	1.102	0.834	22
764 Telecommunications equipment, and parts	19,369,460	2.006	3.579	0.560	0.254	0.347	102
728 Machinery and equipment specialized for particular industries	17,038,212	1.764	1.097	1.608	0.364	0.638	33
752 Automatic data processing machines and units thereof	16,299,412	1.688	2.266	0.745	2.910	1.213	84

(Continued)

Table 9.3a. *Continued*

	VAL3 (000 US$) average 2008–9	Share in country 2008–9	Share in world 2008–9	RCA3 2008–9	Change in RCA, 2008–9/1992–93	Change in RCA, 2008–9/2000–2001	Rank on RAC3 2008–9
778 Electrical machinery and apparatus, n.e.s.	16,078,593	1.665	1.427	1.167	1.250	0.872	43
874 Measuring, checking, analysing instruments	14,909,654	1.544	1.125	1.372	1.187	1.137	38
781 Passenger motor cars, for transport of passengers and goods	14,202,106	1.471	4.334	0.339	0.879	3.810	129
749 Nonelectric accessories of machinery	14,106,562	1.461	0.200	7.289	7.679	6.708	5
674 Universals, plates and sheets, of iron or steel	12,608,768	1.306	0.393	3.320	1.153	1.093	16
511 Hydrocarbons, n.e.s., and their halogenated or derivatives	12,477,420	1.292	0.543	2.378	2.285	1.064	23
759 Parts of and accessories suitable for 751, 752	12,115,736	1.255	1.616	0.776	1.438	0.630	82
582 Condensation, polycondensation and polyaddition products	12,075,190	1.250	0.599	2.086	1.635	1.074	26
784 Parts and accessories of 722, 781, 782, 783	11,796,222	1.221	2.157	0.566	1.183	1.274	99
251 Pulp and waste paper	11,449,994	1.186	0.325	3.652	3.838	1.216	14
792 Aircraft and associated equipment, and parts	10,289,520	1.065	1.309	0.814	0.574	0.847	78
Total above	**649,555,244**	**68.326**					

Source: Based on the UN COMTRADE database.

Table 9.3b. RCA of main import items of Mexico (1992–3/2008–9)

Products	VAL3 (000 US$) average 2008–9	Share in country: 2008–2009	Share in world: 2008–9	RCA: 2008–9	CR:2008–9/ 1992–3	CR:2008–9/ 2000–2001	Rank on RAC: 2008–9
764 Telecommunications equipment, and parts	21,826,617	8.241	3.579	2.302	1.567	1.811	13
334 Petroleum products, refined	16,488,800	6.225	4.722	1.318	1.639	1.615	45
784 Parts and accessories of 722, 781, 782, 783	12,214,453	4.611	2.157	2.138	3.382	0.807	17
776 Thermionic, cold and photo-cathode valves, tubes, and parts	10,122,428	3.822	4.035	0.947	0.710	0.561	84
772 Electrical apparatus such as switches, relays, fuses and plugs	8,441,422	3.187	1.490	2.140	0.839	0.700	15
781 Passenger motor cars, for transport of passengers and goods	6,536,815	2.468	4.334	0.569	4.546	0.992	135
583 Polymerization and copolymerization products	6,257,779	2.363	0.038	62.414	50.224	41.894	1
778 Electrical machinery and apparatus, n.e.s.	6,089,926	2.299	1.427	1.612	0.763	0.820	30
752 Automatic data processing machines and units thereof	5,774,065	2.180	2.266	0.962	1.498	1.472	83
893 Articles of materials described in division 58	5,265,205	1.988	0.902	2.203	0.686	0.692	14
749 Nonelectric accessories of machinery	5,221,738	1.971	0.200	9.838	6.286	5.694	3
713 Internal combustion piston engines, and parts	5,176,593	1.954	1.057	1.849	2.079	0.913	24
699 Manufactures of base metal, n.e.s.	5,002,179	1.889	0.985	1.917	0.539	0.510	21
341 Gas, natural and manufactured	4,633,421	1.749	n.a.	n.a.	0.000	0.000	214

(*Continued*)

Table 9.3b. *Continued*

Products	VAL3 (000 US$) average 2008–9	Share in country: 2008–2009	Share in world: 2008–9	RCA: 2008–9	CR:2008–9/ 1992–3	CR:2008–9/ 2000–2001	Rank on RAC: 2008–9
759 Parts of and accessories suitable for 751, 752	4,598,779	1.736	1.616	1.075	2.829	1.456	68
541 Medicinal and pharmaceutical products	4,488,450	1.695	0.898	1.887	3.453	4.154	22
871 Optical instruments and apparatus	3,921,082	1.480	0.573	2.581	9.366	2.445	12
874 Measuring, checking, analysing instruments	3,676,219	1.388	1.125	1.233	0.941	1.074	50
773 Equipment for distributing electricity	3,661,460	1.382	0.714	1.936	0.411	0.595	20
674 Universals, plates and sheets, of iron or steel	3,583,150	1.353	0.393	3.440	3.244	2.989	9
743 Pumps, compressors, fans and blowers	3,073,363	1.160	0.819	1.417	0.835	0.748	38
728 Machinery and equipment specialized for particular industries	3,050,301	1.152	1.097	1.050	0.764	0.808	73
011 Meat and edible meat offals, fresh, chilled or frozen	2,828,172	1.068	0.235	4.552	3.641	2.836	7
782 Motor vehicles for transport of goods materials	2,729,529	1.031	0.930	1.108	3.625	1.266	62
894 Baby carriages and toys	2,685,839	1.014	0.946	1.072	1.582	2.359	69
684 Aluminium	2,684,459	1.014	0.774	1.309	1.263	1.425	46
Total above	**160,032,248**	**60.419**	**37.312**				

Source: Based on the UN COMTRADE database.

the product may be the result of simple assembly operation, which is a labour-intensive activity, based on imported parts and components with little domestic value added and few domestic technological capabilities.

The application of revealed comparative advantage (RCA) to imports can distinguish comparative advantage in assembly operation from CA in production though it does not measure the extent of the value added involved. When the RCA indicator is applied to imports the formula will be:

$$Rm = [M\ddot{y} / Mj] / [M\,wj / Mw];$$

where R, i, j, w and M stand for RCA, product, country, world and imports respectively. R is the ratio of market share of a country's (here Mexico's or China's) imports of an item to market share of the country in total world imports.

- R greater (smaller) than unity for import of a finished product implies that the country has disadvantage (advantage) in production of that product;
- CR, i.e. changes in R, greater (smaller) than unity for finished products implies further loss (gain) in advantage in production of a product.
- In contrast, R greater (smaller) than unity for imports of a component implies that the country has CA in assembly operation (production of the component);
- CR greater (smaller) than unity means further gain in assembly operations (production of component).

Thus in applying the RCA indicators to the imports of China and Mexico at three-digit levels for the period 1992–2005 in an earlier study we have concluded that China shows significantly better performance in attaining RCA in production, in upgrading its industrial structure and in increasing the domestic value added in its exports of manufactured goods. A number of parts and components produced domestically were used not only in assembly operations but also for direct exportation. Thus their share in the production of manufactured goods for exports increased considerably. The country managed to increase valued added in exports, particularly in electrical and electronic products. It did so not only in those industries which had been initiated through import-substitution, but also in export-oriented industries established in the processing zones. The electrical/electronic products figure among demand dynamic and supply dynamic products (provide linkages with other industries). In other words, the country developed comparative advantage in the production of a number of parts and components and intermediate products, and it also improved comparative advantage in production of a number of other products (e.g. SITC 764, 776, 871, 759, 728 and 729).

Here in this chapter we have extended our analysis to a more recent period covering up to 2008/9. The necessary data are presented in Tables 9.3a and 9.3b. Accordingly China still shows disadvantage in production (advantage in assembly operation) of a number of finished K/T items (e.g. 776, 772, 728, 778 and 749), and P&C (749 and 674). Nevertheless, it has also further developed advantage in production of three other finished goods in more recent years (764, 752 and 781) and P&C (e.g. 759 and 784).

Moreover it has reduced disadvantage (improved advantage) in production of four K/T-intensive finished goods (728, 772, 764 and 778) and two components (682 and 759) in addition to a number of resource-based intermediate products.

Thus in more recent years China has been more successful in improving CA in the production of main items of finished goods than in the previous period. The country has developed comparative advantage in production not only in some electrical goods but also in some nonelectrical K/T-intensive goods produced basically by SOEs. Nonelectrical industries had been initiated through import-substitution, but their performance improved following economic reform and trade liberalization initiated in the late 1970s/early 1980s (Shafaeddin and Pizarro 2010).

Like China, Mexico has achieved RCA in production of a few industries which had been initiated through import-substitution (non-*maquila* industries); their reliance on imported inputs has declined over time despite some increase in imported inputs after NAFTA came into effect in 1995. When trade liberalization was introduced these industries were near the stage of maturity. Passenger cars (SITC 781) and data processing equipment (SITC 752) are such industries. The only other item for which Mexico shows RCA in production in 2008–9 is SITC 776. Otherwise Mexico still shows RCA in assembly operation in all other products shown in the table. This is the case despite the fact that some improvement in RCA is seen for its five finished products during 2000–2001/2008–2009 (SITCs 772, 778, 723, 713 and 773), but the last two are again those initiated during the import-substitution era. Mexico has also reduced its disadvantage in the production of two components (components 784 and 743) and one resource-based industry (SITC 699) during the recent decade.

Generally speaking the share of value added in exports of *maquila* industries (export processing), which were established after trade liberalization, has declined significantly over time despite the expansion of these industries in terms of the number of firms, employees and output. Further, the contribution of local inputs to exports has increased little, while the reliance of exports on imported inputs in the assembly operation has increased. For example, the percentage shares of local inputs to total output in *maquiladora* industries increased from 2.2 per cent in 1998 to only 2.7 per cent in 2006. The percentage share of domestic value added in total outputs declined from 36.3 per cent in 1974 to 21.7 per cent in 1998 and 20.9 per cent in 2006. In contrast, the share of imported inputs, which was 64.3 per cent in 1974, increased to 78.3 per cent in 1998 before declining slightly to 76.9 per cent in 2006 (Pizarro and Shafaeddin 2010, table 2). In other words, Mexico has achieved little in domestic production of finished goods and P&C in the export processing zones.

Generally speaking China, unlike Mexico, has managed to increase production of P&C rapidly. Disaggregate data on production of P&C and finished products are not readily available for China but available data on trade provide some indications. Table 9.4 provides the relevant data for SITC 7 items for recent years. Accordingly it is clear that in the case of China over 2005–9 the improvement in the balance of trade in P&C is far greater than the change in the balance of trade in finished goods. In fact the imports of P&C have declined in absolute terms during the same period while exports of corresponding finished goods have increased by 1.42 times.

Table 9.4. China's trade in P&C and corresponding finished products for SITC 7 (2005–2009) ($ million)

	P&C			Finished products		
	2005 (1)	2009 (2)	Ratio 3=2:1	2005 (4)	2009 (5)	Ratio 6=5:4
Total world						
Exports (X)	97,502	128,949	1.32	199,486	284,249	1.42
Imports (M)	86,185	70,883	0.82	172,618	181,134	1.05
(X)–(M)	11,317	58,066	5.1	26,868	103,115	3.84
(X–M)/M (%)	13.1	81.9	6.25	15.3	56.9	3.7
Total world excluding Hong Kong						
Exports	67,611	88,708.5	1.31	156,375	230,146	1.47
Imports	84,459	69,537.3	0.82	170,770	142,240.3	0.83
X–M	−16,848	19,172.8	n.a.	−14,395	87,905.7	n.a.
(X–M)/M (%)	−19.9	27.6	n.a.	−8.4	61.8	n.a.

Notes: List of parts and components: 7169, 759, 7649, 77129, 772, 77689, 784, 7929, 7139, 78539. List of corresponding finished products: 7169, 751, 752, 764, 7649, 771, 77129, 776, 77689, 722, 781, 785, 78539, 792, 7929.

Source: Calculated by the author, based on UN, COMTRADE database.

The main difference in the performance of the two countries in value added in exports and domestic production of P&C is due to the differential performance of the two countries in processing (assembly) operation. Unfortunately comparative data on value added are not available. Available data on the processing trade of the two countries are shown in Table 9.5. Accordingly it is evident that Mexico started its processing trade earlier than China. Yet Mexico's trade balance ratio for the sector $(X_p–M_p)/X_p$, which had been high in 1980 and increased for a while, has been declining since the economy acceded to the WTO and signed the NAFTA agreement. In contrast, in the case of China the corresponding ratio has improved very fast, despite some fluctuations in the 1990s, and has increased again in more recent years.

In short, Mexico has been less successful in enhancing value added in exports and gaining CA in production in processing industries as compared with China. As in the case of China, trade liberalization in Mexico led to improvement in the production and export performance of industries which had been initiated through import-substitutions. However, unlike China it has shown little success in gaining comparative advantage in production and enhancing value added in exports of industries established in export processing zones. Further, it has been losing its competitiveness in assembly operation relative to China as TNCs have been relocating plants from China to Mexico (Gallagher and Porzecanski 2008; Gallagher, Moreno-Brid and Porzecanski 2008; Dussel Peters 2005, 2007). The country's prospects for expanding value added *maquila* industries are not promising. Mexico has intensified its static comparative advantage in exports,

Table 9.5. Evolution of China's processing trade (1981–2005)

Year	Processing trade ($100m)		Ratios (%)			
	X_p	M_p	$X_p–M_p$	X_p/X_m	$(X_p–M_p)/X_p$	$(X_p–M_p)/M_p$
China						
1981	11.3	15.0	–3.7	5[a]	–32.1	–24.6
1990	254.2	187.6	66.6	55	26.1	35.2
2000	1376.5	925.6	450.9	61.5	32.8	48.7
2005	4,164.0	2,740.1	1,423.9	58.4	34.1	52
2008	6,751.1	3,783.8	2,967.3	59.2	43.95	78.4
Mexico						
1980	25.2	17.5	7.7	45.3	30.5	44.7
1990	138.7	103.2	35.5	49.8	25.6	34.3
2000	794.6	617.1	177.5	54.9	22.3	28.8
2005	974	756.8	217.2	55.6	22.2	28.9
2006	1,118.8	875	243.8	55.1	21.7	27.8

Notes: X_p = processing export; M_p = processing imports; X_m = exports of manufactured goods. [a] 1980.
Source: Based on *China Statistical Yearbook, 2006*, tables 18-4 and 18-5, and Bank of Mexico publications and internet site.

while China has managed to develop its export-oriented industries through a tendency to specialization based on dynamic comparative advantage, upgrading and increase in value added in exports. It is on the road to international competitiveness at a high level of development. What does explain the differences in the performance of the two countries? We will turn to this question in the following sections.

Government Policies on Upgrading and Competitiveness

In this and the following sections we will argue that China and Mexico have been acting differently in their industrial development philosophy since the early 1980s. Mexico has been following policies advocated by neoliberals and neoliberal institutions which see a very limited role for the state in economic activities for integrating into the world economy. In contrast, China has followed a proactive strategy for its globalization pursuits. Mexico's route to international integration has come at the expense of technological development, industrial learning and growth of MVA; China's proactive approach has contributed to a process of technological development, growth of MVA, development of the capabilities of domestic firms and upgrading its industrial structure.

Changes in Mexican industrial strategy since the early 1980s

Since the early 1950s the objective of the government has been to industrialize the country by developing its technological and industrial capabilities. Nevertheless, its industrial and developmental strategies have changed. Until the early 1980s the country followed a government-led model of industrial learning based on import-substitution strategy. Following the balance-of-payments crisis of the early 1980s, Mexico's industrial strategy changed to market-oriented policies and outwards-orientation trade and industrial strategies under pressure from international financial institutions (IFIs) which imposed SAP and SP on the country. Mexico had also established export-processing zones, called *maquiladoras*, for production for the international market in the mid 1960s. *Maquiladoras* included electronics and nonelectrical machinery, some automotive industry and apparel. Nevertheless, import-substitution (IS) was the dominant strategy of the government until the early 1980s.

Although the import-substitution strategy contributed to learning to some extent, it prolonged too much. Hence, like other countries which followed traditional import-substitution strategies too long, Mexico faced deadlock as it had to rely more and more on imports of intermediate products for production mainly for the domestic market. It lacked the ability to penetrate the international market because of its lack of international competitiveness.

In the early 1980s Mexico aimed to create a favourable environment for FDI believing that it would bring technological know-how that would spill over into the whole economy. The government also abolished all subsidies and price controls, privatized most SOEs and provided market-based uniform incentives to all industries and firms. Such a neoliberal approach to industrialization was intensified in the late 1980s. Mexico acceded to the WTO in 1995; it also signed the NAFTA agreement in the same year. Further, it has also signed a number of other free trade and investment agreements (42 as of 2008), including one with the EU and Japan since 1985. The government thought that NAFTA in particular would allow it privileged access to the USA market and the accession to WTO would facilitate its integration into the global economy. Such development towards an open door policy and reduced government role was believed would help Mexico's process of industrialization and international competitiveness.

The government has in fact an industrial strategy the objectives of which are set by it through a national development plan (NDP), and the sectoral plan of the Ministry of Economy. The development of 'strategic sectors' in particular and SMEs in general was to be supported by the government. Strategic sectors included aerospace, automotive, electrical and electronics, energy, biotechnology, software, IT, logistics and tourism (Baz et al. 2010, 9). Such plans were to encompass the vision for the country's development.

Nevertheless, generally speaking, the development strategy including the industrial strategy of the country suffers from a number of deficiencies basically because of the dominant neoliberal economic philosophy. First of all there is a lack of clear vision for its industrialization and development (Baz et al. 2010, 9) beyond the policy of openness or a consensus on what is required to be done in order to achieve development and industrial goals. There are also inefficiencies in both programme design and application hampering industrialization and development. The government objective was to increase the output value/value added ratio of export products from 10 in 1980 to 18 in 1995 for the manufacturing sector as a whole. The actual figure for the *maquila* sector was 635 in 1995 and 864 in 2000 respectively. For the non-*maquila* sector the ratio went up to 150 in 1995 before falling slightly to over 100 in 2000 (Palma 2003, 28–9). In other words,

Box 9.1. Information and communications technology (ICT) industries: Mexico

The Mexican government targeted the computer industry in the late 1970s as part of the strategy of the National Council on Science and Technology (CONACYT) to increase Mexico's national self-sufficiency in technology. CONACYT established the PC Programme (Programa de Computadoras) to develop a domestic computer industry (supported by the surrounding electronics industry) that could not only serve the domestic market, but also emerge as a key exporter for Mexico.

TNCs were limited to 49 per cent foreign ownership of firms in the sector. They had to invest between 3 and 6 per cent of gross sales in R&D and create research centres and training programmes. Domestic parts and components had to account for at least 45 per cent of value added for personal computers and 35 per cent for mini-computers. New Mexican-owned firms could receive fiscal credits and low-interest loans from development banks. In search of domestic markets and export platforms the foreign firms that came in included IBM, Hewlett Packard, Digital, NCR, Tandem and Wang. They were the leaders and accounted for 63 per cent of all computer production. The other foreign firms were responsible for approximately 18 per cent and wholly owned Mexican firms made up another 18 per cent.

The hub of high-technology exports became the western state of Jalisco (specifically the Guadalajara city region) and other regions of the country, particularly in the US–Mexico border region (in the case of TV monitors), and surrounding Mexico City (in the case of electronic appliances). Guadalajara was the ideal region for high-tech FDI, as it had a lower wage average and was characterized by weak unions and proximity to the US. Furthermore, there exist five major universities and numerous technical schools and industrial parks that can host research activities and educate and train the necessary skilled workforce (Gallagher and Zarsky 2007).

What is more the government adopted a number of policies to attract TNCs to Mexico. At the national level one programme (called PITEX) allows firms to import their inputs duty-free as long as more than 65 per cent of their output is exported (Dussel Peters 2003). The Jalisco state government supplemented these federal programs with a regional plan to attract firms and suppliers. The state's Economic Promotion Law reduced or eliminated state and municipal taxes for firms that located plants in the region. In addition the Guadalajara branch of the national chamber of commerce for the IT industry, CANIETI (Camara Nacional de la Industria, Electronica, de Telecomunicaciones e Informatica), works to attract large TNCs to the region and puts on numerous trade shows and workshops. A more regional organization named CADELEC (Cadena Productiva de la Electronica) was founded in 1998 with funding from CANIETI, the United Nations Development Programme (UNDP), and two other federal agencies. CADELEC's mission is to match suppliers with the large TNCs (CADELEC 2004; Palacios 2001).

Source: Gallagher and Shafaeddin (2010).

the share of value added in output of the *maquiladora* export industry dropped from 36.3 per cent in 1974 to 20.9 per cent in 2006 as mentioned already.

Secondly there is a lack of accountability a mechanism for the operation of the programmes and the evaluation of the impact of policies and programmes on the country's productive structure (Baz et al. 2010). Thus government officials do not take the plans seriously. Similarly there is little coordination among various government agencies. Other ministries than the Ministry of Economy design and implement their own policies independently of the Ministry of Economy or NDP. Moreover each state has its own development plan which is not necessarily geared to or coordinated with the NDP.

The reliance on FDI, particularly in *maquiladoras* industries, resulted in the use of advanced technology and processes within the manufacturing sector. From 1982 until NAFTA came into effect in 1995 TNCs in the *maquila* industry introduced a higher level of technological sophistication and automation than before. They applied a somewhat more autonomous level of decision making relative to their corporate headquarters. Further, they increased the number of Mexicans involved in the management and the number of local skilled workers with engineering capabilities (Gallagher and Shafaeddin 2010, based on Carrillo and Hualde 2002). Nevertheless, there was little transfer of technology to the rest of the Mexican economy and very limited linkages with the other industries and sectors, as already discussed. In fact in a study covering 52 Mexican industries Romo Murillo (2002) finds that foreign presence is negatively correlated with backward linkages. Further, FDI led to the crowding-out of domestic investment, as stated before (see also Agosin and Machado 2005) and had a negative impact on R&D. For example, R&D expenditures by the top twenty foreign firms fell from 0.39 per cent of their output in 1994 to 0.07 per cent in 2002 (Dussel Peters 2008). Technological development occurs mainly in the home bases of TNCs without being transferred to Mexico. Further, there was little national technological development and expenditure on R&D by public and private firms and institutions (see Box 9.1) and little interaction between enterprises, universities and research institutes (Cimoli 2000, 280).

FDI has had positive effects on productivity, particularly total factor productivity, mainly in the non-*maquiladora* industries during 1995–2005, and negative effects on wages. Nevertheless, in the *maquiladora* industries unskilled workers benefited at the expense of skilled workers supposedly because the nature of these industries was assembly operation, which requires mainly unskilled labour. A similar study for the period 1984–2000 found little evidence that the expansion of employment in *maquiladora* industries was positively related to the increase in relative wages, or wage-bill share, in favour of educated workers (Airola 2008).

ICT industries are the dominant feature of the high-technology industries initiated mainly during the IS period around the mid 1960s in export-processing zones – *maquiladora* – and inland, through PITEX and expanded by TNCs after the trade and investment liberalization of the 1980s and 1990s (see Box 9.1).

Generally speaking the reliance on TNCs had two main drawbacks. First, as stated before, while the export of manufactured goods expanded rapidly during the 1990s, it started slowing down considerably around 2000 as it faced competition from China despite its privileged access to the USA market on which Mexico relied for 86 per cent of its exports in 2005. For example, between 2000 and 2005 the share of China in the international market for computers increased from 6 per cent to 28.8 per cent while that of Mexico declined from 4.5 per cent to 3.5 per cent (Gallagher and Shafaeddin 2010, table 3). Even in the USA, Mexico is losing market share for 97 per cent of its high-technology exports and many TNCs have been relocating plants out of Mexico into China (Gallagher and Shafaeddin 2010, table 3).

Secondly Mexican domestic information technology (IT) firms were virtually wiped out, except for a few P&C producers, due to trade and investment liberalization. For example, between 1985 and 1997, 71 per cent of domestic firms in Guadalajara closed down (Rivera Vargas 2002). Furthermore, 13 of the 25 indigenous electronics firms that were still operational at the end of 1997 had been closed by 2005.

The poor growth performance of Mexico is sometimes attributed, *inter alia*, to insufficient reform and liberalization at the micro-levels, the government's failure to correct market shortfalls in training and R&D for innovation, and the failure in development of SMEs (Baz et al. 2010). In the national development plan (NDP) both R&D and development of SMEs were in fact regarded as important issues in increasing competitiveness, but training was not even considered in the NDP, and though the government has a training programme it is inadequate.

Human development: Training and education

The training programme of Mexico is inadequate to compensate for the initial problems related to the low-quality, inadequate educational system and low general skills levels of the labour force. There is government failure to provide adequate educational services due to the budget cut. For example, though the coverage of the national education system increased from 4.5 years of education to 8.2 years between 1976 and 2006, only a minority of the population completes secondary school and even fewer have completed higher levels. Further, 'only 27 percent of the working population has schooling beyond basic education' (Baz et al. 2010, 10, 24). Further, there is underinvestment in training by firms due to the lack of appropriability, or by workers, due to the lack of means for financing (ibid., table 3). A programme for training the workforce (BECATE) was established in 1982 but, because of the cut in the budget for training, the number of workers trained decreased over time from 500,000 during 1995–2000 to 200,000 in 2002 and 90,000 (planned) in 2008 (ibid., 14). Moreover the real expenditure per beneficiary was reduced by about 75 per cent in 1995 as compared with 1984 and has remained moreorless the same since then (ibid., 14).

R&D

Mexico established a centre (council) for science and technology (CONACYT) in 1970 to promote scientific and technological development for training high-level researchers. Nevertheless, because of the lack of a consolidated framework and vision for a national system of innovation (NSI),[2] it suffers from a lack of coordination, linkages, planning, and financial and human resources (Baz et al. 2010, 26–47, 90); it is not a component of the country's development plan and it concentrates on new products; new processes and services are neglected (ibid., 42).

Because of the constraints elsewhere, e.g. in the legal framework and the lack of physical and human capital, the government has not been very effective in promoting innovation and technological development. Although the expenditure on R&D in relation to GDP increased by about 5 per cent annually during 1998–2006, it is still low as compared with competitors such as China (ibid., 27; see also pages 238–40 below). Uncertain appropriability, limited access to finance and the high cost of registration patents are among other reasons for low investment in R&D by the private sector. Further, the lack of human capital, limiting regulations of public research institutions and the lack of coordination among the research institutions, universities and enterprises are among other general deficiencies in the NSI of the country (ibid., 29–31). Most of a small number of patent applications (0.05 per 10,000 inhabitants) are submitted by foreign firms.

SMEs policy

Mexico established an SME Fund (Fondo PYME) in 2004. The fund deals with SMEs indirectly through local government and intermediaries but it suffers from design shortcomings: lack of, or deficient, selection criteria and evaluation framework for measuring productivity. It also suffers from a lack of accountability (ibid., 90–91).

In short, Mexico's change of policies in favour of economic liberalization along the line suggested by neoliberals and neoliberal institutions has been accompanied with rapid expansion of FDI and exports of manufactured goods, particularly IT products, produced mainly in export-processing zones, in the 1990s. Nevertheless, it has led to little increase in the value added in exports of these products and higher wages. Similarly it has led to little development of either the backward linkages of the *maquila* industries with the rest of the economy or the upgrading of the industrial structure. Further, the country has not been able to sustain rapid export expansion during the recent decade due to the loss of competitiveness in the international market, particularly *vis-à-vis* China. In other words, Mexico's hands-off approach to the economy has not led to the development of the capabilities of national enterprises. China has followed a different strategy.

China's Sources of Growth of Exports and GDP, and of Competitiveness

The sources of exceptional export, thus GDP growth, and the industrialization and development of China are sometimes attributed to various factors such as undervalued

---

2 The NSI is defined as an 'interactive system of existing institutions, private and public, aiming to create, store and transfer knowledge and skills to define new means of Science and Technology (S&T) within national borders. Interaction among these institutions can be technical, commercial, legal, social or financial' (Intarakummerd et al. 2002).

exchange rate, export subsidies, etc. After discussing some of these issues, we will explain that the government policies were crucial not only in acceleration of growth and MVA but also in achieving competiveness in the international market. The government aimed to expand and upgrade the industrial structure to produce and export 'demand dynamic products' which include mainly high-tech and capital-intensive ones. To do so it tried to enhance the capabilities of domestic firms by promoting R&D, training and encouraging capital accumulation. Meanwhile it subjected enterprises to competitive pressure. The combination of these factors also contributed to enhancing total factor productivity.

Currency devaluation and subsidies

Although China's currency was devalued in the mid 1990s and some production subsidies have been paid to domestic enterprises, and while their influence on exports cannot be denied, these alone cannot explain the rapid growth in China's exports. Similarly it is true that China's labour cost has been cheaper than that of many of its competitors, but this does not seem to be the only factor either. In contrast, its export expansion seems to be mainly due to the contribution of total factor productivity helped by government policies. For example, a study for the period 1997–2005 indicates that the prices of manufacturing China's exports to the USA fell continuously by an annual average rate of 1.5 per cent while export prices of these products from the rest of the world to the United States increased by 0.4 per cent annually (Amiti and Freund 2008). Neither the exchange rate nor the payments of subsidies or low wages can explain *continuous decrease* in export prices.

There are estimates indicating that the nominal exchange rate of RMB (Chinese currency) was undervalued by about 15 per cent in 1996 (Pitylak 2005). Even if we assume that the effective exchange rate of RMB is also undervalued to the same extent, it cannot be attributed to the payment of subsidies and prior devaluation of the currency.

Table 9.6. National budgetary expenditure on Chinese industry (1985–2005)

Expenditures	1985	1995	2000	2005
Expenditure in US$100 million				
Subsidies to loss-making firms	172.7	39.3	33.7	23.6
Appropriation for enterprises circulating capital	4.9	4.2	8.6	2.2
Innovation and S&T promotion funds	35.2	59.2	104.5	182.5
Total	212.7	102.6	146.8	208.3
% Shares of				
Subsidies to loss-making firms	81.2	38.2	23.9	11.3
Appropriation for enterprises circulating capital	2.3	4.1	5.9	1.1
Innovation and S&T promotion funds	16.6	57.7	71.4	87.6

Source: Based on Sourafel et al. (2008, table 2).

Neither can the export performance of the country be attributed to the level of its exchange rate alone. For example, during 1995–2005 RMB was pegged to the dollar and hence its exchange rate remained stable *vis-à-vis* the dollar (Ma and McCauley 2010), but it depreciated against other currencies as the dollar – to which RMB was pegged – depreciated against other currencies. Yet over the same period China's exports to the USA increased by an annual average rate of 27.1 per cent as against 17.7 per cent to the world as a whole. In 2005 RMB was unpegged from the dollar and was based on a basket of currencies of its main trading partners. During July 2005–July 2008 RMB appreciated against the dollar by about 21 per cent (CRS 2011). Over 2005–8 the annual average growth rate of China's exports to the USA declined to 18.75 per cent as against 24.4 per cent for its exports to the world as a whole. Nevertheless, such change in the performance of the country must have been to a large extent due to the change in the differential growth rates of GDP of the USA and the rest of China's trade partners. For example, the GDP growth rate of the USA during 2005–8 was 2.2 per cent as against 3.1 per cent during 1995–2005. The corresponding rates for Europe hardly changed but that of developing countries, excluding China, increased from 3.9 per cent during 1995–2005 to 5.54 per cent during 2005–8 (UNCTAD, *Handbook of Statistics*, 2008, tables 8.2.1, 8.2.2).[3]

There are indications that the main cause of overvaluation of the currency was productivity growth, i.e. the unit labour cost declined because of the contribution of rapid labour productivity growth. A study covering 28 industries for the period 1995–2004 indicates that labour productivity increased considerably faster than labour compensation (Chen, Wu and Ark 2008). Further, productivity growth was more noticeable for K/T industries which benefited from innovation and total factor productivity as well as higher growth rates in exports (Chen, Wu and Ark 2008). We will return to the question of productivity shortly.

Production subsidies were influential in the export expansion of China. Nevertheless, there are indications that subsidies have been used mainly as a reward rather than compensation for loss making. According to a study for the period 1995–2005, when subsidies were allowed before the accession to the WTO and afterwards until 2005; subsidies were more pronounced among profit-making firms rather than loss-making ones (Sourafel et al. 2008). The government budgetary allocation to the industry for 1985–2005 is shown in the following table. Accordingly, first of all, the total amount of allocation to industry for production subsidies decreased over time. Further, the subsidy to the loss-making firms also declined continuously and substantially. Secondly the allocation to innovation and S&T promotion has increased considerably both in absolute terms and in relation to total budgetary allocation over time to the extent that in 2005 it accounted for nearly 88 per cent of total allocation. The related funds are general assistance for innovation rather than specific subsidy for a particular item. It contributes to enhancing productivity and competitiveness indirectly.

At individual product levels the provision of subsidies cannot explain the reduction of export prices to the United States. Table 9.7 shows changes in subsidies per unit of

---

3 The figures are simple averages of the growth rates for 2005–8 and compound rates for 1995–2005.

Table 9.7. Subsidy per US$1,000 of output for two-digit Chinese products

Product	1999	2005	% change
1. Nonmetal mineral products*	5	1	–80
2. Instruments and meters	6	2	–66.6
3. Medical and pharmaceutical products	8	3	–62.5
4. Cultural and sports goods*	4	2	–50
5. Garment and other fibre products*	2	1	–50
6. Electrical equipment and machinery	9	5	–44
7. Food production*	7	4	–42.9
8. Special purpose equipment	8	5	–37.5
9. Textiles industry*	3	2	–33.3
10. Electronic and telecommunications	9	6	–33.3
11. Food processing*	8	6	–25
12. Metal products*	4	3	–25
13. Timber processing*	9	7	–22.2
14. Rubber products*	5	4	–20
15. Ordinary machinery	5	4	–20
16. Other electronic equipment	5	4	–20
17. Beverage industry*	5	4	–20
18. Printing and media reproduction*	7	6	–16.6
19. Transport equipment	8	7	–12.5
20. Smelting and pressing of ferrous metals	3	3	0
21. Plastic products*	3	3	0
22. Leather, fur, down and related products*	1	1	0
23. Raw chemical materials and chemicals	5	5	0
24. Furniture manufacturing*	3	4	+33.3
25. Petroleum refining and coking	2	3	+50
26. Chemical fibres	2	3	+50
27. Paper making and paper products*	4	7	+75
28. Smelting and pressing of nonferrous metals	7	15	+114.3

Note: * Indicates more labour-intensive industries, 15 (out of 28).

Source: Based on Sourafel et al. (2008, table 5).

output for various products at two digit levels. Accordingly subsidies per unit of output have declined between 25 per cent and 80 per cent for 12 items, and 12.5 per cent and 25 per cent for another 7 items. Most of these products are among those with the highest growth rates of exports. Similarly all products (5) for which subsidy per unit of output increased do not figure among the dynamic export products of China. Thus the reduction in export prices are inconsistent with the decrease in subsidies per unit of output unless one assumes that there has been continuous damping by differential pricing of exports and domestic sale. Even if damping may have taken place in a few cases, it cannot explain the high growth rate of exports for a large number of products.

Competitive pressure

The success of China is sometimes attributed mainly to the role played by Chinese firms under the competitive pressure resulting from the liberalization of foreign trade and FDI (Brandt and Thun 2010). While such a pressure was an element in the success of China in export expansion, it could not work in the case of Mexico because on its own it was not sufficient. According to these authors the exposure of domestic firms of China to imported products reduced the share of domestic firms in the internal market during the period beginning 1995, leading to and following China's entry to the WTO. Nevertheless, because of the competitive effects of imports, domestic firms have improved their efficiencies. As a result they have improved their share in the domestic market in more recent years though their share is still below that of 1995 (Brandt and Thun 2009). In certain industries which benefit from natural barriers to entry (of foreign firms), such as the lower end of the domestic market for automobiles, construction equipment and machine tools, the competition among local firms themselves contributed to efficiencies.

The existence of a large and growing domestic market has been attractive for foreign enterprises. It also provides an advantage for domestic enterprises which are more familiar with the domestic market than their rival foreign firms. Yet trade and investment liberalization put competitive pressure on the domestic firms in both domestic and international markets. For example, in the domestic market, between the two manufacturing census years of 1994 and 2004, total domestic sales increased by about 3.4 times even though the share of Chinese firms in total domestic sales declined from 67.7 per cent to 56 per cent. For the foreign firms it increased from 11.3 per cent to 19.1 per cent and that of imports from 21 per cent to 24.9 per cent (ibid., table 1).

Nevertheless, due to the competitive pressure the pace of the decline in the share of domestic firms declined between 2001 and 2005 and began to rise again in 2006 (ibid., 1558). The foreign firms benefit from two advantages: their technological capabilities and their marketing channels for sale in the international market. Thus they have managed to expand market share in exports in industries which technology, know-how and capital intensity were important (ibid., 1558). In cases where Chinese firms are involved in production for export they are active mainly in fields where technological requirements are not very sophisticated. They take advantage of low labour cost for labour-intensive industries but they also attempt to 'broaden the scope of their activities' (i.e. functional upgrading) into design, marketing and branding (ibid., 1557). Moreover, within the same industry (e.g. automotive, construction equipment, machine tools) the Chinese firms were concentrated in the lower segment where product technology was simple. In contrast, the foreign firms were involved mainly in the segment for which quality was more important and technology was more sophisticated.

There has been severe competition between Chinese and foreign firms in the middle segments of sectors and industries. The foreign firms have had to lower their costs and the domestic firms have tried to upgrade. To reduce their costs the foreign firms outsourced some of their intermediate products (e.g. in the above-listed industries) to domestic firms which had advantages. Under competitive pressure from foreign firms the Chinese firms tried to upgrade their capabilities as just stated. To do so they used revenues earned 'from products that are characterized by relatively low technology gaps…[which] provide a secure source of revenue that can be used to help support the shift into technologically more sophisticated and more profitable products' (ibid., 1570). The flow of trained human capital from foreign firms and the resources from state sector (SOEs which benefited from state investment, human capital, etc.) were also useful in the process of upgrading (ibid.).

Brandt and Thun (2009) correctly maintain that 'intense competition and expansion in the [large] domestic market are now offering incentives that are far more powerful than protective tariffs or government fiat' (ibid., 1571). The introduction of domestic competition allowed the manufacturing capabilities which had been developed during the prior import-substitution era to become efficient. Nevertheless, many of the issues they give importance to in the decision making of the local firms of China have also been present in the case of Mexico. Yet Mexico has not been successful. The differential in performance of the two countries is related to the difference in the role of government policies in the two countries, as will be explained shortly.

Tendency for concentration in dynamic products

As stated earlier, both China and Mexico have increased exports of technology and capital-intensive products (sophisticated products) which are mostly among demand dynamic items in the international markets. Yet Mexico, unlike China, has not been able to sustain high export growth rates. The capabilities of China in exporting sophisticated items are subject to some controversy in the literature. Some have confused China's exportation of high capital and technology-intensive items, regarding the country as a special case where its pattern of exports is not consistent with its level of development (e.g. Rodrik 2006). Others have argued that the sophistication of exports from China is not special as the product quality of its exports is not fully considered and China's exports of technology-intensive products are concentrated in coastal areas, which are not representative of the whole country (e.g. Xu 2010). None of these arguments is precise. Regarding Rodrik's argument it should be stated first of all that the exports of K/T items by a country do not necessarily imply capabilities of the country in the *production* of those products, as we have shown earlier in this chapter in the particular case of Mexico. Otherwise Mexico can also be regarded as a special case. China, like Mexico, initiated assembly operation of IT and some other K/T-intensive items based on imported inputs. What is *special* about China is that, unlike Mexico, Costa Rica (see Paus 2005) etc., specialization based on labour-intensive industries and assembly operation was the beginning of a long process aiming to achieve dynamic comparative advantage. By continuously upgrading and replacing domestic production of parts and components for corresponding imported items, China has managed to enhance domestic value added of its exported items by going through a period of rapid learning and innovation. It has started a process of industrialization based on its static comparative advantage, i.e. producing and exporting labour-intensive products such as textiles, clothing, leather products and assembly operation in capital- and technology-intensive (e.g. IT) products. Nevertheless, it has not been satisfied with continuing specialization based on static comparative advantage. It has aimed at upgrading its industrial sector for achieving dynamic comparative advantage.

> The first industrial upgrading happened in 1986, when exports of textiles and clothing exceeded crude oil…[which was] transition from resource-intensive product to labour-intensive [ones]. The Second upgrade happened in 1995, when China's exports of machineries and electronics [non-traditional labour-intensive products [through assembly operation] exceeded textiles and clothing… The third upgrade happened [around 2000]…when high and new tech exports grew rapidly, and the level of product sophistication increased… (Lin and Wang 2008, 15)

Nevertheless, the bulk of China's exports is still based on assembly operations. Thus, though Brandt and Thun (2009) are correct that 'there is…a myth on the level of export sophistication' of China (Lin and Wang 2008, 15), however, they are silent about the fact that the country was in parallel in the process of increasing the share of domestic input in production of sophisticated items. They argue that the country has continuously upgraded its factor endowment by learning and capital accumulation (Lin and Wang 2008, 18). Nevertheless, they do not consider the fact that the process of learning and capital accumulation has not been automatic. Learning cannot be entirely 'market-based' as they claim (Lin and Wang 2008, 30).

Following the World Bank approach the authors emphasize specialization based on static comparative advantage and the need for economic liberalization. They maintain that learning (they regard learning by doing as the only valid type of learning) 'should be used to help a country specialize in certain industries that are consistent with its comparative advantages'. Further, they argue that

> to achieve competitiveness, it is crucial to liberalize prices, and to reduce barriers to entry and exit in most sectors, so that private sector firms can select the right subsectors and products where they have true comparative advantage. (Lin and Wang 2008, 30)

They fail to recognize the fact that Mexico has followed along the line they suggest and has not succeeded, and that the success of China in upgrading its industrial structure was in fact due to its government's strategy and policies.

Turning to Xu's argument, it is true that there are indications that the quality of some Chinese exports is inferior to the quality of similar products exported by the USA and Europe (Kiyota 2008). So is the quality of exports of Mexico. Yet China, unlike Mexico, has been able to maintain high rate of growth of exports and upgrading its industrial structure.

The argument of Xu on the concentration of exports in certain regions of China is also irrelevant to the issue under discussion. In most countries certain industries are concentrated in a particular region. For example, in the UK its aerospace industries are concentrated in the Bristol area and IT industries in Cambridge. Similarly, in the USA IT industries are concentrated in California and Boston. Such a concentration in fact has positive effects on the competitiveness of the country in the international market due to the externalities involved in industrial clustering (see Chapter 5).

Contribution of factor input and productivity

There is no agreement in the literature on the relative contribution of physical capital, human capital and total factor productivity to growth of GDP in China mainly because the methods of measurement applied by different authors are different; so are the periods under study. Nevertheless, one thing is clear; that is, the contribution not only of physical capital and human capital but also total factor productivity, emanating mainly from technical progress, is far greater in the case of China than Mexico. For example, the annual average total factor productivity growth of China increased from less than 1.5 per cent in the 1970s to about 4 per cent and 4.5 per cent in the 1980s and 1990s respectively. In contrast, the corresponding figures for Mexico were nil in the 1970s and 1980s and negative (by nearly −4 per cent) in the 1990s (Baz et al. 2010, 2, based on IMF sources). In fact, in terms of total factor productivity, Mexico has been one of the worst in Latin America (Baz et al. 2010, 2, based on IMF sources). 'Neither openness nor macroeconomic stability has proved sufficient to promote productivity increases in the country's [Mexico] firms…[as] microeconomic conditions are deficient' (Baz et al. 2010, 87).

A study for the period 1991–2004 indicates that China's growth is largely driven by factor input, and new technology plays a less important role than factor inputs (Latham and Yin 2008). In other words, although total factor productivity has been greater in the case of China than Mexico, productivity arising for adoption of new technology could have resulted further in higher growth rates.

According to another estimate, factor inputs (physical capital, labour and human capital) contributed to 76 per cent of growth of output during 1986–2000 and the physical capital has been the most important one during postreform economic growth (Kui-Wai et al. 2009, 24).

However, the role of human capital is underestimated by the author because only 'the average number of schooling years is used as a proxy for the human capital', disregarding other factors such as higher and technical education and training. In fact, while human capital is measured differently by different authors, the estimates by most authors indicate that the contribution of human capital to growth in GDP has been not only significant, but also has increased during 1999–2008 after the reform in the educational system in 1999 (see Tables 9.8 and 9.9 below), as compared with 1978–99 (see Whalley and Zhao 2010 for a short survey). Further, according to these authors the contribution of human capital to growth of GDP has been greater than the corresponding contribution of physical capital during the same periods and has increased further during 2003–8

Table 9.8. Contribution of physical and human capital and total factor productivity to growth of China's GDP, 1978–2008 (%)

	1978–2008	1978–99	1999–2008	2003–2008
Physical capital	35.51	30.07	48.1	48.03
Human capital	46.34	42.98	54.03	58.65
Total factor productivity	18.15	26.95	−2.13	−6.68

Source: Whalley and Zhao (2010, table 5).

Table 9.9. Contribution of physical and human capital and total factor productivity to growth of China's GDP, 1953–2005 (%)

	1953–77	1978–99	2000–2005
Physical capital	50.2	56.9	68.0
Labour	18.3	11.2	7.0
Human capital	44.6	11.2	7
Total factor productivity	−13.1	30.7	19.5

Source: Lin and Wang (2008, table 1).

(see Table 9.8 and Whalley and Zhao 2010). The total factor productivity has, on average, contributed to 3.07 per cent (out of over 9 per cent) of growth. Regarding elements of total factor productivity the technical progress, particularly during 1992–4, and scale effects have been important contributory factors to total factor productivity and growth, but technical efficiency[4] was negative throughout the period under study. Technical progress was the main element; the contribution to growth of technical progress, scale effects and technical efficiency were 3.09 per cent, 0.61 per cent and −0.63 per cent repectively out of an average growth rate of 9.4 per cent (Kui-Wai et al. 2009, 21–2).

The differences in the estimates of total factor productivity by Kui-Wai et al. and Whalley and Zhao seem to be due to their different treatment of human capital as well as coverage of their sample. Whalley and Zhao (2010) attribute the increase in the contribution of human capital to growth during 1999–2008 to a 'major transformation in higher education' since the reform of the educational system in 1999 (Whalley and Zhao 2010, 2). Further, the authors suggest that the reduction in the contribution of total factor productivity to GDP growth rate may be due to inefficient use of human capital in recent years, including an increase in the unemployment of college graduates (Whalley and Zhao 2010, 3). If this is the case, China still has some room to maintain high growth rates based on physical and human capital. The country has the financial resources for capital accumulation, even if the FDI slows down, and a surplus supply of educated workforce.

---

4 A situation where it is impossible for a firm to produce with the given know-how a greater amount of output from the same input or the same output with fewer inputs without increasing the amount of other inputs.

Table 9.10. Contribution of domestic value added (DVA) to exports of China's manufacturing goods, 2002 and 2006 (%)

	Share in DVA		Share in X	
	2002	2006	2002	2006
Ownership:				
Wholly foreign	32.6	27.8	29.4	39.3
Sino-foreign	44.6	44.8	22.6	18.6
SOEs	69.7	70	37.9	19.8
Collectively owned	72.3	70.9	5.8	4.3
Private	83.7	82	4.3	18.0
All firms: Average	53.8	50.9	100	100

Source: Koopman et al. (2008, table 6, 1, 17–18).

There are indications that SOEs in the ICT sector have shown better productivity performance than other SOEs because they have been under more competitive pressure than other SOEs and also because of their efforts in R&D (Yu and Nijkamp 2009). As shown in Table 9.10 SOEs and private (domestic companies) have shown higher ratios of domestic value added (DVA) than other types of enterprises as they have been more active in R&D than other types of enterprises. We will return to the question of R&D and training below.

Policies on Science and Technology (S&T) and R&D

Unlike Mexico where it was assumed, under the influence of IFIs, that technology would be transferred through international trade and FDI, conscious attention to science and technology (S&T) policy and research and development (R&D) has been a cornerstone of China's industrial development and integration into the world economy. The Chinese government learned in practice that technology acquisition from abroad through TNCs alone will not necessarily lead to transfer and development of technology; there was a need for increasing the absorptive capacity of domestic firms and the development of indigenous technological capacity building; and the government managed to do this as its policy space was not limited by the IFIs. The ingredients of the government's strategy included government support, indigenous R&D, innovation within individual firms and the creation of R&D institutions. It also included alliance among firms in an industry and their cooperation with research institutes and universities, as well as foreign firms, targeting particularly the strategic industries.

Government policy on R&D and technological development ranged from direct investment, provision of guidance, institutional and financial support, creating a favourable environment for innovation as well as introduction of competition into the domestic market for the strategic industries (e.g. telecommunications) (Fan, Gao and Watanabe 2007, 359) and development of national standards and patents for main IT

Table 9.11. Development of China's national innovation system

Policy	Dominant feature	Year established
Key technology R&D programme	Encouraging efforts in key technology	1982
Resolution on reform of S&T system (CCCP)	Adopting flexible system on R&D management	1985
Sparkle system 5	Promoting basic research in agriculture	1985
863 programme	High-tech promotion	1986
Torch programme	High-tech communication, high-tech zones	1988
National S&T achievements spreading programme	Promoting product communication	1990
National engineering technology research centre programme	Technology transfer and communication research	1991
Climbing programme	Promoting basic research	1992
Endorsement of UAEs by SSTCC	Promoting university and industry linkage	1992
S&T progress law	Technology transfer; S&T system reform	1993
Decision on accelerating S&T progress (CCCP)	Promoting URI–industry linkage	1992
Law for promoting commercialization of S&T achievements	Regulating the commercialization of S&T	1996
Super 863 programme	Commercialization, break-through in key areas	1996
Decision on developing high-tech industrialization	Encouraging technology innovation and commercialization	1999
Guidelines for developing National University Science Park	Accelerating the development of university science parks	2000N

Source: Gallagher and Shafaeddin (2010, table 4), based on Xiwei and Xiandong (2007).

products (Wang and Wang 2007). The S&T strategy of the government was also aimed at the long-term goal of upgrading the industrial base of the country and it was selective, targeted and responsive to the market dynamic with growing emphasis on the private sector (including TNCs). Beginning in the early 1980s China put in place a number of policies that not only aimed at conducting basic research but also put equal emphasis on the deployment and diffusion of technology. Table 9.11 provides a snapshot of China's key S&T policies between 1982 and 2000 (see also the case of the mobile communications industry and the high-definition disc player industry below).

Institutional set-up and NSI

The government apparatus for guiding the S&T consisted of six different entities: the Chinese academy of Science together with five relevant ministries, including the Ministry of Information Technology which was specifically created for supporting IT industries (Xiwei and Xiangdong 2007, 318). The national system of innovation was geared to basic research as well as R&D in selective activities; although still the share of basic and applied research in total R&D is smaller than in OECD countries, experimental research is given more emphasis (OECD 2009,3). The 863 Programme (1986) aimed at high basic and applied research in seven areas and fifteen topics with the cooperation of private enterprises. The seven areas included, in order of priority given by the planners, information technology, laser, automation, biotechnology, new material technology, astro-technology and energy technology (Fan and Watanabe 2006, 311). The 'climbing programme' of 1992 was oriented towards the acceleration of basic research. In contrast, the Torch programme was market-oriented right from its inception in 1988 and was geared mainly to commercialization of the results of R&D. Its objectives ranged from providing an enabling environment for high-tech industries to the creation of high-tech zones executing projects in the above-stated selected (7) areas, training and facilitating international cooperation (Fan and Watanabe 2006, 312). In 1995 the government passed the 'Decision on Accelerating Scientific and Technological Progress' in order to intensify technological development (Walsh 2003, 105).

The ninth five-year plan (1996–2000) specifically emphasized the development of capabilities to increase domestic value added in assembly operations in the computer industry and its peripherals. This was followed by the emphasis on innovation in integrated circuits and software technology in the tenth five-year plan (2001–5) under the so-called 'Golden Projects' (Xiwei and Xiangdong 2007, 321).

Such development was related to the reform in the S&T system of the country in 1999–2000, which also led to significant acceleration of expenditure on R&D and a number of personnel engaged in R&D activities mainly in the business sector, particularly on experimental development (OECD 2009, 49–51). It also led to acceleration in the expansion of regular institutions of high education. Between 1995 and 2008 the number of new entrants, graduates and total enrolments (including doctoral level) all increased at an average annual growth rate of more than 20 per cent (OECD 2009, 51). For example, the number of enrolments in higher education institutions increased from about 3 million in 1995 to about 18 million in 2006 (OECD 2009, figs 40 and 43).

In 2005 the government introduced a national guideline for the Medium- and Long-Term Plan for Science and Technology Development (2006–20) according to which, *inter alia*, it sets a target for the ratio of R&D expenditure/GDP of 2 for 2010 and 2.5 in 2020. In other words, the R&D expenditure was to increase by an annual average rate of 10–15 per cent (OECD 2009, 3). In the current development plan the related ratio is supposed to increase to 2.2 by 2015.

The features of the NSI

The national system of innovation in China is dynamic in terms of both institutional development and the change in the relative roles of government and private enterprises. The S&T system of China consisted of universities, research institutes and public and private enterprises, including foreign firms. The interrelationship between universities/research institutes and industry is regarded as unique (Chen and Kenney 2008).

Furthermore the NSI went through continuous reforms in terms of policies and the involvement of actors in R&D. To benefit from 'collective efficiency' through clustering, a number of high-tech zones (technology parks) were established (by 1992, 52 high-tech zones had been established (Xiwei and Xiangdong 2007, 319).

The main features of NSI are summarized in Tables 9.12 and 9.13. Accordingly the business sector is becoming the driving force behind the NSI in terms of both input and output, i.e. the number of units involved in S&T activities, the number of personnel involved in R&D, the amount of R&D expenditure as well as the source of finance and the number of applications submitted for patents. While the annual average growth rate of R&D expenditure during 2000–2006 increased by 9.7 per cent by government research institutes, it increased by 20 per cent and 22 per cent by higher education establishments and business sector respectively. The government research institutes and the higher education establishments concentrate mainly on basic and applied research; the focus of the business sector is on experimental development. The reform in the NSI which took place in 1999–2000 led to the downsizing of a number of government institutes and their S&T personnel in favour of higher education establishments and the business sector. Nevertheless, the quality of their services improved, funds available to them were increased and they concentrated on basic and applied research. Meanwhile the higher education establishments increased their activities in engineering, applied research and S&T diffusion. Their R&D expenditure in constant prices increased five times over 1995–2006; over the same period the R&D expenditure by the business sector increased over 20 times. Moreover they enhanced their cooperation with the business sector more and more through such programmes such as 363, Torch, Spark and S&T Achievement (OECD 2009, 19–24).

Policies on TNCs and their contribution to R&D

Although foreign enterprises dominated production particularly in high-tech industries and fabricated metal, their involvement in R&D is smaller than the domestic firms not only in general (OECD 2009, figure 12), but also in high-tech industries in particular

Table 9.12. General characteristics of the three key performers in China's NSI

	Government research	High education	Business sector
R&D funding source	Government funding as a main source	Diversified, mainly government and business sector; increased foreign funding	Rapid increase in self-funding
R&D expenditure annual average growth rate 2000–2006 at constant prices (%)	9.7	20	22
R&D structure	Applied research, basic research	Basic research too low, applied research dominates	Mainly experimental development
Driving force	Reform 1999 and 2000	Expansion since 1999	Privatization; intensified domestic competition; FDI inflow and globalization
Challenges ahead	Increase basic research? Commercialization of research results	Research capacity and its impact in general should be strengthened; increase in basic research; decrease the share of experimental development	Indigenous innovation capacity; international competitiveness; participation of S&T-based SMEs
Participation in globalization	Low participation	Increased participation in both education and research	High application facing both new opportunities and new challenges
Role in the NSI	Decreased share of S&T personnel in total; decreased share of S&T and R&D expenditure	S&T human research supply; applied and basic research; key laboratories; important role in science–industry linkages	Emerging driving force and core of NSI

Source: OECD (2009, table 1).

Table 9.13. Relative importance of the three key performers in China's NSI (2006)

	Government research Institutes	High education sector	Business sector
No. of units (20,059)	3,901	1,792	28,567 LMES, 8,775 have S&T units; 248,813 small enterprises (2004); 22,307 have S&T activities
Share of R&D personnel (FTE) %	18.1	16.1	65.7
Share of government funding %	66.5	20.4	13
Participation in national natural science foundation funding (2005) %	25	73.5	–
Importance in infrastructure and facility building (2005) %	58 states key labs (32.4)	95 state key labs (53.1)	Receive support soon
Share of R&D expenditure %	19.7	9.2	71.1
Share of R&D expenditure in basic research %	46.4	44.9	8.7
Share of R&D expenditure in applied research %	40.7	26.9	32.4
Share of R&D expenditure in experimental research %	13.3	3	83.7
Selling share in contract value in technology market (2005)[a] %	15.3	7.9	59.2
Share of (services) patent application (2005) %	10.8	23.5	64.6

Note: [a] One per cent of the funding to research institutes was allocated to the China Academy of Science. The remaining 19 per cent are technology deals conducted by technology trade agencies, individuals and others.

Source: OECD (2009, table 2), based on *China Statistical Yearbook on Science and Technology* (2006), http://www.stats.gov.cn/tjsj/ndsj/2010/indexeh.htm.

despite their increased activities in R&D more recently (see the section on the role of FDI below). The R&D intensity (the ratio of R&D expenditure to revenue) of domestic and foreign firms in a couple of high-tech industries is shown in the following table as an example. Foreign funding accounts for only 1.6 per cent of total R&D expenditure and 2 per cent of R&D expenditures of the business sector (OECD 2009, table 3). Otherwise the bulk (77.7 per cent) of projects is implemented independently by the local enterprises and another 3.5 per cent in cooperation with other enterprises (OECD 2009, table 5).

Table 9.14. R&D intensity of domestic and foreign firms in 2005 (%)

Industries	R&D intensity	
	Domestic	Foreign
Communication, computer and other electronic products	4.5	0.8
Measuring instruments, machinery for cultural and office products	2.9	0.3
Electrical machinery and equipment	1.9	0.9

Source: Based on OECD (2009, figure 12).

Technology adoption

Following the reform in S&T policy in 1999, building indigenous innovation capacity and reducing the dependence on foreign technology to 30 per cent was emphasized in the National Guidelines for S&T. The technology penetration ratio (expenditure on technology imports [expenditure on domestic R&D (technology exports − technology imports)]) was used as a measure of dependence on imported technology. Thus, to increase the indigenous capacity in R&D and innovation, the expenditure on R&D in relation to the expenditure on import of technology increased significantly. In fact the expenditure on importing technology began to decrease in absolute terms in 2004 (OECD 2009, fig. 28, 44–5).

The relative importance of various agents

Close links were also developed among enterprises, universities and research institutes. Further, commercialization of R&D was encouraged. In particular, over time the role of private enterprises in R&D increased significantly. Over 1987–2003 the number of R&D institutes increased by 67 per cent reaching nearly 19,000 units, and that of the private institutions more than doubled reaching 11,000 (Xu 2010, table 5). The distinction between private and public entities involved in R&D is, however, blurred; some universities and research institutes own enterprises engaged in research (Chen and Kenney 2008). The business sector also provides some funding to the higher education sector (36.6 per cent) and government research institutes (4.5 per cent) (OECD 2009, 27). R&D expenditures of foreign-invested enterprises take place mainly in medium and high-tech industries. Nevertheless, as already stated, domestic enterprises play a more important role in this respect (OECD 2009, 3).

Table 9.15. Expenditure on research and development in China and Mexico*

Countries	Year	Share in GDP	Per capita ($)
China	1996	0.57	15.7
	2005	1.34	89.6
	2007	1.4	77.1
Mexico	1996	0.31	22.4
	2005	0.41	40.4
	2007	0.40	52.1

Note: * GDP and per capita GDP are in PPP.
Sources: UNESCO online database on expenditures on R&D.

While the relative role of the business sector in R&D has been accelerating since 1999, it does not mean that the government role is not important. In fact the government plays a very important role by supporting various S&T policy measures directly, such as direct funding and tax incentives, and by promoting the interaction among key performers through specific S&T programmes and S&T industrial parks and technology business incubators (OECD 2009, 29–30). The S&T parks and incubators are important instruments for promoting academic–industry cooperation. In 2006 there were nearly 46,000 companies in S&T industrial parks, over half of which were domestic shareholding companies and another 15.2 per cent foreign companies and joint ventures (OECD 2009, tables 8 and 9). The government through its funding of R&D activities, despite its relatively small amount, plays an 'important "signalling" role in terms of policy directions and priority fields' (OECD 2009, 30, 50).

Venture capital

Support and funding of venture capital firms by the government has been another channel for promoting R&D and (OECD 2009, 50) indigenous technological capacity. During 1995–2005 alone the number of venture capital organizations increased from 27 to 319, including 50 foreign firms. The amount of related invested capital which was financed mainly by the government increased by over 11 times to US$7.7 billion. The funds were provided through S&T industrial parks, incubators, Torch programmes, etc. (OECD 2009, 45).

Comparison with Mexico

The comparison of China and Mexico is striking both in terms of input to and the results of the S&T policies. Table 9.15 compares the R&D expenditures of China with those of Mexico. China's expenditure on R&D (as a percentage of GDP and in per capita) far exceeds that of Mexico in terms of both level and changes over time. Further, in the current development plan already mentioned, the Chinese government is to increase the R&D/GDP ratio to 2.2 per cent by 2015 and to 2.5 per cent by 2020.

Table 9.16. The number of researchers engaged in science and technology activities in China and Mexico (1996 and 2007)

Actors	Numbers (1000)		Shares	
	1996	2007	1996	2007
China				
Business enterprises	225.4	944.4	40.8	66.4
Government	179.8	230.7	32.8	16.2
Higher education	156.9	248.3	24	17.4
Total	*548*	*1,423.4*	*100*	*100*
Mexico				
Business enterprises	2.3	16.1	11.4	42.5
Government	6.1	7.3	30.6	19.3
Higher education	11.4	13.6	57.3	35.8
Private nonprofit organizations etc.	0.1	0.94	0.7	2.5
Total	*19.9*	*37.9*	*100*	*100*

Source: Based on UNESCO.

China's indicators for R&D are the highest in Asia after Singapore, Republic of Korea and Taiwan; it is also higher than Spain and Italy (based on the same source as Table 9.15). The number of people working on R&D in China was over 1.42 million in 2007 and increased by nearly 2.6 times as compared with 1996. The corresponding figures for Mexico were 37,930 in 2007, which increased by 1.9 times over the same period (Table 9.16). In 2007 the number of researchers per million inhabitants was 1,070, over three times higher than that in Mexico, which was 352 (based on UNESCO, online: http://www.onlineunesco.org/, accessed 10 July 2012). Although the share of business enterprises in total number of researchers increased faster in the case of Mexico than in China, it is still far below that of China. Moreover the distinction between private and public research institutes is blurred in the case of China, as stated earlier.

The results of the implementation of S&T policy are striking in the case of China as compared with Mexico. Table 9.17 shows that, on average, 12 times more patents are filed in China each year than for all the LA countries combined, let alone Mexico. What is more, whereas in Mexico only 4 per cent of all patents are submitted by residents, in China that figure is over 75 per cent. Similar results are also evident in terms of the number of articles published by Chinese scholars as compared with those of Latin American. The number of patents granted increased from 22,558 in 1990 to 581,992 in 2009, out of which domestic patents account for over 86 per cent in 2009 (Table 9.18). Moreover the relative importance of the inventions covered by granted patents has increased sharply over time from 16.9 per cent in 1990 to 22.1 per cent in 2009. More importantly the share of domestic inventions in total inventions jumped from 29.9 per cent in 1990 to about 51 per cent in 2009.

Table 9.17. Selected science and technology indicators for China, Mexico, East Asia and Latin America (2008)

Indicators	Country/region	
	China	*Mexico*
Patent applications nonresidents	95,259 (92,101)	15,896
Patent applications residents	194,575 (163,060)	685
Total	109,834 (255,161)	16,581
Patent applications, residents share	67.1 (63.9)	4.1
R&D expenditure (% of GDP)	1.49	0.50
Science and technical journal articles	41,596	3,902
	East Asia	*Latin America*[a]
Patent applications nonresidents	108,823	20,264[a]
Patent applications residents	196,416	861[a]
Total	305,239	21,125[a]
Patent applications, residents share	64%	4.1[a]
R&D expenditure (% of GDP)	1.49	0.66
Science and technical journal articles	44,064	20,045

Note: [a] 2007.
Source: World Bank, World Development Indicators (2009 and 2010).

Human Development and Training

In tandem with R&D China has a high level of support for tertiary education and training, particularly in science and technology. In 2009 there existed 5,369 schools and institutions of higher education in China, including 796 postgraduate schools and 1,071 vocational and technical colleges (*China's Statistical Yearbook* 2010, table 20-12). In the same year over 371,000 graduated from postgraduate courses in Chinese universities (281 per million of the population or about 1 397 per million urban workforce), of which over 172,000 of them were scientists and engineers. In 2009 over 229,000 people studied abroad, of whom over 108,000 who had graduated returned to China (*China's Statistical Yearbook* 2010, tables 20-10 and 20-11). Similarly in the same year nearly 2.2 million graduated from undergraduate and junior colleges in the field of science and technology (1,664 per million population, or 8,283 per million urban workforce). Further, 5 million graduated from (11,324) secondary vocational schools (or 3,780 per million of population, or 18,794.2 per million urban workforce), out of which 1.3 million of them had been trained for manufacturing activities and another 131,000 in civil and hydraulic engineering (*China's Statistical Yearbook* 2010, tables 20-17 and 20-18). In addition another 152.3 thousand and 46 thousand graduated in science and technology courses through the internet and adult institutions of higher education respectively (*China's Statistical Yearbook* 2010, tables 20-14 and 20-16).

Table 9.18. Applications for patents received and the number of patents granted in China (1990–2009)

Items	1990		2000		2009	
	A	G	A	G	A	G
Inventions	10,137	3,838	51,747	12,683	314,573	128,489
Domestic	5,832	1,149	25,346	6,177	**229,096**	**65,391**
Foreign	4,305	2,689	26,401	6,506	65,477	63,098
Utility models	27,615	16,959	68,815	54,743	85,477	63,098
Domestic	27,488	16,744	68,461	54,407	**310,771**	**202,113**
Foreign	127	11,644	354	336	1,910	1,689
Design	3,717	1,798	50,120	37,919	351,342	244,701
Domestic	3,265	1,411	46,532	34,652	**339,654**	**234,282**
Foreign	452	387	3,588	3,267	11,688	15,409
Total	41,469	22,588	170,682	105,345	976,686	581,992
Domestic	36,585	19,304	140,339	95,236	879,521	501,786
Foreign	4,884	3,248	30,343	10,109	474,900	80,206
Share of domestic (%)	88.2	85.5	82.2	90.4	90.1	86.2

Notes: A – application; G – granted.
Source: UNESCO online, Science and Technology statistics, http://www.onlineunesco.org/.

The S&T reform of 1999–2000 led to significant expansion of institutions of higher education. As a result, for example between 1995 and 2008, the number of new entrants, graduates and total enrolments (including doctoral level) all increased at an average annual growth rate of more than 20 per cent (OECD 2009, 51). For example, the number of enrolments in higher education institutions increased from about 3 million in 1995 to about 18 million in 2006. Similarly the number of students enrolled abroad also accelerated from less than 120,000 in 1999 to nearly 400,000 in 2005 (OECD 2009, fig. 46).

Furthermore, the government created a large number of vocational schools. In 2009 there were nearly 200,000 vocational schools (including secondary vocational schools) in China, out of which 11,324 were created in 2009 alone (People's Republic of China 2009, table 20-17). The number of graduates from secondary vocational schools jumped over 64 times between 1978 and 2009 (Table 9.19). Further, the government policy to send students abroad (see the same table) helped the development of domestic skills in research and development even though some of them never returned to China. For example, in 2008 about 21 per cent of students who graduated abroad did not return home.

The high level of education in science and technology as well as the establishments for vocational education facilitate training of skilled manpower for technological development. In 2008, 49.7 million (nearly 4 million of them in SOEs and collectively owned enterprises) were engaged in science and technological activities, out of which

Table 9.19. The number of graduates in secondary vocational schools and postgraduate students graduating abroad (1978–2009)

Year	Vocational schools (1,000)	Students abroad
1978	79	9
1990	893	35,440
2000	1,763	56,767
2005	1,700	189,728
2008	4,710	344,825
2009	5,097	371,273

Source: *China's Statistical Yearbook* (2009, tables 20-10 and 20-18).

5.8 million were engaged in related higher education activities; 1.6 million of them were scientists and engineers (ibid., tables 20-38, 20-40 and 20-65).

Comprehensive information on the government's other training programmes than the vocational schools is lacking. Nevertheless, there are indications that the government focused on enhancing the high-tech skills and education by establishing state funding training centres (Walsh 2003, 71). Some universities were also involved in training and a number of them benefited from partnership with TNCs for training in addition to R&D (Walsh 2003, 83). The Beijing University of Post and Communication is one example of where there is cooperation with TNCs in training. Foreign investors also provide some training of local staff independently (Walsh 2003, 96).

The combination of these factors allowed rapid expansion of persons engaged in scientific and technical activities in more recent years, as discussed earlier. One shortcoming is the lack of upper management staff despite the fact that some Chinese who have studied and gained experience abroad have returned.

Other Measures to Build Up Capabilities of National Enterprises

In contrast to Mexico the main motive behind China's development of the capabilities of domestic firms was the realization by the government and national enterprises that the transfer of technology from TNCs was not easily possible (Fan, Gao and Watanabe 2007, 360). Under the joint ventures also there was a limit on transfer of technology to Chinese partners (Walsh 2003, 113). The effort to develop capabilities of domestic firms in turn stimulated rivalry among TNCs to be involved in the R&D programmes of domestic firms in order not to miss the large Chinese market.

The Chinese government has followed a gradual and dual policy in developing the capabilities of domestic enterprises. It has gradually increased the role of private firms in the process of industrialization and export expansion. For example, the share of private enterprises in exports has increased to 18 per cent in 1985 and to 60 per cent in 2005 (Naughton 2007). At the same time it has implicitly, or explicitly, established a division of labour between SOEs and private enterprises. The private enterprises have concentrated, as expected, on short-term opportunities and low-cost production and sales to achieve high profitability. In contrast, SOEs concentrated on long-term goals through investment for development of new products[5] rather than profitability per se (Li and Xia 2008). In their efforts SOEs benefited little from spill-over effects of TNCs (Girma and Gong 2008). SOEs were privileged, however, to have better access to government funds and loans from the banking system (Li and Xia 2008)

In their applied R&D, SOEs benefited from a programme called 'National Science and Technology Diffusion' which was specifically designed for and devoted to them. This strategy is criticized for not having market-oriented goals in the case of SOEs. In our view it has been plausible, however, to reform SOEs gradually in order not to let the long-term objectives of the government be undermined, particularly as they had social objectives and responsibilities in addition to their long-term technological goals.

To provide sources of investment for domestic firms, China established two funds: the Export Development Fund for the larger firms and the Fund for Small and Medium Enterprise. The government also offered value added tax (VAT) refunds to exporting firms, and the Chinese export–import bank also provided loans at preferential interest rates.

Chinese domestic firms enjoyed the advantage of familiarity with the domestic market as well as allocation of significant parts of the domestic market to them by the government (e.g. in the telecoms equipment industries) (Fan, Gao and Watanabe 2007, 358). Yet the newcomer local firms of China, like enterprises in other developing countries, suffered from two main disadvantages as compared with TNCs in development of capabilities for and commercialization of new technology: resource disadvantages and reputation (brand) disadvantages, particularly in the IT sector where the technology is complicated and changes rapidly (Fan et al. 2007). Provided with incentives as well as support by the government together with some capabilities developed during the import-substitution period, however, a number of firms have managed to break into the market by developing frontier technologies (see the section on 'The Case of High-Technology Industries'). In addition to the support from the government the leading domestic firms sought collaboration with customers and cooperation with TNCs (Fan et al. 2007).

The Role of FDI

The contribution of TNCs to financial resources needed for R&D has been small. Nevertheless, they have become increasingly involved in R&D in China. Foreign high-tech R&D in China has gone through three phases: explanatory and strategic partnership (early to mid-1990s), expansion (mid- to late 1990s) and consolidation (late 1990s onwards) (Walsh 2003, 86–91). During the 1990s foreign investment in R&D was more of a 'show' than genuine activities as establishing R&D was a precondition for obtaining approval to establish joint ventures. During the second phase the TNCs also started to expand training centres. It was during the third phase, when the TNCs became interested in moving up the value-added production chain to upgrade their products, that they thus needed local R&D (Walsh 2003, 86–91).

---

5 SOEs have also had social objectives (see Li and Xia 2008).

Meanwhile the Chinese government also provided the TNCs with 'a range of preferential policies, including tax rebates, construction loans, access to modern facilities and other incentives', particularly in the case of IT industries (Walsh 2003, xiii, 56). While encouraging foreign firms to undertake R&D in China, the authorities initially entered into partnership with a number of foreign firms to create interfirm rivalry and accelerate technological development (Walsh 2003, 77–8, 80–82). Subsequently wholly foreign-owned firms established R&D facilities in the country (Walsh 2003, 79). Attracting multiple foreign partners was successful particularly in the IT industry. It is estimated that around 120 to 400 foreign R&D centres were operational in 2003 (Walsh 2003, xiv). In the case of IT industries, since the early 1990s almost all main TNCs involved in this industry have established R&D centres in China. In Beijing alone they established 18 main centres between 1993 and 2003.[6] Domestic firms also benefited from the partnership with TNCs, to some extent. For example, Legend, Stone, Founder and Great Wall learned a great deal about modern manufacturing in addition to technology development (Walsh 2003, 79). Nevertheless, the Chinese authorities realized that joint ventures with TNCs alone would not be sufficient for technology transfer.

Generally speaking, as stated before, in China, unlike Mexico, FDI has flooded into domestic investment as government efforts aimed at building the capabilities of domestic firms. As predicted, such capabilities in turn motivated TNCs to invest in R&D. As domestic firms were involved in the development of their technological capabilities, many TNCs were motivated to join them in their R&D in order to share the domestic market, particularly since the government also provided them with other incentives, as already described.

In China efforts to develop indigenous technological capabilities and to bring domestically developed technologies to market have been coupled with a targeted but aggressive acquisition of foreign technologies through foreign direct investment. The strategy has been to either develop a sector or technology nationally or 'import' the technology through FDI. Initially licensing FDI was conditioned to arrangements for transfer of technology and provision of linkages to local firms, joint ventures and partnership. In 2001 such condition was dropped but TNCs were encouraged to invest in R&D, particularly in information technology, 'by offering a range of preferential policies' that includes 'tax rebates, construction loans, access to modern facilities, and other incentives' (Walsh 2003, xiii, 56). Whereas national Mexican firms capture approximately only 5 per cent of the inputs of foreign firms, in China that number is well over 20 per cent (Gallagher and Zarsky 2007).

The Case of High-Technology Industries

China is the most impressive contemporary case of latecomer in high technology development.[7] For 30 years the country has gradually and quietly built manufacturing

---

6 They include Intel, SAP, Motorola, Lucent, Turbolinux, Nokia, IBM, Ericsson, Agilent, Microsoft, Matsushita, NEC and Samsung (Chen and Kenney 2008, table A1).

7 For a brief history of the development of the industry up to 1993 see (Ye 2008).

capacities and integrated into world markets. China has been at the core of TNC location strategies because of its multiple location specific assets: a large and growing internal market *and* a low-cost export platform for manufactured goods. What is more, China provides a match with national linkage capability between TNCs and domestic suppliers. Now the country is on the verge of having formidable flagship firms of its own in the information and telecommunications technology (ICT) industries.

FDI in China's high tech has gone through four phases: sales, marketing, licensing and technical services; manufacturing and production; product design, localization and redevelopment; and finally R&D (Walsh 2003, 75–6). Much is made of China's low wages as a major factor driving TNC outsourcing to China and IT development more generally. There is little doubt that wages have been low: the average manufacturing wage in China was estimated to be 61 cents an hour in 2001, compared with $16.14 in the US and $2.08 in Mexico (OECD 2009, 3).

Nevertheless, the story of China's success and likely emergence as the centre for global IT production goes beyond low wages and generic product manufacturing capabilities. The 863 Programme (1986) was aimed at high basic and applied research in seven areas and fifteen topics with the cooperation of private enterprises. The seven areas included, in order of priority given by the planners, information technology, laser, automation, biotechnology, new material technology, astro-technology and energy technology, as describeded earlier (Fan and Watanabe 2006, 311). The 'climbing programme' of 1992 was oriented towards acceleration of basic research. In contrast, the Torch programme was market-oriented right from its inception in 1988 and was geared mainly to commercialization of the results of R&D. Its objectives ranged from providing enabling environment for high-tech industries, to the creation of high-tech zones, executing projects in above-mentioned selected (7) areas, training and facilitating international cooperation (Fan and Watanabe 2006, 312). In 1995, as already cited, the government passed the 'Decision on Accelerating Scientific and Technological Progress' in order to intensify the technological development (Walsh 2003, 105).

The development of the IT industry is in some part the result of government push and nurturing. In 1986 four Chinese scientists recommended to the government that IT be designated a strategic sector. The request was approved and in 1988 China's National Development and Reform Commission (formerly the State Planning Commission) designated high tech as a 'pillar' industry worthy of strategic industrial policy (MOST 2006). It was coupled with the Ministry of Science and Technology (MOST)'s National High-Tech R&D Program (or 863 Program) that supported the R&D efforts of local governments, national firms and regions. The goal was to foster a vibrant high-tech sector with national firms that could eventually compete as global flagships. The strategy was to establish domestic firms and bring foreign firms to China to build their capacity to produce components and peripherals for pcs. To this end IBM, HP, Toshiba, and Compaq were all invited to come to China and form joint ventures with such Chinese firms as Legend, Great Wall, Trontru and Star. China required the foreign firms to transfer specific technologies to the joint venture, establish R&D centres, source to local firms and train Chinese employees, as already discussed (USDOC 2006). By the 1990s all of the major contract equipment manufacturers also came to China under similar arrangements. According to the Tenth Five Year Plan ending in 2005 the government planned to invest more than \$120 billion in the IT industries in order to raise the share of the sector to 7 per cent of GDP (Walsh 2003, 71). In the current development plan the share of a few strategic (IT) industries is supposed to rise to 8 per cent by 2015.

The strategy has paid off. 'By carefully nurturing its domestic computing industry through tightly controlled partnerships with foreign manufacturers, China has become the fourth-largest computer maker in the world' in the early years of the first decade of the twenty-first century (Dedrick and Kraemer 2002, 28). Now China is the second largest producer of ICT products. Table 9.20 shows that the majority of foreign electronics firms in China are either joint ventures or domestic/state-owned enterprises (SOEs).

Given the large nature of the economy and the fact that China serves as an export platform, China has had a great deal of bargaining power *vis-à-vis* TNCs. First China had location-specific assets that could not be ignored. Not only did China offer an export platform like Taiwan and South Korea did, but it also had a large and growing market at home, which is a major bargaining chip. In essence foreign

Table 9.20. China's major consumer electronics firms by ownership

Sector	Foreign-owned	Joint-ventures	Domestic private firms and SOEs
Mobile phones	Motorola	Motorola/Eastcom Nokia/Capitel, Southern Samsung/Kejian Sagem/Bird	TLC
PCs	HP	IBM/Great Wall	Lenovo*
	Dell	Toshiba/Toshiba Shanghai Epson/Start Taiwan GVC/TCL	Founder Tongfang
'Brown goods'		Sony/SVA Philips/Suzhou CTV Toshiba/Dalian Daxian Great Wall Electronics/TCL	Changhong Konka Hisense Skyworth Hair Panda Xoceco
'White goods'	Siemens	Xianxuehai Samsung/Suzhou Electrolux/Changsha LG/Chunlan Mitsubishi/hair Sanyo/Kelon Sigma/Meiling Hong Leong/Xinfei Toshiba Carrier/Midea	Changling Gree

Source: Gallagher and Shafaeddin (2010) based on Rodrik (2006).

firms traded market access for technology transfer. China's domestic market is growing rapidly, propelled not only by a rise in personal income but also by the active government promotion strategies discussed before.

In addition to domestic market access, global TNCs have been willing to work in the confines of Chinese policy because of China's active support for and subsidies to the high-tech industry. According to a comprehensive study by Dussel Peters (2005) the establishment of high-tech industrial parks has been a key programme. Much of the FDI flows to these parks and national firms, which are also the recipients of numerous incentives and assistance programmes.

Despite the potential market pay-offs, foreign firms started to get nervous about technology transfer arrangements a few years ago, especially as Chinese IT firms are beginning to emerge as flagships. Indeed OECD governments have begun to dub China's policies as 'forced transfers' and have undertaken investigations and task forces in order to eliminate or reduce them (USDOC 2006).

Another key element of the strategy for the development of ICT industries is a high level of support for high-tech R&D and education. According to MOST the bulk of R&D expenditure has been allocated to the IT industry. R&D funds are distributed to SOEs, local governments and Chinese-owned firms. The 2004–8 Five Year Plan called for increased subsidies to SOEs for R&D (MOST 2006, table 5.2). Support for local government is targeted at the cities which house R&D centres within industrial parks. Local governments often match national government funding for R&D programmes.

In short, China's high-tech promotion strategy had two prongs: build up capabilities of domestic firms and stimulate investment and technology transfer by TNCs, and the results of China's high-tech programme have been impressive. By 1989 the Legend group had evolved into Legend Computer and formed a joint venture with Hewlett Packard. By 2000 Legend had emerged as the number one seller of personal computers in the Asia-Pacific and held more than 20 per cent of the Chinese pc market. In early 2005 Legend – morphed into Lenovo – acquired IBM's global desktop and notebook computer divisions. With the IBM deal, Lenovo became, after Dell and HP, the world's third largest pc maker (Spooner 2005). Hassee Computer is another fast-growing domestic computer firm. Domestic manufacturers together have dominated 70 per cent of the market for pc sales in China (Walsh 2003, 108). Founder became a leading firm in developing laser typesetting technologies and electronic publishing. Datang is the leading company in development of 3G (TD-SCDMA) technology. Huawei is a giant maker of telecommunications equipment. A collection of several domestic firms developed their own brand in mobile telephones and high definition disc players (see Tables 9.20 and 9.21 below). Table 9.21 exhibits a few other Chinese firms including lesser known ones that have made significant innovations. Despite numerous problems at the beginning, particularly the lack of recognition of their capabilities and brands, and the Chinese customers' perception of the inferior relative merits of their product as compared with imported products, they succeeded in penetrating both the internal and international markets. They were highly motivated to develop 'leading technologies and leading products'; they focused on a single product, collaborated with leading local firms as provider of equipment and components, sought the cooperation of TNCs and collaborated with their customers. Throughout the process government support was important (Fan et al. 2007).

Table 9.21. Leading innovative domestic high-technology companies in China

Company name	Funding	Major technical achievements
Huawei	1988	Large-scale switch system Next-generation network Optical network Data communication
Shenzhen Zhongxin Technology Co.	1985	Large-scale switch system Next-generation system TD-SCDMA
Datang Telecom Technology	1998	TD-SCDMA SCDMA
Dawning Information Industry Co.	1995	Wormhole routing chip Parallel optimizing compiler Scalability, usability, manageability and availability (SUMA) tech
Beijing Genome Institute	2002	Large-scale genome sequencing
Sibiono Gene Technology	1998	Gene therapy medication for head and neck squamos cell carcinoma
China National Petroleum Co.	1955	Integrated seismic data processing software
	(1988)	ABS technology
		Top drive drilling equipment Multibranch horizontal and large displacement well drilling technology Two-state catalytic cracking technology

Source: Based on Fan et al. (2007).

Overall, by 2003 China's electronics sector generated $142 billion in exports and employed four million workers. Between 1993 and 2003 the growth rate of high-tech exports was 50.2 per cent for computers and peripherals, and 21.9 per cent for telecommunications and related equipment. In 2008–9, high-tech products constituted the top three items of China's exports and the related amounts of their exports on average was nearly $272 billion (UNCTAD, *Handbook of Statistics*, 2010, table 3.2D). Exports of computer equipment alone were nearly $118 billion. Like Lenovo many Chinese firms started as state-owned enterprises (SOEs) and were gradually privatized as they gained capacity and became competitive. In 1993 26 per cent of computer and peripheral firms and 54 per cent of telecommunications firms were SOEs. By 2003 only 6 per cent of computer and 18 per cent of telecoms firms were SOEs. Their share has declined further since then.

Although national firms, including SOEs, are in the minority, they are filing and being granted more patent applications than foreign firms. According to MOST, even in 2002, Chinese firms were granted 112,103 patents whereas foreign firms were granted only 20,296. In 2009 domestic firms accounted for over 86 per cent of patents granted (Table 9.18).

Close to half of these patents were in the form of utility models – patents for incremental innovations where local firms create variations on project and process execution. This reveals that a significant amount of learning is going on in Chinese firms (MOST 2006).

Conclusions

In this chapter we have compared the experience of China and Mexico during the last three decades as they share some similarities in their goals for industrialization and growth as well as their attempts in trade liberalization, economic reform and attraction of FDI. But they show different performance and outcomes. Unlike Mexico, China is on the road to international competitiveness at a high level of development. Mexico has achieved little as compared with China in enhancing value added in exports and gaining comparative advantage in production in processing industries. Mexico has in fact intensified its static comparative advantage in exports through assembly operation. In contrast, while China also started assembly operation in its processing industries it has managed to develop its export-oriented industries through a tendency to specialization based on dynamic comparative advantage, upgrading and increase in value added in exports. We have shown that the difference in their performance is due to their different industrialization and development strategies and the policies they have pursued. Mexico has followed the recommendations of neoliberals, believing that liberalization of international trade and FDI would automatically lead to industrialization and upgrading through the operation of market forces. China in contrast has pursued an approach which can be labelled as 'neodevelopmentalist', through which it has dynamic industrialization and development policies relying not only on market and incentives, but also on government policies for building up the capabilities of domestic enterprise.

More specifically both countries started liberalization of trade, FDI and economic reform around the early 1980s and showed rapid expansion of exports of manufactured goods produced through assembly operations, particularly of ICT products produced mainly in export-processing zones during the 1980s and 1990s. Nevertheless, unlike the case of Mexico, China's export expansion has also been accompanied by rapid growth of MVA and GDP not only during the 1980s and 1990s, but also during the recent decade after its accession to the WTO. In Mexico the expansion of the exports of *maquila* industries has led to little increase either in the value added and higher wages or in development of backward linkages with the rest of the economy. It has not led to the upgrading of the industrial structure. Furthermore Mexico has not been able to sustain rapid export expansion during the recent decade, despite its privileged access to the US market through NAFTA, due to its loss of competitiveness in the international market, particularly *vis-à-vis* China. TNCs have also been relocating plants from China to Mexico.

In Mexico, following the approach advocated by neoliberalists and the 'Washington Consensus', the government assumed that trade liberalization and a hands-off approach to economic activities would automatically lead to growth and upgrading. The government reduced all interference in the technology process in the early 1990s as it was assumed that technology would be transferred through trade and FDI. TNCs were provided with various incentives, particularly in export-processing zones, without demanding their commitment for performance. Economic liberalism also led to the reduction in government investment in R&D, education and training. The government pursued some policies on training, R&D and development of SMEs but they were inefficient and underfunded.

In contrast, China has followed a different strategy. While reforming the economy the Chinese government has taken a more gradual and experimental approach to liberalization and integration into the world economy. It has put in place functional and targeted government policies to develop the capabilities of its national enterprises by emphasizing education and training for human resource development, R&D and learning for development of indigenous technological capabilities through a national innovation system (NSI).

The science and technology (S&T) policy of the Chinese government was responsive to the market dynamic with growing emphasis on the private sector (including TNCs). Nevertheless, through trial and error, the government has learned that reliance on market forces and FDI alone will not automatically lead to the transfer of technology and increased value added in exports. Thus S&T policy and research and development (R&D) have become a cornerstone of China's industrial development. The ingredient of government policies on S&T and NSI included direct involvement and support for indigenous R&D, innovation by individual firms and the creation of R&D institutions. It also included alliance among firms in an industry and their cooperation with research institutes and universities as well as foreign firms, targeting particularly the strategic industries.

Government policy on R&D and technological development ranged from direct investment, provision of guidance, institutional and financial support, creating a favourable environment for innovation and upgrading, as well as the introduction of competition into the domestic market for the strategic industries. It also included development of national standards and patents for main IT products. China's indicators for R&D are the highest in Asia after Singapore, Republic of Korea and Taiwan; it is also higher than Spain and Italy. The number of people working on R&D in China increased by nearly 2.6 times in 2009 as compared with 1996. The corresponding figures for Mexico increased by 1.9 times over the same period. In China the number of researchers per million inhabitants is over three times higher than that of Mexico.

The selective and targeted strategy of the government was aimed particularly at IT industries and the government developed an institutional framework for S&T development and a dynamic national system of innovation (NSI). It consisted of the Chinese Academy of Science, relevant ministries, private enterprises, including venture capital firms, universities and research institutes. Close links were established among these entities in the public and private sectors. Both basic research, and particularly application and diffusion of technology have been emphasized right from the early 1980s. The NSI of China was not perfect but it was a lot more sophisticated than that of Mexico, which was very inefficient and underfunded.

The results of the implementation of science and technology policy are striking for China as compared with Mexico. On average, 12 times more patents are filed in China each year than all the LA countries combined, let alone Mexico. What is more, whereas in Mexico only 4 per cent of all patents are granted to the residents, in China that figure is over 75 per cent. The number of patents granted increased by over 14 times between 1990 and 2009, out of which domestic patents accounted for over 86 per cent in 2009. Moreover the relative importance of inventions in granted patents has increased, reaching 22 per cent of patents granted in 2009. Domestic firms accounted for 51 per cent of total patents granted for inventions in 2009 as against about 30 per cent in 1990. Similar results are also evident in terms of the number of articles published by Chinese scholars as compared with those of Latin American.

The performance of China was impressive not only in exports of high-tech products, but also in increasing domestic value added through the development of domestic indigenous technology. In 2008–9, high-tech products constitute the first three items of exports of China, amounting on average to nearly $272 billion. Development of indigenous capabilities was focused on computers, mobile phones, laser and nanotechnology. For example, Lenovo, produced by Legend Group, has become the world's third largest pc maker after Dell and HP. China also developed its own brand in mobile telephones and high-definition disc players. Like Lenovo, many Chinese firms started as state-owned enterprises (SOEs) and were gradually privatized as they gained capacity and competitiveness.

All in all, while China is to sustain and intensify its international competitiveness on the road to a higher level of development, Mexico seems to continue its developing based on static comparative advantage and remaining at relatively lower level than China's. While China has followed a developmentalist approach, Mexico has gone along the path advocated by neoliberals and proponents of the 'Washington Consensus'.

10

SUMMARY AND CONCLUDING REMARKS

> Trade, [and] thus international competitiveness, are means to development; they are not an objective *per se*... Nations may have different objectives than maximizing world welfare. (List 1856)

Analysing the interrelation between competitiveness and development in this book we have argued that there are two different approaches to competitiveness: static and dynamic, with different implications for long-run development of a country. The static approach is based on the static version of the theory of comparative cost advantage and keeps the pursuing country at a low level of development. The dynamic, or Schumpeterian/ Listian, approach will lead to competitiveness at a high level of development. The static approach is advocated by the proponents of neoliberalism while the dynamic approach is propagated by 'neodevelopmentalists'.

The main developed countries set targets closely, at the highest level of their executive machinery, i.e. in the presidents' or prime ministers' offices, and draft and implement strategies and policies for achieving competitiveness at a high level of development. Yet they try to impose a static approach to competitiveness on developing countries, either directly or indirectly, to limit their policy space. They do so directly through bilateral or regional trade agreements and EPAs, and indirectly though international organizations such as international financial institutions and the WTO.

Following Reinert (1995, 26) we have regarded competitiveness as an element of development. In this sense of the term competitiveness refers to activities, which, while 'being competitive' in the micro sense, also contribute to value added and development, raising income and improving the standard of living of a nation's population. Within such a framework, specialization based on static comparative advantage cannot necessarily lead to a higher level of development. Maintaining and enhancing value added requires, *inter alia*, upgrading, to achieve and sustain competitiveness at a high level of development. In other words, the upgrading of the production structure is a feature of the Schumpeterian approach to competition which implies mobility, that is, 'movement of factors of production from low occupation to high reward ones' (Reekie 1979, 11) or upgrading from low-value uses towards high-value uses (Reekie 1979, 82). The ability to upgrade depends on 'the ability to capture high value added industries which possibly generate rents and positive externalities that spill over to the rest of the economy' (Oxley and Yeung 1998a, xxvi).

Hence activities that support the competitiveness of a national economy include those that 'retain the high value-added production activities which can lead to higher factor earnings and improving living standards' (Oxley and Yeung 1998a, xiv). Such activities are referred to as strategic sectors by Krugman, i.e. sectors which have special value to the economy including 'high-value-added sectors, linkages sectors, sunrise industries, and catalyst industries' (Krugman 1987, 208). In more general terms one may speak of supply dynamic and demand dynamic industries. Supply dynamic industries are those which provide linkages, spill-overs and thus externalities to other activities. Demand dynamic industries include those for which demand rises fast in the international and domestic economy because of their high income elasticity (UNCTAD 2002).

To follow such an approach in discussing issues related to achieving competitiveness at a high level of development we have developed an analytical framework for studying the related issues. In doing so we have also benefited from and developed on the views and theories of a number of leading economists, such as F. List (1856), Kalecki (1955), Schumpeter (1934), Penrose (1959), Hirschman (1958), Porter (1990), Lazonick (1991) and Shafaeddin (2005c).

Analytical Framework

Applying a dynamic Schumpeterian/Penrosian approach to the concept of competitiveness and function of firms, we have regarded firms as a coordinating agent and as part of a coordination system consisting of firms, markets, government and 'nonprice factors' through which economic activities are coordinated. Such a coordination system also has connection with and is influenced by the outside world. A firm is strategically active and is a driving force in such a system around which the other coordination agents operate. In such a system the coordination of most economic activities takes place within the firm rather than through the market. A firm has its own capabilities, motivations – which goes beyond short-term profit making – and undertakes strategic planning in order to achieve its objectives. It has interaction with markets, other firms, consumers, governments, institutions, organizations and infrastructure, in each case both domestic and external. A firm is also influenced not only by the government strategy, but also by incentives provided by, and the pressure imposed on it, by the government. The relative role of a firm in relation to the market and government may vary from one country to another and changes over time within a country.

International Context and Conditions of Competitiveness

Having defined the conceptual framework of our analysis, we have explained in Chapter 2 the context and conditions within which industrial activities and competition take place at the global and national levels. The changes in the global economic situation during the last quarter-century have increased the need for government support for newcomer firms of developing countries for developing supply capabilities and eventually competing in the international market at the high level of development. Yet we have shown that changes in the dominant economic philosophy and international trade rules and in practices of IFIs and bilateral donors have limited the means of doing so by limiting the policy space of developing countries. Globalization and other new methods of production and organization have changed the nature of competition in the international market in three main ways. First it has enhanced the relative importance of the 'strategic competitive advantage' of large established firms *vis-à-vis* comparative cost advantage of the developing countries resulting from cheap labour.

Secondly thus it has intensified the process of Schumpeterian 'dynamic competition' and 'creative distraction'. In such a process large and established firms are continuously active in innovation, product development, quality improvement, shortening of delivery time, etc. As a result the role of 'nonprice attributes' of products in competitive advantages has increased, reducing the relative importance of price and labour cost. Further, development of new methods of production such as flexible specialization, fragmentation of industrial activities and production sharing has intensified the role of large established firms (TNCs) of developed countries.

Finally the growing size, market concentration, rapid technological development and the oligopolistic power and strategic behaviour of established firms (TNCs) have increased barriers to entry into the international market for new independent firms of developing countries. It is true that the process of globalization and trade liberalization has improved the possibilities and opportunities for developing countries to enter the international market for the products which they already produce based on their static comparative advantage, particularly in cases where global firms have relocated plants in these countries. Nevertheless, the limited supply capabilities of domestic firms in many developing countries limit their ability to attract FDI. Moreover, when they do attract FDI, the process of globalization increases the risks from and vulnerability of these countries to the decisions of global firms in the relocation of these plants from one country to another, and to changes in external demand. The recent global financial and economic crisis has also revealed their extreme vulnerability to external sources of demand due to changes in the world economic situation.

Moreover the changes in international trade rules and conditions imposed on developing countries by IFIs and through bilateral donors have also limited the policy space of developing countries to expand supply capabilities and upgrade their industrial structure based on 'dynamic comparative advantage'.

Theories of Competitiveness

In Chapter 3 we have explained that there is a lacuna for a comprehensive dynamic policy framework to achieve competitiveness at a high level of development in the context of developing countries in a way that we have presented in Chapter 1. As we have explained, such a framework needs to encompass both macro- and micro-issues and nonprice factors, and to envisage a firm as a social unit with its own unique culture.

M. Porter's theory of competitive advantage is a step forward in taking into account some of the above-stated issues. Nevertheless, it does not go far enough to investigate the implication of increasing return at the firm level over time. Further, it does not expound sufficiently on the relative role of government, firms and market and their changes during the process of industrialization and development. Lazonick considers the interrelation between increasing return and innovation, and outlines the differences between 'innovating' (large) firms and 'adaptive' SMEs, and deals with the role of government in the development of competitive industries to some extent. However, it lacks a macro-foundation and development perspective, and does not consider firms as sociocultural units. Such deficiencies are overcome by the theory of productive power of F. List. While progressive and relevant to the case of developing countries, the List theory, however, lacks a micro-foundation. The proponents of capability-building theory have developed on the List theory and provided a dynamic theory of competitiveness integrating the evolutionary and new growth theories. However, it does not sufficiently develop on the active role of firm in product, as against cost and price, competitiveness, and on the nonprice strategic behaviour of firms. Moreover the importance of increasing returns to scale at the firm level is not appreciated as the new growth theory remains in the sphere of competitive market structure. Finally it does not fully consider the respective role of various elements of the coordination mechanism at each point in time and their changes in the process of industrialization and development in the way we have explained in the introductory chapter.

Enterprise Strategy and Organization

In Chapters 4 and 5 we have explained the sources of competitiveness at the micro-level. We have discussed the strategy of a firm to create value for its customers, thus enhancing its income and the necessary capabilities for creating supply capacity, operating it efficiently and upgrading its activities in order to sustain its competitiveness through relocation of the rent in the value chain. We have argued that the competitive performance of a firm would depend on its capabilities, strategies and organization of its activities as well as the environment in which it operates. The sources of a firm's capabilities are two-fold: its own distinctive resources (human capital and skill, technological, organization, culture and strategies) and external economies. The external economies are related to the general environment in which a firm operates, including government policies at both macro- and micro-levels; the organization of the industry in which it operates, particularly collective efficiencies involved in industrial clustering and production sharing, as well as the institutional and infrastructural set-up of the country.

Chapter 4 is devoted to the discussion of cost of production, and a firm's strategy and organization, including the application of new methods of production such as a flexible manufacturing system (FMS) and production sharing. The external economies were taken up in the subsequent chapter.

In contrast to the neoclassical theory of the firm, factor cost and product prices are not, we have argued, the only determining factors in competitiveness, and firms are not passive. Further, the international market is not competitive. The increasing return to scale in production, marketing and distribution, economies of scope and X-efficiencies of large established firms influences not only their cost of production but also 'nonprice attributes' of the products they supply; the products they produce are not necessarily homogeneous. Further, the large established firms are not passive; through their 'three pronged investment' in manufacturing, marketing and management; control of technology; strategic behaviour and 'creative destruction' they create barriers to entry for newcomer firms. Therefore, newcomer firms of developing countries are in a disadvantageous position *vis-à-vis* established firms of industrialized countries. In addition to developing efficient supply capabilities newcomer firms also ought to eventually have their own strategy to create a unique position in order to develop value for the consumer and to enjoy 'rent'. Such a strategy requires the upgrading of product, process and organization of production.

Some developing country firms have applied the flexible manufacturing system (FMS), which had been initially developed in Japan, for continuous improvement by integrating 'thinking and doing'. This system requires more than advantage in factor cost. It also has major differences from the system of mass production which is based on advanced planning of production, production of a number of products sequentially and increasing return to scale. In the FMS the system is dynamic, the decision on production is made only when the order is made and thus planning and operation are integrated and the production is flexible. It requires, *inter alia*, multiskilled workforce, multifunctional machinery, a culture of teamwork, 'group-focussed image of change' and close interrelation between the management, the shop floor and the suppliers and distributors for total quality control, problem solving and just-in-time (JIT) delivery.

Developing countries which have applied the FMS, or some elements of it, have experienced some success, but many countries have also faced a number of obstacles. The most important problems of its implementation in developing countries include: the lack of perception by the management about changes in the nature of competition in the global economy or the lack of the necessary commitment from the management and misconception of their function; resistance to change by workers and middle managers; low levels of education and training; the lack of teamwork culture and weak labour-management; and weak interfirm relations. An important finding of the country cases studied and reviewed is that the complexity of the system requires support by the government in providing institutional set-up, infrastructure, education and training, in addition to the need for conducive macroeconomics, industrial policies and close government–business relations.

Organization of Interfirm Relations

The lack of an industrial structure and environment to provide external economies to a firm and the lack of interfirm relations has led some countries to embark on initiating 'clustering' for development of interfirm relations. They have done so in order to enjoy external economies in the form of 'collective efficiency'. We have discussed issues related to the impact of external economies on competitiveness in general and interfirm relations through clustering and production sharing in Chapter 5. In contrast to the neoclassical theory of the firm external economies prevail and play an important role in the competitiveness and development of other firms and the national economy as a whole. The price mechanism fails to stimulate socially optimum levels of investment mainly because of the existence of externalities related to investment coordination, which take the forms of pecuniary externalities and technological externalities. When the number of agents is large, state intervention is required to coordinate investment decisions. Professional experience and investment in skill development also involves dynamic external economies. As the market for knowledge, know-how and technological learning is imperfect, again there is a need for government intervention in the market. There are yet other forms of externalities, including attitude to work, atmosphere creation and reputation, which can be firm specific but would also become country specific where a number of incumbent firms are the source of those types of externalities.

Externalities involved in interfirm relations may prevail in the form of clustering to achieve economies of scale and 'collective efficiency' deriving from local externalities and joint action, and from production sharing. Production sharing enhances the division of labour and economies of scales through vertical integration of production. The main advantage of clustering for SMEs in particular stem not only from proximity of firms, access to the sources of supply of inputs and skills, labour pooling and interchanges of information, knowledge and experience, but also, more importantly, it derives from joint action for organizing the operation of the firms 'according to a definite principle' for benefiting from external economies. Clustering can also contribute to enhancing productivity and competing on 'nonprice attributes' of products produced by the firms involved.

A number of both developed and developing countries have been involved in clustering. While their experience is mixed, a few general observations can be made. First the initial static collective efficiencies have been made through clustering, particularly in developed countries. Secondly, on the whole, firms involved in clustering have shown superior performance in competitiveness over other firms by pursuing dynamic policies for upgrading. Thirdly, nevertheless, the sustainability of competitive advantage has been more difficult in the clusters of developing countries as they have taken a less dynamic approach than the clusters of developed countries. Fourthly skill development has been an important factor in the success of clusters. Fifthly clusters of developing countries have shown better success in resource-based and similar industries where there is low appropriability of knowledge and low barriers to entry than in technologically complex industries. Sixthly the existence of trade networks and trust among member firms has been important in the success of clusters, as has been the role of government through provision of assistance in innovation and upgrading, common services, and through dissemination of information as highlighted by the experience of Japan. Seventhly the global buyers have contributed little to functional upgrading, but when clusters are linked to TNCs, foreign firms can have a positive effect on the competitiveness of local firms through the provision of marketing channels and quality improvement required by demanding foreign clients.

Another contribution of foreign firms to competitiveness is through production sharing, which is a vertical division of labour among firms of different countries leading to assembly operations. Production sharing has, however, contributed to the enhancement of domestic value added when the host government has been active in developing the capabilities of the domestic firms. One downside of production sharing is vulnerability to external factors when the final products are exported to the third market, i.e. developed countries.

Reputation and Trust

The relations of a firm with its stakeholders, its reputation and trust influence its competitiveness. A firm can develop reputation by providing value for the buyers of its products. By developing a favourable reputation a firm creates dynamic external economies of reputation which are beneficial to the other firms and the whole industry and country. The quality of products and after-sale services are, *inter alia*, two important contributory factors in creating and maintaining a favourable reputation for a firm. Further, a combination of 'image' and 'identity' are regarded as the way a firm is perceived by its customers and employers. Image is the view of the company held by its stakeholders and identity is the views of its employees and both are vitally important elements of the reputation of a firm. Such views are influenced, to a large extent, by the development of trust between a firm and its customers, stakeholders and employees. Trust is also important among employees themselves and between the firm and government authorities. Sociopolitical and cultural factors are important in the development of trust among various actors and agencies involved in business relations, particularly in public–private cooperation, which is an important factor in the process of development and attaining competitiveness.

Innovation and Upgrading

Innovation and upgrading of the industrial structure is important in achieving and maintaining international competitiveness and at the same time enhancing development. Innovation in the context of new firms of developing countries takes on a different meaning from that of the established firms of developed countries, which are at the frontier of technology (technology leaders). Thus we have analysed innovation in the context of developing countries, i.e. the technology followers, who need to join the leaders eventually. Distinctions are made among product upgrading, process upgrading and functional upgrading. Accordingly, following Schumpeter, we have referred to various types of innovation required for upgrading including product innovation, process innovation, market innovation, product-service innovation and innovation in procurement. In each case innovation can be incremental, radical or systemic, i.e. a combination of incremental and radical, and part of the techno-economic paradigm, i.e. a set of incremental and radical innovations. Technology can be embodied in machinery and equipment or may be tacit and can be obtained by various types of learning and spill over from one firm to another. Learning is a social process which is cumulative and collective and is influenced, *inter alia*, by cultural factors.

In contrast to the neoclassical theory, innovation plays a more important role than price in competitiveness and upgrading of firms. It is also a driving force behind the growth of not only firms, but also a country. Specialization and competitiveness based on static comparative advantage will be short lived and it will not lead to industries with high rewards to the factors of production. For this purpose continuous upgrading is required for which innovation in its broad sense of the term is essential. The systemic nature of innovation is implied in the national innovation system (NSI). NSI is developed on List's ideas on 'The National System of Political Economy' and is concerned with the generation and distribution of knowledge; it is a social order involving learning and skill formation, and it is sector and country specific. Thus one implication of NSI is that the development of the competitive advantage of a country depends on the development of the capabilities of its national firms. Such capabilities, as we have shown, include, *inter alia*, entrepreneurship, R&D institutional build-up and most of all 'intangible assets' or what List calls 'mental capital', government policies and a firm's strategy for upgrading. Mental capital, in turn, is a complex issue affected by a number of factors in addition to technological capabilities and 'core competences' of a firm.

Following Forbes and Wield (2002) we have demystified myths surrounding technology issues in the context of developing countries. At the early stage of industrialization firms in developing countries may act as a technological 'follower' – referred to as adaptive firms by Lazonick – by undertaking adaptive innovation. In doing so they apply for the first time a method of production, process or organization that may have been practised by other firms – innovating firms – already. Nevertheless, they have to join the technology leaders eventually, and, in other words, they need to develop their own technological capacity so that they could eventually adopt a proactive innovation at the frontier of technology and thus also become an innovating firm. A firm in a developing country would start with capabilities in process innovation by incremental innovation, then move to product innovation and eventually develop its own design, followed by development of a proprietary product and upgrading. The important point is that as innovation involves change it also requires a culture of learning and adaptability, government vision and a firm's strategy.

Trade and FDI, under certain conditions, may make a contribution to the technological development and competitiveness of a country. Nevertheless, we have argued that M. Porter was correct to believe that intensification of globalization and global competition has made the role of home nation and national system of innovation more important rather than less so. The speed of technological change and the lengthening of the period of learning necessitate the nurturing of firms and industries in a developing country. Hence the role of government strategy in building up competitive industrial capacity in developing countries by technological development, innovation, trade and industrial policy and management of FDI, etc. is important.

Government Policies

The process of building up a competitive industrial base in developing countries and catching up with industrialized countries requires: accelerating the productive capacity; making it efficient and competitive in the internal and external markets; and moving up the value-added ladder by upgrading the industrial structure. Contrasting the neoclassical theory, none of the elements of such a process could take place automatically through the operation of market forces alone. The processes of learning and development of endogenous capabilities of national firms necessitate government intervention in both production and export. Government policies should encompass, *inter alia*, dynamic and flexible trade and industrial policies as well as technological strategies complemented by strategic actions at the enterprise level. Accordingly we have presented a typology of developing countries according to their position in the three phases of industrialization listed earlier. At the early stages of industrialization, policies should be geared mainly to the acceleration of supply capabilities. Subsequently the efficiency of the installed capacity requires the attention of policy makers before attempts are made for upgrading which requires, *inter alia*, technological policies. Having reviewed various related theoretical arguments, we have explained what sort of policy is required at each phase of industrialization in order to achieve competitiveness at a high level of development in an ideal situation assuming that there is government will and there are no external regulatory constraints; but in fact there may be constraints in these respects.

The sociopolitical will of the government depends, *inter alia*, on its structure and the vested interests of the dominant governmental group, which might not necessarily be the same as the interests of the public at large. Further, the government may lack the capacity in policy formulation, decision making and implementation. As Myrdal (1970) put it, a 'soft' government cannot tackle development issues. While a disciplined and democratic government is essential, we believe 'soft' should mean incapable. The government capabilities and effectiveness should be developed for which a suitable political environment is needed (Meier 1993), which requires representation and its backing by the public at large. The experience of some Latin American countries and the recent development of the so-called 'Arab Spring' indicate that undemocratic government is not sustainable just because its interests diverge from the interests of the population at large. For example, the rate-of-time discount of the politicians and the 'governmental group' may tend to be higher than that of the community.

Yet further, the policy space of developing countries is limited. The implementation of the required policies is currently constrained by external regulatory issues imposed by the WTO rules and by conditions imposed on them by IFIs and bilateral donors through regional and bilateral trade agreements. Thus, as will be explained shortly, there is a need for changes in international rules and the practices of IFIs and bilateral donors to make them conducive to the development of a competitive industrial structure and its upgrading in a way that raises the standard of living of the population. The alternative is specialization in accordance with the principle of static comparative advantage and competition in the international market at the low level of development.

Comparative Experience of Mexico and China

The comparative performance of China and Mexico during the last couple of decades provides some clues for the possibilities of achieving competitiveness at a high level of development, despite the existence of constraints imposed by the present international economic system and its implications of lessons to be learned for other developing countries. The analysis of comparative performance of the two countries is important because they share some similarities in their goals for industrialization and growth as well as their attempts in trade liberalization, economic reform and attraction of FDI. Further, they both acceded to the WTO (Mexico in 1995 and China in 2000) and have a free trade agreement with the USA. Yet they show different performance levels and outcomes.

As already seen, China is on the road to international competitiveness at a high level of development whereas Mexico has been less successful than China in enhancing value added in exports and gaining comparative advantage in *production* including production in processing industries. Mexico has intensified its static comparative advantage in exports whereas in contrast China has managed to develop its export-oriented industries through a tendency to specialization based on dynamic comparative advantage, upgrading and increasing value added in exports. We have shown that the difference in their performance is mainly due to their different industrialization and development strategies, and the policies of their government. The question is to what extent the experience of China is replicable.

More specifically both countries started liberalization of trade and FDI and economic reform around the early 1980s and attracted considerable FDI. They have also shown rapid expansion in the exports of manufactured goods produced through assembly operations, particularly ICT products and mainly in export-processing zones, during the 1980s and 1990s. Nevertheless, unlike the case of Mexico, China's export expansion has also been accompanied by rapid growth of MVA and GDP not only during the 1980s and 1990s, but also during the recent decade after acceding to the WTO. In Mexico the expansion of exports of *maquila* industries has led to little increase in the value added and resulted in higher wages, and little development of backward linkages with the rest of the economy or upgrading of the industrial structure. Furthermore Mexico has not been able to sustain rapid export expansion during the recent decade due to its loss of competitiveness in the international market, particularly *vis-à-vis* China. In fact TNCs have been relocating many plants from Mexico to China.

In Mexico, following the approach advocated by neoliberals and the 'Washington Consensus', the government assumed that trade liberalization and a hands-off approach to economic activities would automatically lead to growth and upgrading whereas China has followed a different strategy. The government of Mexico reduced all interference in the technology process in the early 1990s as it was assumed that technology would be transferred through trade and FDI. TNCs were provided with various incentives, particularly in export-processing zones, without demanding commitment to performance from them. Economic liberalism also led to the reduction in government investment in R&D, education and training. The government pursued some policies on training, R&D and development of SMEs, but they were inefficient and underfunded. Development of the capabilities of domestic firms was left to the operation of market forces.

In contrast, while reforming the economy, the Chinese government has taken a more gradual and experimental approach to liberalization and integration into the world economy. It has followed a dynamic policy on the development of its 'coordination system' comprising firms, market government and nonprice factors, explained in Chapter 1, for building up the capabilities of its domestic enterprises and their upgrading. It has put in place functional and targeted government policies to develop the capabilities of its national enterprises by emphasizing education and training for human resource development, R&D and learning for development of indigenous technological capabilities through a national innovation system (NSI). Its approach to industrialization and development can be described as neodevelopmental.

The science and technology (S&T) of the Chinese government was responsive to the market dynamic, with growing emphasis on the private sector (including TNCs). Nevertheless, through trial and error, the government has learned that reliance on market forces and FDI alone will not automatically lead to the transfer of technology, an increased value added in exports or upgrading of the industrial structure. Thus S&T policy and research and development (R&D) have become a cornerstone of China's industrial development. The ingredients of the government's policies on S&T and NSI included direct involvement and support for indigenous R&D and innovation investment within individual firms, and the creation of R&D institutions. It also included alliance among firms in an industry and their cooperation with research institutes, universities as well as foreign firms, targeting, in particular, the strategic industries.

Government policy on R&D and technological development ranged from direct investment, provision of guidance, institutional and financial support and a creating favourable environment for innovation and upgrading. Provision of incentives to domestic firms was not unaccompanied by pressure for performance. The government also introduced competition into the domestic market for the strategic industries and developed national standards for main IT products. The China's indicators for R&D are the highest in Asia after Singapore, Republic of Korea and Taiwan; it is also higher than Spain and Italy. In the current development plan China is to increase that ratio from 1.4 in 2007 to 2.2 in 2015. In the last year of the first decade of this century the number of people working on R&D in China increased by nearly 2.6 times as compared with 1996. The corresponding figures for Mexico increased by 1.9 times over the same period. In China the number of researchers per million inhabitants is more than three times higher than that of Mexico.

The selective, targeted and dynamic strategy of the government has been aimed particularly at IT industries. The government developed an institutional framework for S&T development and a dynamic national system of innovation (NSI). It consisted of the Chinese Academy of Science, relevant ministries, private enterprises, universities and research institutes. Close links were established among these entities in the public and private sectors. Both basic research and particularly application and diffusion of technology have been emphasized right from the early 1980s. The NSI of China was not perfect but was a lot more sophisticated than that of Mexico, which was very inefficient and underfunded.

The results of the implementation of science and technology policy are striking in the case of China as compared with Mexico. On average, 12 times more patents are filed in China each year than all the LA countries combined, let alone Mexico. What's more, whereas in Mexico only 4 per cent of all patents are by residents, in China that figure is over 75 per cent. Similar results are also evident in terms of the number of articles published by Chinese scholars as compared with those of Latin American. The number of patents granted increased by over 14 times between 1990 and 2008, out of which domestic patents account for over 86 per cent in 2008. Moreover, the relative importance of inventions in granted patent has increased reaching 22 per cent of patents granted. Domestic firms accounted for 51 per cent of total patent granted for inventions in 2008 as against about 30 per cent in 1990.

The performance of China was impressive not only in exports of high-tech products, but also in increasing domestic value added through development of domestic indigenous technology. In 2008–9, high-tech products constitute the first three export items s of China amounting, on average, to nearly $272 billion. Development of indigenous capabilities was focused on computers, mobile phone, laser and nanotechnology. For example, Lenovo, produced by Legend Group, has become the world's third largest PC maker after Dell and HP. China also developed its own brand in Mobile telephone and high definition disc player. Like Lenovo, many Chinese firms started as state-owned enterprises (SOEs) and were gradually privatized as they gained capacity and competitiveness.

All in all, while China is to sustain and intensify its international competitiveness on the road to higher level of development, Mexico seems to continue development based on static comparative advantage remaining at a relatively lower-level of development than China. While China has followed a developmentalist approach, Mexico has gone along the line advocated by neoliberals and Washington Consensus. In other words, the performance of China is consistent with the theoretical and empirical literature on capability building and views of the proponents of neodevelopmentalism (e.g. Wade 1990; Amsden, 2000; Paus and Gallagher 2008; Chang 2005; Shafaeddin 2005a; Lall 2004).

Policy Implications for Other Developing Countries

China's impressive success in enhancing the capabilities of its domestic firms raises the question whether its experience can be replicated by other developing countries under the current international economic situation. Development policy is country specific and no blueprint can be suggested. This is because socioeconomic features as well as the size of various countries are different. Thus the experience of a country cannot be generalized completely. Nevertheless, some lessons can be learned from the experience of China as compared with that of Mexico. First trade policy cannot be considered in isolation from industrial and other elements of development policies of a country. In particular there is a need for industrial, educational and technological policies. This view is in line with the conclusions of a number of other studies on various developing countries at different levels of industrialization and development (Lall 2004; Rodrik et al. 2004; Rodrik 2007, 2011; Wade 1990, 2007; Shafaeddin 2006b; Di Maio 2008; Amsden 1989).

Secondly capability building of domestic firms for supply capacity building, competitiveness and upgrading is not only crucial, but it is also the main requirement for industrialization and development. Nevertheless, market forces alone are not capable of developing such capabilities in various categories of developing countries, as well as in a country over time. In this respect developing countries with little industrial capacity include low-income African and other least developed countries; those with some industrial capacity are those which went through import-substitution, such as Brazil; those with considerable industrial base which have also penetrated into the international market successfully include a number of East Asian NIEs. The main problem of the first group is to establish production capacities; that of the second group is to make existing production capacities efficient and penetrate into international markets. Hence the burning issue for the third groups is to upgrade their industrial structure. Market forces alone are not adequate to deal with any of the issues concerned, i.e. development of supply capacities, attainment of efficiency and upgrading. Capabilities of government should be developed to formulate, implement and adjust policies for capability building at the macro, sectoral and firm levels. As the country develops, however, the relative role of the market in the economy should increase.

Thirdly trade and industrial policies should be not only development-oriented and country specific, but also selective, mixed, flexible, performance-linked, dynamic and predictable (see also Shafaeddin 2005c, 2009c). The flexibility and dynamism of trade policy require a flexible tariff structure which can be changed over time. A country may choose a group of consumer goods with important internal demands and significant learning effects as a first group of industries to support for capacity building, leaving their imported inputs free of duties. As they are developed measures should be taken to facilitate and support their entry into the international markets by improving their efficiency and quality, and liberalizing them gradually. Meanwhile a second group of industries should be chosen for nurturing on a selective basis, which may include some consumer goods as well as intermediate goods used in the first group. This process of a mixture of government support and liberalization should continue for various groups of industries until some machinery is also produced domestically and the industrial structure is consolidated. For example, initially the machinery used in the production of the first group of industries may be a candidate for capacity building. The process, however, cannot stop there; the industrial structure should be continuously upgraded (for details see Shafaeddin 2005c). Of course such a selective, flexible and dynamic industrial and trade policy requires a flexible and dynamic tariff structure. In particular, while the average tariff rates may be bound (but not at a very low level), the individual tariff rate should be left flexible (see Akyüz 2005). Such a flexible tariff structure would indicate the need for dispersion of individual tariff rates at each point in time and over time during the industrialization process. Thus at each point in time the tariff structure of each country should be based on the stage of development and industrial capacity of the country.

Fourthly trade and industrial policies should also be supplemented by development of what I call 'nonprice factors', and development of the agricultural sector in order to enhance the supply of wage goods. Further, provisions of incentive should be linked to performance requirement of firms, i.e. incentive to be provided in exchange for performance, and supports should be temporary and time bound. FDI should also be managed and targeted on areas which can contribute to the development objectives of the host country.Fifthly, regarding 'nonprice factors', the process of industrialization requires 'COU-Ps-INs' (Shafaeddin 2005c); COU stands for Create capacity, Operate it efficiently and Upgrade the industrial structure, as already mentioned. To do so incentive is necessary but not sufficient and there is a need for a number of Ps and INs: the INs include Investment, Input, Infrastructure, not only in transport and communication, but also other facilities such as marketing channels, distribution networks, etc.; and Institutions, Innovation and Information (Streeten 1987). We use the 'INs' here in its wide sense of the term, which includes knowledge, science and technology, R&D as well as market information requiring investment in human resources through education, skill development and training.

'Ps' stands for Political stability, Predictability of policies, Participatory Politics, Pressure for Performance, Public–Private Partnership, and respect for Property rights, and last, but not least, Production capabilities of local firms in the value chain enhancing Productivity. Here we use production capabilities in a wider sense than supply capabilities and thus it also includes such factors as organizational and institutional issues, which also contribute to productivity, marketing, etc.

There are also two INs which are to be avoided. These are instability in exchange rates and inflation, which are largely related to agricultural development, control of capital flows and macroeconomic policies. Development of food production and other wage goods is essential, particularly during the early stages of industrialization. Availability of cheap food contributes to cheap inputs through its impact on wages. Further, it eases the pressure on the balance of payments and inflationary tendencies, thus contributing to competitiveness of manufactured goods in the internal and international market.

Finally there is a need for the management of FDI and control of capital flow. FDI should be managed in a way that contributes to the objectives of industrialization and development of the country. Capital flows need to be controlled and managed to avoid erratic movement in the flow of imports, exchange rate, interest rate, production cost and the price structure. Devaluation of the local currency may serve a certain purpose when the currency is misaligned and the provision of incentive for the production of tradable goods is required, but it should not replace productivity and quality improvement as a tool of industrial policy and competitiveness. Even repeated use of devaluation cannot lead to a permanent improvement in export competitiveness (see Shafaeddin 2005c, 21–4 for further explanation).

Are the trade and industrial policies advocated above feasible?

The question is whether international economic system is conducive to industrialization and development as outlined above. Of course it is not. In addition to internal constraints, industrialization and development are constrained by external factors including the WTO rules, practices of developed countries through IFIs, bilateral and regional trade agreements as well as own trade, industrial and agricultural policies of these countries. As far as trade agreements are concerned, however, a couple of points are worth emphasizing. First there is still some room to manoeuvre under the WTO rules, particularly in the case of least developed countries. This is so provided developing countries do not lose their remaining policy autonomy through bilateral and regional agreements (Rodrik et al. 2004; Di Maio 2008; Amsden 2000) and do not submit to the conditions of IFIs and proposals of developed countries through NAMA and particularly EPA (Shafaeddin 2010a). 'What constrains sensible industrial policy is largely the willingness to adopt it, not the ability to do so' (Rodrik et al. 2004, 32).

Secondly there is also a need for some changes in the WTO rules to make them development friendly as they are biased against developing countries. The WTO rules should accommodate countries with different levels of industrialization and development, allowing special and differential treatment as a rule; take the concept of 'less than full reciprocity' more seriously; allow selectivity, flexibility and dynamism in the tariff structure of a country over time; thus allow binding average tariffs with significant dispersion; permit the use of export performance requirement in TRIMs; allow easier transfer of technology to developing countries by changing the TRIPs agreement; allow more policy space to developing countries by revising the Agreement on Subsidies, Countervailing Measures and GATS (Shafaeddin 2010c).

Thirdly, in their negotiation through EPA, NAMA and other trade agreements, developing countries should follow a bottom-up approach rather than a top-down one. In other words, rather than going to the negotiating table and discussing some issues without having been clear about their own trade and industrial policies (as they have done so during the Uruguay Round), they should be clear about their own trade, industrial and development policies in general before going to the negotiating table (see Shafaeddin 2005c for details).

The aftermath of recent global economic crises and intensive intervention of developed countries in the market provides a good opportunity for developing countries to bring up the limitations of market forces in the process of industrialization and development. It will allow them to argue in favour of different trade and industrial policies and thus different international trading systems. Of course, 'the [possibility of] failure of talks [in any trade negotiation] should not lead to the acceptance of unfavourable trade agreements', which could lead to further deindustrialization and deprivation (Shafaeddin 2010c). No agreement is better than a bad agreement. Submitting to the pressure of developed countries who wish to avoid changes in the WTO rules and to limit the policy space of developing countries further through NAMA, EPA, IFIs and bilateral and regional agreements would lock developing countries with little or no industrial base in the production of primary commodities, simple labour-intensive industries and, at best, assembly operation. It also prevents those with some industrial capacity from upgrading their industrial structure. Neither the WTO rules and the Washington Consensus nor the theory of static comparative cost theory is god given.

The Need for Further Research

We have touched on a number of issues about which we could not go into detail because of lack of space. These issues include the role and nature of competition policy in a developing country; the developmental implications of bilateral and regional trade agreements between developed and developing countries, including EPA; the developmental implications of environmental issues including the impact on industrialization of the cost of clean technology and possible costs related to potential obligations arising from the climate change conference; the role of South–South trade and cooperation in industrialization; the inhibiting role of SAP and SP programmes of the World Bank and IMF; and, most important of all, the features and political structure of a 'developmental state'. The economic functions of a developmental state have been discussed to some extent in the literature but positive and normative analysis of its political features in a mixed economy requires closer attention.

APPENDICES

1. Main GATT/WTO Agreements

GATT came into force in January 1948 as an interim multilateral agreement after the USA congress failed to ratify the agreement on the creation of ITO (International Trade Organization) and the Havana Charter. In practice GATT turned into a framework for the international trade system. Since then there have been eight rounds of trade negotiations (five in the 1950s and 1960s, the Tokyo Round of 1973–9, the Uruguay Round (UR) of 1986–94 and the latest Doha Round, which started in 2000 but has not yet been concluded. The UR led to the establishment of the WTO and a comprehensive agreement on international trade rules and some related issues.

The UR agreements consist of 13 agreements on goods covering: (1) the General Agreement on Tariffs and Trade 1994, which is basically GATT 1947 and its amendment during various rounds, as well as 6 'understandings' which provide interpretation of some of the articles of GATT; (2) 12 other agreements on goods dealing with agriculture, textiles and clothing, health and safety issues, antidumping procedures, custom valuation, perishable inspection, rules of origin, import licensing, subsidies and countervailing measures, safeguards and TRIMs (Trade Related Investment) issues; (3) it also includes such other agreements as GATS (General Agreement on Trade in Services); TRIPs (Trade-Related Aspects of Intellectual Property Rights); (4) understanding on dispute settlements; and four plurilateral trade agreements concerning civil aircraft, government procurement, dairy products and bovine meat.

While the GATT 1994 agreement is mainly trade enhancing, it also contains some clauses which create constraints for exports of developing countries. Further, its basic features include some restrictions. These are: MFN (most-favoured-nation) treatments, national treatment and transparency. MFN implies the lack of discrimination as between different members of the WTO (regional trade agreements are exceptions). Prohibition on national treatment implies prohibition to give preference to domestic products as against its imports. Transparency provision means that each member country is required to publish its laws and regulations for the information of the international community directly and indirectly through the WTO. In contrast, most other UR agreements restrict the supply capabilities and export expansion of developing countries. We will refer briefly below to the most restrictive ones which particularly affect the industrial development of developing countries.

TRIMs

TRIMs forbids national treatment, i.e. it forbids giving preference to domestically produced input, through specifying brand names or requiring a certain volume or value of a domestic product in absolute or percentage terms in relation to local production or exports. Similarly it forbids limiting the ceiling on the value or volume of purchase or use of an imported product in relation to its local production. The agreement also restricts 'foreign exchange balancing', i.e. linking the purchase of foreign exchange (needed for imports) by foreign firms to foreign exchange earnings. For example, it cannot link the sale of foreign exchange to a firm for importing inputs to a certain percentage (*a* per cent) of the foreign exchange earnings of the company.

Subsidies and Countervailing Duty

This agreement provides regulations on nonactionable, prohibited and actionable subsidies. Subsidies are defined as: provision of public financial contribution (e.g. direct or indirect transfer of funds, tax relief, supply of material or procurement at preferential price); income or price support.

Nonactionable subsidies include those of a general nature, i.e. subsidies which are not linked to any specific industry, or enterprise or group of enterprises/industry. Under certain conditions three exceptions were allowed for a limited time period (five years beginning in 1995) for subsidies paid for R&D, disadvantaged regions and environmental requirements.

Prohibited subsidies include subsidies linked to: (1) export performance; and (2) to the use of domestic products over imported ones. In the former case two groups of countries are excluded: least developed countries as well as countries with GNP per capita of less than $1,000, until the share of exports of a specific product of the country reaches 3.25 per cent of the world exports of that product for two consecutive years. By then it has to phase out the related subsidy in eight years. Initially other developing countries were also exempted, under certain conditions, for eight years from 1 January 1995.

Other types of subsidies than nonactionable and prohibited subsidies (actionable) can be paid provided the measures taken: (1) would not cause or threaten material injury to the (major part of) the domestic industry or cause material retardation of the establishment of an industry of WTO members; or (2) would not nullify or impair benefits under GATT 1994 and in particular should not exceed the effects of the tariff binding; (3) it should not cause or threaten serious prejudice to the interest of another member (see Das 1998, 52–5 for details).

The definition of injury is complicated; it includes:

1. Decline in output, sales, market share, profit, productivity, capacity utilization and return on investments;
2. Factors affecting domestic prices;
3. Negative effects on cash flow, inventories, employment, wages, growth and ability to raise capital investments (Das 1998, 53).

When the lack of observation of the regulation on subsidies affects a member country negatively, it can refer the issue to the Dispute Settlement Body (DSB) of the WTO if the issue cannot be settled through consultation, or impose countervailing duties on imports in cases where injury is involved, after following the related process including investigation.

Antidumping

Dumping means exporting products at abnormally low prices. It is forbidden by GATT 1947 and action against it can be taken by the importing country after an investigation. The investigation has to prove that: (1) dumping exists, and (2) it has caused material injury, or has threatened material injury (for the definition see subsidies and countervailing duty above), to the domestic industry, or has caused material retardation of establishing a domestic industry. Dumping exists when the export price is less than its normal value. The normal value minus the export price is equal to the dumping margin. The normal value is equal to the sale price of the product in the domestic market of the exporting country or the price of the related product exported to a third country or average cost of production plus transaction cost plus an acceptable profit margin.

The remedial measure against dumping is the imposition of an antidumping duty which can be, at most, equal to the dumping margin, after the necessary procedures are completed. Under certain conditions, provisional measures (in the form of provisional duty-by-cash deposit, security or bounds – or undertaking by the exporter to revise its price) can be taken before the completion of the procedures. Of course, if the exporter is unsatisfied with the results of the investigation it can resort to the DSB of the WTO.

Technical Barriers to Trade (TBT) Agreement

This agreement covers technical regulations for the performance of (industrial) products concerning safety, animal or plant life and health or environment. If the standards are put too high, such regulation may work as a barrier to trade. As developing countries at the early stages of development do not have the necessary technical capabilities to produce goods of high quality and standards, they may suffer from such regulations. International regulations and standards are normally used. Nevertheless, if such norms do not exist, an importing country may introduce its own norms (following the Code of Good Practices for Preparation, Adoption and Application of Standards) under certain conditions by giving public notice and notifying other countries for information and comments.

Sanitary and Phytosanitary (SPS) Agreement

The objective of the SPS Agreement is to regulate the safety standards of food, feed, beverages, animals and plants which enter international trade. The objective is to safeguard human, animal and plant life and health from food and feed-borne risks, or pest- and disease-related risks. While the TBT Agreement also deals with heath issues, it is concerned basically with technical standards, while the SPS Agreement is more specific to the above-mentioned products, mainly agricultural and animal products, and issues. Thus to achieve the objective of the SPS Agreement, there is a need to take diverse and complex measures involving the whole supply chain from inputs and production to harvesting, storage, processing, packing and labelling, port facilities and international transport. The related requirements and guidelines entail three sets of international standards provided by the so-called 'three sister organizations': the Codex Alimentarius Commission, the International Plant Protection Convention (IPPC) and the Office International des Epizooties (OIE). The implementation of the agreement requires not only information and awareness, but also various scientific, technical and legal skills and capabilities. It also requires such control facilities as quarantines, standards and accredited laboratories. For example, in the case of plants alone, about fifty different activities and measures are involved (Shafaeddin 2009b, 7). In addition, the intergovernmental organizations and governments as well as the private firms of the importing countries have their own standards and regulations. For example, the EU has 24 regulations and directives. Sometimes the related standards and regulations are not harmonized. Further they are changed rapidly by the importing countries. For example, the number of notifications of new SPS measures to the WTO increased from about 100 in 1995 to over 4,600 in 2005 (Henson 2006, 10). The burden of costs of compliance with the requirements of the SPS Agreement is imposed on exporting countries. The cost of compliance, from 'farm to fork', includes not only those related to the above-mentioned requirements and facilities, but also for establishing and operating an 'Enquiry Point' and 'National Notification Agency' required by the agreement as well as the cost of establishing and operating the necessary laboratories (for details see Shafaeddin 2009b).

Safeguard

The Agreement on Safeguards sets out a complex procedure. Safeguards are temporary measures which can be taken when certain preconditions exist, i.e. there is an increase in imports (in absolute terms or in relation to domestic production) which causes, or threatens to cause, serious injury to the domestic industry. In such a situation the importing country can restrict imports through tariff, import charges and other nontariff measures including quantitative restrictions. Tariffs and import charges can be raised above the bound tariffs. In order to take safeguard measures, an investigation has to be made by the 'competent authority' according to the set procedures to determine the existence of preconditions for taking such measures. In the meantime, all interested parties should be given public notice to present, or defend, their case. The agreement also sets out conditions, modalities, duration and possibilities of repetition of safeguards measures as well as provisional measures – if preliminary determination indicates clear evidence of injury or threat of injuries (see Das 1998, 32–4). The member which takes safeguard measures should also compensate other affected exporters (e.g. by reducing duties on products of their export interests) by reaching an agreement with them through consultation. If no agreement is reached, the affected members can take retaliatory measures by suspending some concessions after three years.

In addition to formulating laws and regulations on safeguards and notifying them to the WTO's Committee on Safeguards, a member should also notify the committee when it initiates the investigation, when the related competent authority concludes the investigation and when it takes safeguard measures. The member affected by safeguard measures can contest the results of the 'competent authority' of the investigating country. If safeguard measures are taken and the affected member is not satisfied, it can raise the issue with the DSB of the WTO.

TRIPs

This is the most damaging agreement for industrialization and development of developing countries, particularly low-income countries as they have limited technological capabilities. It provides protection for the innovators and owners of technology, which are mainly developed countries. It is extremely restrictive in all aspects of intellectual property and transfer of technology (both in product, and processing of goods and services – with a few exceptions related to human and animal health and the production of some plants), including 'copyright, trademarks, geographical indications, industrial design, patents, layout-designs of integrated circuits and undisclosed information' (Das 1998, 115).

As far as patents are concerned, the innovator of a new technology can patent and register it; the owner of the patent will have the monopoly power on his registered patent for at least twenty years – subject to certain constraints and exceptions, including the methods for treatment of humans and animals) (see Das 1998, 117–19). The use of the patent by others is obviously subject to authorization and payment of royalty fees – if the authorization is given.

Similarly an owner of a registered trade mark has monopoly over its use for seven years, which can be renewed each time for another seven years. The industrial design and layout and the design of integrated circuits are similar to trademarks and can be registered for at least ten years. Geographical indications of the origin of a product (e.g. Scotch whisky) are similar to a trade mark, and its use by others is forbidden permanently.

2. Competition Policy

There is some confusion surrounding the issue of competition policy in the context of developing countries. The objective of competition policy in a developing country should be to enhance the capabilities of the domestic firms to compete with established international firms in the internal and international market. Competition does not take place in a perfectly competitive market; it occurs among rival firms which are not necessarily perfectly competitive. The degree of rivalry depends, *inter alia*, on the degree of market concentration; thus the power of each firm to compete with others depends, *inter alia*, on the structure of the industry. In an imperfect market firms are active and compete with each other not only on prices, but also on nonprice factors (see Chapter 7), and there is an interaction between the structure of the industry, i.e. the degree of market concentration for each product (S), and the behaviour of firms (B) and their performance (P). Any policy which affects S, B, or P can be regarded as completion policy.

In practice, however, competition policy means – or should mean – different things to developed and developing countries. In developed countries the sheer concentration of market (S) is not disputed. In fact, the large TNCs dominated each single industry (Shafaeddin 2005c, table 5.3). The competition policy is basically concerned with the conduct and behaviour of firms (B) in order to prevent restrictive business practices. According to OECD: 'National competition policies are [concerned with] prohibition of outright price fixing, of market sharing agreements and anti-dumping conducted by *dominant firms*' (Nicolaides 1994, 36; italics added). Thus the objective of competition policy in developed countries is to prevent excess exploitation of the monopoly/oligopoly position of dominant firms (whether domestic or foreign) against the interests of domestic consumers. Nevertheless, its objective is not to control the conduct (B) of firms abroad. Even if a country intends to do so, it is not easy at the age of globalization.

The structure of the market (S) and the behaviour of TNCs (B) as well as their performance (P) affect development of supply capabilities and competitiveness of developing countries' firms in the international and internal markets. The objective of the competition policy of a developed country outside its territory is different from its domestic objectives.

For example, in the EPA (Economic Partnership Agreement) with ACP the objective of the EU is to get not only greater market access, but also greater guarantee for its investors for interment in those countries. In other words, the objective is to secure the EU's market shares overseas through trade and investment (Martin 2008, 2 and 5). Thus the EU would like to impose a sort of competition policy on ACP countries whose rule would prevent local government:

> [F]rom allowing domestic cartels, monopolies, 'unfair' trade practices and would prevent or make it more difficult for governments to give state aid to their domestic firms or provide other support that would protect their firms from international competition. (Martin 2008, 5)

The stated objective of the (UN) Set of Multilaterally Agreed Equitable Principles and Rules* for competition is to take into account the interests of both developed and developing countries – including industrialization of these countries – by controlling, *inter alia*, a 'concentration of capital and /or economic power' (S) and preventing the restrictive business practices of TNCs and other large enterprises (B). Yet, for example, the EPA-CARIFORUM Agreement restricts the flexibilities of competition policy in the countries of the later group, which had been recognized in the Cotonou Partnership Agreement, necessary to promote the industrialization of ACP countries (Martin 2008, 7–8).

The main objective of competition policy in a developing country is (or should be) not only to regulate the conduct and behaviour (B) of the dominant firms (whether domestic or foreign) in its intern market, but more importantly to tackle market entry barriers (including production, marketing and distribution) created by dominant firms (NCs) which are related to the structure of the market (S). In other words, while often the

---

* Note that the set has not been ratified by the governments.

concentration of competition policy is on B (a defensive approach), the focus should be on proactive policy measures to enhance the ability of the domestic firms to 'compete' with the established firms in the oligopolistic market structure. The market entry barriers are influenced, in developing countries, by the S, B and P of large multinational firms. Thus the government of a developing country may want to encourage some degree of market concentration by establishing, or developing through mergers, large firms to be able to compete with large TNCs in the internal and international markets (Martin 2008, 2–3).

The process of industrialization involves the development of supply capabilities, making it competitive and upgrading the industrial structure, which requires technological development. At the age of globalization, in each phase of such a process, the structure of the market, behaviour of established firms and their performance pose some constraints on newcomer firms to enter the market. A developing country should be concerned with not only the behaviour of dominant firms (as are developed countries), but also with the need for formulating a clear policy on the structure of its domestic market, thus the size of its firms, etc. in response to the S, B, P of dominant TNCs, taking into account its development objectives. Thus, in the first place there is a need for developing its industrial policy in accordance with its development objectives. Trade policy as well as competition policy will be, *inter alia*, the main elements of its industrial policy. Within such a framework, in formulating its trade policy and competition policy, the country should take into account the implications for its choice of trade and industrial policies of: the structure of the international market in the products of main concern to the country; the trade and competition policies of developed countries; the impact of existing (and evolving) international rules and regulations; and the interaction between trade policy and competition policy. Of course, for these purposes development of the capacity for analysing, formulating and implementing such policies is important. So is the ability to negotiate the related issues at the international level. Some countries have formulated competition policy, but in a way which is not conducive to their industrialization; Mexico is an example. The Federal Competition Commission, which was created in 1993 when the Competition Law was passed, suffers from some deficiencies in statutory authority, judicial review process, etc., which limits its ability to address anticompetitive conditions effectively (OECD 2010).

BIBLIOGRAPHY

Abramovitz, M. 1986. 'Catching Up, Forging Ahead and Falling Behind'. *Journal of Economic History* 46.2: 385–406.

———. 1994. 'The Origin of Postwar Catch-Up and Convergence Boom'. In J. Fagerberg, B. Verspagen and N. V. Tunzelmann (eds), *The Dynamics of Technology, Trade and Growth*. Northampton: Edward Elgar.

Agarwala, A. and S. P. Singh (eds). 1958. *The Economics of Underdevelopment*. Oxford: Oxford University Press.

Aghion, P., R. Blundell, R. Griffith, P. Howitt and S. Prantal. 2006. 'Entry and Productivity Growth: Evidence from Micro-level Panel Data'. *Journal of European Economic Association: Paper and Proceedings* 22.3: 265–76.

Agosin, M. and R. Machado. 2005. 'Foreign Investment in Developing Countries: Does it Crowd in Domestic Investment?' *Oxford Development Studies* 33.2: 149–62.

Agosin, M. and D. Tussie (eds). 1993. *Trade and Growth: New Dilemmas in Trade Policy*. New York and London: St. Martin's Press/Macmillan.

Airola, J. 2008. 'A Regional Analysis of the Impact of Trade and Foreign Direct Investment on Wages in Mexico 1984–2000'. *Review of Development Economics* 12.2: 276–90.

Akamatsu, K. 1961. 'A Theory of Unbalanced Growth in the World Economy'. *Weltwirtschaftliches Archive Review of World Economics* 86: 3–25.

Akyüz, Y. 2005. 'The WTO Negotiations on Industrial Tariffs: What is at Stake for Developing Countries?' Paper presented to a Third World Network workshop on 'NAMA Negotiations and Implications for Industrial Development in Developing Countries', Geneva, 9 May.

———. 2008. 'Managing Financial Instability in Emerging Markets, A Keynesian Perspective'. *METU Studies in Development* 2008/1.

Almeid, R. and A. M. Fernandes. 2008. 'Openness and Technological Innovations in Developing Countries: Evidence from Firm-Level Surveys'. *Journal of Development Studies* 44.5: 701–27.

Alvarez, R. 2007. 'Explaining Export Success: Firm Characteristics and Spill-over Effects'. *World Development* 35.3: 377–93.

Amable, B. and B. Verspagen. 1995. 'The Role of Technology in Market Shares Dynamics'. *Applied Economics* 27: 197–204.

Amendola, G., G. Dosi and E. Papani. 1993. 'The Dynamic of International Competitiveness'. *Weltwirtschaftliches Archive* 129.3: 453–71.

Aminian, N., K. C. Fung and H. Iizaka. 2007. 'Foreign Direct Investment, Intra-regional Trade and Production Sharing in East Asia'. RIETI Discussion Paper Series No. 07-E-064.

Amiti, M. and C. Freund. 2008. 'The Anatomy of China's Export Growth'. World Bank Policy Research Paper No. WPS 4628.

Amsden, A. H. 1989. *Asia's Next Giant: South Korea and Late Industrialization*. New York: Oxford University Press.

———. 2000. 'Industrialization under New WTO Law'. Paper prepared for UNCTAD X, 'High-Level Round Table on Trade and Development on Direction for the Twenty-First Century', Bangkok, 12 February.

Archibugi, D. and J. Michie. 1995. 'The Globalization of Technology: A New Taxonomy'. *Cambridge Journal of Economics* 19: 121–40.

_____. 1997. 'Technological Globalization or National System of Innovation?' *Futures* 29.2: 121–37.

_____. 1998. 'Technological Change, Growth and Trade: New Departures in Institutional Economics'. *Journal of Economic Surveys* 12.3: 313–32.

Arndt, H. W. 1955. 'External Economies in Economic Growth'. *Economic Record* 31.61: 192–214.

Arndt, S. 2002. 'Production Sharing and Regional Integration'. Claremont College Working Paper 2002–10.

_____. 2004. 'Trade Diversion and Production Sharing'. Claremont College Working Paper 2004–01.

Arrow, K. 1972. 'Gifts and Exchange'. *Philosophy and Public Affairs* 1: 343–62.

Asheim, B. 1992. 'The Role of Industrial Districts in the Application, Adaptation and Diffusion of Technology in Developed Countries: Inter-firm Linkages and Endogenous Technological Capability-Building'. Paper prepared for UNCTAD/GTZ symposium on the 'Role of Industrial Districts in Application, Adaptation and Diffusion of Technology', Geneva, 16–17 November.

Athukorala, P. and N. Yamashita. 2008. 'Global Production Sharing and US–China Trade Relations'. ACT No. 2008/22, College of Asia and Pacific, Australian National University.

Balassa, B. 1980. 'The Process of Industrial Development and Alternative Development Strategies'. World Bank Staff Working Paper No. 438.

Barshefsky, C. 2007. 'Charlene Barshefsky, on Doha'. *International Herald Tribune*, Managing Globalization Business Blog, 31 January.

Basile, R. and A. Giuta. 2003. 'Things Change: Internationalization and Competitive Advantage of Industrial Districts: An Empirical Analysis'. Paper presented at the 'Conference on Clusters, Industrial Districts and Firms: The Challenge of Globalization', Modena, 12–13 September.

Baumol, W. 2002. *The Free Market Innovation Machine: Analysing the Growth Miracle of Capitalism.* Woodstock, UK: Princeton University Press.

Baz, V., M. C. Capelo, R. Centeno and R. Estrada. 2010. 'Productive Development Policies in Latin America and the Caribbean: The Case of Mexico'. Inter-American Development Bank, Working Paper Series No. IDB-WP-168.

Belderbos, R., G. Capannelli and K. Fukao. 2001. 'Backward Vertical Linkages of Foreign Manufacturing Affiliates: Evidence from Japanese Multinationals'. *World Development* 29.1: 189–208.

Bell, M., B. Ross-Larson and L. E. Westphal. 1984. 'Assessing the Performance of Infant Industries'. *Journal of Development Economics* 16: 101–28.

Bell, M. and M Albu. 1999. 'Knowledge Systems and Technological Dynamism in Industrial Clusters in Developing Countries'. *World Development* 27.9: 1715–34.

Bessant, J. and R. Kaplinsky. 1995. 'Industrial Restructuring: Facilitating Organizational Change at the Firm Level'. *World Development* 23.1: 129–41.

Best, M. H. 1990. *The New Competition: Institutions of Industrial Restructuring.* Cambridge: Polity Press.

_____. 2001. *The New Competitive Advantage: The Renewal of American Industry.* Oxford: Oxford University Press.

Bhagwati, J. 1978. *Foreign Trade Regimes and Economic Development: Anatomy and Consequences of Exchange Control Regimes.* Cambridge, MA: Ballinger Publishing Company.

Bhaskar, V. 1989. 'Export Incentives, Exchange Rates and Commodity Prices'. Commonwealth Working Paper. London: Commonwealth Secretariat.

Boldrin, M. and D. K. Levine. 2008. *Against Intellectual Monopoly.* Cambridge: Cambridge University Press.

Bounfour, A. 2000. 'Intangible Resources and Competitiveness: Towards a Dynamic View of Corporate Performance'. In P. Buigues, A. Jaquemin and J.-F. Marchipont (eds), *Competitiveness and the Value of Intangible Assets.* Cheltenham: Edward Elgar.

Brandt, L. and E. Thun. 2009. 'The Fight for the Middle: Upgrading, Competition, and Industrial Development in China'. *World Development* 38.11: 1555–74.

Bressand, A. 1990. 'From Trade to Networking: a Services and Information Patterns'. Paper presented to the TEP Technology Conference, Tokyo, February.

Brooks, D. and C. Hua. 2008. 'Asian Trade and Global Linkages'. Asian Development Bank, ADB Institute Working Paper No. 122.

Bruton, H. 1998. 'A Reconsideration of Import Substitution'. *Journal of Economic Literature* 36: 903–36.

Brusco, S. 1990. 'The Idea of the Industrial Districts: Its Genesis'. In F. Pyke, G. Becattini and W. Sengenberger (eds), *Industrial Districts and Inter-Firm Co-operation in Italy*. Geneva: International Institute for Labour Studies.

———. 1992. 'Small Firms and Provision of Real Services'. In F. Pyke and W. Sengenberger (eds), *Industrial Districts and Local Economic Regeneration*, 177–97. Geneva: International Labour Office.

Burstein, A., C. Kurz and L. Tesar. 2008. 'Trade, Production Sharing, and the International Transmission of Business Cycles'. NBER Working Paper No. 13731.

CADELEC. 2004. Home page (www.cadalec.com.mx). Cadena Productiva de la Electronica.

Cane A. 1992 'Information Technology and Competitive Advantage: Lessons from Developed Countries'. *World Development* 20.12: 1721–36.

Cantwell, J. 1989. *Technological Innovation and Multinational Corporations*. Oxford and Cambridge, MA: B. Blackwell.

Capecchi, V. 1992. 'A History of Flexible Specialization and Industrial Districts in Emilia-Romagna'. In F. Pyke, G. Becattini and W. Spengenberger (eds), *Industrial Districts and Inter-firm Co-operation in Italy*, 20–36. Geneva: International Labour Office (ILO).

Carlin, W., A. Glyn and J. Van Reenen. 2001. 'Export Market Performance of OECD Countries: An Empirical Examination of the Role of Cost Competitiveness'. *Economic Journal* 111 (January): 128–62.

Carlsson, B. and R. Stankiewicz. 1991. 'On the Nature, Function and Composition of Technological Systems'. *Journal of Evolutionary Economics* 1.2: 93–118.

Carras, M. C. 2001. 'Meaning of Globalization: Groping in the Dark'. *World Affairs* 5.3: 116–24.

Carrillo, V. J. 1995. 'Flexible Production in the Auto Sector: Industrial Reorganization and Ford-Mexico'. *World Development* 23.1: 87–101.

Carrillo, J. and A. Hualde. 2002. 'La maquiladora Electronica en Tijuana: Hacia un Cluster Fronterizo'. *Revista Mexicana de Sociologia* 66.3: 125–71.

Casson, M. 1995. *Enterprise and Competitiveness*. Oxford: Clarendon Press.

Caves, R. E. 1974. 'Multinational Firms, Competition, and Productivity in Host-Country Markets'. *Economica* 41.162: 176–93.

Chandler, A. D. 1990. *Scale and Scope: The Dynamics of Industrial Capitalism*. London and Cambridge, MA: The Belknap Press of Harvard University Press.

———. 2005. *Shaping the Industrial Century: The Remarkable Story of the Evolution of the Modern Chemical and Pharmaceutical Industries*. Cambridge, MA: Harvard University Press.

Chang, E., T. S. Dillon and F. K. Hussain. 2006. *Trust and Reputation for Service-Oriented Environments: Technologies for Building Intelligence and Consumer Confidence*. Oxford: John Wiley & Sons.

Chang, H.-J. 1994. *The Political Economy of Industrial Policy*. New York: St. Martin's Press.

———. 2002. *Kicking Away the Ladder: Development Strategy in Historical Perspective*. London: Anthem Press.

———. 2005. 'Policy Space in Historical Perspective – With Special Reference to Trade and Industrial Policies'. Paper presented at Queen Elizabeth House 50th anniversary conference, 'The Development Threats and Promises', University of Oxford, 4–5 July.

Chang, H.-J. and R. Rowthorn (eds). 1995. *The Role of the State in Economic Change*. Oxford: Clarendon Press.

Chen, K. and M. Kenney. 2008. 'Universities/Research Institutes and Regional Innovation Systems: The Cases of Beijing and Shenzhen'. *World Development* 35.6: 1056–74.

Chen, V. W., H. X. Wu. and B. V. Ark. 2008. 'Measuring Changes in Competitiveness in Chinese Manufacturing Industries across Regions in 1995–2004: A Unit Labour Cost Approach'. The Conference Board, Economic Program Working Papers No. EPWP 08-03.

Chen, Y., 2008. 'Why Do Multinational Corporations Locate Their Advanced R&D Centres in Beijing?' *Journal of Development Studies* 44.5: 622–44.

Chenery, H. B. and T. N. Srinivasan (eds). 1988. *Handbook of Development Economics*, vols 1–2. Amsterdam: North Holland.

Chudnovsky, A., A. Lopez and G. Rossi. 2008. 'Foreign Direct Investment Spillovers and the Absorptive Capacity of Domestic Firms in the Argentine Manufacturing Sector, 1992–2001'. *Journal of Development Studies* 44.5: 645–77.

Cimoli, M. 2000. *Developing Innovation Systems: Mexico in Global Perspective*. New York and London: Continuum Books.

Clarke, R. 1985/89. *Industrial Economics*. Oxford: Basil Blackwell.

Collis, D. and P. Ghemawat. 1994. 'Industry Analysis: Understanding Industry Structure and Dynamics'. In L. Fahey and L. Randall (eds), *Portable MBA in Strategy*. New York: John Wiley & Sons.

Corden, W. M. 1974. *Trade Policy and Economic Welfare*. Oxford: Clarendon Press.

Correa, C. M. 2000. *Intellectual Property Rights, the WTO and Developing Countries: The TRIPS Agreement and Policy Options*. Penang: Third World Network.

Corsino, M., G. Espa, G. and R. Micciolo. 2008. 'R&D, Firm Size, and Product Innovation Dynamics'. Department of Computer and Management Science, University of Trento, Italy, Working Paper No. 3.

Crestanello, P., C. Vicenza and G. Tattara. 2006. 'Connections and Competence in the Governance of the Value Chain: How Industrial Countries Keep their Competitive Power'. The Other Canon Foundation and Tallinn University of Technology, Working Papers in Technology Governance and Economic Dynamics No. 7.

CRS (Congressional Research Service). 2011. 'China's Currency: An Analysis of the Economic Issues'. CRS Report for Congress. http://www.fas.org/sgp/crs/row/RS21625.pdf (accessed 4 May 2012).

Das, B. L. 1998. *An Introduction to WTO Agreements*. Penang: Third World Network.

Dasgupta, P. and J. E. Stiglitz. 1985. 'Learning-by-Doing, Market Structure and Industrial and Trade Policies'. *Oxford Economic Papers* 40.2: 246–68.

Davies, G., R. Chun, R. Vinhas da Silva and S. Roper. 2003. *Corporate Reputation and Competitiveness*. London: Routledge.

Davies, H. 1991. *Managerial Economics for Business Management and Accounting*. London: Pitman Publications.

De Castro, J. A. 1989. 'Protectionist Pressures in the 1990s and the Coherence of North-South Trade Policies'. UNCTAD Discussion Paper No. 27.

Deakin, S. and F. Wilkinson. 1995. 'Contracts, Cooperation and Trust: the Role of Institutional Framework'. ESRC Centre for Business Research, University of Cambridge, Working Paper 10, September.

Dedrick, J. and L. Kenneth Kraemer. 2002. 'Enter the Dragon: China's Computer Industry'. *Perspectives* (February): 28–36.

Delgado, M., M. E. Porter and S. Stern. 2010. 'Clusters and Entrepreneurship'. *Journal of Economic Geography* 10: 495–518.

_____. 2011. 'Clusters, Convergence, and Economic Performance'. http://www.isc.hbs.edu/pdf/DPS_Clusters_Performance_2011-0311.pdf (accessed April 2011).

Di Maio, M. 2008. 'Industrial Policies in Developing Countries: History and Perspectives'. Department of Economics and Finance, University of Macerata, Quaderno di Dipartimento No. 48.

Dosi, G. 1988. 'The Nature of Innovation Process'. In G. Dosi, C. Freeman, R. Nelson, G. Silverberg and L. Soete (eds), *Technical Change and Economic Theory*. London: Pinter.

Dosi, G., L. Marengo and M. Faillo 2008. 'Organizational Capabilities, Patterns of Knowledge Accumulation and Governance Structures in Business Firms: An Introduction'. *Organization Studies* 29.8: 1165–85.

Dussel Peters, E. 1999. 'Reflexiones Sobre Conceptos y Experiencias Internacionales de Industrializacion Regional'. In C. R. Dussel Peters and E. D. Peters (eds), *Dinamica Regional y Competitividad Industrial*. Mexico City: Editorial JUS.

―――. 2003. 'Ser maquila o no ser maquila, ¿es esa la pregunta?' *Comercio Exterior* 53.4: 328–36.

―――. 2005. 'The Implications of China's Entry into the WTO for Mexico'. *Global Issue Papers* 24: 1–41.

―――(ed.) 2007. *Monitor de la Manufactura Mexicana* 3.6. http://www.dusselpeters.com/monitor006.pdf (accessed 4 September 2012).

―――. 2008. *Invesion extranjera directa en Mexico: Desempeño y potencial*. Mexico City: Siglo XXI.

Dwivedi, M. and R. Varman. 2003. 'Nature of Trust in Small Firm Clusters: A Case Study of Kanpur Saddlery Cluster'. Paper presented at the 'Conference on Clusters, Industrial Districts and Firms: The Challenge of Globalization', Modena, 12–13 September.

Dwivedi, M., R. Varman and K. K. Saxena. 2003. 'Nature of Trust in Small Firm Clusters'. *International Journal of Organisation Analysis* 11.2: 93–104.

Eckward, E. W. 1992. 'Cost Competitiveness: New Evidence on Old Issue'. *Applied Economics* 24: 1241–50.

Edquist, C. 1997. 'System of Innovation Approaches: Their Emergence and Characteristics'. In Charles Edquist (ed.), *System of Innovation: Technologies and Organizations*, 1–35. London and Washington: Pinter.

Edquist, C. and M. McKelvey (eds). 2000. *Systems of Innovation: Growth, Competitiveness and Employment*, vols 1–2. Cheltenham: Edward Elgar.

Elkan, V. 1996. 'Catching Up and Slowing Down: Learning and Growth Pattern in an Open Economy'. *Journal of International Economy* 41: 95–111.

Enright, M. 1996 'Why Local Clusters are the Way to Win the Game'. *World Link* 5 (July–August): 24–5.

Esfahani, S. 1991. 'Reputation and Uncertainty toward an Explanation of Quality Problems in Competitive LDC Markets'. *Journal of Development Economics* 35.1: 1–32.

Ethier, W. J. 1979. 'Internationally Decreasing Costs and World Trade'. *Journal of International Economics* 9 (February): 1–24.

―――. 1982. 'National and International Return to Scale in the Modern Theory of International Trade'. *American Economic Review* 72.3: 388–405.

―――. 1988. *Modern International Economies*. New York: W. W. Norton & Company.

Evers, H.-D. 2008. 'Knowledge Hubs and Knowledge Clusters: Designing a Knowledge Architecture for Development'. Centre for Development Research, University of Bonn. http://mpra.ub.uni-muenchen.de/8778 (accessed March 2010).

Etzkowitz, H. and L. Leydesdroff. 1997. *Universities and Global Knowledge Economy: A Triple Helix of University-Industry-Government Relations*. London: Pinter.

―――. 2000. 'The Dynamics of Innovation: From National System and "Mode 2" to Triple Helix of University-Industry-Government Relations'. *Research Policy* 29: 109–23.

Fagerberg, J. 1987. 'A Technology Gap Approach to Why Growth Rates Differ'. *Research Policy* 16.2–4: 87–99.

―――. 1988. 'International Competitiveness'. *Economic Journal* 98: 355–74.

―――. 1994. 'Technology and International Differences in Growth Rates'. *Journal of Economic Literature* 32.3: 1147–75.

―――. 1995. 'User–Producer Interaction, Learning and Comparative Advantage'. *Cambridge Journal of Economics* 19.1: 243–56.

Fagerberg, J. and M. Srholec. 2008. 'National Innovation System, Capabilities and Economic Development'. *Research Policy* 37: 1417–35.

Fagerberg, J., M. Srholec and B. Verspagen. 2009. 'Innovation and Economic Development'. Maastricht Economic and Social Research and Training Centre on Innovation and Technology, United Nations University, Working Paper No. 2009-032.

Fagerberg, J., B. Verspagen and N. V. Tunzelmann (eds). 1994a. *The Dynamics of Technology, Trade and Growth.* Northampton: Edward Elgar.

_____. 1994b. 'The Economics of Convergence and Divergence: An Overview'. In J. Fagerberg, B. Verspagen and N. V. Tunzelmann (eds), *The Dynamics of Technology, Trade and Growth.* Northampton: Edward Elgar.

Fahey, L. 1994. 'Strategic Management: Today's Most Important Business Challenge'. In L. Fahey and L. Randal (eds), *Portable MBA in Strategy.* New York: John Wiley & Sons.

Fahey, L. and M. Randall (eds). 1994. *The Portable MBA in Strategy.* New York: John Wiley & Sons.

Fan, P., X. Gao and C. Watanabe. 2007. 'Technology Strategies of Innovative Chinese Domestic Companies'. *International Journal of Technology and Globalization* 3.4: 344–63.

Fan, P. and C. Watanabe. 2006. 'Promoting Industrial Development through Technology Policy: Lessons from Japan and China'. *Technology in Society* 28: 303–20.

Fan, J. P. H., J. Huang, R. Mork and B. Yeung. 2009. 'Vertical Integration, Institutional Determinants and Impact: Evidence from China'. NBER Working Paper No. 14650.

Fellner, W. J. 1949. *Competition Among the Few: Oligopoly and Similar Market Structure.* London: Knopf.

Fetherston, M., B. Moore and J. Rhodes. 1977. 'Manufacturing Export Shares and Cost Competitiveness of Advanced Industrial Countries'. *Cambridge Economic Policy Review* 3: 87–99.

Fleisher, B., D. Hu, W. McGuire and X. Zhang. 2009. 'The Evolution of an Industrial Cluster in China'. International Food Policy Research Institute Discussion Paper No. 00896.

Fleury, A. 1995. 'Quality and Productivity in the Competitive Strategies of Brazilian Industrial Enterprises'. *World Development* 23.1: 73–85.

Fontaine, J. M. (ed.) 1992. *Foreign Trade Reforms and Development Strategy.* London: Routledge.

Forbes, N. and D. Wield. 2002. *From Followers to Leaders: Managing Technology and Innovation.* London and New York: Routledge.

Freeman, C. 1986. 'The Role of Technical Change in National Economic Development'. In A. Amin and J. B. Goddard (eds), *Technological Change, Industrial Restructuring and Regional Development,* 100–115. London: Allen and Unwin.

_____. 1995. 'The National System of Innovation in Historical Perspective'. *Cambridge Journal of Economics* 19: 5–24.

Freeman, C. and C. Perez.1988. 'Structural Crises of Adjustment, Business Cycles and Innovation Behaviour'. In G. Dosi et al. (eds), *Technical Change and Economic Theory.* London: Pinter.

Fuguet, J. L., D. Penguin, M. F. Renard and N. Richez-Battestin. 1986. 'L'impact de la contrainte extérieure sur des zones d'activités urbaines ou locals'. Report made for DATAR, Aix-en-Provence, France, CEFI, December.

Fukuyama, F. 1996. *Trust: The Social Virtue and the Creation of Prosperity.* New York: Touchstone Books.

Fuller, S. 2000. *The Governance of Science.* Buckingham: Open University Press.

Galbraith, J. K. 1975. *Economics and the Public Purpose.* London: Penguin Books.

Gallagher, K. P. (ed.) 2005. *Putting Development First: The Importance of Policy Space in the WTO and IFIs.* London and New York: Zed Books.

Gallagher, K. P., Juan Carlos Moreno-Brid, and Roberto Porzecanski. 2008. 'The Dynamism of Mexican Exports: Lost in (Chinese) Translation?' *World Development* 36.8: 1365–80.

Gallagher, K. P. and R. Porzecanski. 2008. 'Climbing Up the Technology Ladder? High-Technology Exports in China and Latin America'. Center for Latin American Studies, University of California Berkeley, CLAS Working Papers No. 20.

Gallagher, K. P. and M. Shafaeddin. 2010. 'Policies for Industrial Learning in China and Mexico'. *Technology in Society* 30: 1–19.

Gallagher, K. P. and L. Zarsky. 2007. *The Enclave Economy: Foreign Investment and Sustainable Development in Mexico's Silicon Valley.* Cambridge, MA: MIT Press.

Gaulier, G., F. Lemoine and D. Unal-Kesenci. 2005. 'China's Integration in East Asia: Production Sharing, FDI and High-tech Trade'. Centre d'Etudes Prospectives et d'Informations Internationales, CEPII Paper No.2005-09.

Gereffi, G. 1994. 'The Organization of Buyer-Driven Global Commodity Chains: How US Retailers Shape Overseas Production Networks'. In G. Gereffi and M. Korzeniewicz (eds), *Commodity Chain and Global Capitalism*, 95–122. Westport, CT: Praeger.

Gereffi, G., J. Humphrey and T. Sturgeon. 2005. 'The Governance of Global Value Chain'. *Reviews of International Political Economy* 12.1: 78–104.

Gereffi, G. and O. Memodvic. 2003. 'The Global Apparel Value Chain: What Prospects for Upgrading by Developing Countries?' UNIDO Sectoral Studies Series. http://www.unido.org/fileadmin/import/11900_June2003_GereffiPaperGlobalApparel.4.pdf (accessed October 2009).

Gereffi, G. and T. Tam. 1999. 'Industrial Upgrading and Organizational Chain'. Institute of Development Studies, Sussex University, IDS Working Paper: 1–19.

Gerschenkron, A. 1962. *Economic Backwardness In Historical Perspectives*. Cambridge, MA: Harvard University Press.

Giarratana, M. and S. Torrisi. 2003. 'Emerging Clusters in International Production of Software: Technology, Brand Building and International Linkages'. Paper presented at the 'Conference on Clusters, Industrial Districts and Firms: The Challenge of Globalization', Modena, 12–13 September.

Gibbons, M., C. Limoges, H. Nowotny, S. Schwartzman, P. Scott and M. Trow. 1994. *The New Production of Knowledge: The Dynamics of Science and Research in Contemporary Societies*. London: Sage.

Gilbert, C. L. 1988. 'The Impact of Exchange Rates and Developing Country Debt on Commodity Prices'. *Economic Journal* 99 (September): 773–84.

Girma, S. and Y. Gong, 2008. 'Putting People First? Chinese State-Owned Enterprises' Adjustment to Globalisation'. *International Journal of Industrial Organization* 26.2: 573–85.

Giuliani, E., C. Pietrobelli and R. Rabellotti. 2003. 'Upgrading in Global Value Chains: Lessons from Latin American Clusters'. Paper presented at the 'Conference on Clusters, Industrial Districts and Firms: The Challenge of Globalization', Modena, 12–13 September.

Gjerding, A. 1992. 'Work Organization and Innovation Design Dilemma'. In B. Lundvall (ed.), *National Systems of Innovation: Toward a Theory of Innovation and Interactive Learning*, 95–115. London: Pinter.

Görg, H. and D. Greenaway. 2004. 'Much Ado about Nothing? Do Domestic Firms Really Benefit from Foreign Direct Investment'. *World Bank Research Observer* 19.2: 171–97.

Gorodnichenko, Y., J. Svejnar and K. Terrel. 2008. 'Globalization and Innovation in Emerging Markets'. NBER Working Paper No. 14481. Also published in *American Economic Journal* 2.2: 194–226.

Griffiths, M. A. 2000. 'Japan's Competitive Culture: Origins and Change in a Dynamic Environment'. In L. Lloyd-Reason and S. Wall (eds), *Dimensions of Competitiveness: Issues and Policies*. Cheltenham: Edward Elgar.

Gruber, H. 1992. 'The Learning Curve in the Production of Semiconductor Memory Chips'. *Applied Economics* 24: 885–94.

Guler, M., F. Guillen and J. M. Macpherson. 2002. 'Global Competition, Institutions, and the Diffusion of Organizational Practices: The International Spread of ISO 9000 Quality Certificates'. *Administrative Science Quarterly* 47.2: 207–32.

Hamel, G. and C. K. Prahalad. 1994. *Competing for the Future*. Boston: Harvard Business School Press.

Hanson, G. H. 1996a. 'Agglomeration, Dispersion, and the Pioneer Firm'. *Journal of Urban Economics* 39: 255–81.

_____. 1996b. 'U.S.–Mexico Integration and Regional Economies: Evidence from Border-City Pairs'. NBER Working Paper No. 5425.

Harriss, J. 1995. '"Japanization", Context and Culture in the Indonesian Automotive Industry'. *World Development* 23.1: 117–28.

Hayes, R. H. and S. C. Wheelwright. 1984. *Restoring Our Competitive Edge: Competing Through Manufacturing*. New York: John Wiley.

Helleiner, G. K. 2000. 'Markets, Politics and Globalization: Can the Global Economy be Civilized?' The Tenth Raúl Prebisch Lecture. Geneva: UNCTAD.

Henson, S. 2006. 'The Role of Public and Private Standards in Regulating International Food Market'. Paper presented at the IATRC summer symposium, 'Food Regulation and Trade: International Framework. Concepts of Analysis and Empirical Evidence', Bonn, 28–30 May.

Herzberger, B. and A. Wright. 2005. 'Competitiveness Partnerships – Building and Maintaining Public-Private Dialogue to Improve the Investment Climate'. World Bank/IFC Working Paper No. 3683.

Hessels, L. and H. van Lente. 2008. 'Rethinking New Knowledge Production: A Literature Review and Research Agenda'. *Research Policy* 37: 740–60.

Hirschman, A. O. 1958. *The Strategy of Economic Development*. New Haven, CT: Yale University Press.

Hoesch, A. 1996. 'The Role of Trust in Entrepreneurship and Economic Development: Lessons from East and Southeast Asia for Eastern Europe'. Paper presented at the Development Studies Association annual conference, Reading, September.

Holmström, M. 1994. 'Network, Trust and Shared Services in Bangalore'. Paper submitted to a workshop on 'Industrialization, Organization, Innovation and Institutions in the South', organized by the European Association of Development Institutes and Vienna Institute for Development and Cooperation, Vienna, November.

Huang, Z., X. Zhang and Y. Zhu. 2008. 'The Role of Clustering in Rural Industrialization: A Case Study of Wenzhou's Footwear Industry'. *Chinese Economic Review* 19.3: 409–20.

Humphrey, J. 1995a. 'Introduction to a Special Issue of World Development on Clustering'. *World Development* 23.1: 1–7.

_____. 1995b. 'The Adoption of Japanese Management Techniques in Brazilian Industry'. *Journal of Management Studies* 32.6: 767–87.

_____. 1995c. 'Industrial Reorganization in Developing Countries: From Models to Trajectories'. *World Development* 23.1: 149–62.

Humphrey, J. and H. Schmitz. 1996. 'The Triple C Approach to Local Industrial Policy'. *World Development* 24.12: 1859–77.

_____. 2000. 'Governance and Upgrading: Linking Industrial Cluster and Global Value Chain Research'. Institute of Development Studies, University of Sussex, IDS Working Paper No. 120.

Ikenson, D. 2004. 'Zeroing In: Antidumping's Flawed Methodology under Fire'. Center for Trade Policy Studies, Cato Institute, Trade Bulletin No. 11.

Inomata, S. 2008. 'A New Measurement for International Fragmentation of the Production Process: An International Input–Output Approach'. Japan External Trade Organization, Institute of Developing Economies Working Paper No. 175.

Intarakummerd, P., P.-A. Chairatana and T. Tangchitpiboon. 2002. 'National Innovation Systems in Less Successful Developing Countries: The Case of Thailand'. *Research Policy* 31.8–9: 1445–57.

J.P. Morgan. *Research Outlook*. Online, various issues.

Jonson, B. 1992. 'Institutional Learning'. In B. Lundvall (ed.), *National Systems of Innovation: Toward a Theory of Innovation and Interactive Learning*, 22–32. London: Pinter.

Justo, R. 2003. 'Beyond the Local Productive Systems Model: Towards an Approach Combining Local and Global Sources of Competitiveness'. Paper presented at the 'Conference on Clusters, Industrial Districts and Firms: The Challenge of Globalization', Modena, 12–13 September.

Kaldor, N. 1978. 'The Effects of Devaluations on Trade in Manufactures'. In *Further Essays on Applied Economics*. London: Duckworth.

_____. 1981. 'The Role of Increasing Returns, Technical Progress and Cumulative Causation in the Theory of International Trade and Economic Growth'. *Economie appliquée* 34.6: 593–617.

_____. 1982. 'Devaluation and Adjustment in Developing Countries'. *Finance and Development* (June): 35–7.

Kalecki, M. 1955. 'The Problems of Financing Economic Development'. *Indian Economy Review* 2.3: 1–22.

_____. 1963. 'An Outline of Methods of Construction of Perspective Plan'. In M. Kalecki (ed.), *Essays on Planning and Economic Development*, vol. 1, 9–22. Warsaw: Centre for Research on Underdeveloped Economies.

_____. 1966. 'Forms of Foreign Aid: An Economic Analysis'. *Social Science Information* 1: 21–44.

_____. 1967/1972. 'Social and Economic Aspects of Intermediate Regimes'. In M. Kalecki, *Selected Essays on the Economic Growth of the Socialist and the Mixed Economy*, 162–9. Cambridge: Cambridge University Press.

_____. 1970/1972. 'Problems of Financing Economic Development in a Mixed Economy'. In M. Kalecki, *Selected Essays on the Economic Growth of the Socialist and the Mixed Economy*, 145–59. Cambridge: Cambridge University Press.

_____. 1971. *Selected Essays on the Dynamics of the Capitalist Economy, 1933–70*. Cambridge: Cambridge University Press.

_____. 1972. *Selected Essays on the Economic Growth of the Socialist and the Mixed Economy*. Cambridge: Cambridge University Press.

Kaplinsky, R. 1994. 'From Mass Production to Flexible Specialization: A Case Study of Microeconomic Changes in a Semi-industrialized Economy'. *World Development* 22.3: 337–53.

_____. 1995. 'Techniques and System: The Spread of Japanese Management Techniques to Developing Countries'. *World Development* 23.1: 57–71.

Kaplinsky, R. and M. Morris. 2000. *A Handbook of Value Chain Research*. Prepared for the International Development Research Centre (IDRC).

Kaplinsky, R., M. Morris and J. Readman. 2002. 'The Globalization of Product Markets and Immiserising Growth: Lessons from the South African Furniture Industry'. *World Development* 30.7: 1159–77.

Kaplinsky, R. and A. Posthuma. 1994. *Easternization: The Spread of Japanese Management Techniques to Developing Countries*. Abingdon: Frank Cass.

Kellman, M. 1983. 'Relative Prices and International Competitiveness: An Empirical Investigation'. *Empirical Economics* 8.3–4: 125–38.

Kelsey, J. 2010. 'Legal Analysis of Services and Investment in the CARIFORUM-EC EPA, Lessons for other Developing Countries'. South Centre Research Paper No. 31.

Kemeny, T. 2010. 'Does Foreign Direct Investment Drive Technological Upgrading?' *World Development* 38.11: 1543–54.

Kierzkowski, H. (ed.) 1984. *Monopolistic Competition and International Trade*. Oxford: Clarendon Press.

Kim, S., J. W. Lee and C. Y. Park. 2009. 'Emerging Asia: Decoupling or Recoupling'. Asian Development Bank, Working Paper Series on Regional Economic Integration No. 31.

Kiyota, K. 2008. 'Are US Exports Different from China's Exports? Evidence from Japan's Imports'. Gerald R. Ford School of Public Policy, University of Michigan, Research Seminars in International Economics Discussion Paper No. 576.

Kogut, B. 1985. 'Designing Global Strategies: Comparative and Competitive Value Added Chains'. *Sloan Management Review* 26.4: 15–28.

Koopman, R., Z. Wang and W. Shang-Jin. 2008. 'How Much of Chinese Exports is Really Made in China? Assessing Domestic Value-Added When Processing Trade is Pervasive'. NBER Working Paper No. 14109.

Kravis, I. B. and R. E. Lipsey. 1992. 'Sources of Competitiveness of the United States and of its Multinational Firms'. *Review of Economic and Statistics* 74.2: 193–201.

Kristiansen, S. 2004. 'Social Networks and Business Success'. *American Journal of Economics and Sociology* 63.5: 1149–71.

Krueger, A. O. 1978. *Foreign Trade Regimes and Economic Development: Liberalization Attempts and Consequences*. New York: National Bureau of Economic Research.

Krugman, P. 1984. 'Import Protection as Export Promotion: International Competition in the Presence of Oligopoly and Economies of Scale'. In H. Kierzkowski (ed.), *Monopolistic Competition and International Trade*. Oxford: Clarendon Press.

_____. 1986. 'A Technology Gap Model of International Trade'. In K. Jungenfeld and D. Hague (eds), *Structural Adjustment in Advanced Economies*. London: Macmillan.

_____. 1987. 'Strategic Sectors and International Competition'. In Robert M. Stern (ed.), *US Trade Policies in a Changing World Economy*, 207–32. Cambridge, MA: MIT Press.

_____. 1994 'Competitiveness: A Dangerous Obsession'. *Foreign Affairs* 73.2: 28–44.

Kui-Wai, L., T. Liu and L. Yun. 2009. 'Decomposition of Economic and Productivity Growth in Post-Reform China'. Department of Economics and Finance, City University of Hong Kong, Working Paper No. 200806.

_____. 2005. 'Rethinking Industrial Strategy: The Role of the State in the Face of Globalization'. In K. P. Gallagher (ed.), *Putting Development First: The Importance of Policy Space in the WTO and IFIs*. London: Zed Books.

Lall, S. 1990. *Building Industrial Competitiveness in Developing Countries*. Paris: OECD Development Centre.

_____. 1991. 'Marketing Barriers Facing Developing Country Manufactured Exports: A Conceptual Note'. *Journal of Development Studies* 27.4: 137–50.

_____. 1992. 'Experiencing Industrial Success in Developing Countries'. In V. N. Balasubramanian and S. Lall (eds), *Current Issues in Development Economics*. London: Macmillan.

_____. 1993a. 'Industrial Policy: A Theoretical and Empirical Exposition'. Paper presented at the 'Conference on Industrial Policy and Caribbean Development', University of the West Indies, Port of Spain, Trinidad, October.

_____. 1993b. 'Policies for Building Technological Capabilities: Lesson from Asian Experience'. *Asian Development Review* 11.2: 72–103.

_____. 2004. 'Reinventing Industrial Strategy: The Role of Government Policy in Building Industrial Competitiveness'. United Nations, G-24 Discussion Paper No. 28.

_____. 2005. 'Rethinking Industrial Strategy: The Role of the State in the Face of Globalization'. In K. P. Gallagher (ed.), *Putting Development First: The Importance of Policy Space in the WTO and IFIs*. London: Zed Books.

Lall, S., M. Albaladejo and J. Zhang. 2004. 'Mapping Fragmentation: Electronics and Automobiles in East Asia and Latin America'. *Oxford Development Studies* 32.3: 407–32.

Lall, S., G. B. Navarelli, S. Teitel and G. Wignaraja. 1994. *Technology and Enterprise Development: Ghana under Structural Adjustment*. London: Macmillan.

Latham, W. and H. Yin. 2008. 'Domestic Innovation and Chinese Regional Growth, 1991–2004'. Department of Economics, Alfred Lerner College of Business & Economics, University of Delaware, Working Paper No. 2008–20.

Lazonick, W. 1991. *Business Organization and the Myth of Market Economy*. New York and Melbourne: Cambridge University Press.

_____. 2004. 'Indigenous Innovation and Economic Development: Lessons from China's Leap into the Information Age'. *Industry and Innovation* 11.4: 273–97.

Lazonick, W. and M. O'Sullivan. 1994. 'Skill Formation in Wealthy Nations: Organizational Evolution and Economic Consequences'. Studies in Technology, Innovation and Economic Policy (STEP) Report No. R-23.

Leibenstein, H. 1980. 'X-Efficiency Theory, Productivity and Growth'. In H. Giersch (ed.), *Towards an Explanation of Economic Growth*, 187–212. Tuebingen: Mohr.

_____. 1989. 'Organizational Economics and Institutions as Missing Elements in Economic Development Analysis'. *World Development* 17.9: 1361–73.

Levi-Fauer, D. 1997. 'Friedrich List and the Political Economy of the Nation-State'. *Review of International Political Economy* 4.1: 154–78.

Li, S. and J. Xia. 2008. 'The Roles and Performance of State Firms and Non-State Firms in China's Economic Transition'. *World Development* 36.1: 39–54.

Limoges, C. 1996. 'L'université à la croisée chemins: Une mission à affirmer, un egestion à reformer'. Proceedings of ACFAS.CSE.CST. Government of Quebec, Ministry of Education.

Lin, J. Y. and Y. Wang. 2008. 'China's Integration with the World, Development Process of Learning and Industrial Upgrading'. World Bank Policy Research Working Paper No. 4799.

Linder, S. B. 1961. *An Essay on Trade and Transformation*. New York: John Wiley.

Lipsey, R. G. and K. Carlaw. 1998. 'Technology Policy: Basic Concepts'. In C. Edquist and M. McKelvey (eds), *Systems of Innovation: Growth, Competitiveness and Employment*, vol. 2, 421–55. Cheltenham: Edward Elgar.

List, F. 1856. *The National System of Political Economy*. Translated into English by G. A. Matile. Philadelphia: J. B. Lippincott & Co.

Little, I. M. D., T. Scitovsky and M. Scott. 1970. *Industry and Trade in Some Developing Countries*. Oxford: Oxford University Press.

Liu, W.-H. 2008. 'Do Active Innovation Policies Matter? Findings from a Survey on Hong Kong Electronics SMEs'. Kiel Institute for the World Economy Working Paper No. 1445.

Lloyd-Reason, L. and S. Wall (eds). 2000. *Dimensions of Competitiveness: Issues and Policies*. Cheltenham: Edward Elgar.

Lucas, R. E. 1988. 'On the Mechanics of Economic Development'. *Journal of Monetary Economics* 22.1: 3–42.

_____. 1990. 'Why Doesn't Capital Flow from Rich to Poor Countries?' *American Economic Review* 80.1: 92–6.

Lundvall, B. (ed.) 1992. *National Systems of Innovation: Toward a Theory of Innovation and Interactive Learning*. London: Pinter.

_____. 2004. 'Why the New Economy is a Learning Economy'. Danish Research Unit for Industrial Dynamics, Working Paper No. 04-01.

Ma, G. and R. N. McCauley. 2010. 'The Evolving Renminbi Regime and Implications for Asian Currency Stability'. Bank for International Settlements Working Paper No. 321.

Madsen, E. S., V. Smith and M. Dilling-Hansen. 2010. 'Industrial Clusters, Firm Location and Productivity. Some Empirical Evidence for Danish Firms'. http://www.hha.dk/nat/wper/03-26_esmvs.pdf (accessed 4 September 2012).

Maizels, A. 1988. 'The Impact of Currency Devaluation on Commodity Production and Exports of Developing Countries'. In S. Dell (ed.), *Policies for Development*. London: Macmillan.

Marshall, A. 1920/1960. *Principles of Economics*. London: Macmillan and Co.

Martin, D. F. 2008. 'Implications for Developing Countries of Bilaterally Negotiating Issues of Competition Policy'. London: International Trade and Regional Co-operation Section, Commonwealth Secretariat.

McCoy, M. et al. 2006. 'Facts & Figures of the Chemical Industry'. *Chemical & Engineering News* 84.29: 35–72.

Meier, G. M. 1993. 'The Political Economy and Policy Reform'. *Journal of International Development* 5.4: 381–9.

Meier, N. and D. Seers (eds). 1984. *Pioneers in Development*. Oxford: Oxford University Press.

Metcalfe, J. S. 1997. 'Science Policy and Technology Policy in a Competitive Economy'. *International Journal of Social Economics* 24.7–9: 723–40.

Meyer-Stamer, J. 1995. 'Micro-level Innovation and Competitiveness'. *World Development* 23.1: 143–8.

_____. 1997 *Technology, Competitiveness and Radical Policy Change: The Case of Brazil*. London: Frank Cass.

_____. 1998. 'Path Dependence in Regional Development: Persistence and Change in Three Industrial Clusters in Santa Catarina, Brazil'. *World Development* 26.8: 1495–1511.

Misztal, B. 1996. *Trust in Modern Societies: The Search for the Bases of Social Order.* Oxford: Polity Press.

Mooney, P. R. 2000. 'Concentration in Corporate Power on the Coming Binano Republic'. *Development Dialogue* 1.2: 73–114.

Morrison, A., C. Pietrobelli and R. Rabellotti. 2008. 'Global Value Chains and Technological Capabilities: A Framework to Study Learning and Innovation in Developing Countries'. *Oxford Development Studies* 36.1: 39–58.

Mortensen, J. 2000. 'Intellectual Capital: Economic Theory and Analysis'. In P. Buigues, A. Jacquemin and J.-F. Marchipont (eds), *Competitiveness and Value of Intangibles Assets.* Cheltenham: Edward Elgar.

MOST (Ministry of Science and Technology of the People's Republic of China). 2006. *Science and Technology Statistical Data Book.* Beijing: MOST.

Murphy, K. M., A. Schleifer and W. Vishny 1989. 'Industrialization and Big Push'. *Journal of Political Economy* 97.5: 1003–26.

Myint, H. 1958. 'The Classical Theory of International Trade and Underdeveloped Countries'. *Economic Journals* 68. Reprinted in I. Livingston, *Economic Policy for Development.* London: Penguin Books, 1971.

Myrdal, G. 1957. *Economic Theory and Underdeveloped Regions.* London: Duckworth.

_____. 1970. *Challenges of World Poverty A World Anti-Poverty Programme in Outline* New York: Pantheon Books.

_____. 1971. *Asian Drama: An Inquiry into the Poverty of Nations.* London: Penguin Books.

Nadvi, K. 1992. 'Industrial District Experience in Developing Countries'. Paper prepared for the UNCTAD/GTZ symposium on 'The Role of Industrial Districts in Application and diffusion of Technology', Geneva, 16–17 November.

Naughton, Barry. 2007. *The Chinese Economy: Transitions and Growth.* Cambridge, MA: MIT Press.

Neufeld, I. N. 2001. 'Anti-Dumping and Countervailing Procedures – Use or Abuse? Implications for Developing Countries, Policy Issues in International Trade and Commodities'. UNCTAD, Geneva and New York, Study Series, No. 9.

Nelson, R. R. 1992. 'National Innovation Systems: A Retrospective on a Study'. *Industrial and Corporate Change* 1.2: 347–74.

_____. 1993. *National Innovation Systems: A Comparative Analysis.* Oxford: Oxford University Press.

_____. 1996. *The Sources of Economic Growth.* Cambridge, MA: Harvard University Press.

Nelson, R. R. and G. Wright. 1992. 'The Rise and Fall of American Technological Leadership: The Postwar Era in Historical Perspective'. *Journal of Economic Literature* 30.4: 1931–64.

Nelson, R. R. and S. G. Winter. 1982. *An Evolutionary Theory of Economic Change.* Cambridge, MA: Harvard University Press.

Ng, F. and A. Yeats. 1999. 'Production Sharing in East Asia, Who Does What for Whom, and Why?' World Bank Policy Research Working Paper No. 2197.

_____. 2003. 'Major Trade Trends in East Asia: What are their Implications for Regional Cooperation and Growth?' World Bank Policy Research Working Paper No. 3084.

Nguyen, A. N., N. Q. Pham, C. D. Nguyen and N. D. Nguyen. 2008 'Innovation and Export of Vietnam's SME Sector'. Development and Policies Research Centre Working paper No. 2008/09.

Nicolaides, P. 1994. 'Reconciling Trade and Competition Policies'. *OECD Observer*, 18 April.

Nobuaki, H. and K. Yoshihiro. 2008. 'R&D Partnerships and Capability of Innovation of Small and Medium-Sized Firms in Zhongguancum, Beijing, The Power of Proximity'. Kobe University. ICSEAD Discussion Paper No. 225.

Ocampo, J. A. 1993. 'New Theories of International Trade and Trade Policy in Developing Countries'. In M. Agosin and D. Tussie (eds), *Trade and Growth: New Dilemmas in Trade Policy.* New York and London: St. Martin's Press/Macmillan.

Odigari, H. 1992. *Growth through Competition, Competition through Growth.* Oxford: Clarendon Press.

OECD (Organisation for Economic Co-operation and Development). 1992. *Technology and the Economy: The Key Relationships*. Paris: OECD.

_____. 2005. *Oslo Manual*, 3rd ed. Paris: OECD.

_____. 2008. 'Recent Trends in Internationalization of R&D in the Enterprise Sector'. OECD Working Party on Statistics, Committee on Industry, Innovation and Entrepreneurship, DSTI/EAS/IND/SWP(2006)1/Final.

_____. 2009. 'Measuring China's Innovation System'. OECD Science, Technology and Industry Working Paper 2009/1.

_____. 2010. *Competition Law and Policy in Mexico an OECD Peer Review*. Paris: OECD.

Oikawa, H. 2008. 'Empirical Global Value Chain Analysis in Electronics and Automobile Industries: An Application of Asian International Input-Output'. Institute of Developing Economies Discussion Paper No. 172.

Oliver, N. and B. Wilkinson. 1992. *The Japanization of British Industry*. Oxford: Blackwell.

Oxley, J. E. and B. Yeung. 1998a. 'Structural Change and Industrial Location: Agglomeration, Innovation and Multinational Enterprises'. In *Structural Change, Industrial Location and Competitiveness*. Cheltenham: Edward Elgar.

_____ (eds). 1998b. *Structural Change, Industrial Location and Competitiveness*. Cheltenham: Edward Elgar.

Ozawa, T. 2003. 'Economic Growth, Structural Transformation, and Industrial Cluster: Theoretical Implications of Japan's Post war Experience'. Paper presented at the 'Conference on Clusters, Industrial Districts and Firms: The Challenge of Globalization', Modena, 12–13 September.

Oyelaran-Oyeyinka, B. and D. McCormick (eds). 2007. *Industrial Clusters and Innovation Systems in Africa*. Tokyo: United Nations University Press.

Palacios, Juan. 2001. *Production Networks and Industrial Clustering in Developing Regions: Electronics Manufacturing in Guadalajara, Mexico*. Guadalajara: University of Guadalajara.

Palma, G. 2003. 'Trade Liberalization in Mexico: Its Impact on Growth, Employment and Wages'. International Labour Organization, Employment Paper 2003/55.

Paus, E. 2005. *Foreign Direct Investment, Development and Globalization: Can Costa Rica become Ireland?* London: Palgrave.

Paus, E. and K. P. Gallagher. 2008. 'Missing Links: Foreign Investment and Industrial Development in Costa Rica and Mexico'. *Studies in Comparative International Development* 43.1: 53–80.

Penrose, E. T. 1955. 'Limits to the Growth and Size of Firms'. *American Economic Review* 45.2: 531–43.

_____. 1959. *The Theory of the Growth of the Firm*. Oxford: B. Blackwell.

People's Republic of China. 2006. *Statistical Yearbook*. Beijing.

Pior, M. J. and C. F. Sabel. 1984. *The Second Industrial Divide: Possibilities for Prosperity*. New York: Basic Books.

Pitylak, R. 2005. 'News Reporters and Politics Will Never be Economists: China's Devaluation'. http://www.ryanpitylak.com/Ryan_Pitylak/papers/intl_paper1-final.htm (accessed 4 September 2012).

Platteau, J. P. 1994. 'Behind the Market Stage Where Real Societies Exist'. *Journal of Development Studies* 30.3: 'Part I: The Role of Public and Private Institutions', 533–76; 'Part II: The Role of Moral Norms', 753–817.

Porter, M. 1990. *Competitive Advantage of Nations*. London: Macmillan.

_____. 1994. 'Global Strategy: Winning in the World-wide Market Place'. In L. Fahey and M. Randall (eds), *Portable MBA in Strategy*, 108–41. New York: John Wiley & Sons.

_____. 1996. 'What is Strategy'. *Harvard Business Review*, November–December.

_____. 1998. *On Competition*. Boston, MA: Harvard Business School.

_____. 2008. 'The Five Competitive Forces that Shape Strategy'. *Harvard Business Review*, January, 79–93.

Posthuma, A. C. 1995. 'Japanese Techniques in Africa? Human Resources and Industrial Restructuring in Zimbabwe'. *World Development* 23.1: 103–16.

Prahalad, C. K. and G. Hamel. 1990. *Competing for the Future*. Boston: Harvard Business School Press.

Prebisch, R. 1949. *The Economic Development of Latin America and its Principal Problems*. New York, United Nations Department of Economic Affairs.

———. 1959. 'Commercial Policy in the Underdeveloped Countries'. *American Economic Review: Papers and Proceedings* (May): 251–73.

Prescott, E. C. and J. H. Boyd. 1987. 'Dynamic Coalitions: Engines of Growth'. *American Economic Review* 77.2: 63–7.

Primavera, S. and R. Pezzetti. 2003. 'The Internationalization of Italian Industrial District Firms in Mexico'. Paper presented at the 'Conference on Clusters, Industrial Districts and Firms: The Challenge of Globalization', Modena, 12–13 September.

Pyke, F., G. Becattini and W. Sengenberger. 1992. *Industrial Districts and Inter-firm Co-operation in Italy*. Geneva: International Institute of Labour Studies.

Pyke, F., B. Giacomo and S. Werner. 1990. 'Industrial Districts and Inter-firm Co-operation in Italy'. International Institute of Labour Studies, working paper.

Pyke, F. and W. Sengenberger. 1992. *Industrial Districts and Local Economic Regeneration*. Geneva: International Institute of Labour Studies.

Rabellotti, R. 1995. 'Is there an "Industrial Model"? Footwear Districts in Italy and Mexico Compared'. *World Development* 23.1: 29–41.

Rayment, P. 1983. '"Intra-industry": Specialization and the Foreign Trade of Industrial Countries'. In S. Frowen (ed.), *Controlling Industrial Economics. Essays in Honour of C.T. Saunders*. London: Macmillan.

Reekie, W. D. 1979. *Industry, Prices and Markets*. Oxford: Philip Allan.

Reinert, E. 1994. 'Catching-up from Way Behind: A Third World Perspective on First World History'. In J. Fagerberg, B. Verspagen and N. V. Tunzelmann (eds), *The Dynamics of Technology, Trade and Growth*, 168–97. Northampton: Edward Elgar.

———. 1995. 'Competitiveness and its Predecessors – A 500-Year Cross-National Perspective'. *Structural Change and Economic Dynamics* 6: 23–42.

———. 2006. 'Evolutionary Economics, Classical Development Economics, and History of Economic Policy: A Plea for Theorizing by Inclusion'. The Other Canon Foundation and Tallinn University of Technology, Working Papers in Technology Governance and Economic Dynamics No. 1.

Rivera Vargas, M. I. 2002. *Technology Transfer via the University–Industry Relationship: The Case of Foreign High Technology Electronics Industry in Mexico's Silicon Valley*. London: Routledge.

Riveros, L. A. 1992. 'Labour Cost and Manufactured Exports in Developing Countries: An Econometric Analysis'. *World Development* 20.7: 991–1008.

Rodriguez, F. and D. Rodrik. 1999. 'Trade Policy and Economic Development: A Sceptic's Guide to the Cross-National Evidence'. CEPR Discussion Paper No. 2143.

Rodrik, D. 2004. 'Industrial Policy for the Twenty-first Century'. CEPR Discussion Paper Series No. 4767.

———. 2006. 'What's so Special about China's Exports?' NBER Working Paper No. 11947.

———. 2007. 'Normalizing Industrial Policy'. Commission on Growth and Development Working Paper No. 3. http://dev.wcfia.harvard.edu/sites/default/files/Rodrick_Normalizing. pdf (accessed 4 September 2012).

———. 2011. 'The Future of Economic Convergence'. Paper prepared for the 2011 Jackson Hole symposium of the Federal Reserve Bank of Kansas City, August 25–7.

Rodrik, D., A. Subramanian and F. Trebbi. 2004. 'Institutional Rules: The Primacy of Institutions over Geography and Integration in Economic Development'. *Journal of Economic Growth* 9: 131–65.

Romer, P. M. 1986. 'Increasing Returns and Long-Run Growth'. *Journal of Political Economy* 94.5: 1002–37.

———. 1987. 'Growth Based on Increasing Returns Due to Specialization'. *American Economic Review* 77.2: 52–62.

Romo Murillo, D. 2002. 'Derramas Tecnologicas de la Inversion Extranhera en la Industria Mexicana'. *Comercio Exterior* 53.3: 230–43.

Rosenstein-Rodan, P. 1984. 'Nature Facit Saltum: Analysis of the Disequilibrium Growth Process'. In N. Meier and D. Seers (eds), *Pioneers in Development*, 205–19. Oxford: Oxford University Press.

Ruan, J. and X. Zhang. 2008. 'Finance and Cluster-Based Industrial Development in China'. International Food Policy Research Institute Discussion Paper No. 768.

Sable, C. F. 1992. 'Studies in Trust: Building New Forms of Co-operation in a Volatile Economy'. In F. Pyke and W. Sengenberger (eds), *Industrial Districts and Local Economic Regeneration*, 215–50. Geneva: International Institute of Labour Studies.

Sarkar, P. and H. W. Singer. 1991. 'Manufactured Exports of Developing Countries and Their Terms of Trades since 1965'. *World Development* 19.4: 333–40.

Scherer, F. M. and D. Ross. 1990. *Industrial Market Structure and Economic Performance*. Boston: Houghton Mifflin Company.

Schmitz, H. 1995. 'Collective Efficiency: Growth Path for Small-Scale Industry'. *Journal of Development Studies* 31.4: 529–66.

_____. 1999. 'Global Competition and Local Co-operation: Success and Failure in the Sinos Valley, Brazil'. *World Development* 27.9: 1627–50.

Schmitz, H. and K. Nadvi. 1999. 'Clustering and Industrialization'. *World Development* 27.9: 1503–14.

Schumpeter, J. A. 1934/1976. *Capitalism, Socialism and Democracy*. London: George Allen and Unwin Ltd.

_____. 1961/1974. *The Theory of Economic Development*. Oxford: Oxford University Press.

Schydlowsky, B. D. 1982. 'Alternative Approaches to Short-term Economic Management'. In T. Killick (ed.), *Adjustment and Financing in the Developing World*. Washington, DC: ODI/IMF.

Scitovsky, T. 1954. 'Two Concepts of External Economies'. Reprinted in A. Agarwala and S. P. Singh (eds), *The Economics of Underdevelopment*, 295–308. Oxford: Oxford University Press.

Scott, B. R. 1985. 'U.S. Competitiveness: Concepts, Performance and Implications'. In B. R. Scott and G. C. Lodge. *Competitiveness in the World Economy*, 14–69. Boston: Harvard Business School Press.

Scott, B. R. and G. C. Lodge (eds). 1985. *Competitiveness in the World Economy*. Boston: Harvard Business School Press.

Senghaas, D. 1985. *The European Experience: A Historical Critique of Development Theory*. Dover, NH and Leamington Spa: Longwood.

_____. 1989. 'Friedrich List and the Basic Problems of Modern Development'. *Economics* 40: 62–76.

Shafaeddin, M. 1991. 'Trade Policies and Economic Performance of Developing Countries'. In H. W. Singer and R. Prendergast (eds), *Development Prospects in 1990: Proceedings of the Annual Conference of Development Studies Association*, 77–102. London: Macmillan.

_____. 1992. 'Real Effective Exchange Rate Changes, Export Performances, Diversification and Investment in Developing Countries'. A study prepared for UNCTAD, presented to the Annual Conference of Development Studies Association, Nottingham, September.

_____. 1993. 'Import Shortages and the Inflationary Impact of Devaluation in Developing Countries'. *Industry and Development* 32: 20–32

_____. 1995. 'The Impact of Trade Liberalization on Exports and GDP Growth in Least-Developed Countries'. *UNCTAD Review*, United Nations publication, sales no. E.95.II.D.23.

_____. 1998. 'How Did Developed Countries Industrialize? The History of Trade and Industrial Policy: The Case of Great Britain and the USA'. UNCTAD Discussion Paper No. 139.

_____. 2003. 'Some Implication of Accession to WTO for China's Economy'. *International Journal of Development Issues* 1.2: 93–128.

_____. 2004. 'Is China's Accession to WTO Threatening Exports of Developing Countries?' *China Economic Review* 15: 109–44.

_____. 2005a. 'Friedrich List and the Infant Industry Argument'. In K. S. Jomo (ed.), *The Pioneers of Development Economics: Great Economists on Development*. London and New York: Zed Books.

_____. 2005b. 'Towards an Alternative Perspective on Trade and Industrial Policies'. *Development and Change* 36.6: 1143–62.

_____. 2005c. *Trade Policy at the Crossroads: Recent Experience of Developing Countries*. New York and Basingstoke: Palgrave Macmillan.

_____. 2006a. 'Trade Liberalization and Economic Reform in Developing Countries: Structural Change or De-industrialization?' In A. Paloni and M. Zanardi (eds), *The IMF, the World Bank and Policy Reform*. London: Routledge.

_____. 2006b. *Does Trade Openness Favour or Hider Industrialization and Development?* Geneva and Penang: Third World Network. Based on a paper prepared for the Technical Meeting of the G24 Intergovernmental Group, 16–17 March 2006.

_____. 2006c. 'Is the Industrial Policy Relevant in the 21st Century?' The text of a keynote speech to the 'International Conference on New Approaches to Design of Development Policies', organized by the Arab Planning Institute, Beirut, 20–21 March.

_____. 2006d. 'Beware of NAMA's Slippery Slope to De-industrialisation'. *SUNS*, 15 June.

_____. 2008. 'South–South Regionalism and Trade Cooperation in Asia-Pacific Region'. A study prepared for the UNDP Regional Centre, Colombo, 2007–8.

_____. 2009a. 'NAMA and Industrialization of Africa'. http://mpra.ub.uni-muenchen.de/15050/1/MPRA_paper_15050.pdf (accessed 11 July 2012).

_____. 2009b. *The Cost of SPS Agreement to Developing Countries: An Alternative Strategy for Compliance with WTO rules on SPS*. Geneva and Penang: Third World Network.

_____. 2009c. *Selectivity and Neutrality of Trade Policy Incentives: Implications for Industrialization and the NAMA Negotiations*. Penang: Third World Network.

_____. 2009d. *Impact of the Global Economic Crisis on LDCs' Productive Capacities and Trade Prospects: Threats and Opportunities*. Geneva: South Centre and UNIDO.

_____. 2010a. 'Trade Liberalization, Industrialization and Development, Experience of Recent Decades'. A keynote speech delivered in the fourth ACDC (Annual Conference on Development and Change) at the University of Witwatersrand, Johannesburg, April, forthcoming in the proceedings of the conference.

_____. 2010b. 'The Role of China in Regional South–South Trade in Asia-Pacific: Prospect for Industrialization of Low-Income Countries'. Paper presented to the 'Conference on The Future of Trade Relation in the Global South', organized by the Frederick S. Pardee Centre for the Study of the Long-Range Future, Boston University.

_____. 2010c. 'Political Economy of WTO with Special Reference to NAMA Negotiations'. *European Journal of Development Research* 22.2: 175–96.

Shafaeddin, M. and J. Pizarro. 2010. 'The Evolution of Value Added in Assembly Operations: The Case of China and Mexico'. *Journal of Chinese Economic and Business Studies* 8.4: 373–9.

Shao, Y., S. Chen and B. Cheng. 2008. 'Analyses of the Dynamic Factors of Cluster Innovation: A Case Study of Chengdu Furniture Industrial Cluster'. *International Management Review* 4.1: 51–9.

Sourafel, G. G., Y. Gong, H. Gorg and Z. Yu. 2008. 'Can Production Subsidies Explain China's Export Performance? Evidence from Firm Data'. Kiel Institute for the World Economy Working Paper No. 1442.

South Centre. 2009. 'EPAs and Benchmarking Development'. Doc. SC/AN/TDP/EPA/20, March.

_____. 2010a. 'EPAs: The Wrong Development Model for Africa and Options for the Future'. Document SC/TDP/AN/EPA/23.

_____. 2010b. 'EPA Contentious Issues Matrix: State of Play, Key Problems and Recommendations'. Document SC/TDP/AN/EPA/26.

_____. 2011. 'Economic Partnership Agreements in Africa: A Benefit-Cost Analysis'. Document SC/TDP/AN/EPA/29.

Spooner, John G. 2005. 'The Nouveau Lenovo Wants to Shake Up the PC Market's Status Quo'. ZDnet. http://www.zdnet.com/news/new-lenovo-takes-shape/141589 (accessed 11 July 2012).

Stanley, M. and S. Helper. 2003. 'Industrial Clustering, Social Capital, and International Competition in the U.S. Component Manufacturing Industry'. Paper presented at the 'Conference on Clusters, Industrial Districts and Firms: The Challenge of Globalization', Modena, 12–13 September.

Stewart, F. and E. Ghani. 1991. 'How Significant are Externalities for Development'. *World Development* 19.6: 569–94.

Stewart, F., S. Lall and S. Wagwe (eds). 1992. *Alternative Development Strategies in Sub-Saharan Africa*. London: Macmillan.

Stigler, G. J. 1951. 'The Division of Labour is Limited by the Extent of the Market'. *Journal of Political Economy* 54.3: 185–93.

Stiglitz, J. E. 1988. 'Economic Organization, Information and Development'. In H. B. Chenery and T. N. Srinivasan (eds), *Handbook of Development Economics*, vol. 1, 93–160. Amsterdam: North Holland.

———. 1989. 'Markets, Market Failures and Development'. *American Economic Review: Papers and Proceedings* 79, 2: 197–202.

———. 1998. 'More Instruments and Broader Goals: Moving Toward the Post-Washington Consensus'. United Nations World Institute for Development Economics Research (WIDER), Annual Lectures 2.

Streeten, P. P. 1987. 'Structural Adjustment: A Survey of Issues and Options'. *World Development* 15.12: 1469–82.

———. 1990. 'Comparative Advantage and Free Trade', *World Development* 19.4: 333–40, reprinted in P. Sarkar and H. W. Singer, 'Manufactured Exports of Developing Countries and Their Terms of Trades since 1965' (New Dehli: Indus Publishing Company, 1991), 35–51.

Strøjer, E. M., V. Smith, V. and Dilling-Hansen, M. 2003. 'Industrial Clusters, Firm Location and Productivity, Some Empirical Evidence for Danish Firms'. Department of Economics, Aarhus School of Business ,University of Aarhus, Working Paper 03-26.

Stugeon, T. and O. Memedovic. 2011. 'Mapping Global Value Chains: Intermediate Goods and Structural Change in the World Economy'. UNIDO, Development Policy and Strategic Research Branch Working Paper 05/2010.

Symeonidis, L. 1996. 'Innovation, Firm Size and Market Structure: Schumpeterian Hypotheses and Some New Themes'. OECD Economic Department Working Paper No. 161.

Taeube, F. A. 2003. 'Proximity and Innovation: Evidence from Indian Software Industry'. Paper presented at the 'Conference on Clusters, Industrial Districts and Firms: The Challenge of Globalization', Modena, 12–13 September.

Tayanagi, E. and A. Colovic-Lamotte. 2003. 'What Direction Should the Cluster Policy Take, Top-Down Implementation or Bottom-up Emergence? The Case of Japan'. Paper presented at the 'Conference on Clusters, Industrial Districts and Firms: The Challenge of Globalization', Modena, 12–13 September.

Tesar, L. 2006. 'Production Sharing and Business Cycle Synchronization in Accession Countries'. In L. Reichlin and K. West (eds), *NBER International Seminar on Q4 Macroeconomics*. Cambridge, MA: MIT Press.

Teubal, M. 1987. *Innovation Performance, Learning and Government Policy*. Madison: University of Wisconsin.

———. 1996. 'R&D and Technology Policy in NICs as Learning Processes'. *World Development* 24.3: 449–60.

Tu, Q. and E. Bulte. 2010. 'Trust, Market Participation and Economic Outcome: Evidence from Rural China'. *World Development* 38.8: 1179–90.

UK Cabinet Office. 1996. *Competitiveness: Creating the Enterprise Centre of Europe*. London: HMSO.

UK Government. 1998. 'Our Competitive Future: Building the Knowledge Driven Economy'. http://www.dti.gov.uk/comp/competitive/wh_int1.htm (accessed 4 September 2012).

UN. 1964. *Towards a New Trade Policy for Development. Report by the Secretary General of the United Nations Conference on Trade and Development* [Raúl Prebisch]. New York: United Nations.

_____. 1992. *World Economic Survey*. New York: United Nations.

UNCTAD. *Handbook of Statistics*. New York and Geneva: United Nations. Various issues.

_____. 1997. *Government–Private Sector Interaction, with a Particular Focus on the Participants of SMEs*. Geneva: United Nations.

_____. 2001. *Survey of Good Practice in Public–Private Sector Dialogue*. Geneva: United Nations.

_____. 2000. *Trade and Development Report, 2000*. Geneva and New York: United Nations.

_____· 2002. *Trade and Development Report, 2002*. New York: United Nations.

_____. 2003. *Back to Basics: Market Access Issues in the Doha Agenda*. Geneva and New York: United Nations.

_____. 2005. *Towards a New Trade 'Marshall Plan' for Least Developed Countries: How to Deliver on the Doha Development Promise and Help Realize the United Nations Millennium Development Goals?* Geneva and New York: United Nations.

_____. 2008a. *World Investment Report*. Geneva and New York: United Nations.

_____. 2008b. *Review of Maritime Transport 2007*. New York and Geneva: United Nations.

UNIDO. 2001. *Development of Clusters and Network of SMEs*. Vienna: UNIDO.

United States Government, Domestic Policy Council, Office of Science and Technology Policy. 2006. *American Competitiveness Initiative*. Washington, DC: US Government Printing Office.

United States Presidential Commission on Industrial Competitiveness. 1985. *Global Competition: The New Reality*. Analytical Reports vol. 2. Washington, DC: US Government Printing Office.

USDOC. 2006. *Technology Transfer to China*, ed. B.o.I.a. Security. Washington, DC: United States Department of Commerce.

Veblen, T. 1915. *Imperial Germany and Industrial Revolution*. New York: Macmillan.

Ventura Diaz, V. and J. D. Lima. 2001. 'Production Sharing in Latin American Trade: A Research Note'. CEPAL, Serie Comercio Internacional [International Commerce Series] No. 22.

Von Tunzelmann, N. and V. Acha. 2004. 'Innovation in "Low-Tech" Industries'. In J. Fagerberg, D. Mowery and R. Nelson (eds), *The Oxford Handbook of Innovation*, 407–32. Oxford: Oxford University Press.

Wade, R. 1990. *Governing the Market Economic Theory and the Role of Government in East Asian Industrialization*. Princeton: Princeton University Press.

_____. 1995. 'Resolving the State-Market Dilemma'. In H.-J. Chang and R. Rowthorn (eds), *The Role of the State in Economic Change*, 114–36. Oxford: Clarendon Press.

_____. 2005. 'What Strategies Are Viable for Developing Countries Today? The World Trade Organization and Shirking of Development Space'. In K. P. Gallagher (ed.) *Putting Development First: The Importance of Policy Space in the WTO and IFIs*, 80–101. London and New York: Zed Books.

_____. 2007. 'Rethinking Industrial Policy for Low income Countries'. Paper presented at the African Economic Conference, organized by the African Development Bank and UNECA, Addis Ababa, 15–17 November.

Waldkirch, A. 2008. 'The Effects of Foreign Direct Investment in Mexico since NAFTA'. MPRA Paper No. 7975. http://mpra.ub.uni-muenchen.de/7975/.

Walsh, K. 2003. *Foreign High-Tech R&D in China: Risks, Rewards, and Implications for US–China Relations*. Washington, DC: The Henry L. Stimson Center.

Wang, Q. and H. Wang. 2007. 'Industrial Standard based Competition and Chinese Firm Strategic Choice'. *International Journal of Globalization* 3.4: 422–36.

Wattleworth, M. 1988. 'The Effects of Collective Devaluation on Commodity Prices and Exports'. *Staff Papers - International Monetary Fund* 35.1: 166–80.

Weiss, L. 2005. 'Global Governance, National Strategies: How Industrialized States Make Room to Move under the WTO'. *Review of International Political Economy* 12.5: 723–49.

Whalley, J. and X. Zhao. 2010. 'The Contribution of Human Capital to China's Economic Growth'. NBER Working Paper No. 16592.

Wignaraja, G. 2003. *Competitiveness Strategy in Developing Countries: A Manual for Policy Analysis*. Routledge Studies in Development Economics. London: Routledge.

Wijayasiri, J. and J. Dissanayake. 2008a. 'The Ending of the Multi-Fibre Agreement and Innovation in Sri Lankan Textile and Clothing Industry'. OECD Trade Policy Working Paper No. 75: Trade and Innovation Project, Case Study No. 3.

———. 2008b. *Trade, Innovation and Growth: The Case of Sri Lankan Textile and Clothing Industry*. Colombo: Organisation for Economic Co-operation and Development, Institute of Policy Studies.

Williamson, J. (ed.) 1990. 'What Washington Means by Policy Reform'. In *Latin America Adjustment: How Much has Happened?* Washington, DC: Peterson Institute for International Economies.

Williamson, O. 1975. *Market and Hierarchies*. New York: Free Press.

World Bank. World Development Indicators. Available online at http://data.worldbank.org/datacatalog/worlddevelopment-indicators (accessed 10 July 2012).

———. 1987 *World Development Report*. Washington, DC: World Bank.

———. 1992a. *World Bank Support for Industrialization in Korea, India and Indonesia*. Washington, DC: World Bank.

———. 1992b. *Global Economic Prospects and Developing Countries, 1992*. Washington, DC: World Bank.

———. 1993a. *East Asian Miracle: Economic Growth and Public Policy*. New York: Oxford University Press.

———. 1993b. *Global Economic Prospects and Developing Countries 1993*. Washington, DC: World Bank.

———. 1997. *World Development Report 1997: The State in a Challenging World*. Washington, DC: World Bank.

———. 2001. *World Development Report 2000–2001: Attacking Poverty*. Washington, DC: World Bank.

———. 2003. *Global Economic Prospects 2003*. Washington, DC: World Bank.

———. 2008. *Science, Technology, and Innovation: Capacity Building for Sustainable Growth and Poverty Reduction*. Washington, DC: World Bank.

WTO, ITC and UN. 2008. *World Tariff Profiles*. Geneva: WTO.

Xiwei, Z. and Xiangdong, Y. 2007. 'Science and Technology Policy Reform and its Impact on China's National Innovation System'. *Technology and Science* 29: 317–25.

Xu, B. 2010. 'The Sophistication of Exports: Is China Special?' *China Economic Review* 21: 482–93.

Yao, S. 2009. 'Why Are Chinese Exports Not so Special?' *China & World Economy* 17.1: 47–65.

Ye, M. 2008. *Hands off Continual Control: The Government Role in China's Electronics Industries*. Cambridge, MA: Princeton University.

Young, A. 1991. 'Learning by Doing and the Dynamic Effects of International Trade'. *Quarterly Journal of Economies* 106.1: 326–405.

Young, A. A. 1928. 'Increasing Returns and Economic Progress'. *Economic Journal* 38.152: 527–42.

Yu, J. and P. Nijkamp. 2009. 'Ownership, R&D and Productivity Change: Assessing the Catch-up in China's High-tech Industries'. Department of Spatial Economics, VU University, Amsterdam, Series Research Memoranda No. 0010.

Zebregs, H. 2004. 'Intraregional Trade in Emerging Asia'. IMF Discussion Paper No. PDP/04.

Zeithaml, V., L. L. Berry and A. Parasuraman. 1990. *Delivering Services Quality*. New York: Free Press.

Zhou, Y. 2008. 'Synchronizing Export Orientation with Import Substitution: Creating Competitive Indigenous High-Tech Companies in China'. *World Development* 36.11: 2353–70.

INDEX

Lightning Source UK Ltd.
Milton Keynes UK
UKOW040659251012

201162UK00002B/3/P

9 780857 284600